D1029546

AMS PRESS
NEW YORK

Reprinted from the edition of 1898, Philadelphia
First AMS EDITION published 1971
Manufactured in the United States of America

International Standard Book Number:
Complete Set: 0-404-08970-4
Volume Five: 0-404-08975-5

Library of Congress Number: 75-143179

AMS PRESS INC.
NEW YORK, N.Y. 10003

Translations and Reprints

FROM THE

Original Sources of European History

Vol. V.
(1898)

PUBLISHED BY
THE DEPARTMENT OF HISTORY
OF THE
UNIVERSITY OF PENNSYLVANIA.

TABLE OF CONTENTS.

Vol. V.   No. 1.

Translations and Reprints

FROM THE

Original Sources of European History

MONUMENTUM ANCYRANUM

THE DEEDS OF AUGUSTUS

EDITED BY WILLIAM FAIRLEY, PH.D.

PUBLISHED BY

The Department of History of the University of Pennsylvania.

Philadelphia, Pa., 1898.

ENGLISH AGENCY: P. S. KING & SON, 12-14 King Street, London, S. W.

PREFACE

The method employed in this edition of the *Monumentum Ancyranum* is suggested by the purpose for which it is intended. That purpose is primarily to adapt it as one of the series of *Translations and Reprints from the Original Sources of European History*, published by the Department of History of the University of Pennsylvania. The English version is the core of the work. At the same time the opportunity has been seized to present the original texts in such form as to be of real philological service. That there is room for such an edition of the *Monumentum Ancyranum* there can be no doubt. The critical edition published by Mommsen in 1883, *Res Gestæ Divi Augusti*, must long remain for scholars the sufficient hand-book for the study of the greatest of inscriptions. But that edition, with its Latin notes, is not adapted for ordinary school or college use, or for historical study by those who do not readily use Latin. And although Roman histories constantly refer to this great source for the life and times of Augustus, there has been no accessible English translation. It is true that the English translation of Duruy's *History of Rome* contains a version of the *Monumentum*, but it is not in full accord with the latest text as set forth by Mommsen, and is hidden away in the ponderous volumes of that expensive work.

Aside from Mommsen's edition of 1883, the only recent edition is a French one of 1886 by C. Peltier. But this is simply a condensation of Mommsen. While the present edition depends very largely on Mommsen's work, it is more than a condensation. Not only is the English version given, but all the known studies of the text published since 1883, and in criticism of Mommsen, have been collated. The emendations thus suggested have been placed as footnotes to the Latin and Greek texts. Moreover, the notes have been carefully revised. For the most part they are much reduced in compass, but in many cases they are added to ; and a large number of typographical errors in Mommsen's edition have been corrected. Most of these errors were

(3)

reproduced in the French edition above mentioned. In a work with such a multitude of references it is too much to hope that all errors have been avoided, and the editor will be greatly indebted if users of the book will report them to him.

W. FAIRLEY.

University of Pennsylvania, Philadelphia, Pa.

INTRODUCTION

HISTORY OF THE INSCRIPTION.

Suetonius in his *Life of Augustus* tells us that that Emperor had placed in charge of the Vestal virgins his will and three other sealed documents; and the four papers were produced and read in the senate immediately after his death. One of these additional documents gave directions as to his funeral; another gave a concise account of the state of the empire; the third contained a list of "his achievements which he desired should be inscribed on brazen tablets and placed before his mausoleum." These tablets perished in the decline of Rome. Centuries passed; men had ceased to ask about them, and there was no idea that they would ever be brought to light. Nor were the original tablets ever found. But in 1555 Buysbecche, a Dutch scholar, was sent on an embassy from the Emperor Ferdinand II. to the Sultan Soliman at Amasia in Asia Minor; and a letter of his, published among others at Frankfort in 1595, tells the story of the discovery of a copy of this epitaph of Augustus. He writes: "On our nineteenth day from Constantinople we reached Ancyra. Here we found a most beautiful inscription, and a copy of those tablets on which Augustus had placed the story of his achievements." From this situation of the copy comes the common title, *Monumentum Ancyranum*. Buysbecche made some attempt to copy the Latin inscription, but his work was very hasty and incomplete. What he had discovered was of extreme importance, and his report stimulated such interest that European scholars never rested till as complete a copy as possible was finally made in our own time. The temple on whose walls the inscription was found was one dedicated to Augustus and Rome, as was a common custom during the lifetime of that Emperor. It was a hexastyle of white marble, with joints of such exquisite workmanship that even in this century it was difficult to trace some of them. This temple had served as a Christian church till the fifteenth century, and from that time has been part of a Turkish mosque, some sections of its enclosure being used as a cemetery. The great inscription was cut on the two side walls of the pronaos, or vestibule. It was in six pages, three on the left as one entered, and three on the right. Each page contained from forty-two to fifty-four lines, and each line an average of sixty letters. The pages cover six courses of the masonry in height, about 2.70 metres, and the length of the inscription on each wall is about 4 metres. On one of the outer walls of the temple was a Greek translation of the Latin. This measures 1.38 metres in height by 21 metres in length. Several Turkish houses had been built against the wall containing this Greek version, and this made the reading of it, and still more the copying, an extremely difficult task. The priceless value of the Greek version lies in the fact that it supplements in many cases the breaks in the Latin. For it is needless to say that an inscription so old and so exposed has suffered much from time and violence. Various travelers have described the temple and 'its treasure: Tournefort in his *Voyage du Levant*, Lyons, 1717; Kinneir, *Journey Through Asia Minor*, 1818; Texier, *Description de l'Asie mineure*, Paris, 1839; William Hamilton, *Researches in Asia Minor*, London, 1842; and most completely, Guillaume, Perrot and Delbet, in their *Exploration archéologique de la Galatie, etc., in 1861*, Paris, 1872.

Numerous attempts were made at transcribing the inscription, and a number of editions were published. Buysbecche's fragments found several editors in the century of their discovery. About a hundred years after him Daniel Cosson, a merchant from Leyden, who had lived many years at Smyrna, dying there in 1689, caused an attempt to be made to secure a copy, and with somewhat better results. His copy was edited at Leyden in 1695. In 1701 Joseph Pitton de Tournefort, under direction of Louis XIV, visited Ancyra, and attempted to secure a facsimile of the text. In 1705 Paul Lucas, also sent by Louis XIV, spent twenty days in copying the Latin, and his work was the last of its kind till the present century. While these early copies are far from being as perfect as more recent ones, they have this value: that in a number of cases they show parts of the inscription which progressive disintegration has now rendered illegible.

The Greek text, owing to the buildings reared against it, was much harder to transcribe. In 1745 Richard Pococke published a few fragments, and in 1832 Hamilton copied pages 10, 11, 12 and 13 of the nineteen into which the Greek is divided.

Within recent years all has been done that can possibly be done to secure perfect copies of both Greek and Latin. In 1859 the Royal Academy of Berlin commissioned a scholar named Mordtmann to secure a *papier maché* cast of the Latin, and to transcribe the Greek. He failed in both attempts, and declared that the casts would ruin the original.

Napoleon III. commissioned George Perrot and Edmund Guillaume to explore Asia Minor. In their work above mentioned they give a facsimile copy of the whole of the Latin, and of as much of the Greek as they could get at. Their plates were the basis of an edition of the text by Mommsen in 1865, and another by Bergk in 1873, and of the text given in the *Corpus Inscriptionum Latinarum*.

But Mommsen and the Berlin Academy were not satisfied. Carl Humann had distinguished himself by his researches at Pergamos, and to him they committed the task of securing casts of the whole of both texts. The story of his achievement is extremely interesting. Difficulty after difficulty was met and surmounted. And finally he succeeded in his plan. With materials dug near-by he made plaster casts. The owners of the Turkish houses he succeeded in inducing to allow their walls to be so far torn away as to permit him to get at the entire Greek text. And finally twenty great cases containing the whole series of casts were sent away on pack mules to the coast and thence to Berlin. The Royal Academy now counts these casts among its chief treasures. This was in 1882. In 1883 Mommsen published his great critical edition of the text, on which this edition is based. His work is almost final on the subject, but especially in the matter of conjectural fillings of the *lacunæ* is subject to revision. But an inspection of the text as given in this volume will show that we have the words of Augustus almost in their entirety.

At Apollonia, on the borders of Phrygia and Pisidia, has been found another ruined temple, with remnants of the Greek version of this inscription. At Apollonia the inscription originally covered seven pages. Of these there are still legible the upper portions of pages two, three, four and five. The correspondence between the text at Ancyra and that at Apollonia is almost exact, and where there is a divergence, it has been indicated.

II. Character and Purpose of the Inscription.

German scholars have waged a fierce warfare over the question of the literary character of the *Res Gestæ*, as Mommsen commonly calls it.

He himself refrains from assigning it decidedly to any class of composition. Is it epitaph, or a "statement of account," or " political statement"? Otto Hirschfeld contends strongly it is not an epitaph because it contains no dates of birth or death, and is in the first person. Wölfflin calls it a statement of account. Geppert sides with Hirschfeld. Bormann, Schmidt and Nissen all hold it to be an epitaph. And this appears to be the final agreement. The latest word is the discussion by Bormann, in 1895, in which he still maintains the epitaph view. For these discussions, cf. the bibliography at the end of this volume.

Of course it is an epitaph of unique character. It has certain striking peculiarities, and specially of omission. There is no mention of domestic affairs. The wife of the Emperor is unnamed. Although in enumerating his honors and offices it was necessary to date events by the names of consuls, yet aside from this he mentions no person outside the imperial household, not even such favorites as Mæcenas and Agrippa. His foes, Brutus, Cassius and Antony, are several times alluded to, but never named. The same is true of Lepidus and Sextus Pompeius. Unfortunate events are not noticed. His omission of the disaster to the Roman arms under Varus has been severely criticised as an attempt to deceive; but if the inscription is really an epitaph one cannot wonder at such silence. The omission of the dates of birth and death has been variously explained. Some have thought that he meant his heirs to fill in any such gaps after his death, and to recast the whole into the third person. Or, it has been suggested that it was the desire of Augustus to be counted a divinity, and that therefore he wished to pose as one "without beginning of years, or end of days." It certainly would be incongruous to record the death of a god. With regard to his general purpose Mommsen says: "No one would look for the arcana of empire in such a document, but for such things as an *imperator* of mind shrewd rather than lofty, and who skillfully bore the character of a great man while he himself was not great, wished the whole people, and especially the rabble, to believe about him." Two purposes are manifest throughout the document. One is to pose as a saviour of the state from its foes, and not at all as a seeker after personal aggrandizement; another is to represent his whole authority as having been exercised under constitutional forms. These two ideas appear again and again.

III. Divisions of the Text.

The text may be roughly divided into three sections. Chapters one to fourteen give the various offices held by Augustus, and the honors bestowed upon him; chapters fifteen to twenty-four recount his expenditures for the good of the state and the people; and the remaining chapters, twenty-five to thirty-five, give the statement of his various achievements in war, and his works of a more peaceful character. This classification will not hold rigorously, but is true in the main.

The division into chapters or paragraphs is marked in the Latin text by making the first line of each chapter project a little to the left of the remaining lines. Each such paragraph is relatively complete. And the use of such a topical method marks a new manner of composition quite different from the old annalistic style of Roman historiography.

IV. The Greek Version.

George Kaibel has made a special study of the Greek version, and is led to the opinion that it was made by a Roman rather than by a Greek. It is a grammar and dictionary rendering, rather than the idiomatic work of one quite at home in the use of Greek. This conclusion is based upon linguistic grounds. A further question remains as to where this translation was made, whether at Rome or in the provinces. The fact of the identity of the two copies at Apollonia and at Ancyra would seem to indicate a common Roman source.

V. The Supplement.

This is poorly written both in the Latin and in the Greek; and it is also a very imperfect summary of the document, summing up only what was spent upon games, donations and buildings. The fact that it is in the third person also proves that it is not the work of Augustus. The reckoning by denarii rather than by sesterces points to a Greek origin, and the mention of favors shown by Augustus to provincial towns (cf. c. 4 and notes) would indicate one outside of Rome.

VI. Trustworthiness of the Inscription.

The corroborations of the inscription by other inscriptions, coins and later historians, as well as by allusions in contemporary literature, form an interesting study. And the trustworthiness of the record becomes more manifest the more one compares its statements with those of other writers. Only one point has been found where Augustus makes what might be challenged as a perversion of fact. (Cf. c. 2, note 3.)

VII. Masons' Blunders.

A number of apparent errors in the text are to be attributed in all probability to the stone-cutters at Ancyra. Such are the superfluous *et* of Latin ii, 2; *aede* for *aedem*, iv, 22; *quinquens* for *quinquiens*, iv, 31; *ducenti* for *ducentos*, iv, 45; *provicias* for *provincias*, v, 11; *Tigrane* for *Tigranem*, v, 31. εὔξησα for ηὔξησα, Gr. iv, 8; ʿΡωμάοις for ʿΡωμαίοις, vii, 6; ὕπατον for ὑπάτων, vii, 15; ἄνδρας μυριάδων for ἀνδρῶν μυριάδας, viii, 8; omission of τρὶς before χειλίας, ix, 13; ἐπεσκευσα for ἐπεσκευάσα, x, 18; omission of ναὸν before ἀγοράν, xi, 10; επεύξησα for ἐπηύξησα, xiv, 4; omission of ʾΑρτάξου, xv, 3; μείσζονος for μείζονος, xv, 15; πρυκατηλειμένας for κατειλημένας, xv, 17; ἐπειταδε for ἐπίταδε, xvi, 11; βασιλεες for βασιλεῖς, xvi, 22; βασιλεις for βασιλεὺς, xvii, 4; ἐπείκειαν for ἐπιείκειαν, xviii, 5; ἀγορᾷ Σεβαστῇ for ἀγορὰ Σεβαστή, xix, 1.

VIII. Signs and Abbreviations.

The Latin and Greek texts are printed in such a way as to give the best idea practicable of their actual condition. Roman numerals denote the pages of the inscription, and the Arabic figures the lines. These numerals and the chapter headings are no part of the inscription. The projection of the first line of each chapter in the Latin is the only method of marking the divisions in the original.

Parts of the Greek and Latin text included within brackets, [ ], are conjectural restorations of the portions of the inscription which have perished. The Greek generally is a guide to the Latin and *vice versa*, for the instances are rare where both versions have been lost. The textual notes show that not all scholars have reckoned the same number of missing letters. These variations are quite allowable, for it is impossible to say that just so many letters are missing in any given case, owing to the various sizes of different letters, and varying degrees of closeness of writing.

Where dots (. . .) occur, it signifies that Mommsen reckons as many letters unrestored as there are dots.

The sign § indicates a mark in the original resembling a figure 7, or a very open 3.

The same sign in brackets [§] indicates an unfilled interval in the stone.

The apices over vowels in the Latin indicate similar marks in the original in the case of a, e, o and u, and in the case of i a prolongation of that letter above the line.

Where certain letters of the Latin text are italicized it indicates that while they do not appear in the plaster casts, yet they were traced by Alfred Domaszewski (a fellow-worker with Humann) on the stone itself, by means of certain discolorations from paint, or gilding, or weather, which marked the bottom of the incisions of the letters in several cases where the surface of the stone had been worn away.

In the textual notes, B. stands for Bormann, G. for Geppert, S. for J. Schmidt, Sk. for Seeck, W. for Wölfflin, Apoll. for the inscription at Apollonia, and Anc. for that at Ancyra.

The abbreviations of the names of authors and their works in the historical notes are indicated in the bibliography at the close of the book.

MONUMENTUM ANCYRANUM.

Rérum gestárum díví Augusti, quibus orbem terra[rum] imperib populi Rom. subiécit, § et inpensarum, quas in rem publicam populumque Ro[ma]num fecit, incísarum in duabus aheneís pílís, quae su[n]t Romae positaé, exemplar sub[i]ectum.

I.   C. I.

1 Annós undéviginti natus exercitum priváto consilio et. privata impensá

2 comparávi, [§] per quem rem publicam [do]minatione fac- tionis oppressam

3 in libertátem vindicá[vi. Ob quae sen]atus decretis honor- [ifi]cis in

4 ordinem suum m[e adlegit C. Pansa A. Hirti]o consulibu- [s, c]on[sula]-

I, 3.   ob quae, W. quas ob res ; S. and B. propter quae.

Below is a copy of the deeds of the divine Augustus, by which he subjected the whole world to the dominion of the Roman people, and of the amounts which he expended upon the commonwealth and the Roman people, as engraved upon two brazen columns which are set up at Rome.[1]

c. 1.

In my twentieth year,[1] acting upon my own judgment[2] and at my own expense,[3] I raised an army[4] by means of which I restored to liberty the commonwealth which had been oppressed by the tyranny of a fac- tion.[5]   On account of this the senate by laudatory decrees admitted me to its order,[6] in the consulship of Gaius Pansa and Aulus Hirtius, and at

---

NOTES.

[1] This title at Ancyra extends over the first three pages of the Latin, that is over so much of the 'inscription as is on the left wall of the pronaos; the Greek title extends over seventeen of the nineteen pages of the Greek version.

In its present form, the title cannot be the same as that over the original at Rome. All from "as engraved" is certainly an addition, probably made by the

Μεθηρμηνευμέναι ὑπεγράφησαν πράξεις τε καὶ δωρεαὶ Σεβαστοῦ
θεοῦ, ἃς ἀπέλιπεν ἐπὶ ʿΡώμης ἐνκεχαραγμένας χαλκαῖς στήλαις
δυσί.

I.   C. I.

1 ᾿Ετῶν δεκαε[ν]νέα ὢν τὸ στράτευμα ἐμῇ γνώμῃ καὶ
2 ἐμοῖς ἀν[αλ]ώμασιν ἡτοί[μασα], δι᾽ οὗ τὰ κοινὰ πρά-
3 γματα [ἐκ τῆ]ς τ[ῶ]ν συνο[μοσα]μένων δουλήας
4 [ἠλευ]θέ[ρωσα. ᾿Εφ᾽ ο]ἷς ἡ σύνκλητος ἐπαινέσασά
5 [με ψηφίσμασι] προσκατέλεξε τῇ βουλῇ Γαίῳ Πά[νσ]α
6 [Αὕλῳ ʿΙρτίῳ ὑ]π[ά]το[ι]ς, ἐν τῇ τάξει τῶν ὑπατ[ικῶ]ν

I, 7.   ἅμα, B. μοὶ or ἐμοὶ.

Galatian legate who ordered the magistrates of Ancyra to have the inscription placed
on the temple of Augustus. The last two words in the Latin (placed first in the
English), were probably inserted only by a blunder at Ancyra. "A copy subjoined,"
doubtless stood in the legate's letter, just as we might write "see enclosure." But
what of the remainder of the inscription, "Of the deeds . . . . Roman people"?
It is hardly conceivable that this was the title of the inscription at Rome, because it
embraces only two of the three parts into which the subject-matter falls. It covers the
achievements and the expenditures of Augustus; in reverse order, however, from that
of the document itself; and it omits any allusion to the subject-matter of the first
fourteen chapters, which have to do with the offices and honors conferred upon
Augustus.

It is impossible to say what was the superscription at Rome. Possibly there was
none. The name of Augustus, most likely, was conspicuous somewhere in connection
with the front of the mausoleum, and this inscription may very well have been devoid
of title.

C. I. [1] Augustus was nineteen years old on Sept. 23, 710.

[2] Cicero (*Ad Att.* XVI, 8, 1,) on Nov. 1, 710, writes: "I have letters from
Octavian; great things are doing; he has led over to his views the veterans of
Casilinum and Calatia." Cf. Vell. II, 61. Dio XLVI, 29.

[3] Cf. Cic. (*Phil.* III, 2, 3), "The young Cæsar, without our (the senate's)
advice or consent, raised an army and poured forth his patrimony."

[4] Gardthausen, *Aug.* 1er Th. 2er Bd. p. 524, thinks that this beginning the Res
Gestae with the raising of an army, is an admission of the military foundation of the
principate.

[5] Such a statement is part of Augustus' scheme to pose as a restorer of the old
order. He makes Brutus, Cassius, Pompey and Antony public enemies.

[6] Cicero says (*Phil.* V, 17, 46), that on Jan. 1, 711, "the senate voted that
Gaius Cæsar, son of Gaius, pontiff, should be a senator, and hold praetorian rank in
speaking." Dio (XLVI, 29), says that on Jan. 2 or 3, "Cæsar was made senator as
a quaestor."

5   rem locum s[imul dans sententiae ferendae, et im]perium mihí
    dedit [§].
6   Rés publica n[e quid detrimenti caperet, me] pro praetore
    simul cum
7   consulibus pro[videre iussit.   Populus] autem eódem anno
    mé
8   consulem, cum [cos. uterque bello ceci]disset, et trium virum
    reí publi-
9   cae constituend[ae creavit].

c. 2.

10 Qui parentem meum [interfecer]un[t, eó]s in exilium expuli.
    iudiciís legi-
11 timís ultus eórum [fa]cin[us, e]t posteá bellum inferentis reí
    publicae
12 víci b[is a]cie.

I, 5.   ferendae, W. dicendae; simul ..... ferendae,   B. sententiae dicendaè
        mihi dans; after dedit B. erases [§].
I, 7.   jussit, B. jubens.

the same time gave me consular rank in the expression of opinion;[7] and
gave me the *imperium*.[8]   It also voted that I as propraetor,[9] together
with the consuls, should see to it that the commonwealth suffered no
harm.[10]   In the same year, moreover, when both consuls had perished
in war, the people made me consul,[11] and triumvir for organizing the
commonwealth.[12]

c. 2.

Those who killed my father[1] I drove into exile by lawful judgments,[2] avenging their crime, and afterwards, when they waged war
against the commonwealth, I twice defeated them in battle.[3]

---

[7] Livy (*Ep.* CXVIII), " he received the consular ornaments." App. (*B. C.* III,
51) adds that he was given consular rank in speaking. Cf. Mommsen, *Röm. St.*,
I, pp. 442, 443.
[8] Cf. Cic. (*Phil.* 11, 8, 20), " The senate gave Gaius Cæsar the fasces." Cf.
Tac. *Ann.* I, 10; Livy, *Ep.* CXVIII.
[9] App. *B. C.* III, 51.   Vell. II, 61.
[10] The formula by which in emergencies, extraordinary powers were given to the
ordinary magistrates.   This measure had since 216 B. C., entirely superseded the old

7 [ἅμα τ]ὸ σ[υμβου]λεύειν δοῦσα, ῥάβδου[ς] τ᾽ ἐμοὶ ἔδωκεν.
8 [Περ]ὶ τὰ δημόσια πράγματα μή τι βλαβῇ, ἐμοὶ με-
9 [τὰ τῶν ὑπά]των προνοεῖν ἐπέτρεψεν ἀντὶ στρατηγο[ῦ.]
10 [. . . . .] Ὁ δὲ] δ[ῆ]μος τῷ αὐτῷ ἐνιαυτῷ, ἀμφοτέρων
11 [τῶν ὑπάτων π]ολέμῳ πεπτω[x]ό[τ]ων, ἐμὲ ὑπα-
12 [τον ἀπέδειξ]εν καὶ τὴν τῶν τριῶν ἀνδρῶν ἔχον-
13 [τα ἀρχὴν ἐπὶ] τῇ καταστάσει τῶν δ[η]μοσίων πρα-
14 [γμάτων] ε[ἵλ]ατ[ο

C. 2.

15 Τοὺς τὸν πατέρα τὸν ἐμὸν φονεύ]σ[αν]τ[α]ς ἐξώρισα κρί-
16 [σεσιν ἐνδί]κοις τειμω[ρ]ησάμε[ν]ος αὐτῶν τὸ
17 [ἀσέβημα x]αὶ [με]τὰ ταῦτα αὐτοὺς πόλεμον ἐ-
18 [πιφέροντας τῇ πα]τ[ρ]ίδι δὶς ἐνείκησα παρατάξει.

---

custom of appointing a dictator. (Cf. note [1]) Chap. V. The present formula, however, had been employed long before the disuse of the dictatorship. Cf. Livy III, 4; VI, 19. This extraordinary commission was not restricted to the consuls. Cf. Cæs. B. C. I, 5.

[11] Hirtius was killed April 16, 711, and Pansa died of wounds received on the 15th, in the fighting against Antonius. Cæsar Octavianus and Q. Pedius were elected consuls Aug. 19, 711. Dio LVI, 30; C. I. L. I, p. 400=x, 8375; Tac. Ann. I, 9; Suet. Aug. 100. Vell. (II, 65), says the election was on Sept. 22. But Macrobius, (Sat. I, 35, 25'), assigns the fact that he was made consul in the month Sextilis, as one of the reasons why the name of that 'month was changed to August.

[12] C. I. L. I, p. 466 and App. B. C. IV, 7, fix the formal ratification of the triumvirate by the people, as having been proposed by the tribune Publius Titius and carried in a public assembly on Nov. 27, 711.

C. 2. [1] An instance of Augustus' avoiding the names of his enemies; here, particularly, Brutus and Cassius.

[2] The Lex Pedia, Sept., 711, named from Augustus' colleague in the consulship, constituted an extraordinary tribunal for this class of offenders: the penalty was interdiction from fire and water, i. e., outlawry. Livy, Ep. CXX; Vell. II, 69; App. III, 95; Suet. Aug. 10; Dio XLVI, 49.

[3] The only instance in the Res Gestae of a palpable distortion of fact. The battles at Philippi, in November, 712, are referred to. For the date see Gardthausen, Aug. 2er Th. 1er Halbband, p. 80. In the first fight, Suetonius says (Aug. 13), that Cæsar hardly escaped, ill and naked, from his camp to the wing of Antony's army. He was ill, and had to be carried in a litter, according to Plutarch, Brut. p. 41. In Antony, 22, Plutarch says: "In the first battle, Cæsar was completely routed by Brutus, his camp taken, he himself very narrowly escaping by flight." The decisive defeat of the Republicans was twenty days later.

c. 3.

13 [B]ella terra et mari c[ivilia exter]naque tóto in orbe terrarum
   s[uscepi]

14 °victorque omnibus [superstitib]us cívibus pepercí. § Exte[r-
   nas]

15 gentés, quibus túto [ignosci pot]ui[t, co]nserváre quam ex-
   cídere m[alui].

16 Míllia civirm Róma[norum adacta] sacrámento meo fuerunt
   „circiter [quingen]-

17 ta. § Ex quibus dedú[xi in coloni]ás aut remísi in municipia
   sua stipen[dis emeri]-

18 tis millia aliquant[um plura qu]am trecenta et iís omnibus
   agrós a [me emptos]

19 aut pecuniam pró p[raediis a] me dedí. § Naves cépi sescen-
   [tas praeter]

20 eás, si quae minóre[s quam trir]emes fuerunt. §

I, 14.. superstitibus, Sk. following Hirschfield, veniam petentibus.

I, 1° aliquantum, B. and W. aliquanto; a me emptos, B. following Bergk,
   adsignavi.

I, 19. ‾praediis a me, B. and W. praemiis militiae (me in stone might be iae.)

c. 3.

I ur·lertook civil and foreign wars by land and sea throughout the
whole world, and as victor I showed mercy to all surviving citizens.[1]
Foreign peoples, who could be pardoned with safety, I preferred to preserve rather than to destroy. About five hundred thousand Roman
citizens took the military oath of allegiance to me.[2] Of these I have
settled in colonies or sent back to their *municipia*,[3] upon the expiration
of their terms of service,[4] somewhat over three hundred thousand, and
to all these I have given lands purchased by me, or money for farms,[5]
out of my own means. I have captured six hundred ships, besides
those which were smaller than triremes.[6]

C. 3. [1] The text here is conjectural. Mommsen is almost alone in holding to
"surviving," Zumpt, in his edition of 1869, had read "suppliant" (*supplicibus*),
Bergk, in 1873, "asking pardon" (*deprecantibus*). Hirschfeld, the same sense,
(*veniam petentibus*). Seeck insists on the latter reading, in spite of Mommsen's argu-
ments for his own choice. Augustus did not spare all surviving citizens either after
Philippi or Actium, cf. Dio LI, 2: After Actium "of the senators and knights,
and other leading men, who in any way had helped Antony, he fined some,
many he killed, some he spared." For his conduct after Philippi, cf. Suet. *Aug.*
13. But a coin of 727 (Eckhel VI, 88, Cohen I, p. 66, No. 30), has CÆSAR
COS VII CIVIBUS SERVATEIS, "Cæsar for the seventh time consul, the citizens
having been preserved." It commemorates the civic crown given to Augustus,

c. 3.

19 [Πολέμους καὶ κατὰ γῆν] καὶ κατὰ θάλασσαν ἐμφυ-
20 [λίους καὶ ἐξωτικοὺς] ἐν ὅλῃ τῇ οἰκουμένῃ πολ-
21 [λοὺς ἀνεδεξάμην, νεικ]ήσας τε πάντων ἐφεισάμην
22 [τῶν περιόντων πολειτῶν. τ]ὰ ἔθνη, οἷς ἀσφαλὲς ἦν συν-
23 [γνώμην ἔχειν, ἔσωσα μ]ᾶλ[λον] ἢ ἐξέκοψα. § Μυριάδες

II.

1 'Ρωμαίων στρατ[εύ]σ[ασ]αι ὑπ[ὸ τὸ]ν ὅρχον τὸν ἐμὸν
2 ἐγένοντ[ο] ἐνγὺς π[εντήχ]ο[ντ]α· [ἐ]ξ ὧν κατή[γ]αγον εἰς
3 τὰ[ς] ἀπο[ι]χίας ἢ ἀ[πέπεμψα εἰς τὰς] ἰδία[ς πόλεις] ἐκ-
4 [λυομένους. . . . .
5 . . . .
6 . . . .
7 . . . .
8 . . . .

---

cf. c. XXXIV. There are other coins with Ob Cives Servatos, "On account of the preservation of the citizens."

2 This fact is one of the few which the latest text, based on Humann's work, alone establishes. Merivale's comment on the relation of Augustus to the army is noteworthy : "Their hero (Julius Cæsar) discarded the defence of the legions, and a few months witnessed his assassination. Augustus learned circumspection from the failure of his predecessor's enterprise. He organized a military establishment of which he made himself the permanent head; to him every legionary swore personal fidelity ; every officer depended upon his direct appointment." (C. XXXII.)

3 C. 15 states the number colonized at 120,000. The 200,000 over and above the 300,000 here named, are accounted for in the twenty-five legions, 150,000 men in service at his death, leaving only 50,000 as the number who died in service or were dishonorably discharged during the long rule of Augustus. For a study of the strength and disposition of the Roman army at the death of Augustus, cf. Mommsen's R. G., pp. 67–76.

4 The term of service in 741, was twelve years for praetorian soldiers and sixteen for legionaries, raised in 758 to sixteen and twenty years respectively. Cf. c. 17, N. 2.

5 The reading of Wölfflin and others (see textual note) would give instead of "lands purchased by me," "I have assigned lands," and instead of "money for farms, out of my own means" "money for reward of service." Bormann, *Schr. Nachl.* p. 18–20, does not think that Augustus meant to state that he paid these charges from private sources, but believes that such a statement would be irrelevant in this section, if true, and an anticipation of cc. 15 and 16.

6 Sextus Pompeius lost thirty ships at Mylae, and at Naulochus, out of three hundred which he had, eighteen were sunk and the rest, with the exception of seventeen, burned or captured. Cf. App. *B. C.* V, 108, 118, 121. Plut. *Ant.* 68, says

c. 4.

21 [Bis] ováns triumpha[vi, tris egi c]urulis triumphós et appellá-
[tus sum viciens
22 se]mel imperátor. [Cum deinde plú]ris triumphos mihi se-
[natus decrevisset,

I, 22. deinde, B. autem.

c. 4.

Twice I have triumphed in the ovation,[1] and three times in the
curule triumph,[2] and I have been twenty-one times saluted as imperator.[3]

---

that Augustus took 300 ships at Actium. These captures give, in round numbers, 600
vessels.

C. 4. [1] The ovation was the lesser triumph. The general entered the city clad
as an ordinary magistrate, and on foot, or as here, (see the Greek), on horseback,
decked with myrtle. Suet. *Aug.* 22, says, these ovations were after Philippi, and the
Sicilian war; the former in 714, the latter, Nov. 13, 718. Cf. Dio XLVIII, 31,
XLIX, 15; C. I. L. I, p. 461.

[2] In the curule triumph, for important victories, the general was vested in purple,
and rode in a four-horse chariot, preceded by the fasces. These three triumphs were
celebrated on the 13th, 14th and 15th of August, 725, for the Dalmatian successes, the
victory of Actium and the capture of Alexandria. Cf. C. I. L. I, p. 328 and 478.
Prop. II, 1, 31, ff, gives an eye-witness' account of the second day. Cf. Livy, *Ep.*
CXXXIII; Suet. *Aug.* 22; Verg. *Aen.* VIII; 714, Dio LI, 21.

[3] The acclamation as *imperator*, on account of success in war, must be carefully
distinguished from the title used as a prefix to the name and as a mark of perpetual
authority. The title imperator was regularly and permanently assumed at the beginning of each reign, after that of Augustus. To him it was formally assigned by the
senate, in Jan., 725. C. I. L., V, 1873: *Senatus populusque Romanus imp. Cæsari,*
divi. Juli. f. cos. quinct. cos. design. sext. imp. sept. republica conservata. The term
thus had a double usage and meaning in such cases.

It soon came about that only the *princeps* could assume the special designation
for military successes, no matter whether won by him in person or not. Tacitus says,
Ann. III, 74: "Tiberius allowed Blaesus to be saluted as imperator by the legions.
Augustus conceded the title to some, but Tiberius' allowing it to Blaesus was the last
instance." For a discussion of *Imperator* as permanent title, see Gardthausen, p. 527,
and Merivale, *History of the Romans*, c. XXXI.

Most of the acclamations of Augustus as imperator can be traced. No Greek
inscription records them. A list follows. In the later instances Tiberius was associated.

    I. April 15 (?) 711. After battles about Mutina. C. I. L. X, 8375 and Dio
       XLVI, 38.
    II. Not traced.
    III. Before 717. Cohen, *Vipsan.* 3, gives a coin with the words *imp. divi Juli f.*
       ter. III Vir v. p. c. M. Agrippa cos. desig. Agrippa entered his consulship
       Jan. 1, 717.

C. 4.

9 Δὶς ἐ[πὶ κέλητος ἐθριάμβευσα], τρὶς [ἐ]φ᾽ ἅρματος. Εἰχο-
10 σά[κις καὶ ἅπαξ προσηγορεύθην αὐτο]κράτωρ. Τῆς

IV. Probably connected with the Sicilian victory and ovation of 718.

V. 720 or 721. Probably connected with Dalmatian victories of one of those years. Cf. C. I. L. V, 526.

VI. From Sept. 2, 723, to 725. On account of Actium. Cf. Oros, VI, 19, 14. C. I. L. X, 3826. *Imp. Cæsari divi f. imp. vi, cos. iii* (723). C. I. L. X, 4830, *imp. Cæsari divi f. cos. v* (725) *imp. vi.*

VII. From 725 to 729. C. I. L. VI, 873 : *senatus populusque Romanus imp. Cæsari divi Juli f. cos. quinct.* (725) *cos. desig. sex. imp. sept. republica conservata.* On account of Thracian and Dacian victory of M. Licinius Crassus. Dio LI, 25, says : " Sacrifices and festivals were decreed to Cæsar and to Crassus. He did not, however, as some say, take the name imperator. Cæsar alone assumed that."

VIII. From 729 to 734. Two inscriptions at Nismes (Donat. 96, 6) read : *imp. Cæsari divi f. Augusto cos. nonum* (729) *designato decimum, imp. octavum.* Dio LIII, 26, says it was for a Celtic victory of Marcus Vinicius.

IX. From 734 to 739 (?) Coins have the inscription *Augustus Cæsar div. f. Armen. capt. imp. viii.* These commemorate the Armenian expedition of Tiberius in 734. Possibly Augustus took the title on account of the return of the captured standards from Parthia, which he accounted a greater triumph than many a victory in open warfare.

X. 739 (?) to 742. C. I. L. V, 8088 and others : *Augustus imp. x, tribunicia potestate xi.* The latter falls in the years 742, 743. Probably referable to successes in Rhætian war of 739.

XI. 742. Coins (Cohen, n. 147-150) give : *imp. xi.* The causes were the successes of Tiberius in Pannonia in 742. Dio LIV, 31.

XII. 743 to 744. C. I. L., III, 3117 : *imp. xii tr. pot. xiii* and VI, 701, 702 : *pontifex maximus, imp. xii cos. xi trib. pot. xiv.* Referable to Germanic victory of Drusus. Dio LIV, 33.

XIII. Tiberius Imp. 745. Suet., *Tib.* 9, says that Tiberius received the oration for Pannonian and Dalmatian victories. Cf. Val. 5, 5, 3. Dio LV, 2.

XIV. Tiberius Imp. II. 746-755. Dio LV, 6, refers this acclamation to the Germanic victories of 746. Many coins, milestones and other inscriptions of the period indicated mention this fourteenth acclamation. Cf. C. I. L., II, 3827; 4931; V, 7243; 7817 ; VI, 1244.

XV. 755. For the Armenian victory of C. Cæsar. Dio Cass. LV, 11. C. I. L. X, 3827; *pont. max., cos. iii (xiii) imp. xv, tr. p. xxv, p. p.*

XVI. Untraced.

XVII. Tiberius Imp. III. 759. Dio LV, 28, referring to the German expedition of Tiberius in 759, says, " Nothing great was accomplished. Yet both Augustus and Tiberius received the acclamation as imperators." Cf. C. I. L. V. 6416.

23 eis su]persedi [§]. I[tem saepe laur]us deposuí, § in Capi-
[tolio votis, quae]

24 quáque bello nuncu[paveram, solu]tís. § Ob res á [me aut
per legatos]

25 meós auspicís meis terra m[ariqu]e pr[o]spere gestás qu[in·
quagiens et quin]-

26 quiens decrevit senátus supp[lica]ndum esse dís immo[rtali
bus. Dies autem

27 pe]r quós ex senátús consulto [s]upplicátum est, fuere DC
[CCLXXXX. In triumphis

28 meis] ducti sunt ante currum m[e]um regés aut r[eg]um
lib[eri novem. Consul

29 fuer]am terdeciens, c[u]m [scribeb]a[m] haec, [et agebam
se]p[timum et trigensimum annum

30 tribu]niciae potestatis.

I, 23. decrevisset, S. decerneret; item saepe, S. itaque modo; item saepe
laurus, B. laurumque potius.

I, 29. agebam, B. following Bergk, eram, and omits annum.

After that, when the senate decreed me many triumphs,[4] I declined
them. Likewise I often deposited the laurels in the Capitol [5] in fulfil-
ment of vows which I had also made in battle. On account of enter-
prises brought to a successful issue on land and sea by me, or by my
lieutenants under my auspices, the senate fifty-five times decreed that
there should be a thanksgiving to the immortal gods.[6] The number of
days, moreover, on which thanksgiving was rendered in accordance with
the decree of the senate was eight hundred and ninety.[7] In my triumphs there have been led before my chariot nine kings, or children of
kings.[8] When I wrote these words I had been thirteen times consul,
and was in the thirty-seventh year of the tribunitial power.[9]

XVIII. Tiberius Imp. IV. Probably for successes in Illyricum.

XIX. Tiberius Imp. V, 762. Dio LVI, 17, refers to the Dalmatian war. A coin
of 763-4 (Cohen n. 27) gives: *Ti. Cæsar August. f. imperat. v. pontifex,
tribun. potestate xii.*

XX. Tiberius Imp. VI. 765. The cause is not clear, probably for slight successes
of Tiberius and Germanicus against the Germans in 763, 764. Dio LVI, 25.
A Spanish milestone, C. I. L. II, 4868, gives the data.

XXI. Tiberius Imp. VII. Tac. *Ann.* I, 9, says Augustus was twenty-one times
Imperator. A coin of Lyons (Cohen n. 35-38) has: *Ti. Cæsar Augusti f.
imperator VII.* This dates from the lifetime of Augustus. Tiberius did not
receive a further acclamation.

[4] [a] After his own victory over the Cantabri, that of Varro over the Salassi and
that of M. Vinicius over the Germans, in 729. Cf. Florus, IV, 12, 53.

11 [συνκλήτου] . . . . . ψηφισσ. . .

12 . . . . ων τὴν [δάφνην]

13 . . . .

14 . . . .

15 . . . . . . [Διὰ τὰ πράγ]μ[ατα, ἃ]

16 [αὐτὸς ἢ διὰ τῶν πρεσβευτῶν ἐμῶν] κατώρθω-

17 σα, π[εντ]ηκοντάκις [καὶ] πεντά[κις ἐψ]ηφίσατο ἡ

18 σύ[νκλητ]ος θεοῖς δεῖ[ν] θύεσθαι. ['Ημ]έραι οὖν αὗ-

19 [τα]ι ἐ[κ συ]ν[κλήτου] δ[ό]γματ[ο]ς ἐγένοντο ὀκτα[κ]όσιαι
ἐνενή-

20 [κοντα]. 'Εν [τ]οῖς ἐμοῖς [θριάμ]βοις [πρὸ το]ῦ ἐμοῦ ἅρ-

21 μ[ατος βασι]λεῖς ἢ [βασιλέων παῖ]δες [παρήχθ]ησαν

22 ἐννέα. § ['Υπάτ]ε[υ]ον τρὶς καὶ δέκ[ατο]ν, ὅτε τ[αῦ]τα
ἔγραφον,

23 καὶ ἥμη[ν τρια]κ[οστὸ]ν καὶ ἕβδομ[ον δημαρχ]ικῆ-

III.

1 ἐξουσίας.

II, 16. Before ἐμῶν W. inserts τῶν.

---

[b] After the restoration of the standards by the Parthians in 734. Cf. Borghesi II, 100 ff.

[c] After the victories of Tiberius in Germany in 746. Dio LV, 6

[d] After the victories of Tiberius in Pannonia? Dio LVI, 17.

[5] A part of the ordinary ceremonial of the triumph. Cf. Mommsen, *Röm. St.* I, p. 61, 95, Marquardt, *Staatsverwaltung*, II, p. 582.

[6] For a thanksgiving after the expedition of Tiberius into Armenia cf. Dio LIV, 9. Cf. also Cic. *Phil.* XIV, 11, 29. For two other instances, cf. Mommsen, *R. G.*, appendix, pp. 161–178.

[7] Not an incredible number. Thanksgivings were offered in Julius Cæsar's time of fifteen, twenty, forty and fifty days. Cf. Drumann III, 609, No. 84. Fifty days were decreed for the victories of Hirtius, Pansa and Octavian in 711.

[8] The only names traceable are those of Alexander and Cleopatra, the children of Cleopatra and Alexander brother of Jamblichus, King of the Emesenes. Cf. Dio LI, 2, 21. Prop. 2, 1, 33, tells of "Kings with their necks surrounded with golden chains," in the triumph of Aug. 14, 725.

[9] The emperors assumed the consulship only irregularly and for short periods. Their taking of the "tribunitial power" was not through a regular election to the tribuneship, as was the case with the consulship, for Augustus as a patrician was ineligible; but it was the assumption of a power equal to that of the tribunes. This made the emperors sacrosanct, gave them the initiative and the veto, and well subserved the fiction of their being the representatives and champions of the people. For discussions of this power cf. Merivale, *Hist. of Rom. C.* XXXI; Mommsen, *Röm. St.* II, p. 759, 771–777, 833–845.

c. 5.

31 [Dictatura]m et apsent[i etipraesenti mihi datam . . . . a
    populo et senatu
32 M. Marce]llo e[t] L. Ar[runtio consulibus non accepi. Non
    recusavi in summa
33 frumenti p]enuri[a c]uratio[ne]m an[nonae, qu]am ita ad-
    [ministravi, ut . . . . .
34 paucis diebu]s metu et per[i]c[lo quo erat populu]m uni-
    v[ersum meis impen-
35 sis liberarem]. § Con[sulatum tum dat]um annuum e[t per-
    petuum non
36 accepi.

c. 6.

37 Consulibus M. Vinucio et Q. Lucretio et postea P.] et Cn.
    L[entulis et tertium

    I,ʻ31. datam......... a populo et senatu, W nomine populi et senatus oblatam;
        S. a populo et senatu ultro delatam; et senatu, S. senatuque Romano.
    I, 33, 34. ut......... paucis diebus, W uti intra paucos dies; B. ut paucissimis
        diebus.
    I, 34. quo erat, W and S. praesenti.
    I, 34, 35. meis impensis, W. privata impensa; S. meis sumptibus.

c. 5.

The dictatorship which was offered to me by the people and the
senate, both when I was absent and when I was present, in the consulship of Marcus Marcellus and Lucius Arruntius, I did not accept.[1] At
a time of the greatest dearth of grain I did not refuse the charge of
the food supply, which I so administered that in a few days, at my own
expense, I freed the whole people from the anxiety and danger in which
they then were.[2] The annual and perpetual consulship offered to me at
that time I did not accept.[3]

c. 6.

During the consulship of Marcus Vinucius and Quintus Lucretius, and afterwards in that of Publius and Cnaeus Lentulus, and a

Succeeding emperors, down to 268 A. D., dated their accession from the day of
assuming the tribunitial power. The wording is peculiar in this sentence. May it not
have been that Augustus expected his heir or executors to fill in the exact dates at the
time of his death, as suggested in the introduction?

C. 5. [1] Dio, LIV, 1, writes: "In the following year (732) the Tiber again overflowed;
statues in the Pantheon were struck by lightning, so that the spear was knocked out
of the hand of Augustus. Pestilence was so violent in all Italy that year that there
was no one to till the fields; and I think the same was the case in foreign lands. The
Romans thought that this plague and famine had come upon them, because they had

c. 5.

2 Ἀὐτεξούσιόν μοι ἀρχὴν καὶ ἀπόντι καὶ παρόντι
3 διδομένην [ὑ]πό τε τοῦ δήμου καὶ τῆς συνκλήτου
4 Μ[άρχ]ῳ [Μ]αρχέλλῳ καὶ Λευκίῳ Ἀρρουντίῳ ὑπάτοις
5 ο[ὐκ ἐδ]εξάμην. § Οὐ παρῃτησάμην ἐν τῇ μεγίστῃ
6 [τοῦ] σ[είτ]ου σπάνει τὴν ἐπιμέλειαν τῆς ἀγορᾶς, ἣν οὔ-
7 [τως ἐπετήδευ]σα, ὥστ' ἐν ὀλίγαις ἡμέρα[ις το]ῦ παρόντος
8 φόβου καὶ κι[νδ]ύνου ταῖς ἐμαῖς δαπάναις τὸν δῆμον
9 ἐλευθερῶσα[ι]. Ὑπατείαν τέ μοι τότε δι[δ]ομένην καὶ
10 ἐ[ν]ιαύσιον κα[ὶ δ]ι[ὰ] βίου οὐκ ἐδεξάμην.

c. 6.

11 Ὑπάτοις Μάρχῳ Οὐινουχίῳ καὶ Κοίντῳ Λ[ουκρ]ητ[ίῳ]
12 καὶ μετὰ τα[ῦ]τα Ποπλίῳ καὶ Ναίῳ Λέντλοις καὶ

not made Augustus consul that year; they wished to name him dictator, and with great show of violence compelled the senate, shut up in the curia, to decree this; threatening to burn them unless they did it. So the senate approached Augustus with the twenty-four fasces (insignia of dictatorship, the consul having only twelve), and begged him to accept the dictatorship and the administration of the food supply. He did indeed undertake the latter charge, and ordered that duumvirs, who had held the praetorship five years before, should be yearly appointed to have charge of the distribution of grain, but would by no means accept the dictatorship. When neither by words nor prayers he could move the people, he tore his garments. For he justly wished to avoid the jealousy and hatred of that name, since moreover, he already held a dignity and power superior to that of the dictatorship." Vell. II, 89, 5, says: "The dictatorship which the people persistently thrust upon him, he as constantly repelled."

The dictatorship had fallen into disuse after 552, and was revived, irregularly, by Sulla in 672. Cæsar made it the basis of his power, being made perpetual dictator shortly before his death. After that event, on motion of Antony, the office was abolished.

2 In Chap. 15, Augustus states that in 731 he twelve times distributed grain at his own expense. This assumption of the grain administration in 732 was not strictly a charity. The extract from Dio under Note 1, gives some of the details. It is probable that from this time the tribute in kind was turned into the *fiscus*, or imperial treasury, instead of into the *ærarium*, or treasury of the senate, as heretofore. This new task of the imperial government involved not merely the gratuitous distribution of grain to the ordinary Roman citizens (after 752 even to senators and knights), but also the providing of a sufficient supply of grain for all purchasers at a minimum price, often below the market value. It appears that grain tickets "tessaræ frumentariæ" were distributed to the citizens entitled to free grain, and then, to assist the vast multitude of strangers, freedmen, and *attachés* of the great houses, money tickets, "tessaræ nummariæ," were given out. Cf. Mommsen, *Röm. St.*, II, 992.

3 Vell. II, 89; Suet. *Aug.* 26; Dio, LIV, 10. Dio's statement that Augustus in 735 accepted the consular power (differing from the consulship as the tribunitial power from the tribuneship. Cf. Note 9, Chap. 4.) for life, cannot be correct in face of the

38 Paullo Fabio Maximo et Q. Tuberone senatu populoq]u[e
   Romano consen-
39 tientibus]. . . . .
40 . . . .
41 . . . .
42 . . . .

c. 7.

43 . . . .
44 . . . . . [Princeps senatus fui usque ad
   eum diem, quo scrips]eram [haec,

third time in that of Paullus Fabius Maximus and Quintus Tubero, by
the consent of the senate and the Roman people I was voted the sole charge
of the laws and of morals, with the fullest power;[1] but I accepted the
proffer of no office which was contrary to the customs of the country.[2]
The measures of which the senate at that time wished me to take charge,
I accomplished in virtue of my possession of the tribunitial power.[3] In
this office I five times associated with myself a colleague, with the consent of the senate.[4]

c. 7.

For ten years in succession I was one of the triumvirs for organizing the commonwealth.[1] Up to that day on which I write these words

---

other two authorities cited, who corroborate Augustus here. Chapter 8 tells of two
special assumptions of the consular power for the taking of the second and third census.

C. 6. [1] Before the restoration of the text of this inscription, in this case depending
entirely upon the remains at Apollonia, it used to be taught that Augustus accepted
the formal superintendence of laws and morals. And there seemed to be good ground
for such belief. Horace, c., 740 in *Carm. IV*, 5, v, 22, says, " Morality and law have
subdued foul wrong;" and in *Ep.*, II, 1, v. 1, " Since thou hast protected Italy with
arms, adorned her with morality, and improved her with laws." Ovid wrote, *Tristia*,
II, 233: " The city wearies thee with the care of laws and morals, which thou desirest.
should be like thy own." Suet. *Aug.* 27, says : " He accepted the control of laws
and morals for life, as he had the tribunitial power; and in the exercise of this control,
altho' without the honor of the censorship, he yet thrice took the census of the people,
the first and third times with a colleague, the second time alone." Dio, LIV, 10, 30,
says that in 735 and 742 Augustus accepted this office for periods of five years. But
the inscription shows that Suetonius and Dio were wrong, and that a natural but incor-
rect inference had been drawn from the poets.

This power was offered to Augustus three times: in 735, 736 and 734, and as
often refused. Why was it offered, and why refused? Cf. Dio, LIV, 10; Vell. II,
91, 92; Suet. *Aug.* 19. While Augustus was in Asia in 735 M. Egnatius Rufus, who
is painted as a sort of Catiline, tried to obtain the consulship, and even to supplant

13 τρίτον Παύλλῳ Φαβίῳ Μαξίμῳ καὶ Κοίν[τῳ] Του-
14 βέρωι § τῆς [τε σ]υνκλήτου καὶ τοῦ δήμου τοῦ
15 ʽΡωμαίων ὁμολογ[ο]ύντων, ἵν[α ἐπιμε]λητὴς
16 τῶν τε νόμων καὶ τῶν τρόπων ἐ[πὶ τῇ με]γίστῃ
17 [ἐξ]ουσ[ίᾳ μ]ό[νο]ς χειροτονηθῶ §, ἀρχὴν οὐδε-
18 μ[ία]ν πα[ρὰ τὰ πά]τρ[ια] ἔ[θ]η διδομένην ἀνεδε-
19 ξάμην· § ἃ δὲ τότε δι᾽ ἐμοῦ ἡ σύνκλητος οἰ-
20 κονομεῖσθαι ἐβούλετο, τῆς δημαρχικῆς ἐξο[υ]-
21 οίας ὢν ἐτέλε[σα. Κ]αὶ ταύτης αὐτῆς τῆς ἀρχῆς.
22 συνάρχοντα [αὐτ]ὸς ἀπὸ τῆς συνκλήτου π[εν]-
23 τάκις αἰτήσας [ἔλ]αβον.

IV.   c. 7.

1 Τριῶν ἀνδρῶν ἐγενόμην δημοσίων πραγμάτων
2 κατορθωτὴς συνεχέσιν ἔτεσιν δέκα. § Πρῶτον

III, 14. Last word Apoll., τοῦ, Auc. τῶν.

Augustus, and stirred up sedition in the attempt. This so alarmed the senate and people that they offered Augustus the plenary power of legislation and coercion. The repetition of the offer in 736 was from a similar cause. The reason for that of 743 is unknown. The power thus offered was analogous to the decemvirate, or the Sullan dictatorship. Cf. Mommsen, *Röm., St.*, II, 686.

² This sentence answers the second question asked in Note 1. It was part of Augustus' policy to seem to keep wholly within the lines of the constitution. Hence his refusal to accept any extraordinary office. Yet his tribunitial power was new and extraordinary. Tacitus' comment is caustic, *Ann.*, III, 56: "That specious title (the tribunitial power) importing nothing less than sovereign power, was invented by Augustus at a time when the name of king or dictator was not only unconstitutional but universally detested. And yet a new name was wanted to overtop the magistrates and the forms of the constitution."

³ Dio, LIV, 16, names three laws promulgated by Augustus in 736 : one took cognizance of bribery by candidates for office ; a second dealt with extravagance ; and a third was for the encouragement of matrimony.

⁴ ᵃ in 736 Agrippa was associated with Augustus for five years. Cf. Dio, LIV, 12 ; Vell. II, 90 ; Tac. *Ann.* III, 56. ᵇ in 741 Agrippa again for five years. Cf. Dio, LIV, 12, 28. ᶜ in 748 Tiberius for five years. Cf. Dio, LV, 9 ; Vell. II, 99 ; Suet. *Tib.* 9, 10, 11. ᵈ in 757 Tiberius for ten years. Cf. Dio, LV, 13 ; Vell. II, 103 ; Tac. *Ann.*, I, 3, 10. ᵉ in 766 Tiberius for an indefinite time. Cf. Dio, LVI, 28.

C. 7. ¹ Suet. *Aug.* 27: "He administered the triumvirate for organizing the commonwealth through ten years." Cf. C. I. L. I, p. 461 and p. 466. The first triumvirate lasted from Nov. 27, 711, to Dec. 31, 716 ; the second from Jan. 1, 717, to Dec. 31, 721. But cf. c. 34, N. 1.

45   per annos quadraginta. Pontifex maximus, augur, quin-
     decimviru]m sacris [faciundis,
46   septemvirum epulonum, frater arvalis, sodalis Titius, fetiali]s
     fui.

II.   c. 8.

1 Patriciórum numerum auxí consul quintum iussú populi et
   senátús. § Sèna-
2 tum ter légi. et In consulátú sexto cénsum populi conlegá M
   Agrippá égí. §

I have been *princeps* of the senate through forty years.[2] I have been
pontifex maximus,[3] augur,[4] a member of the quindecemviral college of
the sacred rites,[5] of the septemviral college of the banquets,[6] an Arval
Brother,[7] a member of the Titian sodality,[8] and a fetial.[9]

c. 8.

In my fifth consulship, by order of the people and the senate, I
increased the number of the patricians.[1] Three times I have revised
the list of the senate.[2] In my sixth consulship, with Marcus 'Agrippa
as colleague, I made a census of the people. I performed the lustration

---

[2] Cf. Dio, LIII, 1. This title had been conferred upon the senior senator who
had served as censor. Its only privilege was the [right of speaking first in debate.
The honor had fallen into abeyance with the death of Catulus in 694. It is readily
seen how the revival of such a title and of the right to express his views before any
other senator, gave Augustus a quasi-constitutional initiative in the senate. Gradually
the title dropped its second part, and "prince" began to have something of its modern
significance. Cf. Tacitus, *Ann.* III, 53, for Tiberius' view of its meaning.

Augustus' notation of time here, "through forty years," is similar to the "thirty-
seventh year of the tribunitial power" in Chap. IV, or "the seventy-sixth year" of
Chap. 36.

[3] He was made *pontifex* in 706 by Julius Cæsar. Cf. Cic. *Phil.* V, 17, 46; Vell.
II, 59. For his taking the office of *pontifex maximus* cfl c. 10, N. 3.

[4] The date of Augustus' assumption of the augurate is discussed by Drumann,
IV, 250. Coins are the chief witnesses, and their testimony is confused. The date
probably was 713 or 714.

[5] A coin of Augustus (Cohen, *Jul.* 60; *Aug.* 88) has *imp. Cæsar divi f. III vir
iter. r. p. c. cos. iter. et tert desig.*, which fixes the time as between 717 and 720; it has
also the tripod, the symbol of the quindecemvirate.

[6] We can say only that Augustus received this dignity before 738; for there is a
coin of that year showing the *simpulum*, the *lituus* and the tripod, the symbols respectively of the three foregoing offices, and the *patera*, or bowl, that of the septemviral
office. The four colleges thus associated are the chief ones. Cf. Chap. 9.

3 ἀξιώματος τόπον ἔσχον τῆς συνκλήτου ἄχρι
4 ταύτης τῆς ἡμέρας, ἧς ταῦτα ἔγραφον, ἐπὶ ἔτη τεσ-
5 σαράκοντα. § Ἀρχιερεύς, § αὔγουρ, § τῶν δεκαπέντε ἀν-
6 δρῶν τῶν ἱεροποιῶν, § τῶν ἑπτὰ ἀνδρῶν ἱεροποι-
7 ῶν, § ἀ[δε]λφὸς ἀρουᾶλις, § ἑταῖρος Τίτιος, § φητιᾶλις.

c. 8.

8 Τῶν [πατ]ρικίων τὸν ἀριθμὸν εὔξησα πέμπτον
9 ὕπατ[ος ἐπιτ]αγῇ τοῦ τε δήμου καὶ τῆς συνκλή-
10 του. § [Τὴν σύ]νκλητον τρὶς ἐπέλεξα. § Ἕκτον ὕπα-
11 τος τὴν ἀπ[ο]τείμησιν τοῦ δήμου συνάρχον-
12 [τ]α ἔχων Μᾶρκον Ἀγρίππαν ἔλαβον, ἥτις ἀπο-

---

[7] The name of Augustus is twice found in the *Acta Fratrum Arvalium*, once in May, 767, in recording a vote, and in Dec., 767, in the record of the nomination of his successor.

[8] Tacitus says the Titian Sodality was instituted by Titus Tatius for keeping up the Sabine ritual. Cf. *Ann.* I, 54. The record here is all that'is known of Augustus' connection with it.

[9] The fetials had charge of the formalities in declaring war and peace. Dio L, 4, says that Augustus went through the old-fashioned ceremonies in declaring war against Cleopatra.

These three colleges had fallen into abeyance in the time of Cicero. Augustus undoubtedly revived them. Cf. Suet. *Aug.* 31. Such restoration, and religious conservatism in general, as even in the case of Domitian, marks the policy of the emperors for two hundred years, and was one of their favorite methods of posing simply as restorers of the good old times.

C. 8. [1] In 725. The Saenian law, passed by the people in 724, authorized this proceeding, and the senate's decree followed. Hence the order, "people and senate." Cf. Tac. *Ann.* XI, 25; Dio, LII, 42. An earlier creation of patricians is assigned by Dio to the year 721. But he is probably mistaken, as Tacitus, in the passage just noted, says that Claudius was obliged to create more patricians, "because the number had declined even after being recruited by the dictator Cæsar under the Cassian law, and by Augustus the *princeps* under the Saenian law." Such a creation was not a right of the principate. Cæsar and Augustus did it by special authorization of people and senate. Claudius did it in virtue of his censorship, and this status continued till Domitian absorbed the censorship in the principate, and assumed the right as a permanent one.

[2] During most of the republican history senate numbered, ideally, three hundred. In Cicero's time it had over four hundred members. Julius Cæsar raised it to about nine hundred. Suet. *Aug.*, 35, says: "By two separate scrutinies he (Augustus) reduced to their former number and splendor the senate, which had been swamped by a disorderly crowd; for they were now more than a thousand, and some

3 Lústrum post annum alterum et quadragensimům féc[i]. §
   Quó lústro cívi-

4 um Románórum censa sunt capita quadragiens centum millia
   et sexa-

5 g[i]nta tria millia. [§] [Iteru]m consulari cum imperio
   lústrum

6 [s]ólus féci C. Censorin[o et C.] Asinio cos. § Quó lústro
   censa sunt

7 cívium Romanóru[m capita] quadragiens centum millia et
   ducen-

8 ta triginta tria m[illia. Tertiu]m consulári cum imperio
   lústrum

9 conlegá Tib. Cae[sare filio feci] § Sex. Pompeio et Sex. Ap-
   puleio cos.

10 Quó lústro ce[nsa sunt civium Ro]mánórum capitum quadragiens .

11 centum mill[ia et nongenta tr]iginta et septem millia. §

12 Legibus noví[s latis complura e]xempla maiorum exolescentia

II, 9.   S. inserts meo after filio.
II, 12. complura, B. et multa.

after forty-one years. In this lustration the number of Roman citizens
was four million and sixty-three thousand.[3] Again assuming the consular power in the consulship of Gaius Censorinus and Gaius Asinius,
I alone performed the lustration. At this census the number of Roman
citizens was four million, two hundred and thirty thousand.[4] A third
time, assuming the consular power in the consulship of Sextus Pompeius and Sextus Appuleius, with Tiberius Cæsar as colleague, I performed the lustration. At this lustration the number of Roman citizens
was four million, nine hundred and thirty-seven thousand.[5] By new
legislation I have restored many customs of our ancestors which had

---

of them very mean persons, who, after Cæsar's death, had been chosen by dint of interest and bribery, so that they had the name of Orcini among the people." They were
also called Charonites, because they owed their elevation to the last will of Cæsar, who
had gone into Orcus to Charon. Dio, XL, 48, 63, tells of freedmen in the senate and,
XLIII, 22, of a private soldier; Gell., XV, 4, of a muleteer, cf. Juvenal, Sat. VII,
199.

    Dio, LII, 42, cf. LIII, 1, tells of the first scrutiny, in 725-6. A hint from Augus-
tus was enough to cause the withdrawal first of sixty, then of one hundred and forty
senators. He also tells, LIV, 13, 14, of a further revision in 736, by which the num-

13 [τείμη]σις μετὰ [δύο καὶ] τεσσαρακοστὸν ἐνιαυ-
14 τὸν [σ]υνε[κ]λείσθη. 'Εν ᾗ ἀποτειμήσει 'Ρωμαίων
15 ἐτει[μήσ]α[ντο] κεφαλαὶ τετρακό[σιαι ἑ]ξήκον-
16 τα μυ[ριάδες καὶ τρισχίλιαι. Δεύτερον ὑ]πατι-
17 κῇ ἐξ[ουσίᾳ μόνος Γαΐῳ Κηνσωρίνῳ καὶ]
18 Γαΐῳ ['Ασινίῳ ὑπάτοις τὴν ἀποτείμησιν ἔλαβον·]
19 ἐν [ᾗ] ἀπ[οτειμήσει ἐτειμήσαντο 'Ρωμαί]-
20 ων τετ[ρακόσιαι εἴκοσι τρεῖς μυριάδες καὶ τ]ρι[σ]-
21 χίλιοι. Κ[αὶ τρίτον ὑπατικῇ ἐξουσίᾳ τὰς ἀποτειμή]-
22 σε[ι]ς ἔλα[βο]ν, [ἔχω]ν [συνάρχοντα Τιβέριον]
23 Καίσαρα τὸν υἱόν μο[υ Σέξτῳ Πομπηΐῳ καὶ]

V.

1 Σέξτῳ 'Αππουληΐῳ ὑπάτοις· ἐν ᾗ ἀποτειμήσει
2 ἐτειμήσαντο 'Ρωμαίων τετρακόσιαι ἐνενήκοντα
3 τρεῖς μυριάδες καὶ ἑπτακισχείλιοι. § Εἰσαγαγὼν και
4 νοὺς νόμους πολλὰ ἤδη τῶν ἀρχαίων ἐθῶν κα-
5 ταλυόμενα διωρθωσάμην καὶ αὐτὸς πολλῶν

---

ber was brought down to six hundred. He assigns a third sifting to 743 (LIV. 35),
and a fourth to 757 (LV, 13). Mommsen, however, is inclined to connect the three
revisions of Augustus with the censuses of 726, 746 and 767, and to regard those of
736 and 757 as extraordinary, and therefore not named by Augustus, in his desire to
appear entirely within constitutional lines. Cf. Mommsen, *R. G.*, p. 35.

3 Suetonius evidently depends on this inscription when he says, *Aug.* 27: " Three
times he took the census of the Roman people, the first and third times with a colleague, the second time alone." This first census was in 725-6. Cf. Dio, LII, 42 ;
LIII, 1 ; C. I. L. IX, 422, *imp. Cæsar VI, M. Agrippa II cos.; idem censoria potestate lustrum fecerunt.*

The lustrum was strictly the expiatory offering made at the close of the census.
The census had not been taken for forty-one years. The number of Roman citizens
of military age in 684 had been given as but 450,000. This census of 726 reported
4,063,000. Probably the vast apparent increase rose from the fact of the earlier enumeration counting only such as presented themselves before the censors in the city, while
at the later time the citizens throughout the empire were counted. Clinton, *Fasti Hel-
lenici*, III, 461, estimates a total free citizenship of more than 17,000,000. The total
population of the empire at this time, including citizens, allies, slaves and freedmen,
has been estimated at 85,000,000. Cf. Merivale, *Rom.* cc. XXX, XXXIX.

The Greek of the inscription here reads erroneously 4,603,000.

4 In 746. The result, 4,233,000, shows a gain of 170,000.

5 In 767. Just before the death of Augustus. Result, 4,937,000 ; gain since 746,
704,000.

13   iam ex nost[ro usu reduxi et ipse] multárum rér[um exem]-
     pla imi-
14   tanda pos[teris trádidi.

                              c. 9.

15   Vota pro valetudine mea suscipi per cons]ulés et sacerdotes
     qu[into]
16   qu[oque anno senatus decrevit. Ex iis] votís s[ae]pe fecerunt
     vívo
17   *me* [ludos aliquotiens sacerdotu]m quattuor amplissima collé-
18   [gia, aliquotiens consules. Privat]im etiam et múnicipatim
     *univers*i
19   [cives sacrificaverunt sempe]r apud omnia pulvínária pró
     vale-
20   [tudine mea.

                              c. 10.

21   Nomen meum senatus consulto inc]lusum est in saliáre carmen
     et sacrosan-

     II, 13.   reduxi, B. sanxi; S. revocavi.
     II, 15.   suscipi, B. suscipere,
     II, 16.   iis, S. quibus.
     II, 17.   me ludos aliquotiens, W. mihi ludos interdum; aliquotiens, B. votivos
               modo.
     II, 18.   aliquotiens, W interdum; aliquotiens consules, B. modo consules ejus
               anni.
     II, 19.   sacrificaverunt, B. sacrificia; W. supplicaverunt; semper, B. concer-
               diter; W. unanimiter.
     II, 20.   B. adds fecerunt.

now begun to fall into disuse, and I have myself also committed to
posterity many examples worthy of imitation.[6]

                              c. 9.

     The senate decreed that every fifth year vows for my good health
should be performed by the consuls and the priests. In accordance
with these vows games have been often celebrated during my lifetime,
sometimes by the four chief colleges, sometimes by the consuls.[1] In
private, also, and as municipalities, the whole body of citizens have
constantly sacrificed at every shrine for my good health.[2]

                              c. 10.

     By a decree of the senate my name has been included in the Salian

6 πραγμάτων μείμημα ἐμαυτὸν τοῖς μετέπει-
7 τα παρέδωκα.

c. 9.

8 Εὐχὰς ὑπὲρ τῆς ἐμῆς σωτηρίας ἀναλαμβάνειν
9 διὰ τῶν ὑπάτων καὶ ἱερέων καθ᾽ ἑκάστην πεν-
10 τετηρίδα ἐψηφίσατο ἡ σύνκλητος. ἐκ τού-
11 των τῶν εὐχῶν πλειστάκις ἐγένοντο θέαι,
12 τοτὲ μὲν ἐκ τῆς συναρχίας τῶν τεσσάρων ἱερέ-
13 ων, τοτὲ δὲ ὑπὸ τῶν ὑπάτων. Καὶ κατ᾽ ἰδίαν δὲ καὶ
14 κατὰ πόλεις σύνπαντες οἱ πολεῖται ὁμοθυμα-
15 δ[ὸν] συνεχῶς ἔθυσαν ὑπὲρ τῆς ἐμῆς σω[τ]ηρίας.

c. 10.

16 Τὸ ὄν[ομ]ά μου συνκλήτου δόγματι ἐνπεριελή-

---

6 Suetonius, *Aug.* 34, relates his endeavors to compel matrimony. In Chap. 89, Suetonius writes: "In reading Greek or Latin authors he paid particular attention to precepts and examples which might be useful in public or private life. These he used to extract verbatim, and give to his domestics, or send to the commanders of the armies, the governors of the provinces, or the magistrates of the city, when any of them seemed to stand in need of admonition. He likewise read whole books to the senate, and frequently made them known to the people by his edicts; such as the orations of Quintus Metellus 'For the Encouragement of Marriage,' and those of Rutilius 'On the Style of Building;' to show the people that he was not the first who had promoted those objects, but that the ancients likewise had thought them worthy of their attention." Cf. Livy, *Ep.* LIX; Gell., I, 6.

C. 9. **1** These games were first held in 726, and every fourth year thereafter. The expression "every fifth year" counts the year of the games as the fifth of the old series and also the first of the new. The consuls, or rather the consul Agrippa, Augustus not holding games in his own honor, celebrated the games of 726, the pontifices those of 730, the augurs those of 734, the quindecemvirs those of 738, and the septemvirs those of 742. Cf. c. 7, N. 6. These games are mentioned by Dio, LIII, 1, 2; LIV, 19; Pliny, *Hist. Nat.* VII, 48, 158; Suet. *Aug.* 44. They came to a close with the life of Augustus. We do not hear of them in connection with any subsequent emperor. Vows for his good health had a special fitness, for according to Suetonius, *Aug.* LXXXI, he was almost an invalid. "During his whole course of life he suffered at times dangerous fits of sickness. He was subject to fits of sickness at stated times every year, for about his birthday he was commonly indisposed. In the beginning of spring he was attacked with an inflammation of the midriff; and when the wind was southerly, with a cold in his head. By all these complaints his constitution was so shattered that he could not readily bear heat or cold."

2 Cf. Suet. *Aug.* 59 and 98; Hor. *Carm.* IV, 5, 33; Dio, LI, 19.

22 [ctus ut essem . . .·. . . . et ut q]uoa[d] vívc rem, tribúnicia
potestás mihi

23 [esset, lege sanctum est. Pontif]ex maximus ne fierem in
víví [c]onle-

24 [gaé locum, populo id sace]rdotium deferente mihi, quod
pater meu[s

25 habuit, recusavi; Cepi id] sacerdotium aliquod post annós eó
mor-

26 [tuo qui civilis motús ó]ccasione occupaverat [§], cuncta ex
Italia

27 [ad comitia mea . . . . tanta mu]ltitudine, quanta Romae
nun[q]uam

28 [antea fuisse fertur, coeunte] P. Sulpicio C. Valgio con-
sulibu[s] §.

C. II.

29 [Aram Fortunae reduci iuxta? ae]dés Honoris et Virtutis ad
portam

30 [Capenam pro reditu meo se]nátus consacravit, in qua ponti-

II, 22. sacrosanctus ut essem .... W. sacrosancta ut esset persona mea, or
sacrosancta potestate ut essem.

II, 25. habuit, B. habuerat; cepi id, B. quod.

II, 26. qui civilis motus, B, suscepi qui id tumultus.

II, 27. ad comitia mea......... B. propter mea comitia, or comitiorum caussa;
Sk. inserts coeunte before ad.

II, 28. fertur, Sk. memoriae proditur; omits coeunte.

II, 29. reduci, B. reducis.

hymñ,[1] and it has been enacted by law that I should be sacrosanct, and
that as long as I live I should be invested with the tribunitial power.[2]
I refused to be made *pontifex maximus* in the place of a colleague still
living, when the people tendered me that priesthood which my father
held.   I accepted that office after several years, when he was dead who
had seized it during a time of civil disturbance ; and at the comitia for
my election, during the consulship of Publius Sulpicius and Gaius
Valgius, so great a multitude assembled as, it is said, had never before
been in Rome.[3]

c. 11.

Close to the temples of Honor and Virtue, near the Capena gate,
the senate consecrated in honor of my return an altar to Fortune the
Restorer, and upon this altar it ordered that the *pontifices* and the Vestal

17 φθη εἰ[ς τοὺ]ς σαλίων ὕμνους. καὶ ἵνα ἱερὸς ᾦ
18 διὰ [βίο]υ ΄[τ]ε τὴν δημαρχικὴν ἔχω ἐξουσίαν,
19 νό[μῳ ἐκ]υρώθη. § ᾿Αρχιερωσύνην, ἣν ὁ πατήρ
20 [μ]ου [ἐσχ]ήκει τοῦ δήμου μοι καταφέροντος
21 εἰς τὸν τοῦ ζῶντος τόπον, οὐ προσεδεξά-
22 μ[η]ν. § [ἣ]ν ἀρχιερατείαν μετά τινας ἐνιαυτοὺς
VI.
1 ἀποθανόντος τοῦ προκατειληφότος αὐ-
2 τὴν ἐν πολειτικαῖς ταραχαῖς, ἀνείληφα, εἰς
3 τὰ ἐμὰ ἀρχαιρέσια ἐξ ὅλης τῆς ᾿Ιταλίας τοσού-
4 του πλήθους συνεληλυθότος, ὅσον οὐδεὶς
5 ἔνπροσθεν ἱστόρησεν ἐπὶ ῾Ρώμης γεγονέναι Πο-
6 πλίῳ Σουλπικίῳ καὶ Γαίῳ Οὐαλγίῳ ὑπάτοις.

c. 11.

7 Βωμὸν Τύχης σωτηρίου ὑπὲρ τῆς ἐμῆς ἐπανόδου
8 πρὸς τῇ Καπήνῃ πύλῃ ἡ σύνκλητος ἀφιέρωσεν·

C. 10. [1] Dio writes of the year 725, LI, 20: "When letters were brought about Parthian affairs it was decreed that he should be named in the hymns exactly as were the gods." Tiridates, a Parthian pretender, sought the aid of Augustus. Cf. Chap. 32, and Dio, LI, 18. Augustus balanced Tiridates against Phraates, the legitimate monarch, who sent an embassy, and gave his son to Rome as a hostage.

[2] In 718, when Lepidus had been overthrown, the tribunitial power had been given to Octavian, as formerly to Julius, for life. Inviolability of person̂was one of the privileges of the tribunate. Cf. Oros. VI, 18, 34; Dio, XLIX, 15; LI, 18; LIII, 32. These two later statements relating to the years 724 and 731, Mommsen thinks have to do, the former with the extension of the tribunitial power beyond the city, and the latter to the making it annual, as well as perpetual, so that the years of the principate could be reckoned by it. Cf. Chap. 4, note 9. Cf. also App. B. C. V, 132, and for a discussion of the tribunitial power as an expression of the principate, cf. Mommsen, Röm. St. II, 833, ff.

Wöfflin, cf. textual note, suggests, to fill the gap confessedly left by Mommsen's emendation, a reading which would be translated "that my person should be sacrosanct."

[3] Augustus here characteristically avoids the name of Lepidus. The latter "in the confusion and tumult had seized the supreme pontificate," cf. Livy, Ep. CXVII, "by craft," cf. Velleius II, 63; "Antony transferred the election of the pontifex maximus from the people to the priests again, and through them initiated Lepidus, almost entirely neglecting the customs of the fathers." Cf. Dio, XLII, 53. Lepidus dying in 741, cf. Dio, LIV, 27, Augustus entered upon the office Mar. 6, 742. Cf.

3

31 [fices et virgines Vestales anni]versárium sacrificium facere
32 [iussit die, quo consulibus Q. Luc]retio et [M. Vinuci]o in
    urbem ex
33 [Syria redi, et diem Augustali]a ex [c]o[gnomine nost]ro
    appellavit.

c. 12.

34 [Senatus consulto eodem tempor]e pars [praetorum et tri]bu-
   norum
35 [plebi cum consule Q. Lucret]io et princi[pi]bus [viris ob]-
   viam mihi
36 mis[s]a e[st in Campan]ia[m, qui] honos [ad hoc tempus]
   nemini prae-
37 ter [m]e es[t decretus. Cu]m ex H[ispa]niá Gal[liaque,
   rebus in his p]rovincís prosp[e]-
38 re [gest]i[s], R[omam redi] Ti. Ne[r]one P. Qui[ntilio
   consulibu]s [§], áram
39 [Pácis A]u[g]ust[ae senatus pro] redi[t]ú meó co[nsacrari
   censuit] ad cam-

II, 32.   B. inserts eo before die.
II, 33.   redi, B. redieram.'
II, 36.   S. inserts ante after honos.

virgins should offer sacrifice yearly on the anniversary of the day on
which I returned into the city from Syria, in the consulship of Quintus
Lucretius and Marcus Vinucius, and it called the day the Augustalia,
from our cognomen.[1]

c. 12.

By a decree of the senate at the same time a part of the prætors
and tribunes of the people with the consul Quintus Lucretius and leading citizens were sent into Campania to meet me, an honor which up to
this time has been decreed to no one but me.[1] When I returned from
Spain and Gaul after successfully arranging the affairs of those provinces, in the consulship of Tiberius Nero and Publius Quintilius, the
senate voted that in honor of my return an altar of the Augustan Peace
should be consecrated in the Campus Martius, and upon this altar it

C. I. L., I. p. 387. It was unlawful to deprive a living man of this office, cf. App., B.
C., V, 131.
C. 11. [1] October 12, 735. In C. I. L. I. p. 404, is found an inscription of that date :
Feriae ex senatus consulto, quod eo die imp. Cæsar Augustus ex transmarinis

9 πρὸς ᾧ τοὺς ἱερεῖς καὶ τὰς ἱερείας, ἐνιαυσιον ὑ-
10 σίαν ποιεῖν ἐκέλευσεν ἐν ἐκείνῃ τῇ ἡμέρᾳ,
11 ἐν ᾗ ὑπάτοις Κοίντῳ Δουκρητιῳ καὶ Μάρκῳ
12 Οὐινουκίῳ ἐκ Συρίας εἰς Ῥώμην ἐπανεληλυ-
13 θει[ν], τήν τε ἡμέραν ἐκ τῆς ἡμετέρας ἐπωνυ-
14 μίας προσηγόρευσεν Αὐγουστάλια.

C. 12.

15 Δόγματι σ[υ]νκλήτου οἱ τὰς μεγιστας ἀρχὰς ἄρ-
16 ξαντε[ς σ]ὺν μέρει στρατηγῶν καὶ δημάρχων
17 μετὰ ὑπ[ά]του Κοίντου Δουκρητίου ἐπέμφθη-
18 σάν μοι ὑπαντήσοντες.μέχρι Καμπανίας, ἥτις
19 τειμὴ μέχρι τουτου οὐδὲ ἑνὶ εἰ μὴ ἐμοὶ ἐψηφίσ-
20 θη. § Ὅτε ἐξ Ἰσπανίας καὶ Γαλατίας, τῶν ἐν ταύ-
21 ταις ταῖς ἐπαρχείαις πραγμάτων κατὰ τὰς εὐ-
22 χὰς τελεσθέντων, εἰς Ῥώμην ἐπανῆλθον §
23 Τιβερίῳ [Νέ]ρωνι καὶ Ποπλίῳ Κοιντιλίῳ ὑπάτοις,

VII.

1 βωμὸν Ε[ἰρ]ήνης Σεβαστῆς ὑπὲρ τῆς ἐμῆς ἐπανό-

provincis urbem intravit araq (*ue*) *Fortunae reduci constituta.* There are also gold and silver coins (Eckhel VI, 100, Cohen, *Aug.* nos. 102–108) with the inscription, *Fortunae reduci, Cæsari Augusto senatus populusque Romanus,* Dio, LIV, 10, tells that Augustus after having arranged matters in Sicily, Greece, Asia and Syria, returned to Rome, and that many honors were decreed to him, but that he would accept none of them, "but that an altar should be consecrated to Fortune the Restorer, that the day should be accounted a feast day, and that it should be called the Augustalia."

The location near the Porta Capena was chosen, because it was through that gate Augustus would enter the city, coming by the Appian Way from Brundisium. The altar was dedicated on Dec. 15, C. I. L. X, 8375. Cf. Dio, LI, 19; App. *B. C.* II, 106.

C. 12. [1] Dio, LIV, 10, relates that in this year there were great tumults in connection with the consular comitia, and no election was possible. In consequence of this the senate sent messengers to Augustus urging him to deal with the trouble. Q. Lucretius, one of the delegates, was named consul by Augustus on the spot where they met. It is Mommsen's idea (*R. G.,* p. 48) that the story of Dio, and the statement of Augustus relate to the same event, and that Augustus was not willing to admit that so late in his reign, such disturbances could be, and that he therefore conveys the impression that what was really an appeal for aid was rather an embassy of honor. This Mommsen thinks quite in keeping with the general character and method of Augustus. Bormann, on the other hand (*Schr. Nach.,* p. 29), sees no conflict in the two accounts. He believes that Dio narrates truthfully enough an earlier deputation sent to Augustus, possibly at

40   [pum Martium, in qua ma]gistratús et sac[erdotes et virgines]
     V[est]á[les
41   anniversarium sacrific]ium facer[e iussit.

c. 13.

42 Ianum] Quirin[um, quem cl]aussum ess[e maiores nostri
     volüer]unt,
43   [cum p]er totum i[mperium po]puli Roma[ní terra ,marique
     es]set parta vic-
44   [torii]s pax, cum pr[ius, quam] náscerer, [a condita] u[rb]e
     bis omnino' clausum
45   [f]uisse prodátur m[emori]ae, ter me princi[pe senat]us
     claudendum esse censui[t.

c. 14.

46   Fil]ios meos, quós iuv[enes mi]hi eripuit for[tuna], Gaium
     et Lucium Caesares

    II, 42.   S. inserts tum after quem

ordered the magistrates and priests and vestal virgins to offer sacrifices
on each anniversary.[2]

c. 13.

Janus Quirinus, which it was the purpose of our fathers to close
when there was peace won by victory[1] throughout the whole empire of
the Roman people on land and sea, and which, before I was born, from
the foundation of the city, was reported to have been closed twice in all,[2]
the senate three times ordered to be closed while I was *princeps*.[3]

c. 14.

My sons, the Cæsars Gaius and Lucius, whom fortune snatched
from me in their youth,[1] the senate and Roman people, in order to do

---

Athens, some time before his return, and that Lucretius was named consul there by
Augustus. Then, some time later, the deputation of honor, as recorded in the inscription, was sent into Campania.

    [2] That this annual sacrifice was instituted July 4, 741, appears from C. I. L., I,
395. *Feriae ex. s. c. quodeo die ara Pacis Augustæ in campo Martio constituta est
Nerone' et Varo cos.* Cf. Fasti of Præneste, Jan. 30, C. I. L., I, 313, for day of the
actual dedication; also Ovid, *Fasti* I, 709; Dio, LIV, 25.

    This altar was probably on the Flaminian Way by which Augustus returned from
Gaul.

2 δου ἀφιερωθῆναι ἐψηφίσατο ἡ σύνκλητος ἐν πε-
3 δίῳ Ἄρεως, πρὸς ᾧ τούς τε ἐν ταῖς ἀρχαῖς καὶ τοὺς
4 ἱερεῖς τάς τε ἱερείας ἐνιαυσίους θυσίας ἐκέλευσε ποιεῖν.

c. 13.

5 Πύλην Ἐνυάλιον, ἣν κεκλῖσθαι οἱ πατέρες ἡμῶν ἠθέ-
6 λησαν εἰρηνευομένης τῆς ὑπὸ Ῥωμάοις πάσης γῆς τε
7 καὶ θαλάσσης, πρὸ μὲν ἐμοῦ, ἐξ οὗ ἡ πόλις ἐκτίσθη,
8 ᾧ παντὶ αἰῶνι δὶς μόνον κεκλεῖσθαι ὁμολογεῖ-
9 ται, ἐπὶ δὲ ἐμοῦ ἡγεμόνος τρὶς ἡ σύνκλητος ἐψη-
10 φίσατο κλεισθῆναι.

c. 14.

11 Υἱούς μου Γάιον καὶ Λεύκιον Καίσ[α]ρας, οὓς νεανίας ἀ-

C. 13. [1] The exact conditions necessary for the closing of the temple, viz., "peace won by victories" were first made known in 1882 by this perfected text of the *Res Gestæ*.

[2] Cf. Livy, I, 19 ; Varro, V, 165. The temple of Janus (or as the Romans called it, Janus, without the word temple,) (cf. Latin text and Livy, l. c., and Horace, Carm, IV, 15, 9,) had been closed first under Numa and again after the first Punic War.

[3] Augustus first closed it in 725, after Actium. Cf. Livy, l. c.; Dio, LI, 20; Vell., II; 38; Victor, *De Viris Ill.*, LXXIX, 6; Plut. *De Fort. Rom.*, 9; Oros. VI, 20, 8. C. I. L. I, p. 384, supplies the day, January 11. In 728 it was opened again, on account of the war with the Cantabri. Cf. Dio, LIII, 26, Plutarch, l. c. A second time it was closed in 729, cf. Dio, l. c.; Oros., VI, 21, 1. The time of its next opening cannot be determined ; but in all probability it was reopened that very year, on account of the Arabian campaign. Dio, LIV, 36, records that in 744 the Senate decreed that it should be closed, but that a Dacian rebellion interfered. But Dio must be mistaken, for Drusus was then in the midst of his German campaign. But after the campaigns of Drusus and Tiberius in Germany, closed in 746, up to 753, when Gaius Cæsar started for Armenia, the temple might well have been closed. Parts of Dio are lost here, which may have mentioned such closing. The birth of Jesus Christ, 749, falls in this period of peace. Cf. Milton's *Nativity Hymn*. When it was opened for the third time cannot be said. Tacitus says it was opened when Augustus was an old man. But it can hardly have remained shut after the opening of the Armenian war in 753. Augustus was then sixty-two years old. That age may possibly suit the expression of Tacitus. Horace *Ep.*, II, 1, 255, and *Carm.*, IV, 15, 9, mentions the closing of the temple. Suetonius, *Aug.* 22, says : "Janus Quirinus, which had been shut twice only, from the era of the building of the city to his own time, he closed thrice in a much shorter period, having established universal peace both by sea and land." This is almost a literal transcript of the *Res Gestæ*.

C. 14. [1] Gaius and Lucius, the sons of Agrippa and Julia, the daughter of Augustus,

III.

1 honoris mei caussá senatus populusque Romanus annum quín-
tum et deci-
2 mum agentís consulés designávit, ut [e]um magistrátum
inírent post quín-
3 quennium. Et ex eó die, quó deducti [s]unt in forum, ut
interessent consiliis
4 publicis decrevit sena[t]us. § Equites [a]utem Románi uni-
versi principem
5 iuventútis utrumque eórum parm[is] et hastís argenteís do-
nátum ap--
6 pelláverunt. §

c. 15.

7 Plebei Románae viritim HS trecenos numeravi ex testámento
patris
8 meí, § et nomine meo HS quadringenos ex bellórum manibiís
consul

me honor, designated as consuls in the fifteenth year of each, with the
intention that they should enter upon that magistracy after five years.[2]
And the senate decreed that from the day in which they were introduced into the forum they should share in the public counsels.[3] Moreover the whole body of the Roman knights gave them the title, *principes* of the youth, and gave to each a silver buckler and spear.[4]

c. 15.

To each man of the Roman *plebs* I paid three hundred sesterces in
accordance with the last will of my father;[1] and in my own name,
when consul for the fifth time, I gave four hundred sesterces from the

---

were born, the one in 734 (Dio, LIV, 8), the other in 737 (Dio, LIV, 18) and were
adopted by their grandfather immediately after the birth of the latter. Dio, LIV, 18,
says: "Lucius and his brother Gaius, Augustus at once adopted and made heirs of the
empire, without waiting till they grew to manhood, in order that he might be the more
secure against conspiracies." The will of Augustus (Suet. *Tib.* 23), speaks much as
this chapter does of the death of the two Cæsars : "Since harsh fortune has snatched
from me my sons, Gaius and Lucius, let Tiberius Cæsar be heir to two-thirds of my
estate." Suetonius, *Aug.* 26, says that Augustus took his twelfth and thirteenth consulships, for the purpose of introducing these two boys into the forum.

[2] Dio, LV, 9, under the year 748 writes that these lads were wild and insolent and
that the younger, then eleven years old, actually proposed to the people to make Gaius

12 νήρπασεν ἡ τύχη, εἰς τὴν ἐμὴν τειμ[ὴ]ν ἢ τ[ε] σύνκλη-
13 τος καὶ ὁ δῆμος τῶν ʻΡωμαίων πεντεκαιδεκαέτεις
14 ὄντας ὑπάτους ἀπέδειξεν, ἵνα μετὰ πέντε ἔτηʼ
15 εἰς τὴν ὕπάτον ἀρχὴν εἰσέλθωσιν· καὶ.ἀφʼ ἧς ἂν
16 ἡμέ[ρα]ς [εἰς τὴν ἀ]γορὰν [κατ]αχθ[ῶ]σιν, ἵνα [με]τέχω-
17 σιν, τῆς συ[ν]κλήτου ἐψηφίσατο. § ἱππεῖς δὲ ʻΡω-
18 μαίων σύν[π]αντες ἡγεμόνα νεότητος ἑκάτε-
19 ρον αὐτῶν [πρ]οσηγόρευσαν, ἀσπίσιν ἀργυρέαις
20 καὶ δόρασιν [ἐτ]είμησαν.

c. 15.

21 Δήμῳ ʻΡωμα[ίω]ν κατʼ ἄνδρα ἑβδομήκοντα π[έντ]ε
22 δηνάρια ἑκάστῳ ἠρίθμησα κατὰ δια-
23 θήκην τοῦ πατρός μου, καὶ τῷ ἐμῷ ὀνόματι

consul. Augustus appeared very angry at this, saying it would be a public calamity for the consulship to be borne by one of less age than that at which he himself had assumed it, viz., twenty. Gaius was, however, designated consul in 749, and Lucius in 752. Cf. Tac. *Ann.* I, 3; a coin of Rome has on one side : *Cæsar Augustus, divi. f., pater patriæ;* on the other : *C. L. Cæsares, Augusti f., cos. desig., princ. juvent.* (Eckhel VI, 171). This must have been struck between Feb. 5, 752, when Augustus received the title *pater patriæ,* and January 1, 754, when Gaius entered upon his actual consulship. Cf. C. I. L. III, n. 323, and VI, 900.

Lucius died, Aug. 20, 755, and so did not reach the consulship to which he had been elected. Gaius died in 757. Cf. Dio, LV, II ; C. I. L. I. p. 472.

[3] Cf. Dio, LV, 9 ; C. I. L. I, p. 286 and 565.

[4] Dio, LV, 12, says : " The bodies of Lucius and Gaius were carried to Rome by military tribunes, and the chief men of each city ; and the golden (sic) shields and spears, which they had received from the knights when they assumed the *toga virilis,* were suspended in the curia."

The title of *princeps juventutis* is somewhat difficult to explain. The fact is attested by Zonaras, X, 35, and by an inscription found near Viterbo (cf. Mommsen R. G., p. 53), which reads : *C. Cæsari Aug. f. d. n. pontif. cos. design. principi juventut,* " To Caius Cæsar, son of Augustus, nephew of the divine (Julius) pontifex, consul designate, prince of the youth." Mommsen sums up his investigation of this (Cf. *R. G.* p. 54, ff.) : the knights were divided into *turmæ,* or troops, each officered by *seviri,* three *decurions* and three *optious* or adjutants. Gaius and Lucius were *decurions* of the first *turma,* and their title, " princes of the youth," was a special one, and always thereafter reserved for members of the imperial family. The title does not appear to have been official, or formally bestowed, but was given by common consent of the knights.

C. 15. [1] Cf. Suet. *Cæs.* LXXXIII : " He (Cæsar) bequeathed to the Roman people his gardens near the Tiber, and three hundred sesterces to each man." Dio, XLIV,

9   quintum dedí, iterum autem in consulátú decimo ex [p]atri-
monio

10   meo HS quadringenos congiári viritim pernumer[a]ví, § et
consul

11   urdecimum duodecim frúmentátiónes frúmento pr[i]vatim
ccémpto

12   emensus sum, [§] et tribuniciá potestáte duodecimum quad-
ringenós

13   nummós tertium viritim dedí. Quae mea congiaria p[e]r-
venerunt

14   ad [homi]num millia nunquam minus quinquáginta et du-
centa. §

15   Tribu[nic]iae potestátis duodevicensimum consul XII tre-
centís et

16   vigint[i] millibus plebís urbánae sexagenós denariós viritim
dedí. §

17   In colon[i]s militum meórum consul quintum ex manibiís
viritim

III, 17.   In, W. et.

spoils of the wars;[2] again, moreover, in my tenth consulship I gave
from my own estate four hundred sesterces to each man by way of *congiarium;*[3] and in my eleventh consulship I twelve times made distribu-
tions of food, buying grain at my own expense;[4] and in the twelfth
year of my tribunitial power I three times gave four hundred sesterces
to each man.[5] These my donations have never been made to less than
two hundred and fifty thousand men.[6] In my twelfth consulship and
the eighteenth year of my tribunitial power I gave to three hundred and
twenty thousand of the city *plebs* sixty *denarii* apiece.[7] In the colonies
of my soldiers, when consul for the fifth time, I gave to each man a
thousand sesterces from the spoils; about a hundred and twenty thous-

---

35, is peculiar, saying : " Cæsar left to the people his gardens on the Tiber, and to each
man one hundred and twenty sesterces, as Augustus himself says, or as others say,
three hundred sesterces apiece." May it be that Dio has reversed the facts here, and
that it was " others " who reported the smaller sum and Augustus the larger ? Augustus is substantiated, or followed, by Plut.; *Ant.*, XVI, *Brut.*, XX; App. *B. C.*, II, 143.

Three hundred sesterces equals about fifteen dollars. The date of this disburse-
ment is 710 : its amount, supposing the minimum number of receivers, 250,000, comes
to $3,750,000.

[2] The second (and the seventh, cf. Note 8) donations belong to the year 725 and

24 ἐκ λαφύρων [π]ο[λέ]μου ἀνὰ ἑκατὸν δηνάρια

VIII.

1 ,πέμπτον ὑπατος ἔδωκα, § πάλιν τε δέ[κατο]ν
2 ὑπατεύων ἐκ τ[ῆ]ς ἐμῆς ὑπάρξεως ἀνὰ δηνά-
3 ρια ἑκατὸν ἠρίϑ[μ]ησα, [§] καὶ ἐνδέκατον ὕπατος
4 δώδεκα σειτομετρήσεις ἐκ τοῦ ἐμοῦ βίου ἀπε-
5 μέτρησα, [§] καὶ δημαρχικῆς ἐξουσίας τὸ δωδέ-
6 κατον ἑκατὸν δηνάρια κατ' ἄνδρα ἔδωκα· αἷτ[ι]-
7 νες ἐμαὶ ἐπιδόσεις οὐδέποτε ἧσσον ἠλϑ[ο]ν ε[ἰ]ς
8 ἄνδρας μυριάδων εἴκοσι πέντε. δημα[ρ]χικῆς ἐ-
9 ξουσίας ὀκτωκαιδέκατον, ὕπατ[ος] δ[ωδέκατον]
10 τριάκοντα τρισ[ὶ] μυριάσιν ὄχλου πολειτικ[οῦ ἐ]ξή-
11 [κοντα δηνάρια κατ' ἄνδρα ἔδωκα, κα]ὶ ἀποίκοις στρα-
12 τιωτῶν ἐμῶν πέμπτον ὕπατος ἐ[κ] λαφύρων κατὰ
13 ἄνδρα ἀνὰ διακόσια πεντήκοντα δηνάρια ἔδ[ωκα·]
14 ἔλαβον ταύτην τὴν δωρεὰν ἐν ταῖς ἀποικίαις ἀν-

VIII, 17. οὗτος, W. σύνπας; ἀριθμὸς, S. ἀριθμῷ or ἀριθμὸν.

were connected with the triple triumph. Dio mentions the two together, LI, 21 Four hundred sesterces is about twenty dollars.

3 The third donation was in 730, on the return of Augustus after subduing the Cantabri. Dio, LIII, 28, says: "Augustus gave the people a hundred denarii (four hundred sesterces) apiece, but forbade the distribution until his act should receive the sanction of the senate." It would seem to have been unlawful to give money to the people without the consent of the senate. Probably this was a measure of precaution against demagogues.

The term *congiarium*, which is transferred rather than translated, means a gift, primarily of food or drink, and is derived from *congius*, a measure holding about three quarts, which was perhaps originally brought to be filled with grain or oil, or the like.

4 Cf. c. 5 and Note 2. The date was 731

5 The fifth distribution was in 742. We learn from Dio, LIV, 29, that in that year Agrippa died, leaving to the Roman people his gardens and bath, and that Augustus, as his executor, not only turned over these properties, but made a donation besides, as if it had been so willed by Agrippa. Cf. C. I. L., I. p. 472.

6 As c. 8 furnishes a basis for estimating the total population of the empire, so here we have a guide to the number of people in the city. Merivale, *History of the Romans*, c. XL, gives 700,000 as the limit; Bunsen, 1,300,000; Gibbon, c. XXXI, 1,200,000.

7 Sixty denarii is about twelve dollars. This donation, of 749, and the last one mentioned in this chapter, of 752, have been connected with the introduction in those years of Gaius and Lucius Cæsar, into the forum. Cf. c. 14. The amounts are the same in the two cases, and they vary from the sum given at other times.

18 millia nummum singula dedi; acceperunt id triumphale con-
    giárium
19 in colo[n]ís hominum circiter centum et viginti millia. §
    Consul ter-
20 tium dec[i]mum sexagenós denáriós plebeí, quae tum frú-
    mentum publicum
21 accipieba[t] dedi; ea millia hominum paullo plúra quam du-
    centa fuerunt.

c. 16.

22 Pecuniam [pro] agrís, quós in consulátú meó quárto et posteá
    consulibus
23 M. Cr[asso e]t Cn. Lentulo augure adsignávi militibus, solví
    múnicipís. Ea
24 [s]u[mma sest]ertium circiter sexsiens milliens fuit, quam
    [p]ró Italicís
25 'praed[is] numeravi, § et ci[r]citer bis mill[ie]ns et sescen-
    tiens, quod pro agrís
26 próvin[c]ialibus solví. § Id primus et [s]olus omnium, qui
    [d]edúxerunt
27 colonias militum in Italiá aut in provincís, ad memor[i]am
    aetátis
28 meae feci. Et postea Ti. Nerone et Cn. Pisone consulibus,
    [§] item[q]ue C. Antistio

and men in the colonies received that triumphal donation.[8]   When consul for the thirteenth time I gave sixty *denarii* to the *plebs* who were at
that time receiving public grain; these men were a little more than two
hundred thousand in number.[9] [10]

c. 16.

For the lands which in my fourth consulship, and afterwards in
the consulship of Marcus Crassus and Cnæus Lentulus, the augur, I
assigned to soldiers, I paid money to the *municipia*.   The sum which I
paid for Italian farms was about six hundred million sesterces, and that
for lands in the provinces was about two hundred and sixty millions.[1]
Of all those who have established colonies of soldiers in Italy or in the
provinces I am the first and only one within the memory of my age, to
do this.   And afterward in the consulship of Tiberius Nero and Cnæus

15 θρώπων μυριάδες πλ[εῖ]ον δώδε[κα. ὕ]πατος τ[ρι]σ-
16 καιδέχατον ἀνὰ ἑξήχοντα δηνάρια τῷ σειτομετ[ρου]-
17 μένῳ δήμῳ ἔδω[κα· οὗτο]ς ἀρ[ι]θμ[ὸς πλείων εἴκο-
18 σ]ι [μυ]ριάδων ὑπῆρχ[ε]ν.

c. 16.

19 Χρήματα ἐν ὑπατείᾳ τετάρτῃ ἐμῇ κα[ὶ] μετὰ ταῦτα ὑ-
20 πάτοις Μάρκῳ Κράσσῳ καὶ Ναίῳ Λέντλῳ αὔγου-
21 ρι ταῖς πόλεσιν ἠρίθμησα ὑπὲρ ἀργῶν, οὓς ἐμέρισα
22 τοῖς στρατ[ιώ]ταις. Κεφαλαίου ἐγένοντο ἐν Ἰταλίᾳ
23 μὲν μύριαι π[εντακι]σ[χ]ε[ίλιαι μυ]ριάδες, [τῶ]ν [δὲ ἐ]παρ-
24 χειτικῶν ἀγρῶν [μ]υ[ριάδες ἐξακισχίλ]ιαι πεν[τακό]σ[ιαι].

IX.

1 Τοῦτο πρῶτος καὶ μόνος ἀπάντων ἐπόησα τῶν
2 [κατα]γαγόντων ἀποικίας στρατιωτῶν ἐν Ἰτα-
3 λίᾳ ἢ ἐν ἐπαρχείαις μέχρι τῆς ἐμῆς ἡλικίας. § καὶ
4 μετέπειτα Τιβερίῳ Νέρωνι καὶ Ναίῳ Πείσωνι ὑπά-

8 Up to this point the donations have been enumerated in order of time. But here, between the largesses to citizens in 749 and 752 is introduced one given to veterans in 725. Why this break in the order? Mommsen, *R. G.* p. 2 and 59, thinks that a first draft of this inscription was prepared about 750. In this draft Augustus first mentioned all his gifts to the city people ; and at the end placed the one gift to the soldiers. Then, when in 767, the document was brought down to date, this later gift to the people was placed last, instead of being interpolated after the civil donation of 749 and before the military one of 725. But his reasoning has not convinced other scholars.

9 Cf. Dio, LV, 10.

10 Augustus omits any mention of his bounty to discharged soldiers. Cf. Dio, XLVI, 46; XLIX, 14; LV, 6; Appian, V, 129. The total of the donations in this list is 619,800,000 sesterces = about $30,990,000.

C. 16. 1 Cf. c. 3; Dio, LI, 3, 4; Suet. *Aug.* 17. The last writer says that there was a mutiny at Brundisium in a detachment sent there immediately after Actium, and that they demanded reward and discharge. Augustus was forced to come from Samos to settle the trouble. This was in 724. There were 120,000 veterans to be provided for. Cf. c. 15. 600,000,000 sesterces was the compensation for the lands given to these men, an average of 5000 sesterces ($250) for each holding. But not all Italian proprietors were reimbursed. The Italians who had favored Antony were simply dispossessed. To some other Italians were given lands at Dyracchium and Philippi. His expenditure for land in Italy was $30,000,000. As to colonies outside of Italy, Dio, LIV, 23, tells of many settlements in Gallia (Narbonensis) and Iberia in 739. Eusebius notes colonies at Berytus in Syria, and Patræ in Achaia, as founded in 739. Cf. *Chron.* ad. a. Abr. 2001 ; C. I. L. III, p. 95.

29　et D. Laelio cos., et C. Calvisio et L. Pasieno consulibus, et
　　L. Le[ntulo et] M. Messalla
30　consulibus, § et L. Cáninio [§] et Q. Fabricio ċo[s.] milit-
　　[ibus, qu],ós eme-
31　riteis stipendís in sua municipi[a remis]i, praem[ia n]um-
　　erato
32　persolví [§] quam in ˸rem seste[rtium] q[uater m]illien[s
　　li]b[ente]r
33　impendi.

c. 17.

34 Quater [pe]cuniá meá iuví aerárium, ita ut sestertium míl-
　　lien[s] et
35　quing[en]t[ien]s ad eos quí praerant aerário detulerim. Et
　　M. Lep[i]do
36　et L. Ar[r]unt[i]o cos. i[n] aerarium militare, quod ex con·
　　silio m[eo]
37　co[nstitut]um est, ex [q]uo praemia darentur militibus, quí
　　vicena
38　[aut plu]ra sti[pendi]a emeruissent, [§] HS milliens et
　　septing[e]nti-
39　[ens ex pa]t[rim]onio [m]eo detuli. §

Piso, and also in that of Gaius Antistius and Decimus Lœlius, and in
that of Gaius Calvisius and Luçius Pasienus, and in that of Lucius
Lentulus and Marcus Messala, and in that of Lucius Caninius and
Quintus Fabricius, I gave gratuities in money to the soldiers whom I
sent back to their *municipia* at the expiration of their terms of service,
and for this purpose I freely spent four hundred million sesterces.[2]

c. 17.

Four times I have aided the public treasury from my own means,
to such extent that I have furnished to those in charge of the treasury
one hundred and fifty million sesterces.[1]　And in the consulship of
Marcus Lepidus and Lucius Arruntius I paid into the military treasury
which was established by my advice that from it gratuities might be
given to soldiers who had served a term of twenty or more years, one
hundred and seventy million sesterces from my own estate.[2]

---

[2] The dates are 747, 748, 750, 751 and 752. The amount is $20,000,000. It
was in 741 (Dio, LIV, 25) that Augustus determined upon a gift in money as a substitute for the assignments of land customary up to that time. Why such payments began

5 τοῖς καὶ πάλιν Γαίῳ Ἀνθεστίῳ καὶ Δέκμῳ Λαι-
6 λίῳ ὑπάτοις καὶ Γαίῳ Καλουισίῳ καὶ Λευκίῳ
7 Πασσαίνῳ [ὑ]πάτο[ι]ς [καὶ Λ]ευκίῳ Λέντλῳ καὶ Μάρ-
8 κῳ Μεσσάλ[ᾳ] ὑπάτοις κ[α]ὶ [Λ]ευκίῳ Κανιν[ί]ῳ καὶ
9 [Κ]οίντῳ Φα[β]ρικίῳ ὑπάτοις στρατιώταις ἀπολυ-
10 ομένοις, οὓς κατήγαγον εἰς τὰς ἰδίας πόλ[εις], φιλαν-
11 θρώπου ὀνόματι ἔδωκα μ[υρ]ιάδας ἐγγὺς [μυρία]ς.

c. 17.

12 Τετρά[x]ις χρήμ[α]σιν ἐμοῖς [ἀν]έλαβον τὸ αἰράριον, [εἰς] ὃ
13 [x]ατήνεγκα [χ]ειλίας [ἑπτ]ακοσίας πεντήκοντα
14 μυριάδας. x[αὶ] Μ[ά]ρκῳ [Λεπίδῳ] καὶ Λευκίῳ Ἀρρουν-
15 τίῳ ὑ[πάτοις ε]ἰς τ[ὸ] στ[ρ]α[τιωτ]ικὸν αἰράριον, ὃ τῇ
16 [ἐμῇ] γ[ν]ώ[μῃ] κατέστη, ἵνα [ἐ]ξ αὐτοῦ αἱ δωρ[ε]αὶ εἰσ-
17 [έπειτα τοῖς [ἐ]μοῖς σ[τρατι]ώταις δίδωνται, ο[ἳ εἴκο-
18 σι]ν ἐνιαυτο[ὺ]ς ἢ πλείονας ἐστρατεύσαντο, μ[υ]ρι-
19 άδα[ς] τετρά[x]ις χειλίας διακοσίας πεντήκοντα
20 [ἐκ τῆς ἐ]μ[ῆς] ὑπάρξεως κατήνεγκα.

only in 747 is matter of conjecture; also why they ceased after 752. Probably because the years 742–746 were occupied with the German and Pannonian wars of Tiberius and Drusus, and either there were no discharges, or else no money to spare from the expenses of war. Again in 753 troubles began in the East.

C. 17. [1] Only two of these occasions can be traced. Dio, LIII, 2, mentions one. He says that in 726, when it was determined to exhibit games in honor of Actium, Augustus replenished the empty treasury for that purpose. And there is a coin of c. 738 with the inscription : *Senatus populusque Romanus imperatori Cæsari quod viæ munitæ sunt ex ea pecunia quam is ad ærarium detulit.* Eckhel VI, 105.

Up to 726 the treasury was in charge of the quæstors. Thence to 731 two exprætors, after that year two prætors presided over it, up to the time of Claudius. Cf. Tac. *Ann.* XIII, 29; Dio, LIII, 2 and 32; Suet. *Aug.* 36. The sum mentioned here is $7,500,000. In the Greek τρίς has evidently been omitted before χειλίας.

[2] This was in 759. In 741 (Dio, LIV, 25) Augustus had fixed the term of service at twelve years for the prætorians and sixteen for the legionaries. The gift to the former upon discharge was also larger. In 758 the terms of service were lengthened to sixteen and twenty years. Cf. Dio, LV, 23. In LV, 25, Dio writes of this year 759 : "Augustus contributed, in his own name and in that of Tiberius, money for that treasury which is called the military." The sum so given was $8,500,000. Tributary states and kings also assisted. But income could not keep pace with expenses. The old tax of a twentieth on bequests, except when the heir was a very near relative, or very poor, was revived, much to the discontent of the Roman people. Cf. Dio, LV,

c. 18.

40 Inde ab eo anno, q]uo Cn. et P. Lentuli c[ons]ules fuerunt, cum d[e]ficerent

41   [vecti]g[alia, tum] centum millibus h[omi]num tu[m pl]uribus i[nl]ato fru-

42   [mento vel ad n]umma[rió]s t[ributus ex agro] et pat[rimonio] m[e]o

43   [opem tuli].

IV.   c. 19.

1 Cúriam et continens eí Chalcidicum, templumque Apollinis in

III, 40.   W. Jam before inde.

III, 41.   vectigalia, Sk. publicani.

III, 41–43. inlato......... tuli, S. multo frumentarias et nummarias tessaras ex aere et patrimonio meo dedi.

III, 42   vel......... agro, W. atque nummariis tesseris divisis; tribuṭus, Sk. titulos.

III, 43.   opem tuli, Sk. and W. subveni.

c. 18.

Beginning with that year in which Cnæus and Publius Lentulus were consuls, when the imposts failed, I furnished aid sometimes to a hundred thousand men, and sometimes to more, by supplying grain or money for the tribute from my own land and property.[1]

c. 19.

I constructed[1] the Curia,[2] and the Chalcidicum adjacent

---

25. Other taxes were devised, such as that of one *per cent* on sales. Cf. Tac. *Ann.* I, 78. On sales of slaves two *per cent* was exacted. Cf. Dio, LV, 31.

A glance at the military establishment of Augustus may help to some idea óf its vast expense. Mommsen discusses the matter in detail (*R. G.* pp. 68–76). Augustus seems to have left at his death a standing army of twenty-five legions. Each legion approximated seven thousand men, giving a total of 175,000 soldiers. His legions were numbered from one to twenty-two. The number twenty-five is accounted for as follows: the seventeenth, eighteenth and nineteenth had been exterminated under the leadership of Varus. But there were three legions, one in Africa, one in Syria and one in Cyrenaica, bearing the title third, and the fourth, fifth, sixth and tenth were each double. After Actium, Augustus disbanded the legions numbered above twelve (cf. his colonies of veterans at this time, numbering 120,000 men, c. XV). But by reason of the repetitions above alluded to, the legions bearing the numbers up to twelve, really amounted to eighteen. These duplications may have risen from the absorption into Augustus' army of legions bearing the same numbers from the forces of Lepidus and later from those of Antony. In 759, eight new legions, the thirteenth to the twentieth, seem to have been enrolled, in view of the German and Pannonian wars. This made twenty six. Three were lost with Varus, and their numbers,

c. 18.

21 [Ἀπ᾽ ἐκ]είνου τ[ο]ῦ ἐνιαυτοῦ, ἐ[φ᾽] οὗ Ναῖος καὶ Πόπλιος
22 [Λ]έντλοι ὕπατοι ἐγένοντο, ὅτε ὑπέλειπον αἱ δη-
23 [μό]σιαι πρόσοδοι, ἄλλοτε μὲν δέκα μυριάσιν, ἀλ-
24 [λοτε] δὲ πλείοσιν σειτικὰς καὶ ἀργυρικὰς συντάξεις

X.

1 ἐκ τῆς ἐμῆς ὑπάρξεως ἔδωκα.

c. 19.

2 Βουλευτήρ[ιο]ν καὶ τὸ πλησίον αὐτῷ χαλκιδικόν,

seventeen, eighteen and nineteen, seem never to have been restored to the list. To offset this loss in a measure, two new legions, the twenty-first and twenty-second were levied. Thus the twenty-five remaining at the death or Augustus are accounted for. Such an establishment was enormously and increasingly expensive. Pliny, *Hist. Nat.*, VII, 45.

C. 18. [1] This form of benefaction began in 736. It is a little remarkable that Augustus should not mention the exact years of its continuance, its amount, or the beneficiaries, while he does name the minimum number of men who received aid from time to time. Perhaps he did not go into details because these gifts concerned the provincials and would be of slight interest to the city people for whose reading the inscription was intended. In 742, "when Asia was in need of aid on account of earthquakes, he paid the year's tribute of the province out of his own means." Dio, LIV, 30.

His supplying grain as well as money rose from the fact that taxes were imposed both in kind and in money. Cf. Tac. *Ann.* IV, 6; *Agr*, XIX and XXXI; C. I. Gr. 4957, 47. These passages all speak of taxes both in money and in produce. As to the method of levy, Hyginus is interesting (*De Lim.* p. 205). "The tax on agriculture is arranged in many ways. In some provinces the harvest is chargeable with a certain proportion, here a fifth, there a seventh, elsewhere a cash payment, and for this purpose certain values are determined for the fields by an estimation of the soil; as in Pannonia there is arable of the first class, of the second, meadows, mast-bearing woods, common woods, pastures: upon all these the tax is laid by the single acre, according to the fertility of the soil." This was in the time of Trajan.

C. 19. [1] The structures detailed here and in cc. 20 and 21, fall into three classes. First, those of c. 19, being either new buildings in place of ruined ones, or else entirely new ones, both classes on soil already consecrated; second, those of c. 20, being repairs of public works; third, public works upon soil given by himself, as noted in the first part of c. 21.

Augustus does not mention structures which he erected in the name of others, as the portico of Octavia, (different from the one below, Note 7), the portico of Livia, cf. Dio, XLIX. 43 and LIV, 23 He also omits the temple of Concord dedicated by Tiberius in 763 (C. I. L. I. p. 384), though he paid for it.

The order of the works is chronological for the most part.

[2] This was the Curia Julia, begun in 712. Cf. Dio XLVII, 19; XLIV, 5; XLV, 17. It was dedicated in 725 after Actium. Cf. Dio LV, 22. Here the senate met. Its location was near the forum.

2 Palatio cum porticibus, aedem dívi Iulí, Lupercal, porticum ad cir-

3 cum Fláminium, quam sum appellári passus ex nómine eíus qui pri-

4 órem eódem in solo fecerat Octaviam, pulvinar ad circum maximum,

5 aedés in Capitolio Iovis feretri et Iovis tonantis, [§] aedem Quiriní, §

6 aedés Minervae § et Iúnonis reginae § et Iovis Libertatis in Aventíno, §

7 aedem Larum in summá sacrá viá, § aedem deum Penátium in Velia, §

8 aedem Iuventátis, § aëdem Mátris Magnae in Palátio féci. §

thereto,[3] the temple of Apollo on the Palatine, with its porticoes,[4] the temple of the divine Julius,[5] the Lupercal,[6] the portico to the Circus of Flaminius, which I allowed to bear the name, Portico Octavia, from his name who constructed the earlier one in the same place;[7] the Pulvinar at the Circus Maximus,[8] the temples of Jupiter the Vanquisher[9] and Jupiter the Thunderer, on the Capitol,[10] the temple of Quirinus,[11] the temples of Minerva and Juno Regina and of Jupiter Libertas, on the Aventine,[12] the temple of the Lares on the highest point of the Via Sacra,[13] the temple of the divine Penates on the Velian hill,[14] the temple of Youth,[15] and the temple of the Great Mother on the Palatine.[16]

[3] A shrine of Minerva Chalcidica.

[4] Begun after the Sicilian victories in 718. Cf. Dio XLIX, 15; Vell. II, 81, dedicated Oct. 9, 726. Cf. Dio, LIII, 1; C. I. L. I, p. 403. Suet. *Aug.* 29, says: " He reared a temple of Apollo in that part of his estate on the Palatine which the haruspices declared was desired by the god because it had been struck by lightning; he attached to it a portico and a Greek and Latin library."

[5] An altar was placed at once on the spot in the forum where the body of Julius Cæsar was cremated. In 712 the senate decreed that a temple should be built there. Cf. Dio XLVII, 18. It is shown on coins struck between 717-720. Cf. Eckhel VI, 11, 75. This temple was dedicated Aug. 18, 725. Cf. Dio, LI, 19, 22; C. I. L, I, p. 399.

[6] Dionysius (I, 32), observes that the ancient condition of this place (originally a grotto near the Palatine, sacred to Pan) had been so changed as to be hardly recognizable. This was by reason of the changes made in his time, which nearly coincided with that of Augustus. Cf. C. I. L. VI, 912, 6, 9, and 841. Its precise location is undetermined.

[7] Festus, *De Verb. Sig.* L. 13, writes: " There were two Octavian porticoes,

3 ναόν τε Ἀπόλλωνος ἐν Παλατίῳ σὺν στοαῖς,
4 ναὸν θεοῦ [Ἰ]ουλίου, Πανὸς ἱερόν, στοὰν πρὸς ἱπ-
5 ποδρόμῳ τῷ προσαγορευομένῳ Φλαμινίῳ, ἣν
6 εἴασα προσαγορεύεσθαι ἐξ ὀνόματος ἐκείνου Ὀκτα-
7 ουίαν· ὃ [ς] πρῶτος αὐτὴν ἀνέστησεν, ναὸν πρὸς τῷ
8 μεγάλῳ ἱπποδρόμῳ, [§] ναοὺς ἐν Καπιτωλίῳ
9 Διὸς τροπαιοφόρου καὶ Διὸς βροντησίου, ναὸν
10 Κυρείν[ο]υ, [§] ναοὺς Ἀθηνᾶς καὶ Ἥρας βασιλίδος καὶ
11 Διὸς Ἐλευθερίου ἐν Ἀουεντίνῳ, ἡρώων πρὸς τῇ
12 ἱερᾷ ὁδῷ, θεῶν κάτοικιδίων ἐν Οὐελίᾳ, ναὸν Νεό-
13 τητο[ς, να]ὸν μητρὸς θεῶν ἐν Παλατίῳ ἐπόησα.

the one built near the theatre of Marcellus by Octavia, the sister of Augustus, the other close to the theatre of Pompey, built by Cn. Octavius, son of Cnæus, who was curule aedile, prætor, consul (589) decemvir for the sacred rites, and celebrated a naval triumph for a victory over King Perseus. It was the latter which, after its destruction by fire, Cæsar Augustus rebuilt." Its reconstruction was in 721. Cf. Dio, XLIX, 43, who, however, confounds this Octavian portico with the other built some years after in the name of Augustus' sister, Octavia.

8 The Pulvinar was the place of honor from which the imperial family witnessed the games. Cf. Suet. *Aug.* 45; *Claud.* 4. This restoration followed the burning of the Circus Maximus in 723. Cf. Dio, L, 10.

9 A temple attributed to Romulus, in ruins in the time of Augustus, till restored by him on the suggestion of Atticus. Cf. Nepos, *Atticus*, 20; Livy, IV, 20. The temple was probably restored in 723.

10 Suetonius, *Aug.* 29, writes : " He dedicated the temple to Jupiter the Thunderer, in acknowledgment of his escape from a great danger in his Cantabrian expedition ; when, as he was traveling by night, his litter was struck by lightning, which killed the slave who carried the torch before him." This expedition was in 728–729, and the temple was dedicated Sept. 1, 732. Cf. Dio, LIV, 4 ; C. I. L. I, 400.

11 This was dedicated in 738, on the Quirinal. Cf. Dio, LIV, 19.

12 These three temples have more than an accidental collocation. Just as the Tarpeian mount and the Quirinal hill had their triple divinities, so had the Aventine. Cf. Varro (*De Lin.*) V, 158. The temple of Juno is ascribed to the time of Camillus, and is said to have been built for the Veientines. The date of the other two is unknown, as is that of this restoration by Augustus.

13 Also of unknown origin, location and restoration, other than as mentioned here.

14 Dionysius, I, 68, describes the old temple, not the restoration by Augustus of which we have only this statement.

15 The original temple was dedicated in 563, in the Circus Maximus. Cf. Livy, XXXVI, 36. Burned in 738. Cf. Dio, LIV, 19.

16 The original temple was burned in 756. Cf. Val. Max. I, 8, 11; Dio, LV, 12; Suet. *Aug.* 57.

C. 20.

9 Capitolium et Pompeium theatrum utrumque opus impensá
   grandí reféci
10 sine ullá inscriptione nominis meí. § Rívos aquarum com-
   plúribus locís
11 vetustáte labentés reféci, [§] et aquam quae Márcia appel-
   látur duplicavi
12 fonte novo in rivum eius inmisso. § Forum Iúlium et basilicam,
13 quae fuit inter aedem Castoris et aedem Satúrni, [§] coepta
   profligata-
14 que opera á patre meó perféci § et eandem basilicam consump-
   tam in-
15 cendio ampliáto eius solo sub titulo nominis filiórum m[eo-
   rum i]n-
16 choavi [§] et, si vivus nón perfecissem, perfici ab |heredib[us
   iussi].
17 Duo et octoginta templa deum in urbe consul sext[um ex
   decreto]
18 senatus reféci, nullo praetermisso quod e[o] temp[ore refici
   debebat].

c. 20.

The Capitol and the Pompeian theatre have been restóred by me
at enormous expense for each work, without any inscription of my
name.[1] Aqueducts which were crumbling in many places by reason
of age I have restored, and I have doubled the water which bears the
name Marcian by turning a new spring into its course.[2] The Forum
Julium and the basilica which was between the temple of Castor and
the temple of Saturn, works begun and almost completed by my father,
I have finished; and when that same basilica was consumed by fire, I
began its reconstruction on an enlarged site, inscribing it with the
names of my sons; and if I do not live to complete it, I have given
orders that it be completed by my heirs.[3] In accordance with a decree
of the senate, while consul for the sixth time, I have restored eighty-
two temples of the gods, passing over none which was at that time in
need of repair.[4] In my seventh consulship I constructed the Flamin-

C. 20. [1] The Capitol means the temple of Jupiter Capitolinus.
   [2] Frontinus, *De Aq.* c. 125, speaks of a decree of the Senate in the year 743
"concerning the putting in order of the streams, conduits and arches of the Julian

C. 20.

14 Καπιτώλ[ιο]ν καὶ τὸ Πομπηίου θέατρον ἑκάτερον
15 τὸ ἔργον ἀναλώμασιν μεγίστοις ἐπεσκεύασα ἄ-
16 νευ ἐπιγαφῆς τοῦ ἐμοῦ ὀνόματος. § Ἀγωγοὺς ὕ-
17 δάτω[ν ἐν πλεί]στοις τόποις τῇ παλαιότητι ὀλισ-
18 θάνον[τας ἐπ]εσκευσα καὶ ὕδωρ τὸ καλούμενον·
19 Μάρ[κιον ἐδί]πλωσα πηγὴν νέαν εἰς τὸ ῥεῖθρον
20 [αὐτοῦ ἐποχετεύσ]ας. [§] Ἀγορὰν Ἰουλίαν καὶ βασι-
21 [λικὴν τὴν μεταξὺ τ]οῦ τε ναοῦ τῶν Διοσκό-
22 [ρων καὶ Κρόνου κατα[βεβλημένα ἔργα ὑπὸ τοῦ
23 [πατρὸς ἐτελείωσα κα]ὶ τὴν αὐτὴν βασιλικὴν
24 [καυθεῖσαν ἐπὶ αὐξηθέντι] ἐδάφει αὐτῆς ἐξ ἐπι-
XI.
1 γραφῆς ὀνόματος τῶν ἐμῶν υἱῶν ὑπ[ηρξάμη]ν
2 καὶ εἰ μὴ αὐτὸς τετελειώκ[ο]ι[μι, τ]ελε[ί]ω[θῆναι ὑπὸ]
3 τῶν ἐμῶν κληρονόμων ἐπέταξα. § Δ[ύ]ο [καὶ ὀγδο-]
4 ήκοντα ναοὺς ἐν τῇ πόλ[ει ἔκτ]ον ὑπ[ατος δόγμα]-
5 τι συνκ[λ]ήτου ἐπεσκεύασ[α] ο[ὐ]δένα π[ε]ριλ[ιπών, ὃς]
6 ἐκείνῳ τῷ χρόνῳ ἐπισκευῆς ἐδεῖτο. § [ʺΥ]πα[τος ἕ-

X, 22.   S. inserts τοῦ before Κρόνου.
X, 23.   S. inserts μου after πατρὸς.
X, 24.   καιθεῖσαν ἐπὶ, S. καταφλεχθεῖσαν ἐν.

Marcian, Appian, Tepulan and Aniene waters, which Augustus has promised the Senate that he will repair at his own expense." Aqueducts were repaired in 749–750. Cf. C. I. L. VI, 1244. C. I. L. VI, 1249, gives *Iul. Tep. Mar.*; *imp. Cæsar divi f. Augustus ex s. c.; XXV; ped. CCXL.* C. I. L. VI, 1243, records the repairs of the Marcian aqueduct. Frontinus, *op. cit.*, 12, gives some details of the doubled supply of this source, and says the new spring had to be conducted eight hundred feet to join the older fountain.

³ Julius Cæsar dedicated this forum Sept. 24 or 25, 708. Cf. Dio, XLIII, 22; App. *B. C.*, III, 28; C. I. L. I, p. 402 and 397. Pliny, *Hist. Nat.*, XXXV, 12, 156, mentions its completion by Augustus.

Augustus uses the word *profligata* here for " unfinished," a use which was common enough but not elegant, and is severely criticised by Gellius, XV, 5. The word really means wretched rather than unfinished. That Augustus was not a purist this inscription testifies, and Suetonius also tells us, *Aug.*, 87 and 88, how peculiar he was in diction and orthography.

The basilica which was unfinished at the death of Augustus he refrains from naming while it was not yet dedicated. But we know from Suetonius, *Aug.* 29, and Dio, LVI, 27, that it was built in honor of his grandchildren, Gaius and Lucius.

⁴ There is abundant testimony to this architectural activity. Cf. Suet. *Aug.* 29

19   Con[s]ul septimum viam Flaminiam a[b urbe] Ari[minum
feci et pontes]
20   omnes praeter Mulvium et Minucium.

c. 21.

21   In privato solo Mártis Ultoris templum [f]orumque Augustum
[ex mani]-
22   biís fecí. § Theatrum ad aede Apollinis in solo magná ex
parte á p[r]i[v]atis
23   empto féci, quod sub nomine M. Marcell[i] generi mei esset.
§ Don[a e]x
24   manibiís in Capitolio et in aede dívi Iú[l]í et in aede Apollinis et in ae-
25   de Vestae et in templo Martis Ultoris consacrávi, § quae mihi
consti-
26   terunt HS circiter milliens. § Aurí coronárí pondo triginta et
quin-
27   que millia múnicipiís et colonís Italiae conferentibus ad tri-
umphó[s]

IV, 19. W. omits feci; inserts in ea after pontes.

ian way from the city to Ariminum, and all the bridges except the
Mulvian and Minucian.[5]

c. 21.

Upon private ground I have built with the spoils of war the
temple of Mars the Avenger, and the Augustan Forum.[1] Beside the
temple of Apollo, I built upon ground, bought for the most part at my
own expense, a theatre, to bear the name of Marcellus, my son-in-law.[2]
From the spoils of war I have consecrated gifts in the Capitol, and in
the temple of the divine Julius, and in the temple of Apollo, and in
the temple of Vesta, and in the temple of Mars the Avenger; these
gifts have cost me about a hundred million sesterces.[3] In my fifth
consulship I remitted to the *municipia* and Italian colonies the thirty-

and 30; Dio, LIII, 2; LVI, 40; Livy IV, 20; Ovid, *Fasti*, II, 59; Hor. *Carm.*, III,
6. Nor was this the zeal of a mere archæologist and architect. The emperor was anxious for a revival of religious observance, as a conservative force in his new organization of the state.

   [5] It is remarkable that Augustus should say he "*constructed*" the Flaminian Way,
etc., for it was made nearly two hundred years before this date, 727. Moreover, the
whole chapter is given up to an account of reconstructions, and of course it is meant
that he *repaired* the road and the bridges in question. The Latin verb is wanting and

7 βδ[ο]μον ὁδὸν Φ[λαμινίαν ἀπὸ] ʿΡώμης [Ἀρίμινον]
8 γ[εφ]ύρας τε τὰς ἐν αὐτῇ πάσας ἔξω δυεῖν τῶν μὴ
9 ἐπ[ι]δεομένων ἐ[π]ισκευῆς ἐπόησα.

c. 21.

10 Ἐν ἰδιωτικῷ ἐδάφει ῎Αρεως Ἀμύντορος ἀγοράν τε Σε-
11 βαστὴν ἐκ λαφύρων ἐπόησα. [§] Θέατρον πρὸς τῷ
12 Ἀπόλλωνος ναῷ ἐπὶ ἐδάφους ἐκ πλείστου μέρους ἀγο-
13 ρασθέντος ἀνήγειρα [§] ἐπὶ ὀνόματος Μαρκέλλου
14 τοῦ γαμβροῦ μου. Ἀναθέματα ἐκ λαφύρων ἐν Καπι-
15 τωλίῳ καὶ ναῷ Ἰουλίῳ καὶ ναῷ Ἀπόλλωνος
16 καὶ ʿΕστίας καὶ ῎Α[ρεω]ς ἀφιέρωσα, ἃ ἐμοὶ κατέστη
17 ἐγγὺς μυριάδω[ν δι]σχε[ι]λίων πεντακ[οσίων.]
18 Εἰς χρυσοῦν στέφανον λειτρῶν τρισ[μυρίων]
19 πεντακισχειλίων καταφερούσαις τα[ῖς ἐν Ἰ[ταλί-

---

is restored from the Greek, ἐπόησα, which is unmistakable,—"I made." Mommsen does not comment on the incorrectness of this statement, but Wölfflin regards the Greek verb as a blunder of the stone-cutter at Ancyra, and thinks there was no verb at all at the end of this chapter, but that the mason by mistake took the last word of the preceding chapter which is ἐπόησα. A substitution of ἐπόησα for the proper verb seems more likely, as it seems improbable that the sentence would end without a verb.

These repairs are attested by an inscription on an arch at Ariminum, thus restored by Bormann: Cf. C. I. L. XI, 365.

SENATUS POPULUSQ *ue romanus*
imp. cæsari divi f. augusto imp. sept.
COS. SEPT. DESIGNAT. OCTAVOM *Via flamin* IA *et reliquei*S
CELEBERRIMEIS ITALIÆ VIEIS CONSILIO *et sumptib* US *eius mu*NITEIS.

Cf. also Suet. *Aug.* 30; Dio, LIII, 22. Other roads of Italy were repaired by those who obtained triumphs; of which more were celebrated from 726 to 728 than at any other epoch.

C. 21. [1] Cf. Suet. *Aug.* 29, Its construction was vowed in 712 and it was dedicated in 752. Cf. C. I. L. I, p. 393, May 12. In c. 35, Augustus mentions the quadriga dedicated to him in this forum.

[2] This theatre was begun by Julius Cæsar. Augustus completed it in honor of Marcellus, who died in 731. It was dedicated May 4, 743. Cf. Pliny, *Hist. Nat.*, VIII, 17, 65. Dio, LIV, 36, assigns its dedication to 741.

[3] Suetonius, *Aug.*, 30, says that on one occasion Augustus deposited in the *cella* of Jupiter Capitolinus sixteen thousand pounds of gold (= $3,200,000) and gems and pearls of the value of fifty million sesterces (= $2,500,000). But such statements are fabulous, in view of Augustus' own statement that the total of his gifts of this kind was only one hundred million sesterces (= $5,000,000).

28 meós quintum consul remisi, et posteá, quotienscumque imperátor a[ppe]l-
29 látus sum, aurum coronárium nón accepi decernentibus
   municipií[s]
30 et coloni[s] aequ[e] beni[g]ne adque antea decreverant.

c. 22.

31 *T*[e]*r munus* gladiátorium dedí meo nomine et quinquens
   filiórum me[o]·
32 rum aut n[e]pótum nomine; quibus muneribus depugnaverunt
   homi-
33 nu[m] ci[rc]iter decem millia. [§] Bis [at]hletarum undique
   accitorum
34 spec[ta]c[lum po]pulo pra[ebui meo] nómine et tertium
   nepo[tis] mei no-
35 mine. § L[u]dos feci m[eo no]m[ine] quater [§], aliorum
   autem m[agist]rá·

five thousand· pounds given me as coronary gold on the occasion of my
triumphs, and thereafter, as often as I was proclaimed imperator, I did
not accept the coronary gold which the *municipia* and colonies voted to
me as kindly as before.[4]

c. 22.

Three times in my own name, and five times in that of my sons or
grandsons, I have given gladiatorial exhibitions; in these exhibitions
about ten thousand men have fought.[1] Twice in my own name, and
three times in that of my grandson, I have offered the people the spectacle of athletes gathered from all quarters.[2] I have celebrated games
four times in my own name, and twenty-three times in the turns of

---

[4] In earlier times it had been customary for cities affected by a victory to give
crowns of gold to the triumphing *imperator*. This grew into an abuse and was forbidden by law, unless the gift preceded the decree for the triumph. Later, the value
of the crown was commuted for cash, and it came to be a frequent means of extortion
on the part of provincial governors. To L. Antonius crowns of gold were given by
each of the thirty-five Roman tribes in 713. Cf. Dio, XLVIII, 4. The amount
named here, thirty-five thousand pounds of gold, would appear to have been from the
thirty-five tribes. On the general subject, *aurum coronarium*, cf. Marquardt, *Staatsverwaltung*, II, p. 285.

C. 22. [1] The sons of Augustus were Gaius, adopted in 737, died in 757; Lucius,
adopted at the same time, died in 755; Agrippa Postumus, adopted in 757, exiled

20 ᾷ πολειτείαις καὶ ἀποικίαις συνεχώρη[σ]α τὸ [πέμ]-
21 πτον ὑπατεύων, καὶ ὕστερον ὁσάκις [αὐτ]οκράτωρ
22 προσηγορεύϑην, τὰς εἰς τὸν στέφανο[ν ἐ]παγγε-
23 λίας οὐκ ἔλαβον ψηφιζομένων τῶν π[ολειτει]ῶν
24 καὶ ἀποικιῶν μετὰ τῆς αὐτῆς προϑ[υμίας, κα]ϑ-
XII.
1 ά[περ ἐψηφίσαντο π]ρό[τερον].

c. 22.

2 [Τρὶς μονο]μαχ]ίαν ἔδω]κα τῷ ἐμῷ ὀνόματι καὶ
3 [πεντάκις τῶν υἱῶν μου ἢ υἱ]ωνῶν. ἐν αἷς μονο-
4 [μαχίαις ἐμαχέσαντο ἐ]ν[γὺς μύ]ρι[ο]ι. Δὶς ἀϑλητῶ[ν] παν-
5 τ[αχόϑεν] με[ταπεμφϑέντων γυμνικο]ῦ ἀγῶνος ϑέαν
6 [τῷ δήμῳ π]αρέσχον τ[ῷ ἐ]μῷ ὀνόματι καὶ τρίτ[ον]
7 τ[οῦ υἱωνοῦ μου. Θέας ἐπόη]σα δι᾽ ἐμοῦ τετράκ[ις,]

XII, 1. ἐψηφίσαντο, S. καὶ ἐψήφιστο.

in 760. These were the sons of Agrippa and Julia. On the death of Gaius in 757, Augustus adopted Tiberius. With him Germanicus, nephew and adopted son of Tiberius, and Drusus, Tiberius' own son, became the legal grandchildren of Augustus. None of these could celebrate games in his own name after adoption, as they had no property rights, but were absolutely dependent on the head of their house, according to the *patria potestas* of the Roman law. See this very plainly set forth in Suetonius, *Tib.* 15 : "After his (Tiberius') adoption he never again acted as master of a family, nor exercised in the smallest degree the rights which he had lost by it. For he neither disposed of anything in the way of gift, nor manumitted a slave ; nor so much as received an estate left him by will, or any legacy, without reckoning it as a part of his *peculium*, or property held under his father." Tiberius was forty-six years old when he was adopted.

Seven of these exhibitions can be traced. 1. In 725, on the dedication of the temple of the Divine Julius. Dio, LI, 22. 2. In 726, in honor of the victory of Actium. Dio, LIII, 1. 3. In 738, in accordance with a decree of the senate. This was in the name of Tiberius and Drusus. Dio, LIV, 19. 4. In 742, at the Quinquatria held March 19–23, in honor of Minerva. This was in the name of Gaius and Lucius. Dio, LIV, 28, 29. 5. In 747 ; funeral games in honor of Agrippa. Dio, LV, 8. 6. In 752, at the dedication of the temple of Mars. Vell. II, 100. 7. In 759, in honor of Drusus, in the name of his sons Germanicus and Claudius. Dio, LV, 27 ; Pliny, *Hist. Nat*, II, 26, 96 ; VIII, 2, 4. Possibly the eighth occasion may be found in Suetonius, *Aug.*, 43.

2 Cf. Dio, LIII, 1 ; Suet. *Aug.*, 43. Wooden seats were erected in the Campus Martius for gymnastic contests in 726. Whether Germanicus or Drusus is the grandson mentioned here is unknown.

36 tŭ[um] vicem ter et vicie[ns] [§]. [Pr]o conlegio XV
virorum magis[ter con-

37 l]e[gi]í colleg[a] M. Agríppa [§] lud[os s]aecl[are]s C.
Furnio C. [S]ilano cos. [feci.

38 C]on[sul XIII] ludos Mar[tia]les pr[imus feci], qu[os]
p[ost i]d tempus deincep[s]

39 ins[equen]ti[bus ann]is . . . . [fecerunt co]n[su]les.
[§] [Ven]ati[o]n[es] best[ia]-

40 rum Africanárum meo nómine aut filio[ru]m meórum et
nepotum in ci[r]-

41 co aut [i]n foro aut in amphitheatris popul[o d]edi sexiens
et viciens, quibus

42 confecta sunt bestiarum circiter tria m[ill]ia et quingentae.

c. 23.

43 Navalis proelí spectaclum populo de[di·tr]ans Tiberim, in quo
loco

44 nunc nemus est Caesarum, cavato [solo] in longitudinem
mille

other magistrates.[3]　In behalf of the college of quindecemvirs, I, as
master of the college, with my colleague Agrippa, celebrated the Secular Games in the consulship of Gaius Furnius and Gaius Silanus.[4]
When consul for the thirteenth time, I first celebrated the Martial
games, which since that time the consuls have given in successive
years.[5]　Twenty-six times in my own name, or in that of my sons and
grandsons, I have given hunts of African wild beasts in the circus, the
forum, the amphitheatres, and about thirty-five hundred beasts have been
killed.[6]

c. 23.

I gave the people the spectacle of a naval battle beyond the Tiber,
where now is the grove of the Cæsars.[1]　For this purpose an excava-

---

[3] These were the lesser games of the circus and theatres, given ordinarily by
magistrates holding the lower offices, which Augustus never filled. He took upon himself the care and expense where the proper magistrates were absent or too poor. Cf.
Dio, XLV, 6 ; C. I. L., I, p. 397.

[4] The charge of the Secular Games, celebrated supposedly once in a century,
though in reality oftener, fell to the quindecemvirs. Cf. Eckhel, VI. 102, for a coin
with *imp. Cæsar Augustus lud. saec. XV S. F.* This was in 737. Cf. also C. I. L.,
I, p. 442. The college evidently gave the presidency to Augustus and Agrippa, since

8   διὰ δὲ τῶν ἄλλων ἀρχῶν ἐν μέρει τρὶς καὶ εἰκοσάκις. §

9   'Υρὲρ τῶν δεκαπέντε [ἀνδρ]ῶν, ἔχων συνάρχοντα

10 Μᾶρκον 'Αγρίππ[αν, τὰς ϑ]έας [δ]ιὰ ἑκατὸν ἐτῶν γεινο-

11 μένας ὀν[ομαζομένα]ς σ[αι]κλάρεις ἐπόησα Γαΐῳ

12 Φουρνίῳ κ[αὶ] Ἰαύῳ Σε[ι]λανῳ ὑπάτοις. [§] ῞Υπατος τρισ-

13 χαιδέκατον [ϑέας ᾿Αρεως πρ[ῶτος ἐπόησα, ἃς μετ᾿ ἐ-

14 κεῖνο[ν χ]ρόνον ἑξῆς [τοῖς μ[ετέπειτα ἐνιαυτοῖς

15 δ . . μοι ἐπόησαν οἱ ὑπα- .   .   .   .

16 [τοι]   .   . ν   .   .   .   . ης ϑηρίων ε

17 .   .   .   .

18 .   .   .   .

19 .   .   .   .

20 .   .   .   .

c. 23.

21 Ν[αυμαχίας ϑέαν τῳ δήμῳ ἔδω]κα πέ[ρ]αν τοῦ Τι-

22 [βέριδος, ἐν ᾧ τόπῳ ἐστὶ νῦ]ν ἄλσος Καισά[ρω]ν,

23 ἐκκεχω[κὼς τὸ ἔδαφος] ε[ἰ]ς μῆκ[ο]ς χειλίων ὀκτακο-

24 σίων ποδ[ῶν, εἰς π]λάτ[ο]ς χιλίων διακο[σ]ίων. ἐν ᾗ

it was very convenient that these two members of the sacred body also held the tribunitial power, and so the games came into the charge of the two greatest men of the state in a perfectly natural way. Cf. C. I. L., IX, p. 29, No. 262, for confirmation of Agrippa's membership in the college of quindecemvirs.

5 These games were celebrated on August 1. Dio, LX, 5, and LVI, 46, tells of their being annual, and in charge of the consuls after the death of Augustus. They began in 752. This passage is one of the few where both the Latin and Greek are incapable of restoration.

6 Cf. Suet. Aug. 43. Some of these occasions were: in 743 in connection with the dedication of the theatre of Marcellus. Cf. Dio, LIV, 26. Here six hundred beasts were killed, and the tiger was shown for the first time. Cf. Pliny, Hist. Nat., VIII, 17, 65. In 752, two hundred and sixty lions and thirty-six crocodiles were killed. Cf. Dio, LV, 10. In 765, in the games given by Germanicus, two hundred lions were killed. Cf. Dio, LVI, 27.

Augustus says "amphitheatres," though there was but one such structure. He may have regarded it as being two theatres joined at their straight side and facing each other.

C. 23. 1 Velleius II, 100, writes: "The divine Augustus in the year when he was consul with Gallus Caninius (752) sated the minds and the eyes of the Roman people at the dedication of the temple of Mars with the most magnificent gladiatorial shows and naval battles." Dio, LV, 10, says that traces of the excavation could be

45 et octingentós pedés, [§] in látitudine [m mille] e [t] ducentí. In quo tri-

46 ginta rostrátae náves trirémes a [ut birem] és, [§] plures autem

47 minóres inter se conflixérunt. Q [uibus in] classibus pugnave-

48 runt praeter rémigés millia ho [minum tr] ia circiter. §

c. 24.

49 In templís omnium civitátium pr [ovinci] ae Asiae victor orna-

50 menta reposui, quae spoliátis tem [plis is] cum quó bellum gesseram

51 privátim possederat §. Statuae [mea] e pedestrés et equestres et in

52 quadrigeis argenteae steterunt in urbe XXC circiter, quas ipse

53 sustuli [§] exque eá pecuniá dona aurea in áede Apol [li] nis meó nomi-

54 ne et illórum, qui mihi statuárum honórem habuerunt, posui. §

V.   c. 25.

1 Mare pacávi á praedonibus. Eó belló servórum, qui fugerant á dominis

2 suis et arma contrá rem publicam céperant, triginta fere millia capta §

tion was made eighteen hundred feet long and twelve hundred wide. In this contest thirty beaked ships, triremes or biremes, were engaged, besides more of smaller size. About three thousand men fought in these vessels in addition to the rowers.

c. 24.

In the temples of all the cities of the province of Asia, I, as victor, replaced the ornaments of which he with whom I was at war had taken private possession when he despoiled the temples.[1] Silver statues of me, on foot, on horseback and in quadrigas, which stood in the city to the number of about eighty, I removed, and out of their money value, I placed golden gifts in the temple of Apollo in my own name, and in the names of those who had offered me the honor of the statues.[2]

c. 25.

I have freed the sea from pirates. In that war with the slaves I

XIII.

1 τριάχο[ν]τα ναῦς ἔμβολα ἔχουσαι τριήρεις ἢ δί-
2 χροτ[οι, αἱ] δὲ ἥσσονες πλείους ἐναυμάχησαν. §
3 Ἐν τ[ούτῳ] τῷ στόλῳ ἠγωνίσαντο ἔξω τῶν ἐρετῶν
4 πρόσπ[ο]υ ἄνδρες τρ[ι]σχ[ε]ί[λ]ιοι.

c. 24.

5 [Ἐν ναοῖ]ς π[ασ]ῶν πόλεω[ν] τῆς [Ἀ]σί[α]ς νεικήσας τὰ ἀναθέ-
6 [ματα ἀπ]οκατέστησα, [ἃ εἶχεν] ἰ[δίᾳ] ἱεροσυλήσας ὁ
7 ὑπ' [ἐμοῦ] δ[ι]αγωνισθεὶς πολέ[μος]. Ἀνδρίαντες πε-
8 ζοὶ καὶ ἔφιπποί μου καὶ ἐφ' ἅρμασιν ἀργυροῖ εἱστήκει-
9 σαν ἐν τῇ πόλει ἐνγὺς ὀγδοήκοντα, οὓς αὐτὸς ἦρα,
10 ἐκ τούτου τε τοῦ χρήματος ἀναθέματα χρυσᾶ ἐν
11 τῷ ναῷ τοῦ Ἀπόλλωνος τῷ τε ἐμῷ ὀνόματι καὶ
12 ἐκείνων, οἵτινές με [τ]ούτοις τοῖς ἀνδριᾶσιν ἐτείμη-
13 σαν, ἀνέθηκα.

c. 25.

14 Θάλασσα[ν] πειρατευομένην ὑπὸ ἀποστατῶν δού-

seen in his time (c. 200 A. D.), and that the fight represented a battle of Athenians and Persians, in which the former were victorious. Cf. Suet. *Aug.* 43; Ovid, *Ars Am.* I, 171.

Claudius gave a similar exhibition on the Fucine Lake, but with a hundred triremes and quadriremes, and a force of nineteen thousand men, "as once Augustus did in a pond by the Tiber, but with lighter vessels and a smaller force." Cf. Tac. *Ann.* XII, 56; Suet. *Claud.*, 21; Dio, LX, 33.

C. 24. ¹ Another instance of avoidance of the name of an enemy while distinctly referring to him. Antony had stripped various temples at Samos, Ephesus, Pergamos, and Rhœteum, all in the province of Asia, and had given the spoils to Cleopatra. Dio, LI, 17, says that great numbers of such things were found in her palace when Alexandria was captured. Pliny, *Hist. Nat.*, XXXIV, 8, 58, says: "He (Myro) made an Apollo, which was taken away by the triumvir Antony, but restored to the Ephesians by the divine Augustus." Strabo, XIII, 1, 30, writes of Rhœteum: "Cæsar Augustus gave back to the Rhœtians the shrine and statue of Ajax which Antony had taken away and given to Egypt. He did the like for other cities. For Antony took away the finest votive offerings from the most famous shrines for the gratification of the Egyptian woman, but Augustus restored them." Ib. XIV, 1, 14, writes of the temple of Hera, at Samos: "Antony took away three colossal sitting statues on one base, but Augustus Cæsar restored two of them, Athene and Heracles, to the same base; the Zeus, however, he placed upon the Capitol."

² Suetonius, *Aug.*, 52, says these gifts took the form of tripods. Cf. Dio, LIII, 22; LII, 35; LIV, 35.

3   dominis ad supplicium sumendum tradidi. § Iuravit in mea verba tóta

4   Italia sponte suá et me be[lli], quó víci ad Actium, ducem depoposcit. § Iura-

5   verunt in eadem ver[ba provi]nciae Galliae Hispaniae Africa Sicilia Sar-

6   dinia. § Qui sub [signis meis tum] militaverint, fuerunt senátórés plúres

7   quam DCC, in if[s qui vel antea vel pos]teá consules facti sunt ad eum diem

8   quó scripta su[nt haec, LXXXIII, sacerdo]tés ci[rc]iter CLXX. §

c. 26.

9 Omnium próv[inciarum populi Romani], quibus finitimae fuerunt

10 gentés quae n[on parerent imperio nos]tro, fines auxi. Gallias et Hispa-

11 niás próviciá[s et Germaniam qua inclu]dit óceanus a Gádibus ad ósti-

V, 7.   qui vel antea vel, S. consulares, et qui.

V, 11.   et Germaniam qua includit, W. item Germaniam qua claudit.

delivered to their masters for punishment about thirty thousand slaves who had fled from their masters and taken up arms against the state.[1] The whole of Italy voluntarily took the oath of allegiance to me, and demanded me as leader in that war in which I conquered at Actium. The provinces of Gaul, Spain, Africa, Sicily and Sardinia swore the same allegiance to me.[2] There were more than seven hundred senators who at that time fought under my standards, and among these, up to the day on which these words are written, eighty-three have either before or since been made consuls, and about one hundred and seventy have been made priests.[3]

c. 26.

I have extended the boundaries of all the provinces of the Roman people which were bordered by nations not yet subjected to our sway.[1] I have reduced to a state of peace the Gallic and Spanish provinces, and Germany, the lands enclosed by the ocean from Gades to the mouth

---

C. 25.   [1] The allusion is to Sextus Pompeius, whose fleets, manned largely by slaves, cut off the grain ships on their way to Rome. Again Augustus avoids the name

15 λων [εἰρήν]ευσα· ἐξ ὧν τρεῖς που μυριάδας τοῖς
16 δε[σπόται]ς εἰς κόλασιν παρέδωκα. § ᾽Ὤμοσεν
17 [εἰς τοὺς ἐμοὺ]ς λόγους ἅπασα ἡ ᾽Ιταλία ἑκοῦσα κὰ-
18 [μὲ πολέμου,] ᾧ ἐπ᾽ ᾽Ακτίῳ ἐνε[ί]κησα, ἡγεμόνα ἐξη-
19 [τήσατο, ὤ[μοσαν εἰς τοὺς [αὐτοὺ]ς λόγους ἐπα[ρ]-
20 χε[ῖαι Γαλά[τία ᾽Ισπανία Λιβύη Σι[κελία Σαρ]δώ. Οἱ ὑπ᾽ ἐ-
21 μ[αῖς σημέαις τό]τε στρατευ[σάμενοι ἦσαν συνκλητι-
22 [κοὶ πλείους ἑπτ]α[κοσί]ων· [ἐ]ν [αὐτοῖς οἳ ἢ πρότερον ἢ]
23 [μετέπειτα] ἐγ[ένον]το [ὕπ]α]τοι εἰς ἐκ[ί]ν[ην τὴν ἡ]μέ-
24 [ραν, ἐν ᾗ ταῦτα γέγραπτα]ι, ὁ[γδοήκο]ντα τρε[ῖ]ς, ἱερ[εῖ]ς
XIV.
πρόσπου ἑκατὸν ἑβδομή[κ]οντα.

c. 26.

2 Πασῶν ἐπαρχειῶν δῆμο[υ ῾Ρω]μαίων, αἷς ὅμορα
3 ἦν ἔθνη τὰ μὴ ὑποτασσ[όμ]ενα τῇ ἡμετέρᾳ ἡ-
4 γεμονία, τοὺς ὅρους ἐπεύξ[ησ]α. [§] Γαλατίας καὶ ῾Ισ-
5 πανίας, ὁμοίως δὲ καὶ Γερμανίαν καθὼς ᾽Ωκεα-
6 νὸς περικλείει ἀπ[ὸ] Γαδε[ίρ]ων μέχρι στόματος

XIII, 22. οἱ ἢ πρότερον ἢ, S. ὑπατικοὶ καὶ οὅ.

of an opponent. Cf. Vell., II, 73, who thinks it remarkable that a son of the great Pompey, who had freed the sea from pirates, should himself defile it with piratical crimes. Florus, IV, 8, reflects the same sentiment. App. *B. C.*, V, 77, 80, says that captured pirates under torture confessed that Sextus Pompeius was the instigator of their crimes. When the peace of Misenum was made, Sextus Pompeius stipulated for the freedom of the slaves who had fought under him. It was after the overthrow of Pompey, in 718, that the slaves were returned. Dio, XLIX, 12, adds that slaves whose masters did not claim them were returned to their several cities, there to be crucified. Cf. App. *B. C.*, V, 131; Oros. VI, 18.

² This was in 722, just before the breaking out of hostilities between Antony and Octavian. Cf. Dio, L, 6; Suet., *Aug.* 17.

³ Cf. c. 8, Note 2. There were a thousand senators at this time. Augustus, in his statement, probably means that seven hundred of the thousand then in the senate were on his side, not merely seven hundred who then or later were senators.

The number of consulars, eighty-three, is quite consistent with the facts, as is shown in a careful analysis of the *Fasti Consulares* for the period by Mommsen. *R. G.*, p. 100.

The priests referred to were probably members of the four great colleges and the Arval brotherhood. Cf. c. 7, notes 2–7.

C. 26. ¹ This statement is borne out by what we otherwise know. Taking the provinces in order we find: First, the German frontier is pushed forward from the

12   um Albis flúm[inis pacavi.   Alpes a re[gióne eá quae proxima
     est Ha-

13   driánó marí, [ad Tuscum pacari fec]i nullí gentí bello per
     iniúriam

14   inláto.   § Cla[ssis mea per Oceanum] ab óstio Rhéni ad sólis
     orientis re-

15   gionem u que ad fi[nes Cimbroru]m navigavit, [§] quó neque
     terra neque

16   mari quisquam Romanus ante id tempus adít, § Cimbrique et
     Charydes

V, 13.   pacem feci.   W. pacificavi.

of the Elbe.[2]   The Alps from the region nearest the Adriatic as far as
the Tuscan Sea I have brought into a state of peace, without waging an
unjust war upon any people.[3]   My fleet has navigated the ocean from
the mouth of the Rhine as far as the boundaries of the Cimbri, where
before that time no Roman had ever penetrated by land or sea ;[4] and
the Cimbri and Charydes and Semnones and other German peoples of

Rhine to the Elbe.   Cf. Suet. *Aug.* 21.   Second, in Illyricum and Macedonia he had
erected the new provinces of Pannonia and Moesia.   Third, in Asia Minor he did not
extend the older limits of Bithynia, but out of the kingdom of Amyntas, he made the
new province of Galatia and later added Paphlagonia to it.   Fourth, in Africa, Augustus
rather narrowed than extended the empire by his partition with Juba in 729.   But a
number of Roman proconsuls won laurels there.

 [2] Here the record is of commotions quelled within the recognized limits of
the empire.   In Spain there was the Cantabrian war from 727 to 735.   In Gaul, G.
Carrinas had subdued the Morini, and triumphed, July 14, 726 ; and M. Messala had
suppressed the Aquitani, triumphing Sept. 25, 727.   Cf. Suet. *Aug.*, 20, 21.

 The German campaigns extending at intervals over the years from 742 to the
very end of Augustus' reign it is needless to detail.   This reference to the pacification
of Germany has been the subject of much dispute.   Mommsen in two places (*R. G.*,
p. VI, and 48), uses the word "crafty" (*callidus*) of Augustus, referring to his
alleged glozing over of unsatisfactory events.   Hirschfeld goes further, and in connection with the present passage accuses Augustus (*Wiener Studien*, V, 117) of a
"masterly concealment and whitewashing (übertünchung) of all that could hurt his
reputation."   This charge is made because Augustus omits all mention of the disaster
under Varus.   Against this charge Johannes Schmidt defends Augustus, (*Philologus*,
XLV, p. 394, ff.).   The contest between Schmidt and Hirschfeld is based really upon
opposing views of the purpose of the *Res Gestae*.   Schmidt believed it to be
an epitaph.   In this there would be no place for anything save the fortunate events of
a life.   If *nil de mortuis nisi bonum* be wise, Augustus might well have adapted the
adage to his own case and said, *nil de me morituro nisi bonum.*   But Hirschfeld insists
that the *Res Gestae* constitute not an epitaph, but "an account of his administration,"

7 Ἄλβιος ποταμο[ῦ ἐν] εἰρήνη κατέστησα. Ἄλπης ἀπὸ
8 κλίματος τοῦ πλησίον Εἰονίου κόλπου μέχρι Τυρ-
9 ρηνικῆς θαλάσσης εἰρηνεύεσθαι πεπόηκα, [§] οὐδενὶ
10 ἔθνει ἀδίκως ἐπενεχθέντος πολέμου. [§] Στόλος
11 ἐμὸς διὰ Ὠκεανοῦ ἀπὸ στόματος Ῥήνου ὡς πρὸς
12 ἀνατολὰς μέχρι ἔθνους Κίμβρων διέπλευσεν, οὗ οὔ-
13 τε κατὰ γῆν οὔτε κατὰ θάλασσαν Ῥωμαίων τις πρὸ
14 τούτου τοῦ χρόνου προσῆλθεν· καὶ Κίμβροι καὶ Χάλυ-
15 βες καὶ Σέμνονες ἄλλα τε πολλὰ ἔθνη Γερμανῶν

and therefore contends that the omission of the German disaster was not in good
faith. To this, Schmidt answers that Augustus had nothing to gain by such concealment—indeed that concealment of so notorious a disaster would be absurd. And in
the text itself he finds a recognition of the real state of affairs, inasmuch as Augustus
expressly distinguishes Germany from the provinces, Gallic and Spanish, and while
claiming it for Rome, does not assert that it belongs to her as do organized provinces.
Schmidt also says that *pacavi*, " I pacified " does not necessarily imply that Germany
continued in a state of peace. It may well enough cover the fact that there
was temporary success. But this is hair-splitting. The character of the *Res Gestae*
must be always had in mind. Cf. Introduction. Its deliverances were *ad populum*
and they constituted an epitaph.

3 Suetonius, *Aug.* 21, says : " He waged war upon no people without just and
necessary causes." The present Torbia near Monaco, derives its name from a
Tropœa Augusti, " Trophy of Augustus," some fragments of which still exist.
The inscription has been preserved by Pliny, *Hist. Nat.*, III, 20, 136 : *imp.
Cæsari divi f. Augusto pontifice maxumo imp. XIIII tribunic. potestate XVII s. p. q.
R. quod ejus ductu auspiciisque gentes Alpinæ omnes quæ a mari supero ad inferum
pertiniebant sub imperium p. R. sunt redactæ*—" the Roman senate and people to
Cæsar . . . Augustus . . . because under his leadership and auspices all the Alpine
nations, from the upper to the lower sea have been brought into subjection to the
Roman empire." Then follows an enumeration of forty-six peoples. Pliny adds,
" the Cottian states were not annexed because they had not been hostile ; " and an
arch at Segusio was placed in honor of Augustus, and on it are the names of fourteen
states, six being repetitions from the Torbia monument. Cf. C. I. L. V, 7817 and
7231.

The campaigns here referred to are: First, of Varro Murena against the Salassi in
729. Cf. Strabo, IV, 6, 7, p. 205 ; Dio, LIII, 25 ; Livy, *Epit.*, CXXXV ; Cass.
ad. ann. 729 ; Suet. *Aug.* 21. Second, of Publius Silius against the Vennones and
Camunni in 738. Cf. Dio, LIV, 20. Third, of Tiberius and Drusus against the Ræti
and Vindelici in 739. Cf. Suet. *Aug.* 21. Fourth, against the Ligurians of the Mari-
time Alps in 740. Cf. Dio, LIV, 24. Finally these regions were formed into the
province of Rætia in 747-748.

4 This naval expedition was connected with the German campaign of Tiberius in
758. Cf. Vell. II, 106 ; Pliny, *Hist. Nat.*, II, 67, 167.

17 et Semnones et eiusdem tractús alií Germánórum popu[l]i
per legátós amici-
18 tiam meam et populi Románi petierunt.   § Meo iussú et
auspicio ducti sunt
19 [duo] exercitús eódem fere tempore in Aethiopiam et in
Ar[a]biam, quae appel-
20 [latur] eudaemón, [maxim]aeque hos[t]ium gentís utr[iu]s-
que cop[iae]
21 caesae sunt in acie et [c]om[plur]a oppida capta. In Aethio-
pi*a*m usque a*d* o*p*pi-
22 dum Nabata pervent[um] est, cuí proxima est Meroé. In
Arabiam usque
23 ín fínés Sabaeorum pro[eess]it.exerc[it]us ad oppidum Mariba. §
c. 27.
24 Aegyptum imperio populi [Ro]mani adieci. § Armeniam
maiorem inter-
25 fecto rége eius Artaxe § c[u]m possem facere provinciam,
málui maiórum

that section, by means of legates, sought my friendship and that of the
Roman people.[5]   By my command and under my auspices two armies
at almost the same time have been led into Ethiopia and into Arabia,
which is called "the Happy," and very many·of the enemý of both
peoples have fallen in battle, and many towns have been captured.
Into Ethiopia the advance was as far as Nabata, which is next to
Meroe.[6]   In Arabia the army penetrated as far as the confines of the
Sabaei, to the town Mariba.[7]

c. 27.

I have added Egypt to the empire of the Roman people.[1]   Of
greater Armenia, when its king Artaxes was killed I could have made

---

[5] Strabo, VII, 2, 1, describes an embassy of the Cimbri asking for "peace and
amnesty." They dwelt in the end of Jutland. Cf. Ptolemy, II, 10. Below them were
the Charudes, whom the mason at Ancyra makes Charydes, and the Greek translator,
thinking of the fable, transforms into Chalybes, living just south of the Cimbri. Cf.
Ptolemy, ii, 11, 12.   The Semnones were between the Elbe and the Oder.

[6] When the Egyptian garrisons were weakened on account of the Arabian expedition, Queen Candace took advantage of it and captured a number of towns in
Upper Egypt. These the præfect, C. Petronius, re-took, and inflicted severe punishment upon the Æthiopians. This took place 730–732. Cf. Strabo, XVII, I, 54; Dio,
LIV, 5 ; Pliny, *Hist. Nat.*, VI, 29, 181, 182.

16 διὰ πρεσβειῶν τὴν ἐμὴν φιλίαν καὶ τὴν δήμου ʻΡω-
17 μαίων ἠτήσαντο. ʼΕμῇ ἐπιταγῇ καὶ οἰωνοῖς αἰσί-
18 οις δύο στρατεύματα ἐπέβη Αἰθιοπίᾳ καὶ ʼΑραβίᾳ
19 τῇ εὐδαίμονι καλουμένῃ μεγάλας τε τῶν πο-
20 λεμίων δυνάμεις κατέκοψεν ἐν παρατάξει καὶ
21 πλείστας πόλεις δοριαλώτους ἔλαβεν καὶ προ-
22 έβη ἐν Αἰθιοπίᾳ μέχρι πόλεως Ναβάτης, ἥτις
23 ἐστὶν ἔνγιστα Μερόη, ἐν ʼΑραβίᾳ δὲ μέχρι πόλε-
24 ως Μαρίβας.

XV. c. 27.

1 Αἴγυπτον δήμου ʻΡωμαίων ἡγεμονίᾳ προσέθηκα.
2 ʼΑρμενίαν τὴν μ[εί]ζονα ἀναιρεθέντος τοῦ βασιλέ-

In 1896 Capt. Lyons, R. E., found, at Philæ, an inscription in Latin, Greek and hieroglyphics, of which Prof. Mahaffy gives this translation: "Gaius Cornelius, son of Cnaeus Gallus, a Roman knight, appointed first prefect, after the kings were conquered by Cæsar, son of Divus, of Alexandria and Egypt—who conquered the revolt of the Thebaid in fifteen days, having won two pitched battles, together with the capture of the leaders of his opponents, having taken five cities, some by assault, some by siege, viz., Boresis, Coptos, Ceramice, Diospolis the Great, Ombos, (?); having slain the leaders of these revolts, and having brought his army beyond the cataract of the Nile to a point whither neither the Roman people nor the Kings of Egypt had yet carried their standards, a military district impassable before his day; having subdued, to the common terror of all the kings, all the Thebaid, which was not subject to the kings, and having received the ambassadors of the Ethiopians at Philæ, and guest-friendship from their king (and received their king under his protection) and having appointed him tyrant of the 30-*schoeni* district of Lower Ethiopia—makes this thank-offering to the Dii Patrii, and to the Nile, who aided him in his deeds." *London Athenæum*, March 14, 1896, and *Sitzungsberichte d. kgl. Pr. Akad. d. Wiss. zu Berlin*, 1896, I, pp. 469–480.

7 The Arabian campaign, under C. Aelius Gallus was probably in 729–730. Cf. Dio, LIII, 29; Hor. *Carm.* I, 29, 35; Strabo, XVI, 4, 22, 24. Pliny, *Hist. Nat.* VI, 28, 159, 160.

C. 27. 1 Egypt was made an integral part of the empire after Actium and the death of Cleopatra, in 724. Its connection with the empire was peculiar. W. T. Arnold, *Roman Provincial Administration*, p. 113, says: "The government of Egypt was in many points wholly exceptional. Julius Cæsar had deliberately abstained from making it a province of the country (cf. Suet., *Jul.* 35); and when Augustus added it to the empire he subjected it to an altogether exceptional treatment. The country was his private property, or rather the Emperor's private property; it passed as a matter of course, that is, from emperor to emperor. Augustus appointed a præfect to represent him in the province, just as in earlier times the urban prætors had sent prefects to

26 nostrórum exemplo regn[u]m id Tigrani regis Artavasdis
filio, nepoti au-
27 tem Tigránis regis, per T[i. Ne]ronem trad[er]e, qui tum
mihi priv[ig]nus erat.
28 Et eandem gentem posteá d[esc]íscentem et rebellantem
domit[a]m per Gaium
29 filium meum regi Ario[barz]ani regis Medorum Artaba[zi]
filio regen-
30 dam tradidi [§] et post e[ius] mortem filio eius Artavasdi.
[§] Quo [inte]rfecto [Tigra]-
31 ne, qui erat ex régió genere Armeniorum oriundus, in id
re[gnum] mísí. § Pro-
32 vincias omnís, quae trans Hadrianum mare vergun[t a]d
Orien[te]m, Cyre-
33 násque, iam ex parte magná regibus eas possidentibus, e[t]
antea Siciliam

a province, but I preferred, after the example of our fathers, to deliver
that kingdom to Tigranes, the son of king Artavasdes, and grandson of
king Tigranes; and this I did through Tiberius Nero, who was then my
son-in-law.[2] And afterwards, when the same people became turbulent
and rebellious, they were subdued by Gaius, my son, and I gave the
sovereignty over them to king Ariobarzanes, the son of Artabazes,
king of the Medes, and after his death to his son Artavasdes. When
he was killed I sent into that kingdom Tigranes, who was sprung from
the royal house of the Armenians.[3] I recovered all the provinces
across the Adriatic Sea, which extend toward the east, and Cyrenaica,

represent them in the municipalities of Italy. This præfect was of equestrian, and not
of the highest equestrian rank (Tac. *Ann.*, XII, 60; II, 59; *Hist.* I. 11); no senators
were admitted into the province; and the greatest jealousy was shown of the smallest
interference with it. The reasons for the special jealousy of Egypt shown by Augustus
and his successors were partly the great defensibility of the country (in case of insur-
rection—ED.), partly its immense importance as the granary of Rome. ' It was an
accepted principle with our fathers,' says Pliny, ' that our city could not possibly be fed
and maintained without the resources of Egypt.' " For a fuller treatment cf. Marquardt, *Röm. Staatsverwaltung*, I, 282–298.

[2] Armenia Major had been raised to greatness by Tigranes I (658–699) who had
been a formidable ally of Mithridates. Pompey finally subdued him, 688. Henceforth
Armenia was in a subject condition. Tigranes was succeeded by his son Artavasdes.
In 718, when Antony attacked the Parthians, this king sided with him against Phraates
of Parthia, and another Artavasdes, king of Media. Cf. Dio, XLIX, 25.

3 ὡς δυνάμενος ἐπαρχείαν ποῆσαι μᾶλλον ἐβου-
4 λήθην κατὰ τὰ πάτρια ἡμῶν ἔθη βασιλείαν Τιγρά-
5 νῃ Ἀρταουάσδου υἱῷ, υἱωνῷ δὲ Τιγράνου βασι-
6 λέως δ[ο]ῦν[α]ι διὰ Τιβερίου Νέρωνος, ὃς τότ᾽ ἐμοῦ
7 πρόγονος ἦν· καὶ τὸ αὐτὸ ἔθνος ἀφιστάμενον καὶ
8 ἀναπολεμοῦν δαμασθὲν ὑπὸ Γαίου τοῦ υἱοῦ
9 μου βασιλεῖ Ἀριοβαρζάνει, βασιλέως Μήδων Ἀρτα-
10 βάζου υἱῷ παρέδωκα καὶ μετὰ τὸν ἐκείνου θάνα-
11 τον τῷ υἱῷ αὐτοῦ Ἀρταουάσδῃ· οὗ ἀναιρεθέντος
12 Τιγράνην, ὃς ἦν ἐκ γένους Ἀρμενίου βασιλικοῦ, εἰς
13 τὴν βασιλείαν ἔπεμψα. § Ἐπαρχείας ἁπάσας, ὅσαι
14 πέραν τοῦ Ἰονίου κόλπου διατείνουσι πρὸς ἀνα-
15 τολάς, καὶ Κυρήνην ἐκ μείοζονος μέρους ὑπὸ βασι-
16 λέων κατεσχημένας καὶ ἔμπροσθεν Σικελίαν καὶ Σαρ-

But presently the two Artavasdes changed relations, the king of Armenia passing to the Parthian side and he of Media joining Antony. Cf. Plut., *Ant.*, 52; Dio, XLIX, 33, 44. Antony captured Artavasdes of Armenia and gave him over to Cleopatra, who killed him in 721. His kingdom was assigned to Antony's son Alexander to whom was betrothed Jotape daughter of Artavasdes of Media. The Armenians made Artaxes, son of the late Artavasdes, their king. When Octavian overcame Antony he did not befriend all the Oriental enemies of the latter, but for purposes of his own set up a rival to Phraates of Parthia in Tiridates. Cf. c. 32. And, angered at the Armenians, who had dealt harshly with certain Romans in that kingdom, he held as hostages the brothers of king Artaxes, and set Artavasdes of Media over Armenia Minor as a check upon Artaxes. Cf. Dio, LI, 16; LIV, 9. In 734 Augustus went to the East to arrange affairs there. A campaign against Artaxes was planned, but he was assassinated. Cf. Dio, LIV, 9; Tac., *Ann.*, II, 3; Vell., II, 94, 122; Suet. *Aug.*, 21; Jos., *Ant.*, XV, 4, 3; Eckhel, VI, 98. At this point the action of Augustus, recorded here in the *Res Gestae*, takes place. Augustus follows the example of Pompey, who, in dealing with Armenia in 688 had contented himself with making the Armenian king accept his royalty as a gift from Rome. Cf. Cic. *pro Sext.* 27. The affair was conducted by Tiberius, not yet adopted. Cf. Suet. *Tib.*, 9; Vell., II, 122. Henceforth Armenia was regarded as part of the empire, though its native sovereigns were continued. Cf. Vell., II, 94, 122: "Armenia restored to the control of the Roman people;" "Armenia retaken." "The Medes likewise were subjected." Cf. c. 33.

3 The reign of Tigranes was brief. The Parthians winning some success against Rome, stirred up Armenia. Cf. Tac. *Ann.*, II, 3; Vell. II, 100. They favored the children of Tigranes, Tigranes III and Erato. A Roman faction set up his younger brother Artavasdes. Cf. Tacitus l. c. The suppression of the disorder was enjoined upon Tiberius. But at this juncture, 748, he went into retirement at Rhodes. Cf. Dio, LV, 9. Artavasdes died and the young Tigranes courted the aid of Rome, but

34 et Sardiniam occu*pat*ás bello servili reciperávi. §

c. 28.

35 Colonias in África *Sicilia* [M]acedoniá utráque Hispániá
    Achai[a] As*i*a S[y]*ri*a
36 Galliá Narb*onensi Pi*[si]*dia* militum dedúxi §. Italia autem
    XXVIII [colo]ni-
37 ás, quae vívo *me celeberrimae* et frequentissimae fuerunt, me-
    [is auspicis]
38 deductas h*abet*.

V, 37. meis auspiciis, W. mea auctoritate.

at that time for the most part in the possession of kings, together with
Sicily and Sardinia, which had been engaged in a servile war.[4]

c. 28.

I have established colonies of soldiers[1] in Africa, Sicily, Macedonia, the two Spains, Achaia, Asia, Syria, Gallia Narbonensis and
Pisidia.[2] Italy also has twenty-eight colonies established under my
auspices, which within my lifetime have become very famous and pop-
ulous.[3]

was soon killed, probably by Parthian means, and his sister Erato abdicated.
Cf. fragments of Dio, cited by Mommsen, *R. G.* p. 113, and Dio, LV, 10. Tacitus
confirms the delivery of Armenia to Ariobarzanes by Gaius. Cf. *Ann.*, II, 3; and
Dio, LV, 10. The Parthian faction did not accept him, and it was in a contest over him
that Gaius received a wound, of which he died, Feb. 21, 757. Cf. C. I. L. I, p. 472.
For the succession of Artavasdes, cf. Dio, LV, 10. The Tigranes IV, next mentioned
" of the royal house of the Armenians " was a grandson of Herod the Great, of Judea,
on the one side, and of Archelaus, King of Cappadocia, and probably an Armenian
princess on the other. Cf. Tac. *Ann.* VI, 40; XIV, 26; Jos., *Ant.* XVIII, 5, 4;
Wars, I, 28, 1.

 [4] For Sicily and Sardinia, cf. c. 25 and notes.
By the treaty of Brundisium, Antony had received Macedonia, Achaia, Asia,
Pontus, Bithynia, Cilicia, Cyprus, Syria, Crete, Cyrenaica. The five last named he had
given over to foreign kings. As to Asia and Bithynia, Dio, XLIX, 41 and Plut. *Ant.*
54, are in conflict. But the *Res Gestæ* tends to confirm the latter. Lycaonia and
Pamphylia were taken from the province of Cilicia and given to Amyntas, King of
Galatia. Cf. Dio, XLIX, 32. He extended Egypt again by restoring to it Cyprus.
Cf. Dio, XLIX, 32, 41; Plut. l. c.; Strabo, XIV, 6, 6 : he granted to Cleopatra and
Cæsarion, her son by Julius Cæsar, the coast land of Syria, Tyre and Sidon excepted,
cf. Jos. *Ant.* XV, 4, 1; *Wars*, I, 18, 5; also Coele-Syria, cf. Jos. *Ant.* XV, 3, 8;
Plut. l. c. Ituraea, Judaea and Arabia Nabataea, cf. Dio, XLIX, 32; Jos. *Ant.* XV,
4, 1; 5, 3; *Wars*, I, 18, 5; 20, 3; parts of Cilicia, cf. Strabo, XIV, 5, 3; 5, 6 and
perhaps Crete also, cf. Dio, XLIX, 32 : and Cyrenaica, cf. Plut. l. c. To his younger
son Ptolemy Philadelphus he gave Syria, and part of Cilicia, cf. Dio, XLIX, 41; Plut.

17 δῷ προκατειλημμένας πολέμῳ δουλικῷ ἀνέλαβον.

c. 28.

18 Ἀποικίας ἐν Λιβύῃ Σικελίᾳ Μακεδονίᾳ ἐν ἑκατέ-
19 ρᾳ τε Ἱσπανίᾳ Ἀχαίᾳ Ἀσίᾳ Συρίᾳ Γαλατίᾳ τῇ πε-
20 ρὶ Νάρβωνα Πισιδίᾳ στρατιωτῶν κατήγαγον. § Ἰτα-
21 λία δὲ εἴχοσι ὀχτὼ ἀποικίας ἔχει ὑπ᾽ ἐμοῦ καταχθεί-
22 σας, αἳ ἐμοῦ περιόντος πληθύουσαι ἐτύγχανον.

l. c.: for the elder, Alexander he planned a kingdom made up of Armenia, Media and Parthia, cf. Livy, *Epit.* CXXXI; Plutarch, l. c. These alienations of Roman territory were made the occasion of Octavian's attack upon Antony. Cf. Dio, L, 1; Plut. l. c.

C. 28. [1] Mommsen believes that Augustus founded only military colonies. Zumpt thinks otherwise. Cf. *Comment Epig.*, I, 362.

[2] Known colonies of Augustus are: In Africa, Carthage, cf. C. I. L. VIII, p. 133; Dio, LII, 43; App. *Pun.* CXXXVI. In Sicily, Panhormus, Thermes, Tyndaris, cf. Dio, LIV, 7; Pliny, *Hist. Nat.*, III, 8, 88; 89; 90. Marquardt, *Röm. Staatsverwaltung* I, 246, names seven colonies of Augustus in Sicily. In Macedonia, Dyrrachium, Philippi, cf. Dio, LI, 4. Cassandrea, cf. Pliny, *Hist. Nat.*, IV, 10. In Hither Spain, Cæsaraugusta, cf. coin in Eckhel I, 37, which also gives the numbers of the legions whose veterans were colonized here: *leg. IV, leg. VI, leg. X.* Marquardt *op. cit.*, I, 256, names six colonies of Augustus here. In Farther Spain, Emerita, cf, Eckhel I, 12, and 19, *leg. V, X*; Marquardt, *op. cit.*, I, 257. In Achaia, Patrae, cf. C. I. L. III, p. 95, *leg. X, XII.* In Asia, Alexandrea of the Troad, cf. Pliny, *Hist. Nat.* V, 30. In Syria, Berytus, cf. Eckhel III, 356, *leg. V, VIII;* Heliopolis, cf. Eckhel, III, 334. In Gallia Narbonensis, Reii and Aquae Sextiae, cf. Herzog, *Gall. Narb. inscr.* n. 113, 356. In Pisidia, Antioch, cf. Eckhel III, 18; Cremna, cf. Eckhel III, 20; Olbasa, cf. Eckhel, III, 20; Parlais, cf. Ramsay, *Bull. de Corr. Hell.*, VII, p. 318.

No colonies are assigned to Sardinia, the three Gauls and two Germanies, Raetia, Noricum, Bithynia, Pontus, Galatia, Galatian Pontus, Paphlagonia, part of Phrygia, Lycaonia, Isauria, Cilicia, Cyprus, Crete, Egypt, Cyrenaica. As for parts of the empire under subject kings, such as Thrace, Cappadocia, Mauretania, no account is taken of them, though there were certainly colonies in Mauretania, at Cartenna and Tupusuctu. Ct. Pliny, *Hist. Nat.*, V, 2, 20; C. I. L., VIII, 8857.

[3] Cf. an article by Mommsen, *Hermes*, XVIII, 161 ff. on the "Colonies of Italy from Sulla to Vespasian."

When Augustus wrote, Italy was separated from Illyricum by the river Arsia. Yet Illyricum was not counted by him as a province. It had colonies at Emona, Iader, Salona, and possibly at Epidaurus and Narona. Cf. C. I. L., III, pp. 489, 374, 304, 287, 291. Mommsen thinks this omission was intended by Augustus; that he had been able to satisfy some of his veterans, to whom Italian farms had been promised, with lands over the Italian border in Illyricum, and because he could not call it a province, nor yet a part of Italy, he eludes the difficulty by omitting the Illyrian colonies.

c. 29.

39 Signa mílitaria *complur*[a per] aliós d[u]*c*és ámi[ssa] devicti[s
    hostibu]s re[cipe]ravi]

40 ex His*pania et* [Gallia et a Dalm]ateis. § Parthos trium
    exercitum Roman[o]-

41 rum s*polia et signa re*[ddere] mihi supplicesque amicitiam
    populí Romaní]

42 petere *coegi*. § *Ea autem si*[gn]a in penetrálí, quod e[s]t ín
    templo Martis Ultoris,

43 reposui.

c. 30.

44 Pannonio*rum gentes, qua*[s a]nte me principem populi Romaní
    exercitus nun-

45 quam ad[i]*t, devictas per Ti*. [Ne]ronem, qui tum erat pri-
    vignus et legátus meus,

46 ímperio po*puli Roma*ni s[ubie]ci, protulique finés Illyrici
    ad r[ip]am flúminis

c. 29.

I have recovered from Spain and Gaul, and from the Dalmatians,
after conquering the enemy, many military standards which had been
lost by other leaders.[1] I have compelled the Parthians to give up to
me the spoils and standards of three Roman armies, and as suppliants
to seek the friendship of the Roman people. Those standards, moreover, I have deposited in the sanctuary which is in the temple of Mars
the Avenger.[2]

c. 30.

The Pannonian peoples, whom before I became *princeps*, no army
of the Roman people had ever attacked, were defeated by Tiberius
Nero, at that time my son-in-law and legate; and I brought them under

---

The names of the twenty-eight Italian colonies are somewhat difficult to establish.
Several perplexing questions rise in the attempt. What of the colonies founded by
Antony and Octavian as triumvirs? Were they Antoniæ Juliæ, or some Juliæ and others
Antoniæ? If the former were true and they dropped the name Antoniæ, the result
would be far more than twenty-eight Julian and Augustan colonies. The second
probability is more likely, and that the colonies Antoniæ simply dropped their name
after Actium.

A third difficulty rises in the case of the enlargement of old colonies and their
resettlement, as, *e. g.*, of Minturnæ. Cf. Hyginus, *De Lim.*, p. 177. Mommsen gives
a list which nearly meets the statement of Augustus. 1. Ariminum, *Augusta;*
2. Ateste; 3. *Augusta* Prætoria; 4. *Julia Augusta* Taurinorum; 5. Beneventum,
Julia Augusta; 6. Bononia; 7. Brixia, *Augusta;* 8. Capua, *Julia Augusta;* 9. Cas-
trum novum Etruriæ, *Julia;* 10. Concordia, *Julia;* 11. Cumæ (?), *Julia;* 12. Dev-

c. 29.

23 Σημέας στρατιωτικὰς [πλείους ὑ]πὸ ἄλλων ἡγεμό-
24 νων ἀποβεβλημένας [νικῶν τοὺ]ς πολεμίους

XVI.

1 ἀπέλαβον § ἐξ ʽΙσπανίας καὶ Γαλατίας καὶ παρὰ
2 Δαλματῶν· Πάρθους τριῶν στρατευμάτων ʽΡωμαί-
3 ων σκῦλα καὶ σημέας ἀποδοῦναι ἐμοὶ ἱκέτας τε φι-
4 λίαν δήμου ʽΡωμαίων ἀξιῶσαι ἠνάγκασα. [§] ταύτας
5 δὲ τὰς σημέας ἐν τῷ ᵡΑρεως τοῦ ʼΑμύντορος ναοῦ ἀ-
6 δύτῳ ἀπεθέμην.

c. 30.

7 Παννονίων ἔθνη, οἷς πρὸ ἐμοῦ ἡγεμόνος στράτευ-
8 μα ʽΡωμαίων οὐκ ἤγγισεν, ἡσσηθέντα ὑπὸ Τιβερίου
9 Νέρωνος, ὃς τότ' ἐμοῦ ἦν πρόγονος καὶ πρεσβευτής,
10 ἡγεμονίᾳ δήμου ʽΡωμαίων ὑπέταξα [§] τά τε ʼΙλλυρι-

tona, *Julia;* 13. Fanum Fortunæ, *Julia;* 14. Falerio; 15. Hispellum, *Julia;* 16. Lucus Feroniæ, *Julia;* 17. Minturnæ; 18. Nola, *Augusta;* 19. Parentium, *Julia;* 20. Parma, *Julia Augusta;* 21. Pisae, *Julia;* 22. Pisaurum, *Julia;* 23. Pola, *Julia;* 24. Sæna (?), *Julia;* 25. Sora, *Julia;* 26. Suessa, *Julia;* 27. Sutrium, *Julia;* 28. Tuder, *Julia;* 29, Venafrum, *Julia Augusta.* Cf. Marquardt, *Röm. Staatsver-waltung,* I, 118–132.

C. 29. ¹ Of standards recovered in Spain and Gaul we have no further knowledge. It may be that in the Cantabrian war of 728, 729, some such thing took place.

Appian, *Illyr.* XII, XXV, XXVIII, narrates the capture of standards by the Dalmatians from Gabinius in 706, and their restoration to Augustus in 721. These were then placed in the Octavian portico; and probably later transferred to the temple of Mars.

²The standards had been lost by Crassus and Antony. Cf. Justin, XLII, 5, 11; Livy, *Epit.*, CXLI; Suetonius, *Aug.* 21; Vell., II, 91; Vergil, *Æn.* VII, 606; Horace, *Carm.*, I, 12, 56; III, 5, 4; Dio, LIII, 33; LIV, 8; Cass. *Chron.* ad. 734; Oros., VI, 21; Florus IV, 12; Eutropius, VII, 9. One detachment of Antonius' army, under L. Decidius Saxa, was exterminated in 714, and another in 718 under Oppius Statianus. Cf. Livy, *Ep.* CXXI; Dio, XLVIII, 24.

Tiberius received the standards from the Parthians in 734. Cf. Dio, LIV, 8, etc.; Suet. *Tib.* 9. Eckhel, VI, 95, shows a coin with a Parthian on bended knee presenting a standard to Augustus. Cf. also Horace, *Epis.*, I, 12, 27; Oros., VI, 21, 29; and c. 32 of the inscription.

There were two temples of Mars Ultor, a smaller one on the Capitoline, and a larger in the forum, dedicated in 752. The standards were removed to the larger temple. Cf. Dio, LV, 10; Horace, *Carm.*, IV, 5, 16; *Epis.*, I, 18, 56; Propertius, III, 10, 3; Ovid, *Trist.* II, 295; *Fasti,* V, 549; VI, 459.

47   Dan[u]i. Citr[a quod [D]ac[or]u[m tr]an[s]gressus exer-
citus meis a[u]sp[icis vict]us profliga-

48   tusque [est, et postea tran]s Dan[u]vium ductus. ex[ercitus
me]u[s] Da[cor]um

49   gentes im[peria populi Romani perferre coegit.]

c. 31.

50 Ad me ex In[dia regum legationes saepe missae sunt, nunquam antea visae]

51   apud qu[em]q[uam] R[omanorum du]cem. § Nostram
am[icitiam petierunt]

52   per legat[os] B[a]starn[ae Scythae]que et Sarmatarum q[ui
sunt citra flu]men

53   Tanaim [et] ultrá reg[es, Alba]norumque réx et Hibér[orum
et Medorum.]

c. 32.

54 Ad mé supplices confug[erunt] regés Parthorum Tírida[tes et
postea] Phrát[es]

V, 49.   imperia, W. imperium; perferre, W. accipere; S. sustinere.

subjection to the empire of the Roman people,[1] and extended the
boundaries of Illyricum to the bank of the river Danube.[2] When an
army of the Dacians crossed this river, it was defeated and destroyed,
and afterwards my army, led across the Danube, compelled the Dacian
people to submit to the sway of the Roman people.[3]

c. 31.

Embassies have been many times sent to me from the kings of
India, a thing never before seen in the case of any ruler of the
Romans.[1] Our friendship has been sought by means of ambassadors
by the Bastarnae and the Scythians, and by the kings of the Sarmatae,
who are on either side of the Tanais, and by the kings of the Albani,
the Hiberi, and the Medes.[2]

c. 32.

To me have betaken themselves as suppliants the kings of the

C. 30.   [1] Augustus himself had fought the Pannonians in 719, 720. Cf. Dio,
XLIX, 36–38. The campaigns of Tiberius were from 742 to 745. Cf. Vell. II, 96;
Dio, LIV, 31, 34; LV, 2; Suet. *Tib.*, 9.

[2] This statement varies somewhat from Dio, L, 24, who says Augustus reached the
Danube in 720, and from Suetonius, *Tib.* 16, who assigns the complete subjection of
the district to 759.

[3] The Dacians had become organized and strong in the latter years of the Roman

11 χοῦ ὅρια μέχρι ᾽Ἰστρου ποτομοῦ προήγαγον· οὐ ἐπει-
12 ταδε Δάχων διαβᾶσα πολλὴ δύναμις ἐμοῖς αἰσίοις οἰω-
13 νοῖς κατεχόπη. Καὶ ὕστερον μεταχθὲν τὸ ἐμὸν στρά-
14 τευμα πέραν ᾽Ἰστρου τὰ Δάχων ἔθνη᾽προστάλματα
15 δήμου ῾Ρωμαίων ὑπομένειν ἠνάγκασεν.

C. 31.

16 Πρὸς ἐμὲ ἐξ ᾽Ἰνδίας βασιλέων πρεσβεῖαι πολλάκις ἀπε-
17 στάλησαν, οὐδέποτε πρὸ τούτου χρόνου ὀφθεῖσαι παρὰ
18 ῾Ρωμαίων ἡγεμόνι. § Τὴν ἡμετέραν φιλίαν ἠξίωσαν
19 διὰ πρέσβεων § Βαστάρναι καὶ Σκύθαι καὶ Σαρμα-
20 τῶν οἱ ἐπιτάδε ὄντες τοῦ Τανάιδος ποταμοῦ καὶ
21 οἱ πέραν δὲ βασιλεῖς, καὶ ᾽Αλβανῶν δὲ καὶ ᾽Ἰβήρων
22 καὶ Μήδων βασιλέες.

C. 32.

23 Πρὸς ἐμὲ ἱκέται κατέφυγον βασιλεῖς Πάρθων μὲν

republic. Cf. Justin. XXXII, 3; Jordanis, *Get.*, XI, 67; Strabo, XVI, 2, 39; VII 3, 5; 11; Suet. *Aug.* 44. Julius Cæsar was about to proceed against them when he died. Cf. Suet. *Jul.*, 44; *Aug.*, 8; App. *B. C.*, II, 110; III, 25, 37; *Illyr.*, 13; Vell., II. 59; Livy, *Epit.*, CXVII. In 719 Augustus began his Illyrican campaign by occupying Segesta on the Save, whence he threatened the Dacians and Bastarnæ. Cf. App. *Illyr.*, 22, 23. Antony is responsible for the statement that Augustus sought to secure the goodwill of Cotiso, king of the Getæ (Dacians), by giving him his daughter and by himself marrying a daughter of Cotiso. Cf. Suetonius, *Aug.*, 63. Cotiso refused the alliance and joined the party of Antony. Cf. Dio, L, 6; LI, 22. Antony's story as to the proposed marriages is hardly credible, and may have been invented by him to offset his own alliance with Cleopatra. During the struggle between Antony and Octavian, an invasion of the Dacians was the constant dread of Italy. Cf. Vergil, *Georg.*, II, 497; Hor. *Sat.*, II, 6, 53; *Carm.*, III, 6, 13. When Antony was overthrown M. Crassus undertook the suppression of the Dacians, and triumphed, July 4, 727. Cf. Dio, LI, 23; Tab. Triumph. But Dacian incursions were still frequent. Dio records one in 738, cf. LIV, 20; and one in 744, cf. LIV, 36. Probably it was in this latter incursion that the defeat here alluded to was met by them. Finally an army was sent against them under Lentulus, in 759. Cf. Dio, LV, 30; Strabo, VII, 12 and 13; Suet. *Aug.*, 21; Florus, IV, 12, 19, 20; Tac. *Ann.*, IV, 44.

C. 31. [1] Cf. Suet. *Aug.*, 21; Flor. IV, 12, 62; Oros., VI, 21, 19, says that deputies of Indians and Scythians came to Augustus at Tarracona in 728 or 729; Dio, LIV, 9, that deputies from India came to him at Samos in 734. Strabo gives the name of the Indian king as Porus. Cf. XV. 1, 4 and 73. Cf. also Ver. *Georg.*, II, 170; *Aen.*, VI, 794; VIII, 705; Hor. *Carm.*, I, 12, 56; *Carm. Saec.*, 55, 56; *Carm.*, IV, 14, 41.

[2] For a general statement, cf. Suetonius, *Aug.* 21. For the Scythians, cf. Note I,

VI.

1 regis Phrati[s filius]; [§] Medorum [Artavasdes; Adiabeno-
rum A]rtaxa-
2 res §; Britann[o]rum Dumnobellau[nus] *et Tim* ......;
[Sugambrorum]
3 Maelo; § Mar[c]omanórum Sueboru[m ..... rus]. [Ad
me] rex *Part*horum
4 Phrates Orod[i]s filius filiós suós nepot[esque omnes misit]
*in Ital*iam, non
5 bello superátú[s], sed amicitiam nostram per [liberorum]
suorum pignora
6 petens. § Plúrimaeque aliae gentes exper[tae sunt p. R.]
*fide*m me prin-
7 cipe, quibus anteá cum populo Roman[o nullum extitera]t
legationum
8 et amícitiae [c]ommercium. §

VI, 7. extiterat, S. fuerat.

Parthians, Tiridates, and later, Phraates, the son of king Phraates;[1]
of the Medes, Artavasdes;[2] of the Adiabeni, Artaxares;[3] of the
Britons, Dumnobellaunus and Tim ;[4] of the Sicambri, Maelo;[5]
and of the Marcomanian Suevi, rus.[6] Phraates, king of the
Parthians, son of Orodes, sent all his children and grandchildren into
Italy to me, not because he had been conquered in war, but rather
seeking our friendship by means of his children as pledges.[7] Since I
have been *princeps* very many other races have made proof of the good
faith of the Roman people, who never before had had any interchange
of embassies and friendship with the Roman people.

---

above. For the Bastarnæ, cf. Livy, *Ep.* CXXXIV; Dio, LI, 23, 24. For the Sar-
matæ, cf. Flor. l. c.; Strabo, II, 5, 30; Tac. *Ann.*, VI, 33; Pliny, *Hist. Nat.*, II,
108, 246; VI, 7, 19; VI, 5, 16; VI, 13, 40. Vergil refers to them as Gelones. Cf.
Aen., VIII, 725. Cf. also Hor. *Carm.*, II, 9; III, 8, 23. For the Albani and Iberi,
cf. Dio, XLIX, 24. For the Medes, cf. c. 27 and notes.

C. 32. [1] For Phraates and Tiridates, cf. Justin, XLII, 5; Dio, LI, 18. Tiridates had supplanted Phraates and in turn was driven out by him. He then, in 724,
came to Augustus for aid. But the latter was anxious to regain the lost standards from
Parthia, and simply played off Tiridates against Phraates by setting him over Syria.
Dio, in the passage cited, makes mention of a son of Phraates who was captured by
Tiridates and given up to Augustus. This was possibly the Phraates here mentioned,
though there are difficulties in the way of this explanation. For Augustus implies the
voluntary coming of a reigning king, not the delivery of an abducted prince. We

24 Τειριδάτης καὶ μετέπειτα Φραάτης βασιλέως §
XVII.
1 Φράτου [υἱός, Μ]ηδ[ων] δὲ 'Αρταο[υάσδ]ης, 'Αδιαβ[η]·
2 νῶν ['Α]ρτα[ξάρης, Βριτα]ννῶν Δομνοελλαῦνος
3 καὶ Τ[ιμ........, Σο]υ[γ]άμβρων [Μ]αίλων, Μαρχο-
4 μάνων [Σουήβων]........ρος. § [Πρὸ]ς ἐμὲ βασιλεῖς
5 Πάρθων Φρα[άτης 'Ωρώδο]υ υἱὸ[ς υ]ἱοὺς [αὐτοῦ] υἱω-
6 νούς τε πάντας ἔπεμψεν εἰς 'Ιταλίαν, οὐ πολέμῳ
7 λειφθείς, ἀλλὰ τὴν ἡμ[ε]τέραν φιλίαν ἀξιῶν ἐπὶ τέ-
8 κνων ἐνεχύροις, πλεῖστά τε ἄλλα ἔθνη πεῖραν ἔλ[α]-
9 βεν δήμου 'Ρωμαίων πίστεως ἐπ' ἐμοῦ ἡγεμόνος,
10 οἷς τὸ πρὶν οὐδεμία ἦν πρὸς δῆμον 'Ρωμαίων π[ρε]σ-
11 βειῶν καὶ φιλίας κοινωνία.

know that in 731 Tiridates was in Rome asking that Parthia be assigned to him, and that at the same time Phraates sent an embassy begging the restitution of his son. Cf. Dio, LIII, 33. Augustus laid the matter before the senate, and by their advice restored the prince in exchange for the standards, but did not yield to the plea of Tiridates.

2 Cf. c. 27.

3 A people east of the Tigris, and west of Media Atropatane. Nothing is known of Artaxares. For the Adiabeni and their kingdom, cf. Strabo, XVI, 1, 19 ; Tac. Ann., XII, 13 ; Josephus, Ant., XX, 2, 1.

4 Augustus several times was on the point of invading Britain. Cf. Dio, XLIX, 38, for 720 ; LIII, 22, 25, for 727, 728. The poets have many prophecies of victories in Britain. Cf. Ver. Georg., I, 30, written in 724 ; III, 25 ; Hor. Epode, VII, 7; Carm , I. 35, 29, of the year 727, 728 ; Carm., III, 5; I, 21, 15; III, 4, 33 ; IV, 14, 48. But nothing came of these plans. Cf. Strabo, IV, 5, 3, for embassies from Britain. Coins of Dumnobellaunus have been found. Cf. J. Evans, Coins of the Ancient Britons (London, 1864), p. 198, and the following plate 4, Nos. 6–12.

5 The great defeat of Lollius in 738 was by the Sicambri, joined with the Usipites and Tencteri. Cf. Dio, LIV, 20 ; Vell., II, 97 ; Suet. Aug., 23. There was a temporary peace. Cf. Horace, Carm., IV, 2. 36 ; 14, 51. They rebelled in 742, and were put down, first by Drusus and later by Tiberius. Cf. Dio, LIV, 32, 33, 36. In 746 they were completely subjugated and removed into Gaul. Cf. Dio, LV, 6 ; Vell., II, 97 ; Suet., Aug., 21 ; Tib., 9 ; Tac. Ann., II, 26 ; XII, 39; Strabo, VII, 1, 3. Probably the coming of Maelo was during this surrender of 746.

6 The Marcomani were a branch of the Suevi. Cf. Tac., Germ., XXXVIII; Ann., II, 44, 62.

7 The four sons were Seraspedes, Rhodaspedes, Vonones and Phraates, with the wives of two of them and four children. Cf. Strabo, XVI, 1, 28 ; VI, 4, 2 ; Justin, XLII, 5, 11 ; Vell., II, 94 ; Tac. Ann., II, 1 ; Oros., VI, 21, 29; Suet., Aug. 21, 43 ; Jos., Antiq., XVIII, 2, 4. They were sent to be out of harm's way during

c. 33.

9 Á me gentés Parthórum et Médóru[m per legatos] principes
   eárum gen-
10 tium régés pet[i]tós accéperunt Par[thi Vononem regis Phr]á-
   tis fílium,
11 régis Oródis nepótem; § Médí Ar[iobarzanem] regis Arta-
   vazdis fi-
12 lium, regis Ariobarzanis nep[otem].

c. 34.

13 Ín consulátú sexto et septimo, b[ella ubi civil]ia exstinxeram
14 per consénsum úniversórum [potitus rerum omn]ium, rem
   publicam
15 ex meá potestáte [§] in senát[us populique Romani a]rbitri-
   um transtulí.

VI, 13.   bella ubi, S. postquam bella ; ubi, G. cum.

c. 33.

From me the peoples of the Parthians and of the Medes have
received the kings they asked for through ambassadors, the chief men
of those peoples: the Parthians, Vonones, the son of king Phraates, and
grandson of king Orodes ;[1] the Medes, Ariobarzanes, the son of king
Artavasdes, and grandson of king Ariobarzanes.[2]

c. 34.

In my sixth and seventh consulships, when I had put an end to the
civil wars, after having obtained complete control of affairs by universal
consent, I transferred the commonwealth from my own dominion to the
authority of the senate and Roman people.[1]   In return for this favor

troubles in Parthia, according to all but Josephus, who says they were removed so as
not to hinder the succession of Phraataces, an illegitimate son. When Phraates died,
Phraataces in vain asked Augustus for the return of the princes. This was c. 750. Cf.
Dio, fragments, Ursin. 39.   The two elder princes died in Rome. Cf. C. I. L., VI,
7799.   Vonones was sent back by Augustus. Cf. c. 33, Note 1 ; Phraates was
returned by Tiberius in 788. Cf. Tac., *Ann.*, VI, 31 ; Dio, LVIII, 16. Probably
the princes were sent to Augustus in 744. Cf. Mommsen, *R. G.*, p. 141.

C. 33.   1 The comment of Mommsen here seems too severe. He says : " The
writer magnifies his splendors beyond what is exact : for the Parthians and Medes
asked Augustus, not so much to appoint kings for them, as to restore to them those to
whom the kingdom had fallen by hereditary right." Such a criticism seems to over-
look the force of the word *petitos*, as applied to *reges:* they got the kings they " asked
for."

c. 33.

12 Παρ' ἐμοῦ ἐθνη Πάρθων καὶ Μήδων διὰ πρέσβεων τῶν
13 παρ' αὐτοῖς πρώτων βασιλεῖς αἰτησάμενοι ἔλαβ[ον]
14 Πάρθοι Ὀυονώνην βασιλέως Φράτου υ[ἱ]όν, βασιλ[έω]ς
15 Ὠρώδου υἱωνόν· Μῆδοι Ἀριοβαρζάνην βα[σ]ιλέως
16 Ἀρταβάζου υἱόν, βασιλέως Ἀριοβαρζάν[ου υἱω]νόν.

c. 34.

17 Ἐν ὑπατείᾳ ἕκτῃ καὶ ἑβδόμῃ μετὰ τὸ τοὺς ἐνφυ-
18 λίους ζβέσαι με πολέμους [x]ατὰ τὰς εὐχὰς τῶν ἐ-
19 μῶν πολε[ι]τῶν ἐνκρατὴς γενόμενος πάντων τῶν
20 πραγμάτων, ἐκ τῆς ἐμῆς ἐξουσίας εἰς τὴν τῆς συν-
21 κλήτου καὶ τοῦ δήμου τῶν Ῥωμαίων μετήνεγκα

Phraataces was reigning in 754. Cf. Dio, LV, 10; Vell. II, 101. He was succeeded by Orodes for a short time. Then came the choice of Vonones. Cf. Jos. *Ant.* XVIII, 2, 4; Tac. *Ann.* II, 1. Josephus gives no date. Tacitus implies 770. Augustus, however, returned Vonones, and the date must be much earlier, probably c. 760. A Parthian embassy was in Rome between 757 and 759. Cf. Suet. *Tib.*, 16. Coins also show the name of Vonones in 761. Cf. Gardner, *Parthian Coinage*, p. 46. His reign was very brief. Cf. Tacitus and Josephus, ll. cc.

² Cf. c. 27.

C. 34. ¹ This chapter is possibly the most weighty in the whole inscription, inasmuch as it sets forth the view of his policy which Augustus wished the world to hold. How far his statements in the opening and closing sentences represent his own actual notions of his relations to the sovereign power in Rome is a matter of debate. For a full discussion Mommsen, *Röm. St.* II, p. 723, ff., may be read, and Gardthausen *Aug.* Iᵉʳ Th. IIᵉʳ Bd., pp. 485–540 and IIᵉʳ Th., pp. 277–299.

The question is: Did Augustus in any real sense restore the republic, or did he conceive of himself as monarch, but find it politic to suppress all outward marks of royalty? Was his chief concern to maintain the peace and prosperity of the Roman people, with as little alteration as possible of the old constitutional forms, or was his object the building up of power for his own sake? This is confessedly one of the riddles of history. The best that can be done is to study his actions, estimating their worth and tendency, and leaving the motives of the great statesman where he hid them,—locked in his own bosom.

Undoubtedly, all through the *Res Gestæ*, as is pointed out in the introduction, and as has been noticed from time to time in these notes, one of his great aims is to represent himself as a conservative, moving within constitutional limits. Coins of the period emphasize the view set forth in the opening sentence of this chapter with regard to the restoration of the republic. Cf. Eckhel, VI, 83: *imp. Cæsar divi f. cos. VI, liberatis p. R. vindex;* "The imperator, Cæsar, son of the divine (Cæsar) consul for the sixth time, (726) restorer of the freedom of the Roman people." Cf. C. I. L. VI,

16 Quó pro merito meó sénatu[s consulto Aug. appe]llátus sum
et laureís

17 postés aedium meárum v[estiti publice coronaq]ue civíca
super

18 iánuam meam fíxa est [§] [clupeusque aureu]s in [c]úriá
Iúliá posi-

19 tus, quem mihi senatum [populumque Romanu]m dare virtutis cle-

20 [mentia]e iustitia[e pietatis causa testatum] est pe[r e]ius
clúpei

VI, 16. Aug. S. Augustus.
VI, 17. vestiti, W. velati sunt; S. inserts sunt after vestiti.

on my part I received by decree of the senate the title Augustus,[2] the
door-posts of my house were publicly decked with laurels, a civic crown
was fixed above my door,[3] and in the Julian Curia was placed a golden
shield, which, by its inscription, bore witness that it was given to me by
the senate and Roman people on account of my valor, clemency, justice

---

1527 : "the whole world pacified, the republic restored" Also, C. I. L. I, p. 384 ;
the date referred to is Jan. 13, 727 : "The senate decreed that an oaken crown should
be fixed above the door of the imperator, Cæsar Augustus, because he restored the
Roman republic." Contemporary Roman writers simply echo the views of Augustus.
Cf. Ovid, *Fasti*, I, 589, for Jan. 13. 727, Velleius, II, 89, says : "When the civil wars
were finished in the twentieth year, (724) and the foreign wars brought to a close,
peace was brought back, power restored to the laws, authority to the tribunals, majesty to the senate, the *imperium* of the magistrates reduced to its old time form, the
original and ancient form of the state restored." Cf. Livy, *Epit*, CXXXIV. The Greek
Strabo, also a contemporary, writes, XVII, 3, 25 : "The country committed to him the
headship of her sovereignty, and made him lord of peace, and war for life." Later
writers, even the Romans, are equally free in their judgments. Dio, LII, I, says :
".From this time (725) the affairs of Rome began to be in the control of one man
(μοναρχεῖσθαι)." Cf. Suet. *Aug* 28, Tac. *Ann*, III, 28. Dio's account of the con-
ference in which Agrippa advises a real abdication by Augustus, and Mæcenas urges a
bold assumption of supreme power (LII, 1–40) is regarded as fictitious.

The facts in the case are these: In 711 the Titian law gave the triumvirs a five
years' lease of power. In 716 this was renewed not by formal legislation, but " by
universal consent." Cf. App., *B. C.* V, 95. This triumviral power Augustus wielded
till his sixth consulship, 726, though there was a pretence of its cessation in 721. Cf. c.
7, N, 1, and Mommsen, *Röm. St.*, II, 698. In this and the following years he
divested himself gradually of one extraordinary power after another. He could not at
once fall back to the position of an ordinary magistrate. The armies, the laws, the
provinces, the revenues had all been in his control. These he must gradually restore.
Cf. Dio, LII, 13; LIII, 4, 9, 10. In 726 he began his return to older customs by

22 κυρίῃαν. ἐξ ἧς αἰτίας δόγματι συνκλήτου Σεβαστὸς
23 προσ[ηγορε]ύθην καὶ δάφναις δημοσίᾳ τὰ πρόπυ-·
24 λ[ά μου ἐστέφθ]η, ὅ τε δρύινος στέφανος ὁ διδόμενος

XVIII.

1 ἐπὶ σωτηρίᾳ τῶν πολειτῶν ὑπερά[ν]ω τοῦ πυλῶ-
2 νος τῆς ἐμῆς οἰκίας ἀνετέθη, § ὅπ[λ]ον τε χρυ-
3 σοῦν ἐν τῷ βο[υ]λευτηρίῳ ἀνατεθ[ὲ]ν ὑπό τε τῆς
4 συνκλήτου καὶ τοῦ δήμου τῶν ʽΡω[μα]ίων
5 διὰ τῆς ἐπιγραφῆς ἀρετὴν καὶ ἐπείκειαν κα[ὶ δ]ικαιοσύνην

alternating with Agrippa, his colleague, in the consulship, in having the fasces borne
before him by the lictors for a month. Cf. Dio, LIII, 1. The restoration of the censorship was part of the same programme. Dio, LIII, 2, says that by an edict he declared
all the revolutionary and extraordinary acts of the triumviral period should cease to be
effective with the expiration of his sixth consulship (726). The inscription of Jan.
13, 727, above alluded to, C. I. L. I, p. 384, marks that date as that on which the business of restoring the provinces was finally given over to the senate.

From this time on the senate divided the control of the provinces with him.
Augustus took the troublesome provinces and the frontier ones, leaving to the senate
the older and more peaceable. Over these provinces he received a proconsular
imperium for ten years, which was renewed at the expiration of that term. In
c. 7 he says that he found the tribunitial power a sufficient basis for all the measures
which he wished to put through. Now the proconsulship and tribuneship were
both ordinary and constitutional offices. Augustus' occupancy of each affords an
illustration of the way in which he held ordinary offices in an extraordinary way. For
by the old customs a proconsul must exercise his *imperium* in his province, and never
at Rome. Augustus could not be in ten provinces at once, and must be at Rome most
of the time. Hence a violation of the constitution was necessary. The tribuneship,
instituted for the protection of plebeians could be held only by a plebeian. But Augustus
was a patrician. For this reason he did not take the tribuneship in the ordinary way,
nor by the ordinary title, but designated himself as *tribunicia potestate*, " of tribunitial
authority."

The title *princeps*, "prince " is never used by Augustus as an official designation
in laws and inscriptions, but indicates simply his primacy of rank and is so used throughout the *Res Gestæ*. Cf. cc. 13, 30, 32.

2 Cf. C. I. L. i, p. 384; X. 8375; Livy, *Ep*., 134; Cass. ad. an. 727; Oros.
VI, 20, 8; Vell. II, 91; Suet. *Aug.* 7; Dio, LIII, 16.

3 Cf. coins in Eckhel, VI, 88; Cohen, *Aug.* nos. 43-48, 50, 207-212, 301, 341,
356, 385, 426, 476-8, 482. All these show either the crown or the laurels and many
of them have both. With the crown is generally *ob civis servatos*, "for preserving the
citizens." The civic crown being the reward of any soldier who saved a citizen's
life, Augustus was pre-eminently deemed worthy of it, because he had saved so many
by putting an end to the civil wars, and by his clemency. Cf. Dio, LIII, 16; Suet.
Claud. 17; Sen. *De Clem.* I, 26, 5; Ovid, *Tr.* III, 1, 39, 41, 47; *Fasti* IV, 953;

21 [inscription]em. § Post id tem[pus praestiti omnibus digni-
    tate potes-
22 t]atis au[tem n]ihilo ampliu[s habui quam qui fuerunt m]ihi
    quo-
23 que in ma[gis]tra[t]u conlegae.

c. 35.

24 Tertium dec[i]mum consulátu[m cum gerebam, senatus et
   equ]ester ordo
25 populusq[ue] Románus úniversus [appellavit me patrem
   p]atriae idque
26 in vestibu[lo a]edium meárum inscriben[dum esse et in curia
   e]t in foró Aug.
27 sub quadrig[i]s, quae mihi [ex] s. c. pos[itae sunt, decrevit.
   Cum scri]psi haec,
28 annum agebam septuagensu[mum sextum].

c. 1.

29 Summá pecún[i]ae, quam ded[it in aerarium vel plebei Roma-
   nae vel di]mis·

VI, 22.   quam, G. iis.

and piety.[4] After that time I excelled all others in dignity, but of
power I held no more than those also held who were my colleagues in
any magistracy.[5]

c. 35.

While I was consul for the thirteenth time the senate and the
equestrian order and the entire Roman people gave me the title of
father of the fatherland, and decreed that it should be inscribed upon
the vestibule of my house and in the Curia, and in the Augustan
Forum beneath the quadriga which had been, by decree of the senate,
set up in my honor.[1] When I wrote these words I was in my seventy-
sixth year.[2]

SUPPLEMENT.

c. 1.

The sum of the money which he gave in to the treasury or to the

III, 137; Val. Max. II, 8, 7; Juv. VI, 52, 79; X, 65; XII, 91; Tac. Ann. XV, 71.
    [4] No ancient writer mentions this shield, but a number of coins and inscriptions
portray it. Cf. C. I. L. IX, 5811, wherein two Victories carry a shield inscribed :

6 καὶ εὐσέβειαν ἐμοὶ μαρτυρεῖ. § Ἀξιώμ[α]τι [§] πάντων
7 διήνεγκα, [§] ἐξουσίας δὲ οὐδέν τι πλεῖον ἔσχον·
8 τῶν συναρξάντων μοι.

c. 35.

9 Τρισκαιδεκάτην ὑπατείαν ἄγοντός μου ἥ τε σύν-
10 κλητος καὶ τὸ ἱππικὸν τάγμα ὅ τε σύνπας δῆμος τῶν
11 Ῥωμαίων προσηγόρευσέ με πατέρα πατρίδος καὶ τοῦτο
12 ἐπὶ τοῦ προπύλου τῆς οἰκίας μου καὶ ἐν τῷ βουλευτη-
13 ρίῳ καὶ ἐν τῇ ἀγορᾷ τῇ Σεβαστῇ ὑπὸ τῷ ἅρματι, ὅ μοι
14 δόγματι συνκλήτου ἀνετέθη, ἐπιγραφῆναι ἐψηφίσα-
15 το. [§] Ὅτε ἔγραφον ταῦτα, ἦγον ἔτος ἑβδομηκοστὸν
16 ἕκτον. §

17 Συνκεφαλαίωσις [§] ἠριθμημένου χρήματος εἰς τὸ αἱρά-

"The senate and Roman people have given to Augustus a shield on account of his
valor, clemency, justice and piety;" the very words of the Res Gestæ. For coins,
cf. Eckhel, VI, 95, 103, 121; Cohen, Aug. nos. 50-53, 213-216, 253, 264-267, 283,
286-297, 332. The Victory, which is frequently associated with the shield, probably
indicates that the latter was placed by Augustus near the altar of Victory erected by
him in the Curia Julia.

⁵ Cf. Note 1.

C. 35. ¹ This title was given Feb. 5, 752. Cf. C. I. L. I, p. 386; II, No. 2107.
As in the case of the title, prince of the youth, conferred upon Gaius and Lucius, and
of the continuance of his supreme power by universal consent (cf. cc. 14 and 34),
the appellation, father of the fatherland, was given by general acclamation, leaving to
the senate only the formal ratification of the popular will. Suet. Aug. 58, expressly
states this. Cf. also Ovid, Fasti, II, 128.

ↄ The Augustan Forum was dedicated this same year, 752. Cf. c. 21, Note. In
all probability the quadriga had been in existence some time before this, inasmuch as
it appears on a coin of uncertain date with the inscription: "the senate and Roman
people to Cæsar Augustus, parent and preserver." If the quadriga had been made at
the time this inscription was ordered, the coin would surely have borne the formal title,
"father of the fatherland," not the designation, "parent." Cf. Eckhel, VI, 113.

² The seventy-sixth year of Augustus began Sept. 23, 766. Chapter 8 mentions
his third census, which was completed one hundred days before his death, hence May
11, 767. The Res Gestæ must have been written, then, in the interval between this
date and his start for Campania, on his last journey, as we know he left this document
in the hands of the Vestal Virgins. Cf. Suet. Aug. 97.

SUPPLEMENT.

For a discussion of this supplement, see the Introduction.

6

30   sis militibus : denarium se[xi]e[ns milliens].

C. 2.

31 Opera fecit nova § aedem Martis, [Iovis tonantis et feretri, Apollinis],
32 díví Iúli, § Quirini, § Minervae   [Iunonis reginae, Iovis Libertatis],
33 Larum, deum Penátium, [§] Iuv[entatis, Matris deum, Lupercal, pulvina]r
34 ad circum, [§] cúriam cum ch[alcidico, forûm Augustum, basilica]m
35 Iuliam, theatrum Marcelli, [§] [p]or[ticus . . . ., nemus trans T]iberím
36 Caesarum. §

C. 3.

37 Refécit Capito[lium sacra]sque ae*d*es [nu]m[ero octoginta] duas, thea[t]rum Pom-
38 peí, aqu[arum rivos, vi]am Flamin[iam].

C. 4.

39 Impensa p . . . . . . [in spect]acul[a scaenica et munera] gladiatorum at-
40 [que athletas et venationes et naum]ach[iam] et donata pe-[c]unia a (?)
41   .   .   .   .
     [ter]rae motu § incendioque consum-

Roman people, or to discharged soldiers, was six hundred million denarii.[1]

c. 2.

He constructed new works as follows: the temples of Mars, of Jupiter the Thunderer and the Vanquisher, of Apollo, of the divine Julius, of Quirinus, of Minerva, of Juno Regina, of Jupiter Libertas, of the Lares, of the divine Penates, of Youth, and of the Mother of the gods, the Lupercal, the Pulvinar in the Circus, the Curia with the Chalcidicum, the Augustan Forum, the Basilica Julia, the Theatre of Marcellus, the Portico on the Palatine, the Portico in the Flaminian Circus, the grove of the Cæsars beyond the Tiber.[1]

18 ριον ἢ εἰς τὸν δῆμον τὸν ʿΡω[μαί]ων ἢ εἰς τοὺς ἀπολε-
19 λυμένους στρατιώτας [§]: ἐξ μυριάδες μυριάδων. §
20 ″Εργα καινὰ ἐγένετο ὑπ᾽ αὐτοῦ ναοὶ μὲν ″Αρεως, Διὸς
21 βροντησίου καὶ τροπαιοφόρου, Πανός, ᾽Απόλλω-
22 νος, [§] θεοῦ ᾽Ιουλίου, Κυρείνου, [§] ᾽Α[θη]νᾶς, [§] ″Ηρας
      βασιλί-
23 δος, [§] Διὸς ᾽Ελευθερίου, [§] ἡρώ[ων, θεῶν π]ατρίων, [§],
      Νε-
24 ότητος, [§] Μητρὸς θεῶν, [§] β[ουλευτήριον] σὺν χαλκι-
XIX.

1 δικῷ, [§] ἀγορᾷ Σεβαστῇ [§], θέατρον Μαρχέλλου, [§] β[α]σι-
2 λικὴ ᾽Ιουλία, [§] ἄλσος Καισάρων, [§] στοαὶ ἐ[ν] Παλατ[ί]ῳ,
3 στοὰ ἐν ἱπποδρόμῳ Φλαμινίῳ. § ᾽Επεσκευάσθ[η τὸ Κα]-
4 πιτώλιον, [§] ναοὶ ὀγδοήκοντα δύο, [§]θέ[ατ]ρον Π[ομ]-
5 πηίου, [§] ὁδὸς Φλαμινία, [§] ἀγωγοὶ ὑδάτων. [Δαπ]άναι δὲ
6 εἰς θέας καὶ μονομάχους καὶ ἀθλητὰς καὶ ναυμα-
7 χίαν καὶ θηρομαχίαν δωρεαί [τε] ἀποικίαις πόλεσιν

c. 3.

He restored the Capitol, and sacred structures to the number of
eighty-two, the Theatre of Pompey, the aqueducts, the Flaminian
Way.[1]

c. 4.

His expenses for theatrical representations, for gladiatorial and
athletic exhibitions, for chases and the naval combat,[1] also for gifts in
money to the colonies and ʿcities of Italy,[2] to provincial cities suffering

C. I. [1] Equivalent to 2,400,000,000 sesterces, about $120,000,000. This does
not exactly correspond with the sum of the items mentioned in the *Res Gestæ*. These
sum up 2,199,800,000 sesterces.

C. 2. [1] A mere summary of c. 19, with a bit from c. 20, the only principle of
arrangement being to put temples first, and the rest haphazard. The difference in the
Greek and Latin is curious. No attempt is made to reproduce *pulvinar* in Greek,
although in c. 19 it had been rendered ναόν.

C. 3. [1] A summary of c. 20.

C. 4. [1] A summary of cc. 22, 23.

[2] For aid given to Naples, cf. Dio, LV, 10; to Venafrum, in Campania, C. I. L.
X, 4842.

42   pt[is] a[ut viritim] a[micis senat]oribusque, quórum census
     explévit,
43   in[n]umera[bili]s. §

from earthquake or conflagrations,[3] and to individual friends and to
senators, whose property he raised to the standard;[4] were innumerable.

---

[3] For aid to Paphos, cf. Dio, LIV, 23 ; to a number of towns in Asia, Dio, LIV,
30; to Laodicea and Tralles, Strabo, XII, 8, 18; to Thyatira and Chios, Suet. *Tib.* 8.
[4] Cf. Suet. *Aug.* 41.   The estate necessary to qualify a senator he raised from
800,000 sesterces to 1,200,000, and where senators were worthy, though poor, he made
up their fortunes to that sum.   Cf. Dio, LI, 17; LII, 19; LIII, 2; LIV, 17; LV,
13; LVI, 41.

8 εν Ἰταλίᾳ, πόλεσιν ἐν ἐπαρχείαις [§] σεισμῷ κα[ὶ] ἐνπυ-
9 ρισμοῖς πεπονηκυίαις ἢ κατ᾽ ἄνδρα φίλοις καὶ συν-
10 κλητικοῖς, ὧν τὰς τειμήσεις προσεξεπλήρωσεν: ἄ-
11 πειρον πλῆθος.

CHRONOLOGICAL TABLE.

(Roman numerals refer to chapters.)

A. U. C.

706. Made *pontifex*, VI.

710. Raises army at his own cost, I; gives to each citizen 300 sesterces, according to will of Julius Cæsar, XV.

711. Enters senate, receives consular rank, and the *imperium*, becomes *propraetor*, *imperator*, consul, I; triumvir, I and VII; exiles murderers of Julius Cæsar, II.

712. War of Philippi, II; builds the curia, XIX, app. II.

714. *Imperator* second and third times; ovation, IV.

716. Recovers Sardinia, XXVII.

718. The Sicilian war, III and XIX; fourth time *imperator*, IV; punishes revolted slaves, XXV; recovers Sicily, XXVII; ovation, IV; receives tribunitial power, X, cf. VI; builds temple of Apollo on the Palatine, XIX, app. II.

721. Fifth time *imperator?* IV; recovers standards from Dalmatians, XXIX.

722. Becomes leader against Antony, XXV.

723. Victory of Actium; clemency as victor, III; sixth time *imperator*, IV.

724. Fourth consulship; veterans colonized, XVI; provinces east of the Adriatic, and Cyrenae recovered; Egypt annexed, XXVII; Artavasdes the Mede and Tiridates the Parthian flee to Augustus, XXXII; ornaments replaced in temples of Asia, XXIV.

725. Fifth consulship, VIII, XV, XXI; seventh time *imperator;* triple triumph, IV; declines coronary gold, XXI; gives to 120,000 colonized soldiers 1,000 sesterces apiece.; gives the people 400 sesterces each, XV; gives gladiatorial show, XXII; consecrates gifts in various temples, XXI; closes temple of Janus, XIII; name placed in Salian hymn, X; increases number of patricians, VIII.

726. Sixth consulship, VIII, XX, XXXIV. Takes census; revises list of senators, VIII; made *princeps senatus*, VII; restores city temples, XX, app. III; gives money to the treasury, XVII; gives gladiatorial and athletic shows, XXII; games vowed and celebrated for health of Augustus, IX; restores the commonwealth to the senate and people, XXXIV.

727. Seventh consulship, XX, XXXIV. Continuation of transfer of power to senate and people; is called Augustus.; door-posts decked with laurel; civic crown and golden shield accorded, XXXIV; repairs Flaminian Way, XX, app III; melts down silver statues for offerings, XXIV.

729. Eighth time *imperator;* refuses triumph, IV; closes temple of Janus the second time, XIII; Arabian expedition, XXVI.

730. Tenth consulship; gives the people 400 sesterces each.

731. Eleventh consulship; twelve times supplies food for citizens, XV, cf. V; Ethiopian expedition, XXVI.

A. U. C.

732. Consulship of Marcus Marcellus and Lucius Arruntius; refuses annual and perpetual consulship; also the dictatorship; accepts the administration of grain supply, V; dedicates temple of Jupiter Tonans, XIX.

733. Refuses consulship? V.

734. Receives embassy from India, XXXI; ninth time *imperator?* refuses a triumph, IV; recovers standards ;from Parthia, XXIX; gives Armenia Major to Tigranes, XXVII.

735. Quintus Lucretius and Marcus Vinucius consuls; altar of Fortuna Redux consecrated; Augustalia established, XI; deputation of leading men meet Augustus in Campania, XII; declines the custody of laws and morals, VI.

736. Cnaeus and Publius Lentulus consuls, VI, XVIII; remits tribute, XVIII; again declines custody of laws and morals; associates Agrippa in tribunitial power, VI.

737. Gaius Furnius and Gaius Silanus consuls; secular games, XXII.

738. Augustus supplies money to the treasury, XVII; gives gladiatorial show, XXII; dedicates temple of Quirinus, XIX, app. II.

739. Tenth time *imperator*, IV.

740. Marcus Crassus and Cnaeus Lentulus consuls; pays provincials for lands taken for veterans.

741. Tiberius Nero and Publius Quintilius consuls, XII; deposits laurel in the Capitol, IV; altar of the Augustan Peace dedicated, XII; again associates Agrippa in tribunitial power, VI.

742. Gaius Sulpicius and Gaius Valgius consuls, X; twelfth year of tribunitial power, XV; eleventh time *imperator*, IV; made *pontifex maximus*, X; gives gladiatorial show, XXII; gives the people 400 sesterces each, XV.

743. Paullus Fabius Maximus and Quintus Tubero consuls, VI; twelfth time *imperator*, IV; for the third time refuses the custody of laws and morals, VI; dedicates theater of Marcellus, XXI, app. II.

745. Thirteenth time *imperator;* deposits the laurel in temple of Jupiter Feretrius, IV; Tiberius Nero subdues the Pannonians, XXX.

746. Gaius Censorinus and Gaius Asinius consuls; second census taken; list of senate revised, VIII; children of Phraates sent to Rome; Maelo, King of the Sicambri, surrenders himself, XXXII; fourteenth time *imperator;* refuses a triumph, IV.

747. Tiberius Nero and Cnaeus Piso consuls; veterans discharged, with gratuities, XVI; Alpine peoples added to the empire, XXVI; gives gladiatorial show, XXII.

748. Gaius Antistius and Decimus Laelius consuls; veterans discharged, with gratuities, XVI; associates Tiberius in tribunitial power, VI.

749. Eighteenth year of tribunitial power; twelfth consulship; gives sixty denarii each to ‾320,000 citizens; Gaius Cæsar consul designate, made prince of the youth, received into senate, XIV; aqueducts repaired, XX, app. III.

750. Gaius Calvisius and Lucius Passienus consuls; veterans discharged, with gratuities, XVI.

751 Lucius Lentulus and Marcus Messala consuls; veterans discharged, with gratuities, XVI.

A. U. C.

752.   Thirteenth consulship, XV, XXII, XXXV; Lucius Caninius and Quintus
       Fabricius consuls; veterans discharged, with gratuities, XVI ; gives the
       citizens sixty denarii each, XV ; Lucius Cæsar consul designate, prince of the
       youth, and admitted to senate, XIV; dedicates temple of Mars Ultor, XXI,
       app. II ; martial games instituted, XXII; naval contest exhibited, XXIII;
       title *pater patriae* conferred, XXXV.

755.   Lucius Cæsar dies, XIV, cf. XX; fifteenth time *imperator*, IV; Armenia sub-
       dued by Gaius Cæsar and given to Ariobarzanes, XXVII.

757.   Gaius Cæsar dies, XIV, cf. XX; again associates Tiberius in tribunitial
       power, VI.

758.   Fleet penetrates to limits of the Cimbri ; the Cimbri, Charudes and Semnones
       send ambassadors, XXVI; King Vonones given to the Parthians, XXXIII.

759.   Marcus Lepidus and Lucius Arruntius consuls, XVII; seventeenth time
       imperator, IV; Dacians subdued, XXX; gives gladiatorial show, XXII;
       military treasury established, XVII.

762.   Nineteenth time *imperator*, IV.

766.   Associates Tiberius the third time in tribunitial power, VI.

767.   Sextus Pompeius and Sextus Appuleius consuls, VIII; thirty-seventh year of
       tribunitial power, IV; seventy-sixth year of Augustus, XXXV; third census
       taken; list of senate revised, VIII.

BIBLIOGRAPHY.

Abbreviations as used in the Notes are put in parentheses.

I. EDITIONS.

Mommsen, Theodor : Res Gestæ Divi Augusti ex Monumentis Ancyrano et Apolloniensi. pp. LXXXXVII, 223. With eleven photogravure plates. Berlin, 1883. (*R. G.*)

This work is so exhaustive and so full that it puts all preceding editions and discussions out of date. Hence this bibliography enumerates only such editions and discussions as have appeared since 1883.

C. Peltier and R. Cagnat : Res Gestæ Divi Augusti, d'après la derniere recension de Th. Mommsen. Paris, 1886.

II. DISCUSSIONS OF THE MONUMENTUM.

Bormann, Ernest: Bemerkungen zum Schriftliche Nachlasse des Kaisers Augustus. Marburg, 1884. Universitäts Einladung. pp. 1–46.

Bormann, Ernest : Verhandlungen der dreiundvierzigsten Versammlung Deutschen Philologen in Köln, 1895. pp. 180–191. Leipzig, 1896.

Geppert, Paul : Zum Monumentum Ancyranum. Gymnasiums Programm. pp. 1–18. Berlin, 1887.

Hirschfeld, Otto : Wiener Studien, 1885. pp. 170–174.

Mommsen, Theodor : Historische Zeitschrift, Neue Folge, XXI. pp. 385-397.

Nissen, H. : Rheinisches Museum, XLI. 1886. pp. 481–499.

Plew, J.: Quellenuntersuchungen zur Geschichte des Kaisers Hadrian, nebst einem Anhang über das Monumentum Ancyranum. Strassburg, 1890. pp. 98–121.

Schiller, H. : Bursians Jahresbericht, XLIV, 85–86.

Schmidt, Johannes : Philologus, XLIV, 1885. pp. 442–470; XLV, 1886. pp. 393–410; XLVI, 1887. pp. 70–86.

Seeck, Otto : Wochenschrift für Klassische Philologie, 19 Nov., 1884. Col. 1473–1481.

v. Wilamowitz Ulrich : Hermes, XXI, 1886. pp. 623–627.

Wölfflin, E.: Sitzungsberichte der philosophisch-philologischen und historischen Klasse der Akademie der Wissenschaften zu München, 1886. pp. 253–282.

III. WORKS OF REFERENCE MOST FREQUENTLY CITED.

Gardthausen, V.: Augustus und seine Zeit. 1er Th., 1er Bd., pp. VIII, 484; 2er Th., 1er Hlb., pp. 276. Leipzig, 1891. 1er Th., 2er Bd., pp. 485-1032; 2er Th., 2er Hlb., pp. 277-649. 1896. Not yet completed; the standard work on the subject. Second part contains the references. (*Aug.*)

Marquardt, Joachim : Römische Staatsverwaltung.

Mommsen, Theodor : Römische Geschichte. (*Röm. Gesch.*)

Corpus Inscriptionum Latinarum. (C. I. L.)

IV. CLASSICAL AUTHORS CITED.

Ammianus Marcellinus (Amm.) : *Rerum Gestarum Libri.*

Appianus (Appian) : *Bella Civilia* (*B. C.*); *Illyrica* (*Illyr.*).

Cæsar, Gaius Julius (Cæs.) : *De Bello Gallico* (*B. G.*) ; *De Bello Civili* (*B. C.*).

Cassiodorus (Cass.) : *Chronicon* (*Chron.*).

Cicero, Marcus Tullius (Cic.): *Epistolae, ad Atticum* (*ad Att.*) ; *pro Sextio* (*pro Sext.*) ; *Philippica* (*Phil.*).

Dio Cassius Cocceianus (Dio) : *Historia Romana.*

Dionysius: *Archæologia Romana.*

Eusebius: *Chronicon* (*Chron.*).

Eutropius: *Breviarium Historiæ Romanæ.*

Festus, Sextus Pompeius: *De Verborum Significatione.*

Florus, Lucius Annæus (Flor.): *Epitome Rerum Romanarum.*

Frontinus, Sextus Julius (Front.): *De Aquæductibus Urbis Romæ Libri II* (*De Aq.*).

Gellius, Aulus (Gell.): *Commentarii Noctium Atticarum.*

Horatius Flaccus, Quintus (Hor.): *Carmina* (*Carm.*) ; *Satiræ* (*Sat.*) ; *Carmen Sæculare* (*Carm. Sæc.*) ; *Epistolæ* (*Ep.*) ; *Epodon* (*Epod.*).

Hyginus, Gromaticus: *De Limitum Constructione* (*De Lim.*).

Jordanes: *De Getarum Origine et Rebus Gestis.*

Josephus Flavius (Jos.): *Jewish Wars* (*Wars*) ; *Jewish Antiquities* (*Ant.*).

Justinus (Justin): *Historiarum Philippicarum Libri XLIV.*

Juvenal, Decimus Junius (Juv.): *Satiræ* (*Sat.*).

Livius, Titus (Livy): *Annales ; Epitomæ* (*Ep.*).

Macrobius, Ambrosius Aurelius Theodosius (Mac.): *Saturnaliorum Conviviorum Libri VII* (*Sat.*).

Nepos, Cornelius (Nep.): *De Viris Illustribus.*

Orosius, Paulus (Oros.): *Historiarum adversus Paganos* (*adv. Pag.*).

Ovidius Naso, Publius (Ovid): *Metamorphoses* (*Met.*); *Fasti ; Tristia* (*Tr.*), *Ars Amatoria* (*Ars Am.*).

Plinius Secundus, Gaius (Plíny): *Historia Naturalis* (*Hist. Nat.*); *Moralia*. *De Fortuna Romanorum* (*De Fort. Rom.*).

Plutarchus (Plut.): *Vita Antonii* (*Ant.*); *Vita Bruti* (*Brut.*)

Propertius, Sextus Aurelius (Prop.): *Elegiæ.*

Ptolemæus, Claudius (Ptol.): *Geographia.*

Seneca, Lucius Annæus (Sen.): *De Clementia ad Neronem Cæsarem Libri II* (*De Clem.*).

Strabo : *Geographia.*

Suetonius, Tranquillus Gaius (Suet.): *Vitæ Duodecim Cæsarum; Julii* (*Jul.*); *Augusti* (*Aug.*); *Tiberii* (*Tib.*); *Claudii* (*Claud.*).

Tacitus, Gaius Cornelius (Tac.): *Historiæ* (*Hist.*); *Annales* (*Ann.*); *Germania* (*Ger.*); *Agricola* (*Agr.*).

Valerius Maximus (Val): *De Factis Dictisque Memorabilibus Libri IX.*

Varro, Marcus Terentius: *De Lingua Latina.*

Velleius Paterculus, Gaius (Vell.): *Historiæ Romanæ Libri II.*

Vergilius Maro, Publius (Ver.); *Æneid* (*Æn.*); *Georgica,* (*Georg.*).

Victor, Sextus Aurelius (Vict.): *Historia Romana.*

Zonaras, Joannes: *Annales.*

Vol. V. No. 2.

Translations and Reprints

FROM THE

Original Sources of European History

PROTEST OF THE COUR DES AIDES
OF PARIS—April 10, 1775.

EDITED BY JAMES HARVEY ROBINSON, PH. D.,

Professor of History in Columbia University.

With an English Version by

GRACE READE ROBINSON.

PUBLISHED BY

The Department of History of the University of Pennsylvania.

Philadelphia, Pa., 1899.

ENGLISH AGENCY: P. S. KING & SON, 2 & 4 Great Smith St., Westminster, London, S. W.

INTRODUCTION.

THE rare pamphlet here reprinted furnishes us with a singularly clear and authentic picture of the French government before the Revolution. It describes with admirable lucidity and insight the whole oppressive system of taxation which prevailed under the *Ancien Régime*, and frankly exposes many of the notorious abuses which it was the great achievement of the Revolution to destroy forever. It is a sort of official report presented to the young king Louis XVI., about a year after his accession to the throne, by one of the superior tribunals of France, in the hope that the monarch might remedy the evils portrayed therein. As Louis was then but twenty years old, and presumably unacquainted with the technicalities of legal procedure and public administration, the magistrates adopted a simple, elementary style of presentation, which greatly enhances the value of the document for students of to-day.

During the few months he had been on the throne the king had given many proofs of a real solicitude for the welfare of his people ; he was evidently conscientious and well-meaning. He had early dismissed the unscrupulous and discredited advisers of his grandfather, Louis XV., and replaced them by better men. Among the new ministers the most distinguished was the well known economist and experienced government official, Turgot, who was put at the head of the finances,[1] and immediately began his wide-reaching reforms. There is no reason, however, to suppose that Turgot inspired the *Remontrances* or " Protest " of which we are speaking, although a denunciation by one of the king's highest tribunals of the iniquitous system of taxation and administration which weighed so heavily upon the people, could hardly fail to forward his plans.

The *Remontrances* were drawn up by the First President of the court, the upright Malesherbes, who is perhaps best known on account

[1] Louis XVI. came to the throne May 10, 1774, and Turgot was appointed Controller General on August 24 of the same year.

of his heroic defense of Louis XVI. when the king came to be tried by
the Convention in 1792. Malesherbes was a staunch friend and supporter of Turgot, and doubtless consulted him in the preparation of
the elaborate report before us; but it had fallen to his lot to draft a
good many *remontrances* since he had become First President, twenty-
five years before, and while none of his earlier ones are so extensive as
these of 1775, some of them are very like them in scope, and in the
character and frankness of their criticisms.[1]

The *Cour des aides* of Paris,[2] in whose name the report was submitted to the sovereign, was an ancient tribunal, the functions of which
had been clearly defined early in the fifteenth century. Its jurisdiction included, first and foremost, those cases to which the taxes—*e. g.*,
the excise (*aides*), the salt tax, the *taille*, etc.—gave rise. It tried
suits involving the farmers of the revenue and their contracts with the
government, as well as cases which concerned the privileges and exemptions of the nobility and clergy in the matter of taxation. Consequently it speaks as one having authority when it calls the young
king's attention to the scandalous abuses, connected with the taxes.

The right of the superior courts of France, especially of the *parlements*, to remonstrate with the king when he presented an edict for
their registration was a privilege of long standing, and one of which
they frequently took advantage in order to hamper the king's ministers.
Louis XIV. had finally commanded the courts to register edicts without
any delay whatever, but their right of protest had been restored to
them by the Regent. Toward the end of the reign of Louis XV. the
repeated interference of the *parlements* and the protests of the *Cour
des aides* led the king, at the instigation of the chancellor, Maupeou,
to abolish these tribunals altogether (in 1771) and substitute in their
place a different, and in many ways better, judicial organization. But
Louis XVI., against the advice of Turgot, Vergennes and other thought-
ful men, was induced to reinstate the former tribunals, in November,
1774. Pains were taken, however, in the decree re-establishing them
to place certain restrictions upon them, which it was hoped might
prevent in the future their interference with legislation. It was in

---

[1] Some of these are reprinted by Eugène de Vignaux in his *Mémoires sur Lamoi-
gnon de Malesherbes*, Paris, 1876.

[2] *Cours des aides* had been established in the provinces from time to time, but only
one, that of Montpellier, continued in independent existence down to 1789; the
others had been suppressed or united with other tribunals.

connection with a protest against these restrictions that the long *Remontrances* which we reproduce were sanctioned by the *Cour des aides*. The three years during which the action of the old tribunals had been suspended were naturally viewed by the re-established magistracy as a dark and mournful period, " when the absence of the ministers of justice and the silence of the law left unrestrained the avidity of the tax-gatherer and the tyranny of the ministers." The reader will note frequent references in the *Remontrances* to the despotic conduct of the king's ministers, with whom the courts were generally on very bad terms. While some allowance must, of course, be made when the court dwells upon its own particular grievances, the conduct of Louis XV.'s last cabinet, made up of L'abbé Terray, Maupeou, the Duc d'Aiguillon and others, probably merited all the reprobations of the magistrates.

Malesherbes read the *Remontrances*, which it had taken him some months to prepare, to his court April 10, 1775, and about the middle of May they were laid before the king. The ministers, upon learning the nature of the document, were naturally fearful lest it might be made public. The precautions which they took to prevent this have usually been ascribed to the malign influence of the courtiers, who were ready to check even the most salutary reforms. But let us give the devil his due. The *Cour des aides*, it should be observed, contents itself with denouncing the oppression and unfairness of the existing taxes, and discreetly excuses itself from suggesting any substitutes, by declaring that it is not its business to invent new forms of taxation. Now it may well be that even Turgot himself was fearful lest this long list of abuses, drawn up by a body which passed as the most expert judges in such matters, might, if published, greatly hamper the collection of the revenue and so increase the existing deficit. Anxious as he was for a speedy regeneration of the state, he may have co-operated with conservative ministers, like Maurepas and Miromesnil, the keeper of the seals, in the attempt to prevent the possible printing of the *Remontrances*.[1] However this may have been, the keeper of the seals requested the representatives of the *Cour des aides* to bring with them the minutes of the *Remontrances*, that is, the record which the court kept of its own resolutions. This he retained with the hope of securing its secrecy, explaining the king's views as follows :

" His Majesty is well aware that the excessive taxation is one of the

---

[1] *Cf.* Gomel, *Histoire Financière de la Révolution Française*, Paris, 1892, I., 473.

worst misfortunes of his subjects, and he regards as his first duty the lightening of his people's burdens, whether by reducing the taxes, or by correcting the abuses which may exist in either their assessment or collection. But the king knows, too, that if abuses really exist they ought not to be made public until the time comes to remedy them, and that it is dangerous to increase the ill feeling of the taxpayer against those whose co-operation is necessary to the levying of the taxes. His Majesty does not doubt that you have made the same reflections, and that in drawing up these *Remontrances* your intention was assuredly not to make them public, but simply to second his Majesty's wisdom. You will not, therefore, be surprised by the unusual measures that the king has taken to avoid their publication." [1]

These precautions did not, however, prevent the public from getting wind of the matter and learning the general character of the *Protest*. Bachaumont—who kept a careful diary of occurrences, important and unimportant—reports as early as May 26 that "People are talking a great deal of the *Remontrances* of the *Cour des aides* concerted between M. Turgot and M. Malesherbes, the aim of which is to open the way for the plans of the former regarding the financial system, its betterment, and especially the reform of the abuses." [2]   On June 1 he reverts to the same subject, gives a brief account of the contents of the report, says that it exhibits the "intolerable atrocity" of the prevailing method of taxation, and speaks of the retention of the minutes by the council on the ground that the language of the court was too "lively and picturesque" to be appropriate for the public ear.

Nevertheless, by July, the *Remontrances* had been printed. Bachaumont writes (July 19), "The *Cour des aides*, following its custom, has suppressed its *Remontrances*, which have been secretly printed and are being sold with the greatest mystery. No work of its class could be better written. It contains nothing of the vague declamation and tiresome rhetoric with which such productions are often filled, but sets forth irrefragable principles and clear deductions, which are expressed in a wholesome, austere and nervous style. It is full of striking truths hard for kings to listen to, but which must nevertheless be told them." The admission of Malesherbes at this time to the king's council, the author adds, does

---

[1] Quoted by Gomel, *op. cit.*, I., 474.

[2] *Mémoires secrets pour servir à l'histoire de la République des Lettres en France.* Londres, 1784 *sq.* VIII., 47.

honor to the uprightness of the monarch's intentions and proves his
aversion to flattery.[1]

The *Remontrances* do not seem to have become generally known
until 1778, when new editions appeared. Bachaumont describes,
April 28, 1778, the same edition of which we have made use.[2] On
April 30, a copy of it was exhibited to the *Cour des aides* by the king's
representatives, with the request that the work be suppressed, since it
contained matter which should never have been made public. The
court promptly acceded to the king's wishes and decreed its suppression.

To one unacquainted with the habits of French magistrates and
ministers in the latter half of the eighteenth century, the authenticity
of this address to the king might seem incredible. One would naturally
infer that it had been composed by some *philosophe,* like Diderot, who
put his violent denunciations into the mouth of a dignified judge in
order to give them weight. Nevertheless the general tone adopted by
Malesherbes in the discussion which received the official sanction of
the *Cour des aides* was perfectly in accord with the habits of the time.
Any one who will take the trouble to look over the *remontrances* of the
Parlement of Paris[3] or of the provincial *parlements*, or the earlier utter-
ances of the *Cour des aides*, from 1756 on, or will read Turgot's pre-
ambles to his edicts removing the restrictions on the grain trade and
abolishing the *corvées,* or Necker's *Compte rendu* of 1781, will discover
the same tendency in government officials publicly and unreservedly
to expose the evils of which all were conscious. The reforms of the
National Assembly in 1789–90 will seem far less abrupt than they are

[1] *Mém. Secr.,* VIII., 120–121,

[2] "*Elles* [the *Remontrances*] *sont dateés du 6 Mai, 1775, et ont 180 pages, indépendamment de deux lacunes qu'on y remarque.*" *Op. cit.,* XI., 209. With the
kind permission of Professor George L. Burr, the librarian of the President White
Library of Cornell University, we reproduce the exact and complete text of the only
copy of the famous *Remontrances* which is known to exist in this country. The
edition generally used by French writers forms a part of a collection published at
Bruxelles in 1779, *Mémoires pour servir à l'histoire du droit public français ou
Recueil de ce qui s'est passé à la Cour des aides de 1756–1775.* Portions of this have ·
been reprinted by De Vignaux in his *Mémoires sur Malesherbes.* The date, May 6,
is probably a mistake. *Cf.* Jobez, *La France sous Louis XVI.,* I., 236–7 and 243
and n.

[3] *Cf.* Vol. II. of Flammermont's *Remontrances du Parlement de Paris au XVIIIe.
Siècle.*

usually represented to have been, if we realize that the different governmental bodies had long been vigorously inculcating the desire for a
change, by persistently calling the nation's attention to the absurdity,
wastefulness, and injustice of the existing order.

The *Remontrances* here reproduced are, as has been pointed out,
very clear and intelligible. Almost all the technical terms are carefully explained to the young ruler. Nevertheless, since French judicial
procedure differs in some important respects from ours, for example,
in the matter of appeals, there may be a few places which will not be
completely understood by the reader. Still it has not been deemed
best to attempt to elucidate such differences in detail; they play but
a very small part in the exposition, and an explanation would in most
cases prove both difficult and irrelevant to the main object of the publication.

TRÈS-HUMBLES

ET TRÈS-RESPECTUEUSES

REMONTRANCES

*QUE présentent au Roi notre trés honoré Souve-
rain & Seigneur, les Gens tenans sa Cour des
Aides à Paris.*[1]

SIRE,

[1] Votre Cour des Aides vient de réclamer pour elle-même & pour
toute la Magistrature contre quelques articles de l'acte de son rétablissement; mais il lui reste un devoir encore plus important à remplir;
c'est la cause du peuple que nous devons à présent plaider au Tribunal
de VOTRE MAJESTÉ. Nous devons vous présenter un tableau fidele
des droits & des impositions qui se levent dans votre Royaume, & qui
sont l'objet de la jurisdiction qui nous est confiée; nous devons faire
connoître à VOTRE MAJESTÉ au commencement de son regne, la
vraie situation de ce peuple, dont le spectacle d'une Cour brillante ne
lui rappelle point le souvenir. Qui sçait même si les témoignages de
joie & de tendresse que VOTRE MAJESTÉ a reçus, dans le moment
de son avénement, de tous ceux qui ont pu approcher de sa Personne
de ce peuple un peu moins malheureux que celui des Provinces, ou
déja heureux par ses espérances, ne l'entretiennent pas dans une erreur
funeste sur le sort du reste de la Nation? Cette Nation, SIRE, a
toujours signalé son zele & son attachment pour ses Maîtres, en faisant
les plus grands efforts pour maintenir la splendeur de leur trône : mais
au moins faut-il que VOTRE MAJESTÉ sçache ce que ces secours immenses coûtent au malheureux peuple.

[2] Cependant l'examen approfondi de tous les impôts seroit un

---

[1] The original spelling, which differs in a few respects only from that of to-day, has
been retained, as well as the capitalization; the paragraphs however, have frequently
been combined, as they often included but a sentence or two, and have been
numbered to correspond with the paragraphs of the English translation which follows,

travail infini auquel VOTRE MAJESTÉ ne peut pas se livrer elle-même. Nous présenterons des mémoires particuliers sur chaque objet; & VOTRE MAJESTÉ pourra en renvoyer la discussion à ceux qu'elle honorera de sa confiance. Mais dans ce jour, SIRE, dans ce jour précieux où nous parlons à VOTRE MAJESTÉ pour être entendus d'elle-même, nous nous bornerons à lui rendre sensibles les causes générales & fondamentales de tous les abus, & à établir des vérités assez simples pour que VOTRE MAJESTÉ puisse s'en convaincre, qu'elle puisse, pour ainsi dire, s'en pénétrer : & quand vos intentions seront connues, quand vos instructions auront été données, ce sera à vos Ministres à s'y conformer dans l'examen détaillé qui sera fait avec eux des différentes parties.

[3] Aucune considération ne doit nous arrêter, SIRE, quand nous avons des objets si importants à présenter à VOTRE MAJESTÉ. C'est cependant avec regret que nous nous verrons obligés de porter nos regards sur ce temps malheureux où l'absence des Ministres de la Justice & le silence des Loix a laissé une libre carriere à l'avidité des Financiers & au despotisme des Administrateurs. VOTRE MAJESTÉ a fait cesser les malheurs publics, & nous voudrions que le souvenir en fût entiérement effacé par cet acte éclatant de votre justice. Si nous n'avions à nous plaindre que de la persécution soufferte par les Magistrats, & même si nous n'avions à dénoncer que les infractions faites pendant ces temps de trouble à l'order judiciaire, nous penserions que tout étant réparé, tout doit être enseveli dans l'oubli. Mais il est une importante vérité, SIRE, que nous ne pouvons éviter de mettre sous vos yeux sans trahir notre devoir : c'est que la prétendue nécessité d'affermir l'autorité souveraine a servi de prétexte à des exactions exercées avec impunité sur vos Sujets; qu'il a été fait une ligue entre les ennemis des Tribunaux, & ceux qui faisoient gémir le peuple sous le poids des impôts arbitraires; que ceux-là ont prêté leur appui pour anéantir la Magistrature, & leur ministere pour la remplacer, & que le prix de ce funeste service a été de livrer le peuple à leur cupidité.

[4] Il nous est douloureux, SIRE, d'avoir à vous dénoncer ce système d'oppression dans des jours de clémence. Mais des Loix onéreuses au peuple ont été promulguées dans la forme qu'on regardoit alors comme légale, & elles subsistent encore aujourd'hui, puisque VOTRE MAJESTÉ a validé tout ce qui s'étoit fait pendant l'inaction de la Justice. Nous voyons aussi plusieurs places importantes encore occupées par ceux qui ont abusé de leur pouvoir; & si de nouveaux abus

excitent l'animadversion de la Justice, on ne manquera pas de faire valoir, en faveur des coupables, le prétendu mérite de s'être sacrifiés pour le maintien de l'autorité Royale ; & sous prétexte de les mettre à l'abri de la vengeance de leurs ennemis, on voudra mettre leur administration à l'abri des recherches de la Justice. Il est donc bien important, SIRE, d'affranchir VOTRE MAJESTÉ du fardeau d'une reconnoissance si préjudiciable à son peuple, & de lui faire connoître que ceux qui prétendoient travailler pour l'autorité Royale, ont réellement & efficacement travaillé pour s'arroger sur tous les Ordres de l'Etat un pouvoir exorbitant, & inutile au service de VOTRE MAJESTÉ.

[5] Nous desirerions, SIRE, que d'autres que nous pussent vous faire parvenir ces fâcheuses vérités. Que n'est-il possible que VOTRE MAJESTÉ abandonne aujourd'hui ces funestes maximes de Gouvernement, ou plutôt cette politique introduite depuis un siecle par la jalousie des Ministres, qui a réduit au silence les Ordres de l'Etat, excepté la seule Magistrature ! Que n'est-il possible à la Nation elle-même de s'expliquer sur ses intérêts les plus chers ! Alors, SIRE, avec quelle joie nous remettrions en d'autres mains le soin de vous faire connoître tous les excès aux quels s'est porté ce même Ministere qui vouloit nous anéantir ! Mais puisque nous seuls jouissons encore de ce droit antique des François, de ce droit de parler à nos Rois, & de réclamer avec liberté contre l'infraction des Loix & des droits nationaux, nous ne devons point user envers nos ennemis d'une générosité qui nous rendroit coupables envers la Nation entiere.

[6] Le premier tableau que nous ayons à présenter à VOTRE MAJESTÉ, est celui des droits connus sous le nom de Droits des Fermes. Nous ne vous annonçons pas, SIRE, une vérité nouvelle, en vous disant que ces droits sont moins onéreux par les sommes mêmes que le tresor royal reçoit du peuple, que par les frais de la régie, & les gains des Fermiers, qui certainement sont trop forts, puisque les Ministres du dernier regne ont sçu en reprendre une partie, non pas pour le profit de VOTRE MAJESTÉ, mais pour en gratifier leurs favoris. Cette vérité qui est dans la bouche du public entier, ne peut pas être ignorée de VOTRE MAJESTÉ.

[7] Elle sçait aussi qu'indépendamment des sommes d'argent tirées de ses Sujets, l'Etat est privé, par les droits des Fermes, d'une multitude de citoyens, employés les uns à faire la fraude, les autres a l'empêcher. Eh ! quels citoyens ? Ceux précisément qui pourroient être les plus tiles, les uns par la force du corps & le courage, les autres par l'industrie

& l'activité : car il est notoire que le métier de Commis, & peut-être même le métier de fraudeur, malgré ses risques, valent mieux que le métier de soldat, & que les places de finances procurent à ceux qui les obtiennent, des avantages plus certains & plus considérables que l'agriculture, le commerce ou les manufactures ; qu'il ne reste donc dans ces professions utiles que ceux qui n'ont pas eu assez de bonheur ou de talent pour parvenir à la finance.

[8] VOTRE MAJESTÉ n'ignore pas non plus qu'outre les droits payés sur chaque denrée, il en est dont la production est défendue ou gênée dans le Royaume pour l'intérêt de la Ferme ; que tel est le tabac, dont la culture est interdite à vos Sujets, pendant qu'il s'en achete tous les ans de l'étranger pour plusieurs millions ; que tel est aussi aujourd'hui le sel, denrée d'un bien plus grand prix, & un des dons les plus précieux que la nature ait faits à la France, si la main du Financier ne repoussoit sans cesse ce présent que la mer ne cesse d'apporter sur nos côtes ; qu'il est des parages où la fabrication du sel n'est permise qu'à quelques privilégiés, & que les Commis de la Ferme assemblent les paysans, dans certains temps de l'année, pour submerger celui que la mer a déposé sur le rivage ; que sur d'autres côtes la fabrication du sel, permise en apparence, est cependant assujettie à de telles contraintes, que le Fermier peut ruiner, & ruine réellement celui qui l'entreprend contre son gré ; que presque par-tout l'excès du prix du sel prive le peuple de l'avantage qu'il pourroit tirer de cette précieuse denrée pour les salaisons, pour la nourirture & la conservation des bestiaux, & pour une infinité d'arts utiles, même pour l'engrais des terres.

[9] VOTRE MAJESTÉ sçait aussi que les autres droits sur les denrées nuisent tous à la production & au commerce ; que la France produiroit plus de vins sans les droits d'Aides ; qu'il s'y fabriqueroit plus de marchandises sans les droits de Traites. Le détail de ces privations seroit infini ; & nous reconnoissons, SIRE, que nous ne pourrions vous en donner un tableau complet, car chaque jour nous en apprend de nouvelles : mais cette esquisse suffit pour faire connoître le tort que les droits des Fermes font à votre Royaume, indépendamment des sommes que le peuple paie & pour le gain des Fermiers, & pour les frais de régie.

[10] Il n'est pas possible non plus que VOTRE MAJESTÉ ne soit pas instruite de la rigueur des Loix pénales prononcées contre la contrebande. Elle sçait que ceux qui se rendent coupables de ce délit, ne sont quelquefois point habitués à le regarder comme un crime ; qu'il y a des Provinces entieres où les enfans y sont élevés par leurs peres,

n'ont jamais acquis d'autre industrie, & ne connoissent d'autres moyens pour subsister ; & que quand ces malheureux sont pris, ils subissent le genre de captivité destiné aux grands crimes, & quelquefois la mort. Nous ne doutons pas que VOTRE MAJESTÉ ne soit attendrie au récit de ces cruautés, & qu'elle n'ait demandé comment, dans l'origine, on a pu prononcer la peine de mort contre des citoyens pour un intérêt de finance.

[11] Mais il est encore une autre tyrannie dont il est possible que VOTRE MAJESTÉ n'ait jamais entendu parler, parce qu'elle n'offre point un spectacle si cruel, & qui cependant n'est pas moins insupportable au peuple, parce qu'elle est sentie par tous les citoyens du dernier état, par ceux qui vivent tranquillement de leur travail & de leur commerce : elle consiste en ce que chaque homme du peuple est obligé de souffrir journellement les caprices, les hauteurs, les insultes même des Suppôts de la Ferme. On n'a jamais fait assez d'attention à ce genre de vexations, parce qu'elles ne sont éprouvées que par des gens obscurs & inconnus. En effet, si quelques Commis manquent d'égards pour des personnes considérées, les Chefs de la finance s'empressent de désavouer leurs subalternes, & de donner satisfaction : & c'est précisément par ces égards pour les Grands, que la Finance a eu l'art d'assujettir à un despotisme sans bornes & sans frein tous les hommes sans protection. Or la classe des hommes sans protection est certainement la plus nombreuse dans votre Royaume ; & ceux qui ne paraissent protégés par personne, sont ceux qui ont plus de droit à la protection immédiate de VOTRE MAJESTÉ.

[12] Il est donc de notre devoir de développer à VOTRE MAJESTÉ les vraies causes de cette servitude à laquelle le peuple est soumis dans toutes les Provinces. Cette cause est, SIRE, dans la nature du pouvoir que les Préposés de la Ferme ont en main ; pouvoir arbitraire à beaucoup d'égards, & avec lequel par conséquent il leur est trop aisé de se rendre redoutables.

[13] Premiérement, le code de la Ferme générale est immense, & n'est recueilli nulle part. C'est une science occulte que personne, excepté les Financiers, n'a étudié ni pu étudier : en sorte que le particulier à qui on fait un procès, ne peut ni connoître par lui-même la loi à laquelle il est assujetti, ni consulter qui que ce soit ; il faut qu'il s'en rapporte à ce Commis même, son adversaire & son persécuteur. Comment vaut-on qu'un laboureur, un artisan, ne tremble pas, ne s'humilie pas sans cesse devant un ennemi qui a contre lui de si terribles armes?

[14] D'autre part, les loix de la Ferme ne sont pas seulement inconnues, elles sont aussi quelquefois incertaines.   Il y a beaucoup de
droits douteux que le Fermier essaie d'exercer suivant les circonstances.
On conçoit que les Employés de la Ferme font ces essais par préférence
sur ceux qui ont le malheur de leur déplaire.   On conçoit aussi qu'on
ne les fait jamais que sur ceux qui n'ont pas assez de crédit pour se
défendre.

[15] Enfin il est d'autres loix malheureusement trop certaines, mais
dont l'exécution littérale est impossible par l'excès de leur rigueur.   Le
Fermier les a obtenues sçachant très-bien qu'il ne les fera pas exécuter ;
& il s'est réservé d'en dispenser quand il le voudra, mais à condition
que cette dispense, sans laquelle le particulier redevable des droits seroit
ruiné, sera une faveur accordée arbitrairement ou par lui ou par ses
Préposés.   Tel est un des systêmes favoris de la Finance, qu'il faut absolument dévoiler à VOTRE MAJESTÉ.   Oui, SIRE, on a entendu le
Financier dire au citoyen : *Il faut que la Ferme ait des graces à vous
accorder & à vous refuser: il faut que vous soyiez obligés de les lui
venir demander.*   Ce qui est dire en termes équivalens : *Ce n'est pas
assez d'apporter votre argent pour satisfaire notre avidité; il faut
satisfaire par des bassesses l'insolence de nos Commis.*   Or, quand il
seroit vrai que l'avidité du Fermier tourne au profit du Roi, il est certain au moins que l'insolence de cette multitude de Commis qui inon-
dent les provinces, lui est absolument inutile.

[16] Nous nous sommes plus étendus, SIRE, sur les abus de ce genre
que sur les autres, soit parce qu'ils ne sont pas assez connus, soit parce
que nous croyons qu'il est impossible d'y remédier sans porter obstacle
aux recouvremens.   Enfin, SIRE, nous croyons qu'on n'a jamais mis
sous vos yeux les moyens employés par la Ferme générale pour réussir
dans ses contestations contre les particuliers.

[17] Le premier de ces moyens, SIRE, il ne faut pas se le dissimuler, est de n'avoir point de Juge, ou, ce qui est à peu près même
chose, de n'avoir pour Juge que le tribunal d'un seul homme.   Les
Cours des Aides, & les Tribunaux qui y ressortissent, sont, par leurs institutions, Juges de tous les impôts : mais la plus grande partie de ces
affaires ont été évoquées, & sont renvoyées devant un seul Commissaire
du Conseil, qui est l'Intendant de chaque province, & par appel, au
Conseil de Finance, c'est-à-dire, à un Conseil qui réellement ne se tient
ni en présence de VOTRE MAJESTÉ, ni sous les yeux du Chef de la
Justice, auquel n'assistent ni les Conseillers d'Etat, ni les Maîtres des

Requêtes, & qui n' est composé que d'un Contrôleur-Général & d'un seul Intendant des Finances ; où par conséquent l'Intendant des Finances est presque toujours le seul Juge ; car il est rare qu'un Contrôleur-Général ait le temps de s'occuper des affaires contentieuses.

[18] Nous rendons justice, SIRE, avec tout le public, aux Magistrats qui occupent à présent ces places ; mais les vertus personnelles d'un homme mortel ne doivent point nous rassurer sur les effets d'une administration permanente. Ce que nous déférons à VOTRE MAJESTÉ est un système de justice arbitraire sous lequel le peuple gémit depuis un siecle, & gémiroit sans cesse, si on ne réclamoit que dans le temps où le pouvoir est dans la main de ceux qui veulent en abuser. Il faut donc profiter du moment heureux où la justice de VOTRE MAJESTÉ a présidé à tous ses choix, pour établir en présence de VOTRE MAJESTÉ & de ses Ministres, la maxime incontestable que ce n'est point donner des Juges au Peuple, que de ne lui donner que le tribunal d'un seul homme. Or pour tous les genres d'affaires qui ont été enlevées par des évocations à la Justice réglée, ce tribunal d'un seul homme est le seul qui ait été donné au Peuple. Dans les provinces c'est l'Intendant qui prononce sur le sort des citoyens, seul dans son cabinet, & souvent dans son travail avec le Directeur des Fermes ; & à Paris, où se jugent les appels, c'est encore l'Intendant des Finances¹ qui statue irrévocablement, seul dans son cabinet, & souvent dans son travail avec le Fermier-Général : & sur cela, SIRE, nous croyons pouvoir interpeller la bonne foi de ceux mêmes à qui ce pouvoir exorbitant est confié ; c'est à eux que nous demandons s'il n'est pas vrai que cette justice arbitraire soit la seule qu'on rende à vos sujets dans toutes les matieres évoquées.

[19] Ajoutons que dans celles qui ne sont pas encore évoquées, & où le recours à la Justice réglée semble encore permis, le Fermier-Général a trouvé le moyen de rendre ce recours illusoire, & que ce n'est pour le malheureux peuple qu'une occasion de faire des frais inutiles, par l'usage introduit de porter les requêtes en cassation contre les Arrêts des Cours des Aides, au Conseil des Finances, c'est-à-dire, toujours à ce tribunal composé du seul Contrôleur-Général & du seul Intendant des Finances. Car, d'une part, les Fermiers soutiennent que dans le Conseil le mal-jugé doit être un moyen de cassation, lorsqu'il s'agit des droits du Roi, & que tous les droits qui leur sont affermés doivent jouir de ce privilége. D'autre part, on a établi au Conseil des

---

¹ The functions of the six Intendants of finance are described below, paragraph 112.

Finances une jurisprudence sur les cassations absolument contraire aux Loix certaines, & constamment observees dans le vrai Conseil de VOTRE MAJESTÉ ; c'est qu'en cassant un Arrêt de Cour souveraine, on juge le fond sans le renvoyer à un autre tribunal. Dès-lors il n'existe plus de différence entre la requête en cassation présentée à votre Conseil, & l'appel interjetté à un Juge supérieur ; & le recours au Conseil n'est qu'un degré de jurisdiction de plus. Tel est donc l'ordre des Jurisdictions pour tous les droits des Fermes.

[20] Sur les objets évoqués, comme le contrôle & les francs-fiefs, on se pourvoit d'abord devant la seule personne de l'Intendant de la province, ensuite devant la seule personne de l'Intendant des Finances ; & sur les objets non évoqués, comme les Aides, on se pourvoit d'abord en l'Election, ensuite à la Cour des Aides, mais toujours, à la fin, devant la seule personne de l'Intendant des Finances.

[21] Nous sçavons qu'on donne des motifs plausibles de ces évocations & de ces attributions. On dira à VOTRE MAJESTÉ qu'on a voulu épargner aux Fermiers & à leurs adversaires les frais & la longueur de la Justice réglée, & qu'on a voulu aussi éviter une partialité que les Financiers prétendent toujours avoir éprouvée de la part des Juges ordinaires. On vous expliquera même la cause de cette prétendue partialité, en avouant que les droits sont si rigoureux, & les réglemens pour la régie si contraires à l'ordre judiciaire commun, que ces réglemens ne peuvent être bien observés que par des Juges qui, étant initiés dans l'administration, ont senti la nécessite de les faire exécuter.

[22] Mais si le premier de ces motifs étoit sincere, on auroit proposé aux Cours des Aides d'enregistrer des loix qui établissent une procédure abrégée & sans frais ; loix que ces Cours adopteroient avec empressement, mais qu'on ne leur a jamais proposées, parce qu'on n'a pas voulu perdre des prétextes d'évocation. Et quant au reproche de partialité, s'il étoit vrai qu'on n'eût eu d'autres intentions que de donner au Fermier des Juges initiés dans l'administration, les appels des Intendans & les requêtes en cassation se porteroient au vrai Conseil de VOTRE MAJESTÉ, qui est composé de Magistrats qui ont administré les provinces, & non pas au seul Contrôleur-Général & au seul Intendant des Finances. Il faut donc avouer que le vrai motif des évocations, la vraie intention du Gouvernement, est de ne donner d'autres Juges au Fermier pour tous ses procès, que le Ministre & les Administrateurs des Finances ; c'est-à-dire qu'on a voulu que le Fermier fût son Juge à lui-même, & celui de tout le public, toutes les fois qu'il auroit un crédit prépondérant dans les bureaux.

[23] Nous n'entrerons point, SIRE, dans le détail de toutes ces évocations, parce que l'énumération en seroit infinie, & que nous nous faisons quelque peine d'insister trop long temps sur cet objet qui nous est personnel, puisqu'il intéresse notre jurisdiction. D'ailleurs il nous seroit impossible de donner des preuves de la plupart des abus qu'entraîne cette administration, parce que ces affaires n'étant portées à aucun tribunal réglé, l'abus le plus constaté par la notoriété publique ne l'est par aucune piece juridique : mais VOTRE MAJESTÉ suppléera aisément à cet égard aux Remontrances des Cours, en écoutant le témoignage universel du public.

[24] C'est par-là qu'Elle apprendra jusqu'à quel point les Financiers ont abusé de leur pouvoir arbitraire dans la régie de tous les droits compris dans le bail des Fermes, sous le nom de domaine, qui sont tous enlevés à la connoissance de la Justice réglée. Elle sçaura que ceux qu'on nomme droits de contrôle, d'insinuation, de centieme denier, droits qui portent sur tous les actes passés entre les citoyens, s'arbitrent suivant la fantaisie du Fermier ou de ses Préposés ; que les prétendues loix en cette matiere sont si obscures & si incompletes, que celui qui paie ne peut jamais sçavoir ce qu'il doit ; que souvent le Préposé ne le sait pas mieux, & qu'on se permet des interprétations plus ou moins rigoureuses, selon que le Préposé est plus ou moins avide ; & qu'il est notoire que tous ces droits ont eu sous un Fermier une extension qu'ils n'avoient pas eu sous les autres : d'où il résulte évidemment que ce Fermier est le législateur souverain dans les matieres qui sont l'objet de son intérêt personnel ; abus intolérable, & qui ne se seroit jamais introduit, si ces droits étoient soumis à un tribunal, quel qu'il fût ; car quand on sçait qu'on aura des Juges, il faut bien avoir des loix fixes & certaines.

[25] VOTRE MAJESTÉ sçaura que dans les derniers temps ces extensions ont été portées à des excès inconnus jusqu'alors ; que le Fermier ne se contente plus d'être instruit des secrets des familles consignés dans les actes qui se passent journellement, mais qu'il recherche tout ce qui s'est passé depuis vingt ans, sous prétexte que les droits n'ont pas été exigés avec assez de rigueur, pendant que le particulier sur lequel il auroit été éxercé une concussion, n'auroit pas deux ans pour réclamer.

[26] Vous sçaurez, SIRE, que les vexations de ce genre ont été portées à un tel excès, que pour s'y soustraire les particuliers sont réduits à faire des actes sous signature privée plutôt que pardevant

Notaires ; & que dans les cas où il est indispensable de contracter en
forme authentique, on exige souvent des rédacteurs d'altérer les actes
par des clauses obscures ou équivoques, qui donnent ensuite lieu à des
discussions interminables : en sorte qu'un impôt établi sous le spécieux
prétexte d'augmenter l'authenticité des actes, & de prévenir les procès,
force au contraire vos subjets à renoncer souvent aux actes publics, &
les entraîne dans des procès qui sont la ruine de toutes les familles.

[27] Quant au droit de franc-fief, qui est aussi nommé droit
domanial, c'est une finance qui s'exige des roturiers ou non-nobles pour
les fiefs qu'ils possédent ; & ce droit a été soumis aussi à la justice
arbitraire. Ce droit est une année de revenu qu'on fait payer tous les
vingt ans pour jouir tranquillement dans les dix-neuf autres années.
Mais quand il y a mutation pendant les vingt ans, on fait payer le droit
entier au nouvel acquéreur, sans accorder à l'ancien indemnité pour
les années pendant lesquelles il devait jouir ; usage qui est peut-être
aujourd'hui consacré par quelque Réglement, mais qui certainement
a été dans l'origine une concussion. VOTRE MAJESTÉ sçaura aussi
qu'on a ajouté huit sous pour livre à un droit qui est de la totalité du
revenu ; qu'on fait l'évaluation des biens sans déduction des frais, &
bien d'autres injustices de détail. Mais ce qui étonnera le plus VOTRE
MAJESTÉ, sera d'apprendre que, sous prétexte du paiement de ce
droit, le Fermier-Général fait juger aujourd'hui par la Justice arbitraire
la question d'état la plus intéressante, celle de la noblesse.

[28] On a attribué aux Intendans la connoissance des contestations
sur les franc-fiefs, comme sur le contrôle & autres droits semblables ;
c'est-à-dire, qu'on a voulu les constituer Juges de l'exécution de la Loi
bursale, de la quotité du droit pour le franc-fief ; & à présent quand
le particulier soutient qu'il n'en doit aucun, parce qu'il est noble, &
qu'il plaît au Fermier de contester sa noblesse, on veut que cette
contestation soit portée au même tribunal : en sorte que le Gentilhomme dépend du jugement d'un seul homme pour jouir de l'état qui
lui a été transmis par ses ancêtres. Il est aisé de concevoir jusqu'où
ont dû être portés les abus d'une telle Justice, & VOTRE MAJESTÉ
en sera plus convaincue par des faits que la notoriété publique pourra
lui apprendre.

[29] Elle sçaura, par example, qu'en 1723 le feu Roi avoit exigé de
tous ceux qui avoient été anoblis sous le regne précédent, un droit de
confirmation à cause de son avénement à la Couronne ; mais que la
Loi n'avoit point prononcé la peine de déchéance contre ceux par qui

ce droit n'auroit pas été payé ; que cette déchéance a depuis été pro-
noncée par des Arrêts du Conseil non revêtus de Lettres-patentes ;
comme si on pouvoit être condamné à perdre son état d'après des Arrêts
qui n'ont point le caractere de Loix enregistrées ; qu'enfin ces Arrêts,
dont le dernier est de l'année 1730, avoient toujours été réputés pure-
ment comminatoires, & que les Fermiers-Généraux eux-mêmes avoient
avoué publiquement qu'ils n'avoient jamais été exécutés. En effet,
l'exécution en paroissoit impossible, parce qu'il répugne à tous les principes de punir la faute de n'avoir pas payé une taxe par la déchéance
de la noblesse, peine infamante à laquelle on ne condamne jamais que
ceux qui sont convaincus de crimes capitaux ; & qu'il est encore moins
possible de faire tomber cette peine sur les enfans de celui qui n'a pas
payé, de déclarer déchus de la noblesse des citoyens qui l'ont reçue
avec la naissance, & ont toujours vécu conformément à cet état, parce
que leur pere a négligé autrefois de satisfaire une Loi bursale dont il
n'a peut-être pas eu connoissance.

[30] Ce sont là de ces rigueurs auxquelles tout le monde se refuse :
la justice ainsi que l'humanité ne permettent jamais l'exécution littérale
de semblables Loix ; & voilà pourquoi cet Arrêt du Conseil de 1730, &
tant d'autres Loix du même genre, sont restés sans effet. Mais telle
est, SIRE, la nature du pouvoir arbitraire, que la justice & l'humanité
elle-même perdent tous leurs droits quand un seul homme est sourd à
leur voix. Il s'est trouvé un Fermier qui a voulu faire revivre cet Arrêt
de 1730, oublié depuis qu'il existe, & un Ministre qui lui a abandonné
toutes les familles qui n'avoient pas payé le droit de confirmation.
Ainsi celui dont le pere ou l'aïeul ont obtenu l'anoblissement le plus
glorieux pour prix de leur sang & de leurs services, & qui ayant, à leur
exemple, passé sa vie dans la dispendieuse profession des armes, ne
s'est pas trouvé en état de payer la taxe, pourra aujourd'hui être déchu
des droits de la noblesse, parce qu'il en a rempli les devoirs ; & sa
famille sera reléguée par l'impitoyable Financier, dans la classe des
roturiers ; tandis que peut-être ce Financier lui-même, anobli par une
charge vénale, jouira des mêmes privileges que la plus haute noblesse.

[31] VOTRE MAJESTÉ voit, par cet exemple, jusqu'à quel point
un Ministere dur a pu abuser des évocations autrefois trop légérement
accordées, & Elle croira aisément qu'on ne s'en est pas tenu à abuser
des anciennes, & que, sur-tout pendant l'absence de la Magistrature, on
a profité des malheurs publics pour soumettre de nouveaux genres
d'affaires au pouvoir arbitraire, sans craindre aucunes réclamations.

[32] Nous donnerons pour exemple les visites domiciliaires qui se font pour la recherche du tabac de contrebande. Le prix excessif qu'on a mis au tabac, a donné, depuis quelques années, un tel attrait à la fraude, que pour l'empêcher on a employé des moyens qui tous les jours deviennent plus violens, & cependant sont toujours inutiles. Les Fermiers-Généraux ont obtenu de ces Loix qui exciteroient une guerre intestine dans le Royaume, si on vouloit les faire exécuter littéralement. Leurs Commis sont autorisés à faire les visites les plus séveres dans toutes les maisons indistinctement & sans aucune exception, sans respect pour le rang, pour la naissance, pour les dignités. De semblables Loix avoient déja été obtenues par les Fermiers en différens temps, & pour différens objets ; mais il existoit toujours un frein contre l'excès de l'abus ; c'est celui de la Justice réglée, qui peut sévir contre le Commis qui abuse du droit que lui a donné la Loi. Aujourd'hui ce frein n'existe plus ; le dernier Ministere a saisi le moment de l'absence de la Cour des Aides pour enlever ce genre d'affaires à la Justice réglée, & l'attribuer à des Commissaires du Conseil.

[33] Il est, SIRE, bien d'autres évocations semblables : on pourroit citer celle des droits sur les cartes, celle des droits de la caisse de Poissy, & tant d'autres. Nous n'avons voulu en donner à VOTRE MAJESTÉ que quelques exemples ; le reste est réservé pour les mémoires particuliers. Quand la totalité aura été mise sous les yeux de VOTRE MAJESTÉ & de ses Ministres, nous espérons, SIRE, qu'eux-mêmes reconnoîtront la nécessité de ne les pas laisser subsister.

[34] Il semble cependant que le Fermier-Général auroit pu se dispenser d'employer tant de moyens illégaux pour se soustraire à la Justice réglée, quand on considere les moyens légaux qui lui ont été aussi donnés pour réussir contre ses adversaires, dans quelque Justice que ce soit. Ces moyens sont tels qu'il n'est plus permis aux Juges de chercher où est la vérité ni où est la justice, & qu'ils sont presque toujours forcés de juger d'après des pieces qui, aux yeux de la raison seroient légitimement suspectes.

[35] C'est ce que VOTRE MAJESTÉ va voir clairement, quand nous lui aurons exposé par quelle voie le Fermier découvre & constate les fraudes ; car c'est à la découverte de la fraude que tendent presque tous ses procès. Nous allons être obligés, SIRE, de vous entretenir du détail fastidieux d'une guerre continuelle qui se fait entre les deux especes d'hommes les plus méprisables, d'une part, des contrebandiers, & de l'autre, des espions : mais comme s'est le peuple innocent qui

en souffre, & que ce tableau peut faire impression à VOTRE MAJESTÉ, nous ne croyons pas devoir le lui épargner.

[36] Les moyens de découvrir la fraude se réduisent aux procès-verbaux des Commis, & à la délation. Quant aux procès-verbaux des Commis, voici ce que la Loi a établi. Le Fermier-Général a droit d'exercer, par le ministere de ses Commis, & avec quelques formalités de Justice, les plus rigoureuses recherches dans les chemins, & souvent jusques dans les maisons des particuliers. Si dans ces visites les Commis croient avoir trouvé une fraude, ils en dressent procès-verbal ; & sur ce procès-verbal, signé de deux Commis, les faits sont regardés comme constants, & la fraude comme prouvée.

[37] Si le particulier accusé de fraude par le procès-verbal, prétend que les Commis sont calomniateurs, il ne peut le soutenir en Justice qu'en s'inscrivant en faux ; & il est nécessaire d'expliquer à VOTRE MAJESTÉ ce que c'est qu'une inscription de faux. Il ne suffit pas à l'accusé de prétendre que les faits allégués contre lui sont dénués de preuves ; il faut qu'il prouve directement le contraire. Or cette preuve, par sa nature, est le plus souvent impossible. Comment prouver un fait négatif ? Comment prouver aux Commis la fausseté des faits par eux allégués, quand tout s'est passé dans l'intérieur d'une maison, sans autres témoins que l'accusé & les Commis eux-mêmes ?

[38] De plus, les formalités prescrites pour l'inscription de faux sont d'un détail infini, & l'omission d'une seule prive l'accusé de sa juste défense. De plus, il faut, pour être admis à s'inscrire en faux, con-signer une amende que la plupart des gens du peuple sont hors d'état de payer. De plus, on ne leur donne qu'un temps très-court pour se déterminer, c'est-à-dire, pour consulter des gens de Loi, pour chercher des preuves juridiques, pour emprunter l'argent nécessaire pour la consignation. Il est donc vrai, il est évident, il est reconnu qu'un homme du peuple n'a aucun moyen possible pour se pourvoir contre ces procès-verbaux signés de deux Commis.

[39] Or on a souvent vu qu'un de ces Commis ne sçavoit ni lire ni écrire ; on lui avoit seulement appris à former les caracteres de son nom. Les Fermiers-Généraux ont soin d'en avoir un par brigade qui sçache écrire : c'est celui-là qui rédige le procès-verbal ; un de ses camarades le signe, & il ne leur paroissoit pas nécessaire que celui-là sçût ce qu'on lui donnoit à signer. Votre Cour des Aides, informée de cet abus, quelques temps avant la dispersion de la Magistrature, rendit un Arrêt de Réglement qui défendit aux Commis qui ne

sçavoient pas lire, de signer des procès-verbaux. Les Fermiers-Généraux oserent s'en plaindre, comme d'un Réglement qui rendoit leur régie impossible ; & nous croyons, SIRE, que pendant l'absence de la Cour des Aides cet Arrêt a été mal exécuté.

[40] Mais il est un autre abus auquel la Cour des Aides ne peut pas remédier par son autorité, parce qu'il consiste dans une convention secrete entre le Fermier & ses Commis ; convention expressément défendue par les Ordonnances, mais dont on ne peut jamais avoir de preuves juridiques. Il est notoire que, malgré la défense de la Loi, le Fermier promet à ses Commis une part dans les amendes auxquelles ils font condamner les particuliers par leurs procès-verbaux, & que c'est là une partie de leur solde. Ainsi la fraude est réputée prouvée contre un citoyen par la seule affirmation de deux hommes qui, non-seulement sont aux gages du Fermier-Général son adversaire, mais attendent un salaire proportionné à la somme à laquelle ce citoyen sera condamné.

[41] Telle est la voie juridique pour constater la fraude par les procès-verbaux. Mais il falloit aussi aux Fermiers des moyens pour découvrir où elle peut être, & pour diriger les démarches de leurs Commis. C'est pour y parvenir qu'on a voulu qu'il pût se trouver dans chaque société de marchands, dans chaque maison, dans chaque famille un délateur qui avertît le Financier qu'en tel lieu & en telle occasion il y aura une prise à faire. Ce délateur ne se montre point ; mais les Commis, avertis par lui, vont surprendre celui qui a été dénoncé, & acquierent la preuve, ou plutôt se la fabriquent eux-mêmes par leur procès-verbal. Quand un avis a réussi, il est donné une récompense au dénonciateur, c'est-à-dire à un complice, à un associé, à un commensal, à la femme qui a dénoncé son mari, au fils qui a dénoncé son pere.

[42] Daignez, SIRE, réfléchir un instant sur ce tableau de la régie des Fermes. Par la foi accordée aux procès-verbaux, le prix est continuellement mis au parjure ; par les délations, c'est à la trahison domestique qu'on promet récompense. Tels sont les moyens par lesquels plus de cent cinquante millions arrivent tous les ans dans les coffres de VOTRE MAJESTÉ.

[43] Ce n'est point à nous, SIRE, de vous indiquer d'autres impôts qui puissent remplacer ce produit immense ; ce n'est pas même à nous à examiner si les seules ressources de l'économie pourroient y suppléer. Il est cependant nécessaire de venir au secours d'un peuple opprimé par cette monstrueuse régie ; & s'il est vrai que l'économie seule ne

suffise pas pour que VOTRE MAJESTÉ puisse renoncer au produit entier de ses Fermes, il est au moins bien des adoucissemens qu'on pourroit apporter aux malheurs publics, si la diminution des dépenses permettoit le sacrifice d'une portion des revenus. Voilà pourquoi nous avons dû mettre sous vos yeux le terrible spectacle du plus beau Royaume de l'univers, gémissant sous une tyrannie qui fait tous les jours de nouveaux progrès.

[44] On loue, SIRE, & on implore en même temps votre bien-faissance ; mais nous, défenseurs du peuple, c'est votre justice que nous devons invoquer ; & nous sçavons que presque tous les sentimens dont l'ame d'un Roi est susceptible, l'amour de la gloire, celui des plaisirs, l'amitié même, le desir si naturel à un grand Prince, de rendre heureux ceux qui approchent de lui, sont des obstacles perpétuels à la justice rigoureuse qu'il doit à ses peuples, parce que ce n'est qu'aux dépens du peuple qu'un Roi est vainqueur de ses ennemis, magnifique dans sa Cour, & bienfaisant envers ceux qui l'environnent.

[45] Et si la France, & peut-être l'Europe entiere est accablée sous le poids des impôts ; si la rivalité des Puissances les a entraînées à l'envi dans des dépenses énormes, qui ont rendu ces impôts nécessaires ; & si ces dépenses sont encore doublées par une dette nationale im-mense, contractée sous d'autres regnes ; il faut que VOTRE MAJESTÉ se souvienne que vos ancêtres ont été couverts de gloire, mais que cette gloire est encore payée par les générations présentes ; qu'ils captiverent les coeurs par leur libéralité, qu'ils étonnerent l'Europe par leur magnificence, mais que cette magnificence & cette libéralité ont fait créer les impôts & les dettes qui existent encore aujourd'hui.

[46] Il faut aussi que VOTRE MAJESTÉ se rappelle sans cesse que le vertueux Louis XII, malgré sa passion pour la guerre, ne se crut jamais permis d'employer les moyens qui auroient été onéreux à ses sujets ; & que malgré la bonté qui étoit sa vertu caractéristique, il eut le courage de s'exposer aux reproches d'avarice de la part de ses cour-tisans, parce qu'il sçavoit que si l'économie d'un Roi peut être censurée par quelques hommes frivoles ou avides, sa prodigalité fait couler les larmes d'une nation entiere.

[47] Cette grande vérité, SIRE, est aujourd'hui reconnue de toutes les nations, à qui l'expérience de bien des siecles a appris à ne de-mander à leurs Rois que les vertus qui feront le bonheur des hommes ; & si, à votre avénement, toute la France a fait éclater, par ses acclama-tions, son amour pour le sang de ses Maîtres, la sévérité de notre mi-

nistere, SIRE, nous oblige de vous avouer qu'une partie de ces transports étoit aussi due à l'opinion qu'on a conçue de VOTRE MAJESTÉ
dès ses plus tendres années, & à l'espérance qu'une sage économie
feroit bientôt diminuer les charges publiques.

[48] Cependant, SIRE, tandis que cette économie vous est demandée par les vœux universels de toute la nation, ceux qui ne font
consister la grandeur souveraine que dans le faste, sont toujours ceux
qui approchent le plus près du trône ; & pendant que le misérable à
qui la dureté des impôts arrache la subsistance, est éloigne de vos regards, les objets de votre bienfaisance & de votre magnificence sont
continuellement sous vos yeux. Il a donc fallu leur opposer le tableau
effrayant, mais non exagéré, de la situation des peuples.   Puisse-t-il
vous être toujours présent, SIRE ! S'il l'eût été aux Rois vos prédécesseurs, VOTRE MAJESTÉ pourroit suivre aujourd'hui les sentimens
de son cœur ; & quand on lui fait connoître que l'humanité répugne à
la rigueur des Loix bursales établies dans son Royaume, Elle ne balan-
ceroit pas à les révoquer, & ne seroit pas arrêtée par cette nécessité
de payer les dettes de l Etat, qui fait sans cesse obstacle à la réformation des abus les plus odieux.

[49] Au reste, SIRE, sans entreprendre de proposer à VOTRE
MAJESTÉ cette réformation générale des droits des Fermes, il pourra
vous être présenté sur plusieurs parties des mémoires particuliers, qui
seront discutés avec vos Ministres : car il n'est pas possible que VOTRE
MAJESTÉ entre elle-même dans le détail de tout ce qui a été inventé
par les Fermiers-Généraux pour faire payer les droits, & par les fraudeurs
pour s'y soustraire.   Mais ce que nous pouvons demander à présent à
VOTRE MAJESTÉ elle-même, c'est de faire examiner les extensions
de tous les droits faites sous le dernier Ministere, & les évocations accordées avec une profusion dont il n'y avoit pas d'exemple.

[50] Vous nous avez ordonné, SIRE, de nous soumettre sans examen à tout ce qui a reçu le caractere de Loi pendant que nous étions
éloignés de nos fonctions, & une force majeure nous a empêchés de
veiller aux droits & aux intérêts du peuple : il est donc nécessaire que
VOTRE MAJESTÉ elle-même daigne en prendre le soin ; & dans
l'examen qu'Elle fera faire, nous la supplions de faire distinguer avec
grande attention ce qui est réellement utile à la perception, de ce qui
n'a été introduit que par la complaisance aveugle du Ministere pour
les Financiers, & pour satisfaire leur despotisme.   Il est juste sur-tout
que VOTRE MAJESTÉ fasse retrancher de ces nouvelles loix tout ce

qui établit une justice arbitraire. Nous convenons que puisqu'il faut percevoir des droits excessifs, il faut être soumis à des loix rigoureuses ; mais au moins faut-il que ce soient des loix précises : car aucun motif, aucune considération, aucun intérêt ne peut autoriser VOTRE MAJESTÉ à faire dépendre le sort du peuple de l'avidité du Fermier, ou du caprice de l'Administrateur.

[51] Enfin, SIRE, quoique notre fonction ne soit point de vous donner des projets, & que nous devions éviter sur-tout de nous livrer à des systêmes incertains, il est cependant une vérité si importante, si evidente, & tellement faite pour être sentie par VOTRE MAJESTÉ elle-même, que nous nous croyons obligés de la mettre sous vos yeux ; c'est qu'il y auroit un avantage certain pour VOTRE MAJESTÉ, & immense pour le peuple, à simplifier les droits qui existent, & les loix qui en assurent la perception.

[52] Nous avons déja observé que la procédure établie pour les Fermes est un code effrayant par son immensité : or il n'est aucun homme versé, soit dans la Jurisprudence, soit dans l'administration, qui n'atteste qu'il n'y a de bonnes loix que dans les loix simples. Si on considere les droits dont la perception a donné lieu à ce code, on verra que ces droits mis sur chaque denrée, sont différens, suivant le genre de commerce qui s'en fait, suivant les lieux où ils se perçoivent, suivant la qualité des personnes. La fraude, toujours active & toujours in-dustrieuse, en profite, & se fait jour, pour ainsi dire, à travers les sinuosités de la loi. La Finance invente tous les jours de nouveaux moyens pour la poursuivre ; & ces moyens employés contre les fraudeurs gênent tous les citoyens dans la propriété de leurs biens, & dans la liberté de leurs personnes.

[53] C'est ce qui a fait multiplier à l'infini ces Commis, qui portent une curiosité si importune sur toutes les actions de la vie ; c'est ce qui a fait accorder aux Financiers le droit de visiter les marchandises, d'entrer jusques dans les maisons, de violer le secret des familles ; c'est aussi cette inégalité des droits perçus dans les différens pays, qui a obli-gé les Rois vos prédécesseurs à couper leur Royaume dans tous les sens, par des lignes qu'il faut faire garder comme autant de frontieres, par une armée innombrable de Commis.

[54] Voilà, SIRE, à quoi on remédieroit en simplifiant les droits : les Fermiers de VOTRE MAJESTÉ y gagneroient une grande partie des frais de régie, & la contrebande deviendroit aussi plus difficile ; car rien ne la favorise autant que la complications des droits & l'obscurité

des réglemens ; & le peuple en retireroit l'avantage d'être moins tour-
menté par les recherches des Employés de la Ferme ; recherches qui
ne sont nulle part plus incommodes que dans les pays que l'on regarde
comme sujets à la fraude, & nommément dans les limites de ce qu'on
appelle le pays des cinq grosses Fermes, le pays d'Aides, le pays de
grandes Gabelles, &c.

[55] Cependant, SIRE, nous ne prétendons pas dire à VOTRE
MAJESTÉ que cette simplification soit un ouvrage facile. On voit
avec évidence, dans la spéculation, qu'elle est possible, & qu'elle sera
très-utile à l'Etat ; mais pour y procéder, il faut connoître dans le plus
grand détail, non-seulement le produit de chaque droit dans chaque
territoire, mais la vraie source de ce produit, & prévoir avec justesse
quelle augmentation ou quelle diminution chaque changement apportera dans le recouvrement. Ce n'est pas seulement le produit
actuel qu'il faut connoître, mais le produit possible. Il faut calculer
non-seulement les intérêts de la Ferme, mais ceux du cultivateur, du
fabricateur, du commerçant & du consommateur de chaque denrée.
Nous osons cependant assurer VOTRE MAJESTÉ que ce travail peut
se faire, malgré toutes ces difficultés. Il existe certainement des
matériaux immenses & dans les registres de la Ferme-générale, & dans
les bureaux des Ministres & des Intendans des Finances, & même chez
beaucoup de Commerçans ; il n'est question que de déterminer par qui
& comment ils seront employés.

[56] Sera-ce les Fermiers-Généraux eux-mêmes qu'on chargera de
ce travail? C'est ce qu'on a voulu faire plus d'une fois, SIRE. C'est
à eux qu'on a demandé des projets ; mais nous devons avertir VOTRE
MAJESTÉ qu'en même temps que la simplification des droits est
avantageuse à la Ferme, les plus habiles Fermiers ont en cela un intérêt
personnel contraire à celui de la Ferme, parce que la science qu'on
rendra inutile, est celle qu'ils ont acquise avec de grands travaux, &
que par cette science profonde, & la complication de la machine qu'ils
font mouvoir, ils se sont rendus nécessaires au Gouvernement, & font
tous les jours la loi aux Ministres. D'ailleurs peut-on douter que les
Financiers, érigés en législateurs, n'ajoutent à la rigueur des droits tout
ce qui servira à cimenter ce despotisme intolérable, & inutile au service
de VOTRE MAJESTÉ, auquel ils ont déja asservi la nation?

[57] Il faut certainement consulter les Fermiers-Généraux ; &
malgre l'observation que nous venons de faire à VOTRE MAJESTÉ,
on en a déja vu qui ont montré assez d'amour pour le bien public, pour

y sacrifier tous les intérêts & tous les préjugés de leur état : & cependant, en les consultant, il ne faut jamais oublier en quoi leur intérêt est
contraire a celui du peuple & à celui de VOTRE MAJESTÉ.

[58] Vous avez beaucoup, SIRE, à attendre, dans ce travail, du zele
& des lumieres des Magistrats chargés de l'administration de vos
Finances ; nous croyons même qu'il est important qu'il soit fait sous
leur direction. Mais sera-ce par eux-mêmes ? Un travail si étendu
peut-il être fait par un seul homme ? Et cet homme peut-il être celui
dont le temps est déja consommé par le courant des affaires journalieres de son administration ? Ils emploieront sans doute des coopéra-
teurs : mais si c'est un bureau attaché à la seule personne du Magistrat,
on tombera toujours dans les inconvéniens déja si souvent éprouvés,
d'être dans la dépendance d'un seul homme, d'avoir ce seul homme
pour défenseur du peuple contre tous les efforts réunis de toute la
Finance ; à quoi il faut ajouter que sa mort entraînera un jour la perte
de toutes les connoissances acquises & de tous les travaux faits dans la
partie de l'administration qu'il seroit peut-être le plus nécessaire
d'éclairer.

[59] Il seroit juste, SIRE, que tous les détails de la régie des Fermes
fussent connus de VOTRE MAJESTÉ, pour qui les droits sont perçus,
& du peuple qui les paie ; & que quand ce peuple vous adresse ses
plaintes, quand il demande du soulagement aux malheurs qu'il éprouve,
le remede pût vous en être indiqué, & que VOTRE MAJESTÉ pût en
juger par elle-même. Puisque cela est impossible dans l'état actuel de
la complication des Loix, il faut certainement travailler à les simplifier :
mais jusqu'à ce que ce travail soit achevé, jusqu'à ce que ce nouveau
corps de Loix soit donné à la France, n'est-il aucun frein qu'on puisse
mettre à ce despotisme des Fermiers, fondé sur l'ignorance où est tout
le public des Loix & de leur régie ? Il en est un, SIRE ; & vous
pouvez ordonner dès à présent aux Fermiers-Généraux de faire publier
des tarifs exacts & circonstanciés des droits qu'ils ont à percevoir, &
une collection courte, claire & méthodique des réglemens qu'il faut observer, & qu'il importe au public de connoître.

[60] Peut-être dira-t-on à VOTRE MAJESTÉ que ce travail sera
long & difficile ; cependant si on veut être de bonne foi, on conviendra
qu'il n'est aucune partie des droits affermés dont plusieurs Fermiers &
plusieurs Directeurs ne soient spécialement occupés ; que chacun
d'eux a sur sa partie un traité complet, qui lui sert à fournir d'un
moment à l'autre les mémoires dont la Ferme-générale a besoin ; qu'ils

ont aussi des instructions abrégées qui servent à diriger leurs Commis ;
& il seroit juste que le public en eût communication, puisque le public
a sans cesse à se défendre des entreprises de ces Commis. Le travail
est donc fait, il n'y a plus qu'à le publier.

[61] Mais nous devons prévenir VOTRE MAJESTÉ que les Fermiers ne se prêteront qu'avec répugnance à cette publication, & cette
répugnance même en prouvera la nécesstié. On ne veut pas que le
peuple lui-même connoisse ses droits ; on veut le tenir dans une sou-
mission aveugle pour la Ferme-générale : on craint qu'il ne se forme
dans chaque province des practiciens qui, après avoir étudié les loix
financieres, pourront guider les particuliers dans leurs contestations
contre le Fermier. Or il est de votre devoir, SIRE, de procurer cette
facilité à vos malheureux sujets. Vous leur devez l'appui des loix ; &
cet appui devient illusoire, quand les loix ne sont pas connues de ceux
qui ont le droit de les invoquer.

[62] En vous présentant, SIRE, le tableau général des droits des
Fermes, nous n'avons voulu entrer dans le détail d'aucune affaire particuliere. Nous nous croyons cependant obligés de supplier VOTRE
MAJESTÉ de prendre en considération les Remontrances qui furent
faites au feu Roi au mois d'Août 1770, & qui jusqu'à présent sont restées
sans réponse.[1] . . . .
. . . .
. . . .

[63] Pourquoi n'oserions-nous pas espérer, SIRE, que cette importante vérification pourra vous déterminer à l'acte de justice qui illustrera
le plus le commencement de votre regne ; à choisir les hommes les plus
dignes de la confiance de la Nation, & les charger de l'examen de tous
les ordres qui retiennent encore aujourd'hui des citoyens dans l'exil ou
dans la captivité?

[64] Nous portons encore plus loin nos espérances ; & si VOTRE
MAJESTÉ se détermine à faire faire cet examen, nous ne doutons pas
qu' à cette occasion on n'établisse des principes dans une matiere où
l'on n'en connut jamais. Il en résultera au moins cette vérité, que
des ordres attentatoires à la liberté des citoyens ne doivent jamais être
accordés à des particuliers, ni pour leurs intérêts personnels, ni pour
venger leurs injures, parce que dans un pays où il y a des loix, les particuliers n'ont pas besoin d'ordres extrajudiciaires, & que d'ailleurs ae

---

[1] NOTE DE L'ÉDITEUR.—Il s'est trouvé ici une lacune dans le manuscrit sur lequel
on a imprimé, & qui avoit pour objet les lettres de cachet. . . . See note, ¶ 64 of the
Translation.

tels ordres sont donnés aux puissans contre les foibles, sans réciprocité, ce qui est la plus criante de toutes les injustices.

[65] Peut-être pensera-t-on qu'il y a des cas privilégiés où c'est pour l'ordre public qu'il faut des actes d'autorité qui ne soient point revêtus des formalités de la Justice. On dira qu'il est quelquefois utile de suppléer à la lenteur de la Justice réglée, qui laisseroit évader des coupables ; que pour la police & la sûreté des grandes villes, il faut pouvoir s'assurer des gens légitimement suspects ; que souvent l'intérêt public se réunit à celui des familles pour sequestrer de la société un sujet qui ne pourroit que la troubler, & contre lequel on n'a d'autres preuves que celles qui sont administrées par cette famille même, qui cherche à se soustraire à l'infamie d'une procédure légale.

[66] Mais quand on aura discuté toutes ces considérations en votre présence, & qu'on aura mis sous vos yeux les abus qui en ont été faits, vous reconnoîtrez, SIRE, que ce sont de vains prétextes, qui n'auroient jamais dû faire livrer à la puissance arbitraire la liberté des citoyens ; ou du moins qu'il faut réserver aux opprimés la faculté de réclamer contre la violence.

[67] Vous reconnoîtrez que s'il est des cas où ce soit la Justice elle-même qui vous demande des ordres prompts & secrets, parce qu'on craint que la lenteur de la procédure ne favorise la fuite des criminels, un Roi législateur pourroit donner à la Justice plus d'activité, sans employer des moyens illégaux, & qu'alors la célérité requise ne priveroit pas celui qui auroit été injustement arrêté, de son recours contre le calomniateur.

[68] Que si l'ordre public veut qu'on s'assure d'un homme légitimement suspect, la légitimité des soupçons doit être constatée, en sorte que celui qui a été la victime innocente de ces précautions politiques, puisse demander & obtenir une indemnité, & qu'il sçache au moins pourquoi & par qui cette violence est exercée.

[69] Enfin, que quand on use de ménagement pour une famille qui est venue implorer elle-même les secours du Gouvernement contre un sujet qui la déshonore, il n'est pas encore nécessaire que ce genre de justice soit sans aucun recours. En effet, ce n'est que l'éclat des procédures qu'on veut éviter. Or, sans faire de procédures publiques, il est possible de consigner les motifs de l'ordre du Roi dans un acte signé de celui qui a expédié l'ordre, & de ceux qui l'ont obtenu ; de conserver cet acte au moins pendant tout le temps de la détention du prisonnier, & de lui en donner communication.

[70] Ce prisonnier, quel que soit son crime, devroit être admis à présenter sa justification, & même à demander que les causes de l'ordre rigoureux fussent examinées de nouveau par d'autres que ceux qui l'ont fait décerner, & qu'il en fût rendu un nouveau compte au Roi, qui chosiroit pour cet examen les hommes de la réputation la plus intacte & la plus imposante. Et comme il est très-difficile, & souvent même impossible à un prisonnier de faire parvenir sa réclamation jusqu'au Roi, il seroit nécessaire de faire faire de temps en temps, & toujours par des personnes étrangeres à l'administration, & de l'intégrité la plus reconnue, une visite de toutes les prisons Royales, & une revue exacte de toutes les lettres de cachet.

[71] Quand on sçaura que ces précautions sont prises par VOTRE MAJESTÉ contre les surprises qui pourroient lui être faites, & sur-tout quand on se rappellera que votre regne aura commencé par un examen sévere de tout ce qui a été reproché à la précédente administration, croyez, SIRE, que les abus de ces ordres donnés en votre nom, seront très-rares. Nous ne pouvons que vous faire entrevoir les avantages qui résulteront de cette recherche ; mais si elle s'exécute, vous jugerez, par la reconnoissance de la Nation, de l'importance du bienfait. Nous nous sommes livrés, SIRE, à une digression que nous ne nous reprochons point, puisqu'elle a été pour nous l'occasion de vous présenter des réflexions peut-être utiles sur le genre d'abus qui a le plus excité de plaintes de la part d'une partie de la nation, & sur lequel il est le plus facile de lui donner satisfaction.

[72] Il est temps de revenir aux impôts. Les vexations occasionnées pour la perception des droits des Fermes ont une excuse ; c'est la nécessité de procurer à VOTRE MAJESTÉ le revenu considérable qui est le produit de ces droits : mais il semble qu'il ne devroit pas en être de même des impositions qui se levent directement sur le peuple. Si la somme qu'on veut lever étoit fixée, comme elle le devroit toujours être, on n'auroit plus qu'à choisir la forme de répartition la plus juste, la plus simple, la moins dispendieuse. L'administration est donc inexcusable quand elle introduit dans la levée de ces impôts un despotisme aussi inutile qu'odieux, quand elle ajoute à l'impôt même des frais de régie, qui sont toujours supportés par le peuple. Voilà cependant, SIRE, ce qu'on éprouve dans la levée de tous les impôts directs, de la taille, de la capitation, du vingtieme ; & une partie de ces inconvéniens se fait même sentir dans toutes les prestations de service corporel qui s'exigent du peuple, comme la milice & la corvée.

[73] Mais la discussion de ces abus nous conduira nécessairement à de bien plus grandes questions. La perception des droits sur les denrées ne tient pas à la forme du gouvernement de l'Etat ; mais la répartition des impôts directs tient essentiellement à la constitution de la Monarchie. Les vices de cette répartition font partie d'un systême général d'administration qui depuis longtemps s'introduit dans votre Royaume, & le remede ne peut se trouver que dans la réformation qu'il plaira à VOTRE MAJESTÉ d'apporter dans l'administration générale.

[74] Ainsi nous examinerons la régie de chaque impôt direct, & VOTRE MAJESTÉ y verra le développement de ce systême funeste : mais il faut auparavant remonter à l'origine ; il faut faire connoître à VOTRE MAJESTÉ le principe général & ses conséquences ; & peut-être serez-vous étonné, SIRE, quand vos verrez jusqu'à quel point on a abusé du prétexte de votre autorité contre cette autorité elle-même.

[75] Vous nous permettez, SIRE, de nous servir du terme de *despotisme*, tout odieux qu'il est ; dispensez-nous de recourir à des circonlocutions embarrassantes, quand nous avons des vérités importantes à vous rendre sensibles. Le despotisme contre lequel nous réclamons aujourd'hui, est celui qui s'exerce, à votre insçu, par des émissaires de l'Administration, gens absolument inconnus à VOTRE MAJESTÉ. Non, SIRE, nous ne venons point offrir à VOTRE MAJESTÉ des dissertations inutiles, & peut-être dangereuses, sur les limites de sa puissance souveraine ; c'est au contraire le droit de recourir à cette puissance, que nous allons revendiquer pour tous les citoyens, & nous ne nommerons *despotisme* que le genre de l'administration qui tend à priver vos sujets de ce droit qui leur est si précieux, & à soustraire a votre justice ceux qui oppriment le peuple.

[76] L'idée qu'on s'est faite du despotisme, ou de la puissance absolue, dans les différens temps & chez les différens peuples, n'est pas la même. On parle souvent d'un genre de gouvernement qu'on nomme *le despotisme Oriental :* c'est celui dans lequel non-seulement le Souverain jouit d'une autorité absolue & illimitée, mais chacun des exécuteurs de ses ordres use aussi d'un pouvoir sans bornes. Il en résulte nécessairement une tyrannie intolérable : car il est une différence infinie entre la puissance exercée par un maître dont le véritable intérêt est celui de son peuple, & celle d'un sujet qui, enorgueilli de ce pouvoir auquel il n'étoit pas destiné, se plaît à en aggraver le poids sur ses égaux ; genre de despotisme qui, étant transmis graduellement à des Ministres de différens ordres, se fait sentir jusqu'au dernier citoyen ; en sorte qu'il n'est personne, dans un grand Empire, qui puisse s'en garantir.

[77] Le vice de ce gouvernement est tout à-la-fois dans la constitution & dans les mœurs.   Dans la constitution, parce que les peuples qui y sont sujets, n'ont ni tribunaux, ni corps de loix, ni représentans du peuple.   Point de tribunaux ; voilà pourquoi l'autorité est exercée par un seul homme.   Point de loix fixes & positives ; voilà pourquoi celui qui a l'autorité en main, statue d'après ses propres lumieres, c'est-à-dire, ordinairement d'après ses affections.   Point de représentans du peuple ; voilà pourquoi le despote d'une Province peut l'opprimer contre la volonté & à l'insçu du Souverain, & avec l'assurance de l'impunité.

[78] Les mœurs contribuent aussi à cette impunité ; car les peuples soumis à ce genre de despotisme sont toujours des peuples en proie à l'ignorance.   Personne ne lit, personne n'entretient de relation ; les cris de l'opprimé ne se font point entendre au-delà du pays qu'il habite.   L'innocent n'a donc point en sa faveur de recours à l'opinion publique, qui est un frein si puissant contre la tyrannie des subalternes.

[79] Telle est donc la malheureuse situation de ces peuples, que le Souverain même le plus juste ne peut faire sentir les effets de sa justice qu'à ceux qui approchent de lui, ou dans le petit nombre d'affaires dont il peut prendre connoissance par lui-même.   Tout ce qu'il peut faire pour le reste de ses sujets, est de choisir le moins mal qu'il peut les dépositaires de son autorité, & de les exhorter aussi à faire les meilleurs choix qu'ils pourront pour les places inférieures.   Mais quelque chose qu'il fasse, le citoyen du dernier ordre gémit toujours sous l'autorité d'un despote du dernier grade, & lui est aussi soumis que les Grands de l'Etat le sont au Souverain lui-même.

[80] Il semble qu'une telle forme de gouvernement ne peut pas exister chez les Nations qui ont des loix, des mœurs & des lumieres : aussi dans les pays policés, lors même que le Prince jouit d'un pouvoir absolu, la condition des peuples doit être très-différente.   Quelque absolue que soit l'autorité, la justice peut être rendue par délibération, & dans les Tribunaux astreints à des loix certaines.   Si les Juges s'écartent de ces loix, on peut recourir à des Tribunaux supérieurs, & enfin à l'autorité souveraine elle-même.   Tous les recours sont possibles, parce que tous les actes d'autorité sont écrits, constatés, déposés dans des registres publics ; qu'il n'est point de citoyen qui ne puisse trouver un défenseur éclairé, & que le public même est le censeur des Juges.   Et non-seulement la justice est rendue aux particuliers, mais les Corps, les Communautés, les Villes, les Provinces entieres peuvent

aussi l'obtenir, & pour pouvoir défendre leurs droits, doivent avoir des assemblées & des représentans.

[81] Ainsi dans un pays policé, quoique soumis à une puissance absolue, il ne doit y avoir aucun intérêt, ni général, ni particulier, qui ne soit défendu ; & tous les dépositaires de la puissance souveraine doivent être soumis à trois sortes de freins, celui des loix, celui du recours à l'autorité supérieure, celui de l'opinion publique.

[82] Cette distinction entre les différens genres de pouvoir absolu n'est point nouvelle. Ces définitions ont été souvent données par des Jurisconsultes, par les Auteurs, tant anciens que modernes, qui ont écrit sur la législation. Elles sont le résultant de ce qu'on lit dans les histoires & les relations des différens pays : mais il nous étoit nécessaire de les retracer, parce que nous avons une grande vérité à en déduire. Nous devons faire connoître à VOTRE MAJESTÉ que le gouvernement qu'on veut établir en France est le vrai despotisme des pays non policés ; & que chez la Nation la plus instruite, dans le siecle où les mœurs sont les plus douces, on est menacé de cette forme de gouvernement où le Souverain ne peut pas être éclairé lors même qu'il le veut le plus sincérement.

[83] La France, ainsi que le reste de l'Europe Occidentale, étoit régie par le droit féodal : mais chaque Royaume a éprouvé différentes révolutions depuis que ce gouvernement est détruit. Il est des Nations qui ont été admises à discuter leurs droits avec le Souverain, & les prérogatives y ont été fixées. Dans d'autres, l'autorité absolue a si promptement prévalu, qu'aucun des droits nationaux n'a été examiné ; & il en est résulté au moins un avantage pour ces pays, c'est qu'il n'y a aucun prétexte pour y détruire les corps intermédiaires, & enfreindre la liberté naturelle à tous les hommes, de délibérer en commun sur des intérêts communs, & de recourir à la puissance suprême contre les abus des puissances subalternes.

[84] En France, la Nation a toujours eu un sentiment profond de ses droits & de sa liberté. Nos maximes ont été plus d'une fois reconnues par nos Rois ; ils se sont même glorifiés d'être les Souverains d'un peuple libre : cependant les articles de cette liberté n'ont jamais été rédigés ; & la puissance réelle, la puissance des armes, qui, sous le gouvernement féodal, étoit dans les mains des Grands, a été totalement réunie à la puissance Royale.

[85] Alors, quand il y a eu de grands abus d'autorité, les représentans de la nation ne se sont pas contentés de se plaindre de la mauvaise

administration; ils se sont crus obligés à revendiquer les droits
nationaux.   Ils n'ont pas parlé seulement de justice, mais de liberté;
& l'effet de leurs démarches a été que les Ministres, toujours attentifs
à saisir les moyens de mettre leur administration à l'abri de tout examen, ont eu l'art de rendre suspects & les Corps réclamans, & la réclamation elle-même.   Le recours au Roi contre ses Ministres a été
regardé comme un attentat à son autorité.   Les doléances des Etats,
les remontrances des Magistrats ont été transformées en démarches
dangereuses, dont le Gouvernement devoit se garantir.   On a persuadé
aux plus puissans Rois de la terre qu'ils avoient à craindre jusqu'aux
larmes d'un peuple soumis; & c'est sous ce prétexte qu'on a introduit
en France un gouvernement bien plus funeste que le despotisme, &
digne de la barbarie Orientale; c'est l'administration clandestine par
laquelle, sous les yeux d'un Souverain juste, & au milieu d'une nation
éclairée, l'injustice peut se montrer, disons plus, elle se commet notoire-
ment.   Des branches entieres d'administration sont fondées sur des
systêmes d'injustices, sans qu'aucun recours, ni au public, ni à l'autorité
supérieure, soit possible.

[86] C'est ce despotisme des Administrateurs, & sur-tout ce systême
de clandestinité, que nous devons dénoncer à VOTRE MAJESTÉ; car
nous n'aurons point la témérité de discuter les autres droits sacrés du
trône.   Il nous suffit que VOTRE MAJESTÉ ait désavoué, dans l'acte
de rétablissement de la Magistrature, les maximes de tyrannie qui avoient
été exécutées sous un ministere aujourd'hui proscrit; & nous nous con-
formerons aux intentions de VOTRE MAJESTÉ, en n'agitant point des
questions qui n'auroient jamais dû être élevées.

[87] Mais ce n'est point blesser la *juste subordination*, que de mettre
sous vos yeux une suite d'infractions faites à la liberté nationale, à la
liberté naturelle de tous les hommes, qui vous mettent aujourd'hui
dans l'impossibilité d'entendre vos sujets, & d'éclairer la conduite de
vos Administrateurs.

1°. On a cherché à anéantir les vrais représentans de la nation.

2°. On est parvenu à rendre illusoires les réclamations de ceux qu'on
n'a pas encore pu détruire.

3°. On veut même les rendre impossibles.   C'est pour y parvenir
que la clandestinité a été introduite.   Il en est de deux genres; l'une
qui cherche à dérober aux yeux de la nation, à ceux de VOTRE
MAJESTÉ elle-même, les opérations de l'administration; l'autre qui
cache au public la personne des Administrateurs.   Voilà, SIRE, le

précis du système que nous dénonçons à VOTRE MAJESTÉ, & que nous allons développer.

[88] Nous annonçons comme la premiere démarche de ce despotisme, celle d'anéantir tous les représentans de la nation, & si VOTRE MAJESTÉ veut bien réfléchir sur la réunion de plusieurs faits dont aucun n'est douteux, elle y trouvera la démonstration de cette vérité.

[89] Les Assemblées générales de la Nation n'ont point été convoquées depuis cent soixante ans, & long-temps auparavant elles étoient devenues très-rares, nous oserons même dire presqu' inutiles, parce qu'on faisoit sans elles ce qui rendoit leur présence le plus nécessaire, l'établissement des impôts.

[90] Quelques Provinces avoient des Assemblées particulieres ou Etats provinciaux : plusieurs ont été privées de ce précieux privilege ; & dans les Provinces où ces Etats existent encore, leur ministere est resserré dans des bornes qui deviennent tous les jours plus étroites. Ce n'est pas une assertion téméraire de dire que dans nos Provinces on entretient entre les dépositaires du pouvoir arbitraire & les représentans des Peuples, une espece de guerre continuelle, où le despotisme fait tous les jours de nouvelles conquêtes.

[91] Les Provinces qui n'avoient pas d'Etats provinciaux étoient nommées pays d'Election ; & il y existoit réellement des Tribunaux nommés Elections, composés de personnes élues par la Province elle-même, qui, au moins pour la répartition des impôts, remplissoient quelques-unes des fonctions des Etats provinciaux. Ces Tribunaux existent encore sous le nom d'Elections ; mais ce nom est tout ce qu'il leur reste de leur institution primitive. Ces Officiers ne sont plus réellement élus par la Province ; & tels qu'ils sont, on les a mis dans la dépendance presqu' entiere des Intendans pour les fonctions qui leur restent. Nous aurons une autre occasion de parler des Elections, en parlant de l'impôt de la taille ; nous ferons même connoître à VOTRE MAJESTÉ en quoi elles différoient des Etats provinciaux : il suffit d'observer à présent que les vrais Elus des Provinces n'existent plus.

[92] Il restoit au moins à chaque Corps, à chaque Communauté de Citoyens le droit d'administrer ses propres affaires, droit que nous ne dirons point qui fasse partie de la constitution primitive du Royaume, car il remonte bien plus haut ; c'est le droit naturel, c'est le droit de la raison. Cependant il a été aussi enlevé à vos Sujets ; & nous ne craindrons pas de dire que l'administration est tombée à cet égard dans des excès qu'on peut nommer puériles.

[93] Depuis que des Ministres puissans se sont fait un principe politique de ne point laisser convoquer d'Assemblée nationale, on en est venu, de conséquence en conséquence, jusqu'à déclarer nulles les délibérations des Habitans d'un village, quand elles ne sont pas autorisées par l'Intendant ; en sorte que si cette Communauté a une dépense à faire, quelque légere qu'elle soit, il faut prendre l'attache du Subdélégué de l'Intendant, par conséquent suivre le plan qu'il a adopté, employer les ouvriers qu'il favorise, les payer suivant son arbitrage ; & si la Communauté a un procès à soutenir, il faut aussi qu'elle se fasse autoriser par l'Intendant ; il faut que la cause de la Communauté soit plaidée à ce premier Tribunal avant d'être porté à la Justice ; & si l'avis de l'Intendant est contraire aux Habitans, ou si leur adversaire a du crédit à l'Intendance, la Communauté est déchue de la faculté de défendre ses droits.

[94] Voilà, SIRE, par quels moyens on a travaillé à étouffer en France tout esprit municipal, à éteindre, si on le pouvoit, jusqu'aux sentimens de citoyen : on a, pour ainsi dire, interdit la Nation entiere, & on lui a donné des tuteurs.

[95] L'anéantissement des Corps réclamans étoit un premier pas pour anéantir le droit de réclamation lui-même. On n'a cependant pas été jusqu'à prononcer en termes exprès, que tous recours au Prince, toutes démarches pour les Provinces fussent défendues ; mais VOTRE MAJESTÉ n'ignore pas que toute requête dans laquelle les intérêts d'une Province ou ceux de la Nation entiere sont stipulés, est regardée comme une témérité punissable, quand elle est signée d'un seul particulier, & comme une association illicite, quand elle est signée de plusieurs. Il avoit cependant fallu donner à la Nation une satisfaction apparente, quand on avoit cessé de convoquer les Etats : aussi les Rois avoient-ils annoncé que les Cours de Justice tiendroient lieu des Etats, que les Magistrats seroient les représentans du Peuple.

[96] Mais après leur avoir donné ce titre, pour consoler la Nation de la perte de ses anciens & véritables représentans, on s'est souvenu dans toutes les occasions que les fonctions des Juges étoient restreintes à leur seul territoire & à la Justice contentieuse, & on a mis les mêmes limites au droit de représentation.

[97] Ainsi tous les abus possibles peuvent être commis dans l'administration sans que le Roi en soit jamais instruit, ni par les représentans du Peuple, puisque dans la plupart des Provinces il n'y en a point ; ni par les Cours de Justice, puisqu'on les écarte, comme in-

compétentes, dès qu'elles veulent parler de l'administration ; ni par les particuliers, à qui des exemples de sévérité ont appris que c'est un crime d'invoquer la justice de leur Souverain.

[98] Malgré tous ces obstacles, le cri public, genre de réclamation qu'on ne peut jamais tout-à-fait étouffer, étoit toujours à craindre pour les Administrateurs & peut être a-t-on craint aussi qu'un jour un Roi ne voulût, de son propre mouvement, se faire rendre compte de tous les secrets de l'administration. On a donc voulu que ce compte fût impossible à rendre, ou au moins qu'il ne pût être rendu que par les seuls Administrateurs, sans être exposé à aucune contradiction ; & c'est pour cela qu'on a fait tant d'efforts pour introduire par-tout l'administration clandestine.

[99] Pour prouver cette vérité dans toute son étendue ; il faudroit entrer dans le détail de toutes les parties du Gouvernement ; mais quelques exemples suffiront pour la rendre sensible. Nous les choisirons dans les impôts qui font notre principal objet, & nous n'hésiterons point de citer les administrations qui ont le plus mérité l'approbation publique ; car nous devons toujours faire connoître à VOTRE MAJESTÉ les vices intrinseques d'une administration, quoiqu'ils soient réparés pendant un temps par les qualités personelles de l'Administrateur.

[100] Par exemple, il est reconnu dans toute l'Europe que rien n'a plus signalé le dernier regne que la construction des chemins qui facilitent le commerce, & doublent la valeur des biens du Royaume. Le gouvernement a cru jusqu'à présent que la corvée étoit nécessaire pour ce grand ouvrage & la corvée n'est autorisée par aucune Loi du Royaume.[1] Il semble qu'il auroit fallu la faire reconnoître juridiquement ; & alors on auroit pu établir des regles certaines & publiques sur la répartition de ce travail souvent plus accablant pour le Peuple que la taille elle-même.

[101] Ce n'est pas le parti qu'on a pris : on craignoit, disoit-on, la sensation qu'exciteroit dans le Royaume une Loi qui, en réglant la corvée, sembleroit l'autoriser. En conséquence toutes les opérations se sont faites en secret, & il n'a paroît pas même un Arrêt du Conseil imprimé concernant une imposition qui, depuis si long-temps, fait gémir les Peuples. Chaque Province n'apprend que le projet d'un chemin est arrêté, que quand on en commence l'exécution ; & si le choix de cette route est contraire au bien de la Province, il est trop

---

[1] See note, ¶ 100 of the Translation.

tard pour s'y opposer.   Si le travail est réparti avec injustice ou avec
trop de dureté, ceux qui voudroient se plaindre n'ont ni Juges légaux
devant qui se pourvoir, ni regles certaines à opposer à la rigueur des
ordres qu'ils ont reçus, ni moyens juridiques pour constater l'injustice
qui leur a été faite.

[102] On dit aujourd'hui que VOTRE MAJESTÉ veut adoucir la
rigueur de la corvée ; ou y substitue une imposition d'un autre genre.
La Nation attend ces changemens avec confiance, & déja avec reconnoissance ; & nous osons espérer que ce qui sera substitué à la
corvée, ne sera point infecté de la même clandestinité.   Nous avons
cependant dû vous représenter les abus qu'entraînoit cette administration, comme un des exemples les plus frappans du système général.

[103] Il en est de même du vingtieme ; & à cet égard l'abus a encore moins de prétexte ; car on pourroit dire sur la corvée, que la
célérité nécessaire pour les ouvrages ne permettoit pas d'attendre la
discussion de toutes les injustices particulieres : mais le vingtieme est
une imposition mise tous les ans sur les mêmes terres depuis pres de
quarante années, presque sans interruption.   Croiroit-on que depuis
ces quarante années les rôles de cette imposition ne sont point encore
déposés dans aucuns registres où les particuliers puissent les consulter.

[104] Ce n'est point une formalité omise par négligence ; car cet
abus fut représenté au Roi par sa Cour des Aides en 1756.   Le Ministere de ce temps céda à l'évidence : le feu Roi consentit que ce dépôt fût fait ; mais les Ministres qui sont venus, après avoir employé
pendant plusieurs années tous les détours possibles pour s'opposer indirectement à l'effet de cette parole sacrée, on finit par obtenir qu'elle
soit expressément révoquée.

[105] Nous ne rapporterons point ici tout ce qui s'est passé à ce
sujet, pour ne pas fatiguer VOTRE MAJESTÉ du récit d'une affaire
finie : si cependant VOTRE MAJESTÉ vouloit en être instruite, ces
faits ne sont point oubliés, & il seroit aisé de les mettre sous ses yeux.
Mais aujourd'hui nous nous contenterons d'observer que la plupart des
infidélités des Preposés du vingtieme sont nécessairement inconnues &
impunies, à la faveur de cette clandestinité.   Par exemple, quand un
Préposé trahit l'intérêt du fisc, en ménageant le contribuable qu'il veut
favoriser, & que, pour cacher aux Ministres cette prévarication, il rem-
plit le vuide en augmentant injustement les autres quotes, ceux qui se
trouvent lésés ne peuvent faire connoître cette iniquité, parce qu'ils ne
le pourroient que par l'inspection du rôle entier, & que ce rôle est secret.

[106] VOTRE MAJESTÉ voit par cet exemple, que le genre d'abus qui favorise la clandestinité des rôles, est précisément celui qui est le plus contraire à l'intérêt du Roi, à l'intérêt de finance, à l'intérêt fiscal. Ce n'est donc point pour cet intérêt que les Administrateurs ont fait défendre le dépôt des rôles ; c'est donc uniquement pour mettre leur administration à l'abri de tout examen, & pour procurer l'impunité à leurs Préposés.

[107] Et quand toutes les précautions prises pour cet objet se trouvent insuffisantes, quand les vexations sont si évidentes qu'on ne sçauroit les pallier, il arrive encore le plus souvent que ceux qui en sont coupables obtiennent l'impunité par l'effet de l'autre genre de clandestinité, de celle que nous avons nommée clandestinité de personnes, & qui consiste en ce que le plus souvent on ne sçait pas, on ne peut pas même découvrir à qui chaque abus d'autorité doit être imputé.

[108] L'administration de votre Royaume se fait, SIRE, auprès de la personne de VOTRE MAJESTÉ, par les Ministres aidés de leurs Commis, & dans certaines parties, par les Intendans des Finances, aidés pareillement de leurs Commis : dans les Provinces elle se fait par les Intendans & leurs Subdélégués. Nous allons considérer ces différentes personnes en commençant par le dernier ordre, & par ceux qui approchent le plus près du peuple.

[109] Le Subdélégué d'un Intendant est un homme sans qualité, sans pouvoir légal, qui n'a le droit de signer aucune Ordonnance : aussi toutes celles qu'il fait rendre sont signées par l'Intendant. On sçait cependant dans les Provinces que c'est le Subdélégué qui a prononcé sur beaucoup de détails dans lesquels l'Intendant lui-même ne peut pas entrer. Si ce Subdélégué abuse de son pouvoir, ce n'est qu'à l'Intendant qu'on peut se pouvoir : mais comment les gens du peuple oseroient-ils exercer ce recours, quand ils voient que c'est sous le nom de l'Intendant lui-même que l'Ordonnance a été rendue, & que sans doute ce Magistrat supérieur se croira compromis, & obligé de soutenir son Ordonnance ?

[110] Ce qui se passe à cet égard du Subdélégué à l'Intendant, est aussi ce qui se passe de l'Intendant au Ministre, & du Ministre à VOTRE MAJESTÉ elle-même.

[111] L'Intendant évite autant qu'il peut de prononcer en son nom. Dans toutes les affaires qui pourroient le compromettre, il prend le partie de faire rendre un Arrêt du Conseil, ou de se faire autoriser par une lettre du Ministre ; & le particulier de la Province qui voudroit

se pourvoir contre le jugement de l'Intendant, & porter ses plaintes au
Conseil ou au Ministre, reste sans replique, quand il se voit condamné
d'avance par une décision du Ministre, ou un Arrêt du Conseil.

[112] Pour les Intendans des Finances, qui sont placés entre les Intendans des Provinces & les Ministres, ce sont des puissances tout-à-fait
inconnues de tous ceux qui sont éloignés de la capitale & du séjour
de la Cour. On sçait en général que ces Magistrats existent, & qu'ils
ont une grande autorité dans le Royaume ; cependant on ne voit point
quels sont les genres d'affaires pour lesquels il faut recourir à eux,
parce que réellement il n'en est aucun qui dépende directement d'eux,
& personne spécialement ne leur est subordonné & n'est tenu de reconnoître leurs ordres. C'est dans leur travail avec le Contrôleur-
Général qu'ils font toute leur administration, en lui faisant signer des
lettres, ou de ces Arrêts du Conseil qu'on nomme Arrêts de Finance ;
& le particulier qui croit avoir à se plaindre de ces décisions, ne peut
s'en prendre ni à l'Intendant des Finances, qui ne signe rien, & ne
peut être tenu de rien, puisque le Ministre n'est pas obligé à suivre son
avis, & s'en écarte quelquefois ; ni au Contrôleur-Général, qui diroit
avec raison qu'il ne peut pas répondre de tout ce que lui font signer
les six Intendans des Finances.

[113] Enfin le Ministre lui-même n'a aucun état dans le Royaume,
aucune autorité directe. C'est cependant en lui que réside toute la
puissance, parce que c'est lui qui certifie la signature de VOTRE
MAJESTÉ. Il peut tout, & ne répond de rien ; car le nom respec-
table dont il lui est permis de se servir, ferme la bouche à quiconque
oseroit se plaindre.

[114] Ainsi, pendant que l'Habitant d'un village n'ose se pourvoir
contre la vexation d'un Subdélégué qui s'est fait autoriser par l'Ordonnance d'un Intendant, nous, Habitans de la capitale, nous personnellement, Magistrats chargés par état de faire parvenir la vérité aux
oreilles de VOTRE MAJESTÉ, combien de fois nous nous sommes vus
taxés d'audace pour avoir réclamé contre les ordres surpris au Roi par
ses Ministres !

[115] Osons dire à VOTRE MAJESTÉ la vérité toute entiere. Il
en a été mis sous nos yeux dont la fausseté étoit physiquement dé-
montrée, & d'autres dans lesquels il étoit évident que ce nom sacré
avoit été prostitué pour des sujets indignes de l'attention du Roi ; &
quand nous avons fait voir clairement les petites passions subalternes
qui avoient fait obtenir ces ordres, les petites vengeances, les petites

protections, ne nous a-t-on pas dit que c'étoit manquer à la Majesté
Royale, que de révoquer en doute qu'un ordre signé du Roi fût réellement donné par lui-même? Et si VOTRE MAJESTÉ vouloit que
ces faits, que nous ne faisons qu'alléguer, fussent articulés & prouvés,
nous serions en état de la satisfaire.

[116] De plus, ces mêmes Ministres ont attiré à eux, depuis un
siecle, le détail de tant d'affaires de tous les genres, qu'il leur est
impossible de les expédier eux-mêmes. Il s'est donc établi un nouveau
genre de puissance intermédiaire entre vos Ministres & vos autres
Sujets, qui n'est ni celle des Commandans ni celle des Intendans des
Provinces; c'est celle des Commis, personnages absolument inconnus
dans l'Etat, & qui cependant parlant & écrivant au nom des Ministres,
ont comme eux un pouvoir absolu, un pouvoir irrésistible, & sont même
encore plus qu'eux à l'abri de toutes recherches, parce qu'ils sont
beaucoup moins connus.

[117] Ainsi un particulier sans appui, sans aucune relation avec la
Cour, par exemple, un homme qui vit dans sa Province, peut recevoir
l'ordre le plus rigoureux, sans sçavoir ni par qui cet ordre a été décerné,
pour en obtenir la révocation, ni quelles en sont les causes, pour faire
entendre sa justification. L'ordre est signé du Roi; mais ce particulier
obscur sçait bien que le Roi n'a jamais entendu prononcer son nom.
La signature du Roi est certifiée par un Ministre; il sçait aussi qu'il
n'est pas connu des Ministres. Il ignore si c'est par l'Intendant de
sa Province que l'ordre a été obtenu, ou si un de ses ennemis a trouvé
accès auprès des Commis de Versailles, du premier, du second ou du
troisieme rang, ou si c'est un de ces ordres en blanc qui sont quelquefois donnés aux différentes puissances de chaque Province : il l'ignore,
& il reste dans l'exil, peut-être dans les fers.

[118] Nous avons cru nécessaire, SIRE, de présenter à VOTRE
MAJESTÉ ces notions des différens genres de despotisme, & surtout
de clandestinité; nous pouvons à présent en faire l'application aux
trois impositions directes, la taille, la capitation, le vingtieme.

[119] La taille, le plus ancien des impôts directs, est celui qui se
leve sur les roturiers non privilégiés, dans les Provinces qu'on appelle
pays d'Election, c'est-à-dire dans celles qui n'ont point d'Etats
provinciaux; & comme la taille est personnelle, on la fait payer aussi
aux fermiers des Ecclésiastiques, des Nobles & des privilégiés. Ainsi
c'est une imposition qui est aujourd'hui supportée par presque tous les
propriétaires des terres.

[120] On a joint à la taille plusieurs impositions qu'on nomme accessoires, & tous les ans on en ajoute de nouvelles. Ces accessoires égalent à présent, ou même surpassent le principal de la taille. On dit que depuis long-temps le principal de la taille n'est jamais augmenté ; cependant le peuple qui en supporte le poids, se plaint souvent de l'augmentation. Ce n'est qu'une dispute de mots : on n'augmente pas le principal, mais on augmente les accessoires.

[121] Il faut exposer à VOTRE MAJESTÉ comment se font, chaque année, l'imposition & la répartition de la taille & de ses accessoires. Il y a quatre opérations.

1°. Le brevet de la taille contient l'imposition sur toutes les Généralités : ainsi, soit qu'on veuille lever une somme accessoire à la taille sur tout le Royaume ou sur quelque Généralité en particulier, c'est par ce brevet qu'elle s'impose, & c'est aussi par ce brevet qu'on répartit entre les Généralités la somme totale imposée sur le Royaume. C'est au Conseil que s'arrête le brevet de la taille.

2°. Les commissions contiennent l'imposition sur toutes les Elections. Par conséquent si on veut lever une somme sur quelque Election en particulier, c'est par les commissions qu'on l'impose. C'est aussi dans les commissions qu'est faite la répartition entre les Elections de la somme imposée sur chaque Généralité. Les commissions, ainsi que le brevet, sont envoyées du Conseil.

3°. Ce qu'on appelle le département, est l'acte par lequel on impose chaque paroisse ou communauté. On impose donc au département les sommes qu'on veut lever sur une paroisse en particulier, ce qui arrive souvent pour constructions de presbyteres, rejet de frais de Justice ou autres dépenses ; & c'est aussi au département que se fait la répartition entre les paroisses de la somme imposée sur l'Election. Le département se fait dans la Province même, & c'est aujourd'hui par l'Intendant seul, & sans aucuns recours. Les Elus & autres personnes qui ont droit d'assister à l'assemblée du département, n'y ont plus de voix délibérative, & les Cours ne peuvent plus prendre connoissance de ce qui s'y passe.

4°. Le rôle de la taille contient l'imposition sur chaque contribuable, ou, ce qui est la même chose, la répartition entre les contribuables de la somme imposée sur tout la paroisse ou communauté. Le rôle de la taille se fait par les contribuables eux-mêmes, c'est-à-dire, par ceux qui sont à leur tour Asséeurs ou Collecteurs. Cependant l'Intendant a droit d'imposer d'autorité & d'office un contribuable qu'il croit favorisé par les Collecteurs. Il a aussi le droit d'envoyer dans les paroisses des Commissaires, qui font assembler les habitans, qui font faire en leur présence le rôle de la taille, qu'on appelle alors rôle d'office. La fonction de ces Commissaires devroit se terminer à instruire les contribuables des réglemens faits pour la confection des rôles, & à les obliger à s'y conformer : cependant l'autorité d'un homme envoyé par l'Intendant est telle dans les Provinces, que ces Commissaires font faire le rôle comme ils veulent ; & cela est tellement reconnu, que souvent les Intendans donnent des instructions imprimées pour prescrire à leurs Commissaires les règles suivant lesquelles ils veulent que la répartition soit faite. Au reste, quoique les quotes d'office soient faites par les Intendans, & les rôles d'office par les Commissaires, cette quatrieme répartition n'est pas autant soumise à l'autorité arbitraire que les trois premieres ; car les particuliers lésés ont droit de se pourvoir en Justice.

[122] Nous allons considérer ces quatre opérations d'abord sous l'aspect d'impositions, ensuite sous celui de répartitions. En les considérant comme impositions, on voit évidemment que pendant que les Cours ne cessent de soutenir que leur enregistrement libre est nécessaire pour l'établissement des impôts, pendant que cette maxime est regardée par la Nation comme son unique ressource depuis qu'elle n'a plus de représentans, & que les Rois eux-mêmes sont convenus en mille occasions du principe, il s'impose cependant tous les ans de nouvelles sommes sur le peuple sans enregistrement, & par des actes d'autorité arbitraire, tels que le brevet de la taille, les commissions, & l'opération du département.

[123] S'il faut donner à VOTRE MAJESTÉ une idée des abus qui peuvent résulter de cette forme arbitraire d'imposition, il est un fait récent & notoire que nous pouvons choisir pour exemple. Depuis 1771, on a imposé, comme accessoire de la taille, les sommes qu'on a crues nécessaires tant pour le remboursement des offices de Magistrature qu'on vouloit supprimer, que pour le paiement des gages des Officiers par qui on vouloit faire tenir les nouveaux Tribunaux : aujourd'hui la Magistrature est rétablie, & les nouveaux Tribunaux sont détruits, cependant l'imposition subsiste.

[124] On pense peut-être, SIRE, dans votre Conseil, que la suite des opérations faites pendant ces quatre années entraîne encore aujourd'hui une dépense trop considérable pour être prise sur les revenus ordinaires de VOTRE MAJESTÉ ; & à cet égard ces opérations

peuvent être comparées à une guerre qui a fait créer des impôts qu'on
laisse encore subsister quelque temps après la paix, pour payer les
dettes contractées.   Bientôt la cause cessera, & devons-nous espérer
qu'alors l'imposition sera aussi supprimée? Oui, SIRE, nous l'espérons,
nous ne nous permettons pas même d'en douter; mais nous devons
avouer que notre espérance n'est fondée que sur la confiance personnelle que toute la Nation a dans votre justice : car depuis long-temps
personne en France ne se flatte de voir jamais cesser un impôt qui
peut être renouvellé tous les ans par un acte secret d'autorité arbitraire, comme le brevet de la taille; & si VOTRE MAJESTÉ vouloit
se faire rendre compte de toutes les impositions générales ou particulieres qui se levent dans le Royaume, & qui ont été ainsi établies par
l'autorité arbitraire, Elle verroit peut-être que la plupart ont eu pour
motifs des besoins momentanées qui ont cessé, & que cependant on
a continué de lever l'impôt.

[125] A présent, SIRE, nous allons considérer les quatre opérations
l'une après l'autre sous le second aspect, c'est-à dire, comme répartition.
Commençons par le brevet de la taille, qui contient la premiere répar-
tition entre les Généralités.   Nous avons déja dit qu'il s'arrête au
Conseil de Finance.   Mais VOTRE MAJESTÉ sait qu'à l'exception du
Contrôleur-Général & d'un Intendant des Finances, aucun de ceux
qui assistent à ce Conseil ne peut être instruit de la situation des
Provinces, ni des besoins de l'Etat : c'est donc le Ministre seul qui fixe
tous les ans & la somme de l'imposition, & la premiere répartition.
Nous ignorons, SIRE, & toute la France ignore par quel principe ce
Ministre se détermine : nous sçavons seulement qu'avant la fixation du
brevet personne dans le Royaume n'a vu prendre aucune information
de l'état des Provinces.   Le brevet de la taille est donc réellement un
acte fait par l'autorité arbitraire, sans avoir pris des connoissances
suffisantes pour l'objet qui exigeroit le plus que tous les ordres de l'Etat
fussent consultés.

[126] Il en est à peu près de même des commissions, qui contiennent la seconde répartition, puisqu'elles se font au même Conseil de
Finance, par conséquent par la seule volonté du Ministre & de
l'Intendant des Finances.   Il y a cependant une différence en ce
qu'avant d'expédier les commissions, on demande l'avis des Intendans
de chaque Province.   C'est donc sur le rapport du seul Intendant qu'on
statue sur le sort de chaque Province.   Or cet Intendant lui-même
est obligé de s'en rapporter à des subalternes; car il ne peut pas connoître lui seul & par lui-même l'état de toute sa Généralité.

[127] D'ailleurs il faut observer que cet Intendant a souvent un intérêt contraire à celui de sa Province. En effet, on ne sauroit dissimuler que l'Intendant est un homme qui court la carriere de la fortune ; qu'il a sans cesse besoin des graces de la Cour ; qu'il ne peut les obtenir que par un Ministre, à qui souvent on est sûr de plairs en lui facilitant les moyens de tirer tout le parti possible des impôts. Il est vrai aussi que l'état précaire & incertain de ces Magistrats les oblige à de grands égards pour tous les gens de leur Province qui ont du crédit à la Cour.

[128] Nous sommes cependant bien éloignés, SIRE, d'élever des doutes sur la sincérité des avis que les Intendans envoient à votre Conseil ; nous ne doutons pas qu'ils n'aient le zele & le courage néces- saires pour défendre les intérêts de la Province qui leur est confiée ; nous croyons aussi que la plus exacte justice préside aux comptes qu'ils vous rendent des facultés réciproques de toutes les Elections de leur Généralité.

[129] Il faut cependant avouer qu'il n'est pas juste que ce soit par les seuls Intendans que la situation des peuples vous soit présentée, & qu'il est étonnant que ni les Corps ni les particuliers de chaque Province n'aient été admis à donner des mémoires en faveur du peuple avant la fixation du brevet & des commissions.

[130] Nous observons encore à VOTRE MAJESTÉ que ce brevet & ces commissions sont non-seulement des actes d'autorité arbitraire, mais aussi des actes clandestins dans leur exécution : car jamais ni le brevet ni les commissions ne sont imprimés, ni annoncés publiquement ; on envoie seulement les commissions à l'Election, qui doit s'y con- former lors du département, pour faire la troisieme répartition. La Province n'apprend donc son sort que dans le moment de ce départe- ment, c'est-à-dire, quand tout est irrévocablement terminé. Elle ne connoît jamais le sort des autres Provinces ; car nulle part dans le Royaume on ne voit le tableau général.

[131] Ainsi non-seulement les Provinces sont jugées sans être entendues, lorsqu'on arrête le brevet & les commissions, mais il leur est absolument & physiquement impossible de se pourvoir devant VOTRE MAJESTÉ elle-même par opposition. Si une Province, en effet, est imposée à des sommes excessives pour des besoins imaginaires, pour des dépenses insensées, elle n'en est avertie que dans l'instant où ces sommes vont être levées. Si cette même Province a été traitée injustement dans la répartition générale, soit parce que sa situation n'a

pas été assez bien connue, soit par l'effet d'une prédilection du Ministre pour d'autres Provinces, non-seulement il ne lui est pas permis de
se pourvoir contre l'injustice, mais il ne lui est pas même possible de
la connoître.

[132] Cette clandestinité, SIRE, est un systême très-réfléchi : car
il est nécessaire de rappeller à VOTRE MAJESTÉ qu'en l'année 1768
la Cour des Aides avoit ordonné à chaque Election *de lui envoyer tous*
les ans, dans la huitaine après le département, un état contenant la
somme totale des impositions à répartir sur les paroisses ; lequel état
devoit contenir le montant principal de la taille & de ses accessoires, de
la capitation, & des sommes qui s'imposent au marc la livre d'icelles,
& devoit donner une connoissance exacte des sommes réparties chaque
année sur les tailles. La Cour des Aides, SIRE, vouloit avoir ce tableau
général uniquement pour le présenter au Roi ; & il est bon d'observer
qu'il n'étoit pas possible qu'elle en fît d'autre usage ; car des loix
enregistrées & observées depuis plus d'un siecle, ne lui permettent pas
de faire aucun acte d'autorité sur ce qui se passe au département.

[133] Croirez-vous, SIRE, que l'Administration a eu le crédit de
faire casser un tel Arrêt ?   Il est difficile de deviner sous quel prétexte ;
car vraisemblablement on n'alla pas jusqu'à dire au feu Roi, en termes
exprès, qu'on vouloit empêcher que personne ne pût lui faire connoître
la situation de son peuple ; nous ne croyons pas non plus qu'on ait osé
avancer en sa présence la maxime barbare & trop souvent proférée,
que le peuple supporte toujours aisément son malheur, pourvu que le
Gouvernement ait l'art de le lui cacher.

[134] Permettez-nous, SIRE, une derniere réflexion sur l'arbitraire
de ces deux répartitions.   On conçoit aisément que des Ministres à
qui le despotisme étoit cher, aient voulu s'arroger à eux-mêmes, sous le
nom du Conseil de VOTRE MAJESTÉ, le droit d'imposer arbitrairement la somme qu'il leur plairoit sur le peuple ; mais on ne conçoit pas
quel intérêt ils ont pu avoir à priver le peuple du droit de se faire
entendre sur la répartition.   Aussi croyons-nous que ces Ministres si
impérieux n'auroient pas établi eux-mêmes la forme de répartition qui
existe aujourd'hui, si les réflexions que nous venons de faire à VOTRE
MAJESTÉ leur eussent été présentées dans toute leur simplicité.

[135] Mais il est un aveu que nous devons faire à VOTRE MAJESTÉ
dans ce jour où nous nous sommes prescrit le devoir de lui dire tout
espece de vérité sans aucune réticence ; c'est que nos prédécesseurs
ont eu vraisemblablement à se reprocher de n'avoir pas dévoilé autant

qu'ils l'auroient dû ce systême de clandestinité dans le temps qu'il fut introduit. Alors il n'y avoit déja plus d'Etats généraux ni provinciaux, ni même de représentans des Provinces chargés par le peuple de faire la répartition des impositions. Cette répartition se faisoit par des Juges subrogés à ces anciens représentans de la Nation, & il y avoit appel de ces Juges aux Cours des Aides. Ces Magistrats réclamerent ; mais leurs efforts se terminerent à demander l'exécution des loix qui étoient alors en vigueur, c'est-à-dire, à demander que la répartition fût faite par eux, au lieu de l'être par le Conseil. Ces réclamations ne parurent donc qu'une dispute de jurisdiction, une affaire personnelle à ces Cours, & peu intéressante pour l'Etat.

[136] Mais si ces mêmes Cours avoient revendiqué pour le peuple entier le droit naturel qu'ont tous les hommes d'être entendus avant d'être jugés, si elles avoient insisté sur la nécessité de connoître l'état des Provinces avant d'asseoir les impositions, si elles avoient sur-tout fait connoître aux Rois la différence du despotisme à la clandestinité, il ne nous paroît pas possible que le systême actuel eût été adopté ni par les Rois, ni par les principaux Ministres ; car ils n'y ont aucun intérêt ; & les Administrateurs subalternes sont les seuls qui en profitent, puisque ce sont eux qui, à la faveur des ténebres, peuvent se rendre indépendans de l'autorité supérieure.

[137] Nous allons passer à la troisieme répartition, celle qui se fait au département, entre les Paroisses ou Communautés de chaque Election. Autrefois cette répartition n'étoit pas arbitraire, elle se faisoit par les Elus, qui étoient alors des personnes réellement élues par la Province. On ne pouvoit cependant pas assimiler l'assemblée de ces Elus à une assemblée d'Etats provinciaux, & la différence est bien sensible. Des Etats provinciaux accordent ou refusent des dons gratuits ; des Etats provinciaux reglent toutes les parties de l'administration ; des Etats provinciaux sont les défenseurs de tous les droits de la Province, & ces droits sont ordinairement ceux dont la conservation étoit promise à chaque Province lors de sa réunion à la couronne. La fonction des Elus ne s'étendoit pas à tous ces objets : ils faisoient au département comme Asséeurs généraux de la Province, la répartition de l'imposition entre toutes les Paroisses & Communautés, comme dans chaque Paroisse ou Communauté il y a des Asséeurs particuliers qui répartissent entre tous les contribuables la somme imposée sur la Communauté.

[138] Il faut observer, pour prévenir toute équivoque, que ces anciens Elus avoient aussi la fonction quÆÆux qui portent aujourd'hui

le nom d'Elus ont conservée, celle de Juges dans le tribunal de l'Election : mais ce n'est pas sous cet aspect que nous les considérons ici, c'est comme Asséeurs généraux de la Province.

[139] Or cette fonction d'Asséeurs généraux a excité la jalousie de l'Administration, & voici les différens coups qui ont été portés successivement à la liberté nationale dans cette partie.

Premiérement, on a supprimé les vrais Elus, ceux qui étoient réellement choisis par le peuple, & on leur a substitué des Officiers nommés par le Gouvernement, & propriétaires d'offices vénaux.

Secondement, on a fait entrer l'Intendant de la Province au département, on lui a donné la présidence, & on a fini par ôter la voie délibérative aux Elus & à tous ceux qui ont droit d'assister au département. On a aussi défendu aux Cours supérieures de prendre connoissance de ce qui s'y passe ; en sorte qu'aujourd'hui la répartition qui se fait au département est l'ouvrage de seul Intendant, sans recours & sans appel.

[140] VOTRE MAJESTÉ remarquera aisément que la seconde opération rendoit la premiere inutile. En effet, on conçoit que le despotisme ait voulu faire supprimer les vrais Elus, tant qu'ils ont eu un pouvoir ; mais depuis que le Commissaire du Conseil[1] est devenu le maître absolu au département, & que personne n'y a plus que voix consultative, il n'y a aucune raison & même aucun prétexte pour ne pas rendre aux Provinces le droit d'y envoyer des représentans qui puissent défendre leurs intérêts.

[141] Troisiémement enfin, il fut fait en 1767 une derniere enterprise, dont il faut rendre compte à VOTRE MAJESTÉ. Dans cette année l'esprit de clandestinité prévalut à un tel point, qu'on voulut que la répartition qui se fait au département fût cachée à tous ceux qui ont droit d'y assister. Dans cette vue on imagina de faire deux brevets de taille, l'un qui fût porté au département, l'autre qui restât secret, & dont l'Intendant seul fît la répartition dans son cabinet. On ne mit dans le premier brevet que la taille principale, qui, dit-on, ne varie jamais, & sur laquelle par conséquent il est inutile de consulter la Province, & on réserva pour le brevet secret les accessoires, toutes les impositions nouvelles, tout ce qui est sujet à variation d'une année à l'autre ; on y fit entrer même toutes les diminutions sur les accessoires de la taille, accordées à des malheureux que des désastres

---

[1] *I. e.*, the Intendant.

ont mis dans l'impossibilité de pouvoir payer; diminutions qui leur sont dues, mais qui ne doivent être accordées qu'à ceux à qui on les doit réellement, si on rapporte en augmentation sur les uns ce qui a été diminué sur les autres. Voilà, SIRE, sur quoi on a voulu que l'Intendant pût statuer seul, sans la présence importune de ceux qui assistent au département.

[142] Votre Cour des Aides fit au feu Roi, dans l'année 1768, des Remontrances dans lesquelles le système de ces deux brevets fut développé; mais comme, depuis plus d'un siecle, la Cour des Aides ne prend aucune connoissance juridique de ce qui se fait au département, elle ne put que faire des Remontrances, & ne rendit aucun Arrêt. Ces Remontrances furent vraisemblablement renvoyées par le feu Roi aux Administrateurs, c'est-à-dire à ceux mêmes qui avoient voulu introduire cette nouvelle clandestinité dans la répartition.

[143] Mais à présent que nous espérons que VOTRE MAJESTÉ voudra bien nous entendre, nous attestons que de toutes les opérations faites par le despotisme, il n'en est aucune où ce funeste esprit de clandestinité se soit plus manifesté que dans ce système des deux brevets. En effet, puisque les Elus n'ont plus de voix délibérative au département, qu'ils n'y ont plus aucun pouvoir, nous ne concevons pas quelles intentions honnêtes on a pu avoir en écartant de pareils témoins.

[144] Il nous reste, SIRE, à vous parler de la quatrieme & derniere répartition, de celle qui se fait entre les contribuables par le rôle de chaque Paroisse. Quand les réglemens sur la taille ont été faits, le despotisme n'avoit pas encore fait tous les progrès qu'on a vus depuis, & dont nous parlerons à l'occasion de la capitation & du vingtième: ainsi on ne croyoit pas encore que l'autorité arbitraire pût statuer sur le sort de chaque particulier individuellement. Cette autorité ne s'est donc pas encore entiérement emparée de cette quatrieme répartition; cependant elle y a déja porté plusieurs atteintes. Nous en avons déja indiqué deux principales; l'une consiste dans l'usage où sont plusieurs Intendans de faire faire tous ou presque tous les rôles en présence de Commissaires, l'autre consiste dans les diminutions accordées par l'autorité du seul Intendant.

[145] Quant aux rôles par Commissaires, ou rôles d'office, il est certain que la présence du Commissaire dans une assemblée de gens de la campagne, est trop imposante pour laisser ni aux Collecteurs la liberté de faire leur rôle suivant *leur ame & conscience*, ni aux particuliers qui se croient lésés, celle de se pourvoir. Cet inconvénient

avoit été prévu par la Cour des Aides, lorsque ces rôles par Commissaires furent permis. Elle pensa qu'il ne faudroit en faire que rarement, & pour quelque cas extraordinaire, par exemple, quand on vient de faire un nouveau réglement sur la confection des rôles, & qu'on veut l'expliquer aux Habitans des Communautés. Cette Cour crut y pourvoir en défendant aux Commissaires de rien recevoir des contribuables, & pensa que ces commissions ne seroient pas fréquentes quand elles ne seroient pas utiles, & que les Intendans ne seroient pas engagés à les multiplier par le desir de donner des places à leurs protégés : cependant dans plusieurs Généralités tout se fait par Commissaires, & sûrement on les paie fort cher. On a donc rendu inutile la précaution prise par la Cour des Aides. Il n'y a cependant pas d'apparence que les Intendans fassent supporter ces frais par le Roi ; mais il est vraisemblable qu'on impose sur les Paroisses une somme destinée à cette dépense. C'est une concussion, puisque la Loi l'a défendu : c'est cependant ce que l'Intendant peut toujours faire impunément, puisque l'imposition absolue des Paroisses se fait au département, où il est le maître.

[146] Quant aux diminutions accordées aux particuliers qui ont fait des pertes, nous avons déja observé qu'on les regarde comme des graces provenues de la libéralité du Roi, & que c'est sous ce prétexte qu'on les fait annoncer par l'Intendant au département. Car si ce ne sont pas des graces, & que la somme dont un particulier est diminué se reporte sur le général des Habitans, ce doit être à ceux qui font les rôles à statuer sur les diminutions ; autrement une diminution seroit une gratification que l'Intendant accorderoit à ses favoris, en la faisant payer par le peuple. C'est encore ce que la Cour des Aides a prévu, & à quoi elle a voulu pourvoir, en ordonnant expressément que les modérations ou décharges accordées par l'Intendant, ne pourront en aucun cas être réimposées sur les redevables : mais les Intendans ont encore éludé cette disposition, en faisant cette réimposition au département, où ils sont les maîtres ; & nous avons déja observé qu'ils ont eu grand soin de faire mettre les diminutions dans le brevet secret, de peur que leur conduite à cet égard ne fût critiquée.

[147] Au fond, la diminution accordée à un particulier sur son imposition n'est point une grace ; c'est une justice, & souvent même une nécessité ; car il est nécessaire de faire une remise à celui que la grêle ou un incendie a mis dans l'impossibilité physique de payer. Ce ne seroit donc point de la puissance arbitraire des Intendans que dev-

roient dépendre les diminutions, & ils devroient encore moins faire une telle opération dans un acte secret & clandestin où toutes les injustices sont à couvert. La Cour des Aides a dévoilé & démontré clairement tous ces artifices, & les abus qui en doivent résulter, dans ses Remontrances de 1768, sur lesquelles nous avons déja observé qu'il n'a pas été rendu justice au peuple, parce que l'examen en fut renvoyé aux auteurs des abus qu'on dénonçoit, & les Intendans sont restés maîtres d'accorder des graces à leurs protégés aux dépens du peuple, sous le nom de diminution d'imposition.

[148] Il est encore d'autres injustices & d'autres infractions aux réglemens commises dans la confection des rôles de tailles ; il est peut-être aussi des changemens nécessaires à apporter aux loix existantes. On dit que la plupart de vos Administrateurs le pensent, & peut-être votre Cour des Aides pensera-t-elle de même. Ces changemens exigeront une longue discussion, qui doit être faite avec vos Ministres ; mais dès à présent nous devons demander à VOTRE MAJESTÉ elle-même d'obvier au moins à la clandestinité des trois premieres répartitions. Nous supplions VOTRE MAJESTÉ de commencer par se faire représenter les Remontrances faites par sa Cour des Aides en 1768. Elle y verra la discussion des deux brevets de taille ; Elle y verra aussi spécialement ce qui concerne les diminutions ; & nous espérons qu'après que ces éclaircissemens auront été mis sous les yeux de VOTRE MAJESTÉ, tout ce systême de clandestinité & d'iniquité ne subsistera plus.

[149] Mais ce n'est point à cela, SIRE, que se termineront nos demandes & nos espérances sous le regne de VOTRE MAJESTÉ ; nous la supplions aussi de rendre à ces Assemblées provinciales qu'on nomme départemens, la consistance & l'authenticité qu'elles n'ont plus depuis un siecle. Nous la supplions d'y faire porter toutes les impositions qui se levent chaque année sur la Province, sans aucune exception, c'est-à dire, non-seulement la taille & ses accessoires, mais la capitation, le vingtieme, ce qui s'impose pour la construction des presbyteres & autres dépenses locales, & même la milice & la corvée. Nous la supplions d'ordonner que toutes ces impositions soient annoncées publiquement, que les répartitions soient faites, que les rôles en soient publiés dans un temps qui permette à ceux qui se croient lésés, de recourir à votre justice.

[150] Enfin, SIRE, il nous semble qu'il est temps de rendre à vos Peuples le droit qu'ils avoient anciennement de nommer des repré-

sentans pour assister à cette Assemblée où il est statué sur le sort de la Province.   Nous avons déja fait connoître que la présence de ces Elus ne pourra point faire comparer l'Assemblée du département à des Etats provinciaux, ainsi le despotisme lui-même n'en pourra prendre aucun ombrage.   Elle ne portera non plus aucun préjudice aux Elus en titre d'office, qui ne perdront rien des fonctions actuellement attachées à leurs charges.[1]   Enfin cet établissement n'apportera aucun changement à cette Assemblée provinciale qu'on nomme le département : il peut donc être fait dès à présent, sans aucune dépense, sans aucune opération préalable.   Ce n'est point, SIRE, une innovation que nous proposons à VOTRE MAJESTÉ, puisque c'est l'ancienne constitution du Royaume que nous la supplions de faire revivre, en accordant à chaque Province ce qui est accordé par-tout à chaque particulier, le droit d'être entendue avant d'être jugée.

[151] On a supprimé les anciens Elus parce qu'ils avoient une puissance en qualité d'Asséeurs des impositions, & qu'il y avoit alors des Ministres qui vouloient détruire toute puissance qui n'étoit pas émanée d'eux ; mais aujourd'hui que c'est l'Intendant qui fait cette

---

[1] *Nota.*   Pour éclaircir la question & ne laisser aucun nuage, nous pensons qu'il ne faudroit rendre aux représentans qu'élira la Province, que la séance au département, & non la fonction de Juges au tribunal de l'Election ; en voici les raisons :

1°. Si on vouloit leur donner les fonctions de Juges, le Roi seroit obligé à rembourser les Elus en titre d'office ; au lieu qu'il ne leur sera rien dû quand on ne donnera aux vrais Elus que l'assistance au département, & qu'eux-mêmes Elus en titre d'office n'en seront point privés, & continueront d'y assister.

2°. Les Elus sont actuellement des Juges Royaux, mais Juges inférieurs, Juges à la charge de l'appel.   Ils ont des affaires contentieuses à juger, ce qui les oblige à être initiés dans la Jurisprudence & à la pratique, & les fonctions journalieres exigent d'eux de résider dans la ville où est le siege de leur Tribunal.   Il s'ensuit que si ceux qui seront choisis par la Province, devoient tenir le tribunal de l'Election, le choix ne pourroit être fait qu'entre ceux qui habitent la ville, & à qui il convient de se livrer aux fonctions de Juges, & de siéger dans un Tribunal qui n'est pas souverain.

Or quand une Province aura à choisir des représentans pour défendre ses intérêts, soit au département, soit par des mémoires addressés au Roi, il faut que ce choix important puisse tomber sur tous les habitans de la Province sans exception, il faut qu'on puisse toujours choisir le plus digne.   Cependant il y a tel homme qui se croira honoré d'être le défenseur des droits de sa Province, qui s'assujettira volontiers à aller tous les ans, dans le temps du département, dans la ville où il se tient ; mais il ne voudra ni résider dans cette petite ville, ni consacrer sa vie entiere au jugement des procès particuliers.   Il faut donc que les représentans de la Province assistans au département, soient des personnes différentes des Juges tenant le Tribunal de l'Election.

[The editor adds an unimportant note of his own, which we omit.]

assiette de sa seule autorité, les prétextes cessent; & si jusqu'à présent
les Rois n'ont pas rendu cette justice à la Nation, c'est sans doute
parce qu'elle ne leur a jamais été demandée. Nous avons déja avoué
que dans tous les temps les Magistrats ont trop peu insisté sur le
rétablissement de ce qui est étranger à leur jurisdiction ; voilà pourquoi,
dans le temps qu'on donna aux Intendans voix prépondérante aux
départemens, les Cours ne firent pas observer que puisque cet acte de
despotisme étoit fait, il falloit au moins rendre aux Provinces le droit
de choisir elles-mêmes leurs Elus. Peut-être demandera-t-on de quelle
utilité sera à la Nation la simple assistance de ces représentans qui
n'auront aucun pouvoir réel : mais ignore-t-on à combien d'abus la
seule présence d'un homme considéré peut mettre obstacle? Les
Administrateurs du dernier regne ne l'ignoroient certainement pas,
puisque par leur système des deux brevets ils ont voulu dérober leurs
opérations à la connoissance même des Elus en titre d'office, qui
certainement ne leur en imposoient pas autant que des gens choisis
par la Province.

[152] D'ailleurs il n'est pas vraisemblable qu'on refuse à de véritables Elus le droit de recourir à VOTRE MAJESTÉ quand leurs
représentations n'auront pas été écoutées du département, puisqu'ils y
seront sans pouvoir. Ils ne pourront jamais retarder l'exécution ; mais
ils jouiront du droit naturel qu'ont tous vos Sujets, & il leur sera permis
d'en faire usage pour le bien de la Province. Nous devons aussi
prévenir VOTRE MAJESTÉ que si ces Elus choisis par la Province
font rarement des représentations contre la conduite des Intendans,
ou même si celles qu'ils feront se trouvent quelquefois mal fondées, il
ne faudra pas en conclure que leur existence soit inutile ; car le vrai
bien qu'ils auront fait sera le mal que leur présence aura empêché.

[153] Nous pensons donc, SIRE, que si VOTRE MAJESTÉ veut
bien rendre aux Provinces ces antiques représentans, & qu'il ne soit
fait par leur ministere aucune plainte bien fondée de l'administration,
ce sera une premiere preuve de l'utilité de cet établissement ; & que
si, malgré la rareté ou le peu de succès de leurs plaintes, l'administration fait encore des efforts & cherche des prétextes pour se débarrasser
de cette censure incommode, ce sera le complément de cette preuve.

[154] Enfin quand nous avons représenté les inconvéniens des deux
premieres répartitions qui se font arbitrairement dans votre Conseil,
nous ne vous avons indiqué aucun moyen d'y remédier, parce que
jusqu'à présent il n'y a personne dans les Provinces qui en connoisse

assez bien la situation pour la faire connoître à votre Conseil.   Mais
quand il y aura dans le ressort de chaque Election, des citoyens qui
auront assisté avec mission dans un département, où la répartition de
tout ce qui se leve sur la Province aura été faite en leur présence, ils
seront en état de donner des mémoires instructifs, & nous ne doutons
pas que VOTRE MAJESTÉ ne leur permette & ne leur ordonne même
de faire passer de tels mémoires aux Ministres de la Finance, & à tous
ceux qui composent le Conseil : alors les Intendans auront des contradicteurs, & le peuple des défenseurs.

[155] Et nous croyons, SIRE, que les Intendans qui régissent à
présent vos Provinces, ne craindront point d'être exposés à cette
contradiction.   Nous croyons qu'eux & les Ministres qui composent
actuellement votre Conseil, desireront ardemment d'être éclairés &
guidés dans une opération aussi importante que la répartition des
impôts, qui cependant jusqu'à présent ne se pouvoit faire qu'au hasard.

[156] Les deux autres impositions dont nous allons entretenir
VOTRE MAJESTÉ, sont établies sur des principes différens de ceux
de la taille.   Nous avons déja observé que la taille est le plus ancien
des impôts directs, & que pendant long-temps ce fut le seul.   Elle fut
créée par Charles VII, pour subvenir à la solde des troupes réglées
qui, vers ce siecle, furent établies dans presque toute l'Europe.   Cependant la Noblesse étoit toujours assujettie au service militaire de
fief ; il étoit donc juste qu'elle fût exempte de la taille.

[157] Mais dans les siecles suivans le service militaire fut tout-à-
fait oublié, & la Noblesse ne servit plus l'Etat que dans des troupes
enrégimentées & soudoyées.   Dans le même temps on commença à
moins respecter les privileges de la Noblesse, parce qu'étant accordés
à des charges vénales, ils devinrent le partage de la richesse.   Alors
les Administrateurs des finances conçurent le projet de les enfreindre ;
mais ce fut d'abord indirectement, & la plus forte de ces infractions
fut d'imposer les roturiers pour les biens qu'ils tenoient à ferme des
Nobles ou autres exempts.   Enfin Louis XIV, dans ses dernieres
guerres, créa deux impôts auxquels les Nobles & les privilégiés furent
assujettis directement en leur nom ; ce fut d'abord la capitation, &
ensuite le dixieme.

[158] Nous nous étendrons peu sur la capitation ; nous croyons que
ce que nous aurions à en dire seroit superflu.   En effet, cette imposition est trop vicieuse, sous quelque aspect qu'on la considere, pour que
les Ministres de VOTRE MAJESTÉ n'en soient pas convaincus.   Elle

a été établie dans des temps malheureux où l'on saisissoit sans examen toutes les ressources qui se présentoient. En 1713, lors de la paix faite après une guerre malheureuse, Louis XIV ne crut pas pouvoir remplir l'engagement qu'il avoit pris avec ses peuples de la supprimer, & cette imposition a eu depuis le même sort que beaucoup d'autres ; on a mieux aimé conserver un impôt vicieux & enregistré, que d'en substituer un plus raisonnable, mais qu'il auroit fallu soumettre à la critique de l'enregistrement.

[159] D'ailleurs, un intérêt encore plus puissant a rendu cette imposition plus précieuse que toutes les autres aux yeux de quelques Administrateurs ; c'est l'arbitraire qui y regne. Il est tel, que les excédens de capitation, dont la somme est incertaine & variable, son entiérement à la disposition des Administrateurs ; & c'est cette somme qui est réservée depuis long- temps pour les dépenses favorites & secretes.

[160] VOTRE MAJESTÉ concevra à présent pourquoi on a fermé les yeux sur les inconvéniens évidens de la capitation. Peut-être dira-t-on aujourd'hui à VOTRE MAJESTÉ que ces excédens de capitation sont nécessaires, parce que ce sont les seuls fonds avec lesquels on puisse faire des dépenses utiles pour les Provinces. Si cela est, il faudroit que VOTRE MAJESTÉ s'informât des moyens qu'on employoit avant que la capitation fût connue en France.

[161] Au fond, SIRE, non-seulement la capitation de vos Sujets est fixée à la volonté d'un seul homme, non seulement les rôles en sont secrets, mais ceux qui sont chargés de cette répartition, & qui voudroient ne la pas faire arbitrairement, n'ont aucune regle qui puisse les guider.

[162] Autrefois un Gentilhomme de chaque Généralité devoit être associé à l'Intendant pour faire les rôles de la Noblesse : cette formalité est tombée en désuétude, & il faut y avoir peu de regret ; car ce Gentilhomme n'étoit point choisi par la Province ; il étoit nommé par le Gouvernement, & toujours sur la présentation de l'Intendant : ainsi ce n'étoit qu'un témoin oisif de ses opérations.

[163] Il est cependant quelques ordres de citoyens dont la capitation n'est point arbitraire. Par exemple, la capitation des taillables est devenue un accessoire de la taille. On permet aussi, dans quelques grandes villes, aux Communautés d'artisans de répartir cette imposition sur elles mêmes, & on a remédié par ce moyen à l'arbitraire pour la répartition entre ces contribuables. Mais d'après quelle loi, d'après

quelle regle la somme générale doit-elle être imposée sur chaque corps d'artisans? C'est ce que nous ignorons, & ce qui vraisemblablement dépend tout-à-fait de la volonté des Administrateurs.

[164] Il est aussi d'autres Sujets de VOTRE MAJESTÉ dont la capitation est fixée ; ce sont ceux qui la paient par retenue sur les gages de leurs offices. Mais si celle-là n'est pas arbitraire, elle est injuste. Elle ne le seroit pas, si la capitation étoit un impôt réel qui affectât chacun des biens des contribuables. Elle est injuste, puisque c'est un impôt personnel qu'on devroit proportionner à toutes les facultés de ceux qui sont imposés. Or il y a souvent une très-grande différence de fortune entre ceux qui possedent une charge semblable ; cependant ils paient la même capitation.

[165] Pour celle qui ne se leve ni par retenue des gages, ni par contribution des Corps & Communautés, ni comme accessoire de la taille, c'est un impôt absolument arbitraire, c'est un asservissement honteux de tous les citoyens aux Administrateurs. Si nous voulions faire connoître à VOTRE MAJESTÉ tous les abus qui en ont résulté, nous craindrions d'être soupçonnés d'exagération. Par exemple, seroit-on cru de VOTRE MAJESTÉ, si on lui alléguoit qu'on a vu des Intendans se glorifier d'avoir menacé des habitans de leur Généralité de les doubler à la capitation, s'ils ne se prêtoient à des arrangemens que sans doute ces Administrateurs croyoient utiles à la Province, mais auxquels ils n'avoient pas le droit de forcer directement des citoyens?

[166] Il nous est impossible, SIRE, de vous donner la preuve de tous les faits de ce genre, puisqu'un des vices principaux de cette imposition est la clandestinité. Il est cependant un abus qui se commet tous les ans, & qui est d'un genre si grave, que nous nous croyons obligés d'en avertir VOTRE MAJESTÉ, quoique nous ne puissions pas le prouver ; mais il sera aisé à VOTRE MAJESTÉ de le vérifier.

[167] Daignez, SIRE, faire constater s'il est vrai que dans beaucoup de Villes on impose chaque année tous les Officiers de Justice à une capitation plus forte que celle qu'on peut leur faire payer, ce qui les force à venir demander une grace à l'Intendant, & les met aussi dans la dépendance absolue de ce Magistrat. Et sur qui s'exerce cette tyrannie? Sur les Juges qui ont à statuer sur le sort des hommes, par conséquent sur l'ordre de citoyens auquel il seroit le plus nécessaire de conserver sa liberté & son indépendance. Voilà, SIRE, à quoi servent les impositions arbitraires & clandestines, & jusqu'où peuvent se porter des despotes qui sont sûrs de n'être ni surveillés ni critiqués. En effet,

sans diminuer le pouvoir des Intendans, si on les obligeoit seulement à publier les rôles de la capitation, il ne seroit pas possible qu'ils y laissassent voir une quote sur chaque juge qui seroit diminuée tous les ans, excepté dans l'année où ce Juge leur auroit déplu.

[168] Nous ne vous disons rien de plus, SIRE, sur la capitation ; nous sommes seulement obligés de revendiquer notre jurisdiction sur cet objet. La capitation est un impôt ; par conséquent votre Cour des Aides devroit en connoître, & elle ne peut se dispenser de réclamer son droit dans toutes les occasions, parce qu'elle ne doit jamais renoncer volontairement à aucune portion de la jurisdiction qui lui a été donnée pour le bien du peuple, & pour le maintien de la justice.

[169] Mais ce que nous demandons bien plus vivement à VOTRE MAJESTÉ, c'est de révoquer tout-à-fait la capitation, qui est une source intarissable d'injustices, ou au moins d'en changer entiérement la nature ; & nous rendons, SIRE, aux Magistrats Municipaux de Paris & aux Intendans de Provinces la justice de croire qu'ils desirent ardemment d'être déchargés de cette répartition fantastique, & aussi désagréable pour des Magistrats qui aiment la regle, qu'elle est chere à ceux qui veulent en abuser.

[170] Il est temps, SIRE, de parler à VOTRE MAJESTÉ du vingtieme, cet impôt qui est aujourd'hui l'objet des plus fortes réclamations du peuple, parce qu'il avoit été regardé comme une ressource extraordinaire réservée pour les temps malheureux, jusqu'au moment où l'on a profité de l'absence de la Magistrature pour en faire un impôt perpétuel. Nous serions exposés, SIRE, aux reproches les plus justes de toute la Nation, si nous ne faisions les plus grands efforts pour obtenir de VOTRE MAJESTÉ d'en fixer la durée. S'il est vrai que la prolongation de cette imposition pendant la paix fût nécessaire pour payer les dettes de la guerre, falloit-il ôter au peuple l'espérance d'en voir le terme ? Et quelle nécessité d'accabler la Nation par cette perspective de perpétuité ?

[171] Depuis quarante ans cette imposition a été renouvellée presque sans discontinuation ; & VOTRE MAJESTÉ sçait combien peu de résistance a éprouvé chacun de ces renouvellemens. C'étoit seulement une occasion de mettre sous les yeux du Roi la malheureuse situation de son peuple ; auroit-on dû priver de cette consolation un peuple si réellement malheureux ? Mais nous ne craignons pas, SIRE, que sous votre regne, des représentations faites pour le peuple ne soient qu'une simple consolation.

4

[172] Nous supplions VOTRE MAJESTÉ de se rappeller ce qui vient de lui être dit de la capitation. Si après la guerre de 1701 le terme de cette imposition eût été fixé, & qu'on se fût contenté de la prolonger par des renouvellemens successifs, peut-être se seroit-il trouvé un moment favorable où les Cours en auroient fait reconnoître les abus, & au moins les Administrateurs ne se seroient pas portés à tant d'excès, s'ils avoient eu à craindre qu'à chaque renouvellement leur conduite fût critiquée.

[173] C'est ce qui étoit arrivé, SIRE, à l'occasion du vingtieme, avant qu'il fût rendu perpétuel. On avoit reconnu en 1763 que cet impôt, déja si onéreux par lui-même, l'étoit devenu encore davantage par l'inquisition qu'on exerçoit pour le lever; & dans le temps d'un renouvellement le Parlement de Paris y avoit remédié par une clause qui ne fut point désapprouvée par le Roi, & qui fut imitée par toutes les autres Cours. L'objet du Parlement étoit de mettre un terme aux inquisitions, & pour cela on défendit d'augmenter les quotes de l'année 1763. Mais cette clause, qui remédioit aux abus, déplut à ceux qui vouloient les conserver; aussi quand l'impôt a été rétabli en notre absence, la clause n'a été mise ni dans la loi même, ni dans l'enregistrement fait par ceux qui occupoient nos places.

[174] Le peuple n'a pas tardé à ressentir les cruels effets de cet impôt rétabli sans la clause de 1763; car dans l'instant même presque tous les sujets de VOTRE MAJESTÉ ont vu augmenter considérablement leurs quotes, sans qu'il leur fût donné aucune raison de cette augmentation subite, & on a annoncé dans tout le Royaume de nouvelles recherches, & une rigueur dont il n'y avoit pas encore eu d'exemples; comme si les Administrateurs avoient voulu se venger de la contrainte où ils avoient été depuis 1763 jusqu'en 1771; oserons-nous dire, SIRE? comme s'ils avoient voulu faire sentir au peuple tout ce qu'il avoit perdu en perdant ses anciens Magistrats.

[175] Les choses en sont venues au point qu'aujourd'hui la perpétuité même de l'impôt est peut-être moins accablante pour le peuple, que le despotisme qu'il entraîne. Voilà, SIRE, l'objet duquel il est nécessaire que VOTRE MAJESTÉ daigne s'occuper, & nous croyons qu'il n'en est aucun qui soit plus digne de son attention : car c'est la nature même des impositions qu'il faut examiner; ce sont les principes fondamentaux de cette partie de l'administration que nous allons tâcher d'éclaircir.

[176] En effet, si nous ne demandions à VOTRE MAJESTÉ que

de fixer la durée du vingtieme, ce seroit uniquement votre amour pour
vos peuples que nous aurions à invoquer ; mais pour faire connoître la
nécessité de rétablir la clause de 1763, ou d'y substituer quelque autre
disposition équivalente, il faut donner à VOTRE MAJESTÉ une
notion simple & juste de cet impôt, qui a été connu en France au
commencement de ce siecle, sous le nom de dixieme, & depuis sous
celui de vingtieme, de sou pour livre du dixieme, &c. & pour rendre
cette définition claire & sensible, il faut remonter au principe, il faut
déterminer la vraie nature des impôts réels.

[177] On nomme, SIRE, impôt réel celui qui se leve, non sur la
personne des contribuables, mais sur leurs biens ; en sorte que c'est
chaque bien, chaque fonds de terre qui est imposé proportionnellement
à son produit. Toutes les fois qu'on veut établir un tel impôt, il semble
qu'on doit commencer par déterminer la somme totale que le Roi veut
percevoir sur son peuple, & chercher ensuite la forme de répartition
& de perception la moins dispendieuse pour le Roi, & qui livre le moins
le peuple au pouvoir arbitraire, & aux vexations qui en sont la suite
nécessaire.

[178] Ce n'est point là ce qu'on a fait dans l'imposition du dixieme
& des vingtiemes ; on a voulu que chaque particulier portât au trésor
Royal une certaine portion de son revenu ; & pour faire exécuter cette
loi, on a établi, sur-tout dans les derniers temps, une régie qui a le
double défaut de coûter au Roi des frais considérables, & de soumettre
le peuple au pouvoir arbitraire. Sur cela nous représentons à VOTRE
MAJESTÉ, premiérement, qu'une imposition réelle dont la somme
totale n'est pas fixée, est une injustice commise envers la nation ;
secondement, que ce genre d'imposition est vicieux en lui-même, parce
qu'il entraîne nécessairement & les frais & l'arbitraire.

[179] Nous osons dire à VOTRE MAJESTÉ qu'un tel impôt est
une injustice commise envers la Nation, d'après le grand principe qu'un
Roi ne doit jamais imposer sur ses sujets ni plus ni moins que ce
qu'exigent les besoins de l'Etat. En effet, si un impôt tel que le
dixieme ou les vingtiemes, produit moins qu'il ne faut pour le besoin
de l'Etat, il faut chercher d'autres ressources, & on en trouve qui sont
moins onéreuses au peuple qu'un impôt direct. Si au contraire le
dixieme ou vingtieme produit plus qu'il n'est nécessaire, vous ne pouvez
pas douter, SIRE, que ce surplus ne soit employé à des dépenses pour
lesquelles il n'auroit pas été juste de mettre un nouvel impôt sur vos
peuples.

[180] Nous avons dit aussi que ce genre d'imposition entraîne nécessairement les frais & l'arbitraire. Pour rendre cette vérité sensible, il faut faire connoître à VOTRE MAJESTÉ les différentes formes de répartitions employées dans les différentes Provinces pour les impositions dont la somme est fixée. Nous en examinerons le plus sommairement qu'il sera possible les avantages & les inconvéniens réciproques, & il sera aisé de se convaincre que l'imposition du vingtieme réunit tous les inconvéniens ; qu'elle occasionne plus de frais, plus de despotisme & plus d'injustices de tous les genres qu'aucune espece de répartition, & que la clause de 1763 étoit un remede nécessaire à apporter à des abus qui ne pouvoient plus être supportés.

[181] Il est des pays où, quand la somme de l'imposition est déterminée, on en laisse faire chaque année la répartition par les contribuables eux-mêmes. Il en est d'autres où l'on fait un cadastre, c'est-à-dire, une évaluation fixe de tous les biens des contribuables, d'après laquelle les sommes imposées chaque année se trouvent réparties par une simple opération d'arithmétique, & sans que personne s'en mêle. Il y a des raisons de préférence pour & contre ces deux systêmes de répartition.

[182] On peut dire en faveur de la répartition annuelle par les contribuables, qu'elle n'entraîne aucuns frais, & ne soumet point le peuple au despotisme des Préposés envoyés par le Gouvernement. On peut dire aussi que les contribuables sont les seuls qui puissent faire la répartition avec justice, parce qu'il n'est point de cultivateur qui ne connoisse très-bien la valeur de la terre de son voisin, & qu'il est impossible qu'un étranger acquiere jamais cette connoissance. Aussi soutient-on que tous les cadastres sont injustes, qu'on en convient dans les Provinces cadastrées, & que cette injustice provient, ou de ce que le cadastre a été fait originairement par des gens incapables de le bien faire, parce qu'ils étoient étrangers à la paroisse, ou de ce que depuis que le cadastre est fait, il est survenu des variations dans la valeur des biens, ce qui peut-arriver & arrive très-souvent par mille causes différentes.

[183] Les partisans du cadastre disent que dans les Provinces cadastrées il n'y a non plus ni frais de répartition, ni arbitraire. Il est vrai que dans le temps de la confection du cadastre il y a des frais énormes, & une autorité despotique dans la personne des Commissaires au cadastre qui ont à statuer sur le sort de tous les particuliers ; mais ce temps malheureux une fois passé, la tranquillité du peuple est assurée

pour toujours. En effet, dans les pays de cadastres, non-seulement il n'y a ni frais ni arbitraire, mais il n'y a point non plus de procès ; au-lieu que la répartition annuelle entre les contribuables est une source intarissable de divisions, de haines & de contestations.

[184] Quant à l'objection que les contribuables ont plus de con-noissances de leurs facultés réciproques que ne peut en avoir un Com-missaire étranger, on répond qu'ils ont aussi des intérêts personnels & des passions qui les empêchent d'opérer avec justice. Or on prétend avoir remédié à tout à-la-fois, en faisant faire le cadastre par un Com-missaire. Cet homme étranger à la paroisse ne doit avoir d'autre intérêt que celui de la justice ; & si les connoissances du local lui manquent, il y supplée en écoutant contradictoirement les contribua-bles, dont l'universalité a toujours intérêt à contredire chaque déclara-tion particuliere.

[185] On dit aussi en faveur du cadastre, & contre la répartition annuelle par les contribuables, que cette connoissance de leurs facultés réciproques qu'ont les contribuables, ne peut servir que pour la réparti-tion entre les habitans d'une même Communauté ; mais il y a aussi des répartitions à faire entre les Communautés de chaque Province, & entre toutes les Provinces du Royaume, & on soutient que celles-là ne peuvent être faites avec justice que par un cadastre, & par des Commissaires envoyés par le Gouvernement.

[186] Il est bon de faire observer à VOTRE MAJESTÉ que cette derniere objection contre la répartition par les contribuables, n'a lieu que parce qu'on ne veut pas que les Communautés & les Provinces aient des représentans : car si elles en avoient, rien n'empêcheroit que toutes les Communautés ne s'assemblassent par ces représentans, & ne répartissent elles-mêmes sur elles-mêmes la somme imposée sur la Province, comme les habitans d'une Communauté peuvent répartir eux-mêmes & sur eux-mêmes la somme imposée sur la Communauté. Peut-être réuniroit-on tous les avantages en faisant faire un cadastre par les contribuables eux-mêmes, & non par des Commissaires : dès qu'il seroit fait, il n'y auroit plus jamais ni frais, ni arbitraire, ni procès ; & comme il auroit été fait par ceux qui connoissent par eux-mêmes la valeur des biens, & entre qui l'intérêt commun est que chacun soit imposé avec justice, il y a lieu de croire que cette répartition seroit plus juste que toute autre.

[187] Ce genre de cadastre auroit encore un avantage, c'est que quand il surviendroit une variation dans la valeur des biens, qui rendroit

nécessaire une réformation de cadastre, la Communauté elle-même verroit cette nécessité, & pourroit procéder à cette réformation, sans attendre qu'elle fût ordonnée par le Gouvernement.

[188] Enfin en faisant faire ainsi le cadastre, on y gagne tous les frais de la confection, qui sont énormes, & qui le plus souvent empêchent d'employer cette forme de répartition. En effet, ces frais sont premiérement ceux du séjour d'un Commissaire étranger successivement dans tous les villages d'une Province, & ceux-là n'auroient pas lieu. Secondement ceux de l'arpentage ; & nous croyons aussi qu'on pourroit s'en passer ; car nous concevons que l'arpentage est nécessaire à un Commissaire étranger, qui, ne connoissant pas par lui-même la valeur des terres, ne peut que s'informer en général de celles qui sont bonnes, mauvaises ou médiocres, & imposer chaque fonds à raison du nombre d'arpens qu'il contient, & qu'il croit être de bonne, mauvaise ou médiocre qualité : mais les gens du pays, qui ont la science directe de la valeur de chaque piece de terre, n'ont pas besoin de ce travail, & peuvent faire leur cadastre sans arpentage préalable.

[189] Disons plus : le cadastre se fera de lui-même, sans que le Gouvernement l'ordonne, pourvu que l'impôt réparti sur les contribuables soit un impôt réel, un impôt dont chaque quote s'applique à chaque piece de terre, & que chacune de ces pieces de terre soit exactement désignée. En effet, quand il y aura eu une fois un rôle bien fait dans une Paroisse, tous les fonds s'y trouveront évalués. On sçaura que le rôle de cette année étoit bien fait, parce qu'une Communauté d'Habitans est un public, & qu'aucun ne se refuse à une vérité évidente. Ce rôle reconnu pour bon sera donc le cadastre.

[190] Si jusqu'à présent l'impôt de la taille qui se répartit par les contribuables, n'a point produit de cadastre entre les taillables, malgré les rôles qui se font tous les ans, c'est que la taille n'est point un impôt réel, que les quotes ne s'appliquent point à chaque bien, qu'on impose chaque contribuable pour la totalité des biens qu'il possede, ce qui change d'une année à l'autre ; qu'on fait aussi entrer dans le motif de la quote le commerce & l'industrie ; qu'il y a des privileges personnels ; en sorte que le bien pour lequel on a imposé une année le roturier taillable, est possédé une autre année par un exempt : ainsi les rôles d'une année sont inutiles pour les années suivantes.

[191] Voilà, SIRE, à peu près ce qu'il y a à dire sur les deux formes usitées pour la répartition d'une imposition dont la somme est fixée. Il peut y avoir sur cela différentes opinions, entre lesquelles

nous ne prendrons aucun parti, car nous ne voulons présenter à VOTRE MAJESTÉ sur cet objet que des vérités incontestables. Or la vérité incontestable est que l'impôt du dixieme ou des vingtiemes, l'impôt où l'on n'a point une somme à répartir, mais où l'on exige de tous les particuliers une certaine portion du produit de leurs biens, a par sa nature plus d'inconvéniens, entraîne plus de frais, occasionne plus d'injustices qu'aucune des différentes répartitions dont nous venons de donner le tableau. Voilà ce qu'il faut démontrer à VOTRE MAJESTÉ, & nous lui ferons connoître ensuite qu'à ces vices dérivans de la nature de l'imposition, on a ajouté en France une clandestinité inutile.

[192] Nous avons observé que dans les répartitions entre les contribuables il n'y a point de frais & point d'arbitraire, mais qu'il y a des procès continuels ; & que dans le cadastre il n'y a ni frais, ni arbitraire, ni procès, lorsque le cadastre est fait ; mais que la confection exige de grands frais, & que l'autorité arbitraire y préside, à moins qu'on ne fasse faire le cadastre par les contribuables eux-mêmes.

[193] Dans l'impôt du vingtieme, si on veut le percevoir avec exactitude, on a tous les ans & continuellement les mêmes frais de régie qui sont nécessaires une fois pour la confection d'un cadastre : il faut aussi que le Peuple soit soumis à perpétuité à ce pouvoir arbitraire auquel il est soumis pour un temps pendant la confection du cadastre. Enfin il y a continuellement des procès, comme dans les pays où la répartition se fait tous les ans par les contribuables, & n'a pas encore produit une évaluation certaine.

[194] Tous ces inconvéniens de l'imposition du vingtieme ont une cause commune ; c'est que dans le système de cet impôt le Roi a en son nom un procès continuel avec chaque particulier de son Royaume, & que ce procès dépend de l'évaluation de chaque piece de terre.

[195] Il faudroit donc, pour que l'impôt fût bien perçu, qu'il y eût dans chaque lieu un homme du Roi chargé de stipuler ses intérêts. Il faudroit donc couvrir la France entiere d'une armée de Commis ; & si jusqu'à présent le nombre de ces Commis n'est pas si considérable, c'est que l'impôt n'est pas encore perçu avec toute la rigueur dont il est susceptible, & à laquelle il est certain qu'on le portera un jour, si VOTRE MAJESTÉ n'y met un frein en corrigeant la loi. Aussi il est certain que cette rigueur, & les frais qu'elle entraîne, ont continuellement augmenté depuis que cet impôt existe, excepté pendant le temps qu'a duré la clause de 1763. Outre ces frais perpetuels, nous disons

qu'il y a aussi un arbitraire perpétuel ; car il n'est pas possible que la pouvoir de ces Préposés ne soit pas arbitraire. Ils ont, dit-on, l'Intendant pour Juge ; mais est-il possible que l'Intendant prononce en connoissance de cause sur autant de procès qu'il y a de fonds de biens dans sa Généralité ? Et comment tous ces procès pourroient-ils être instruits ? Il faut donc absolument qu'il s'en rapporte au Préposé. Ce Préposé est donc le vrai Juge des Peuples.

[196] Or peut-on douter, SIRE, que le Gouvernement ne donne à chacun de ces Préposés une gratification lorsqu'il a fait augmenter la totalité des quotes du vingtieme dans son département ? En effet, sans cet encouragement, quel seroit l'homme qui iroit s'exposer gratuitement à la haine de tout un pays ? Cependant il s'ensuit que non-seulement un pouvoir arbitraire préside à cette imposition, mais que celui à qui ce pouvoir est confié, a intérêt de vexer le Peuple : & néanmoins il faut avouer que cet encouragement à la vexation n'est pas encore suffisant pour l'intérêt de la Finance ; car il y a toujours des contribuables qui sçavent donner au Préposé des motifs encore plus puissans pour les ménager. Et daignez, SIRE, considérer à cette occasion, que tel est le double inconvénient des impositions arbitraires ; on y vexe le foible sous prétexte de l'intérêt du Roi, & on y favorise le puissant ou l'intrigant contre l'intérêt du Roi.

[197] Enfin nous disons aussi que le vingtieme doit être, comme la taille, une source intarissable de procès. Il est évident que cela doit arriver jusqu'à ce que le procès général du Roi avec tous les particuliers de son Royaume soit irrévocablement terminé, c'est-à-dire, qu'on ait fait un cadastre par le moyen des rôles du vingtieme. Or nous croyons, SIRE, qu'il ne se fera jamais par cette voie, ou que ce ne sera que très-lentement & très-imparfaitement : en voici la raison, que VOTRE MAJESTÉ trouvera sensible.

[198] Il est reconnu qu'il n'y a que les Habitans d'un pays qui connoissent réciproquement la valeur de leurs biens : le cadastre ne peut donc être bien fait que quand il l'est par eux, ou au moins avec eux. Aussi avons-nous indiqué comme la meilleure méthode pour faire faire un cadastre, celle d'en charger les Communautés elles-mêmes. Cependant nous avons aussi observé que quand on envoie un Commissaire au cadastre, ce Commissaire peut s'aider des lumieres des Habitans, parce que l'intérêt général du pays est que l'opération soit bien faite, & que la déclaration de chaque particulier ait pour contradicteur la Communauté entière. Mais un Préposé au vingtieme ne

peut s'aider des lumieres de personne, parce que personne n'a intérêt
à l'éclairer, & qu'au contraire l'intérêt général est de tromper cet
homme, qui est l'ennemi commun de tout le pays.

[199] Nous avons aussi annoncé à VOTRE MAJESTÉ qu'à ces
inconvéniens qui dérivent de la nature de l'imposition d'un dixieme
ou d'un vingtieme, on a joint sans nécessité ceux de la candestinité :
on y trouve même les deux genres de clandestinité que nous avons
définis, celle des opérations, & celle des personnes.

Clandestinité d' Opérations.

[200] Nous avons déja exposé à VOTRE MAJESTÉ avec quelle
ténacité le Ministere a empêché que les rôles du vingtieme ne fussent
déposés ; ce qui étoit avouer qu'on vouloit qu'il y eût impunité toutes
les fois qu'il auroit été accordé des faveurs ou exercé des déprédations.

Clandestinité de Personnes.

[201] Il faut qu'à cet égard VOTRE MAJESTÉ sçache ce qui
s'étoit introduit pendant le dernier Ministere.   Autrefois celui qui se
croyoit trop imposé s'adressoit à l'Intendant de la Province.   On
sçavoit bien que l'Intendant s'en rapporteroit au Préposé ; mais au
moins l'Intendant, le Préposé, le contribuable habitoient dans la même
Province où le bien étoit situé ; ainsi on pouvoit s'entendre contradictoirement, & il n'étoit pas impossible de vérifier des faits allégués de part
& d'autre.   Sous le dernier Ministere, il a semblé que les Ministres
eux-mêmes fussent jaloux de cette autorité des Intendans des Provinces ;
& il y a eu un instant où ceux qui s'adressoient à l'Intendance, rece-
voient pour réponse qu'actuellement c'étoit au Conseil du Roi qu'il falloit
s'adresser directement ; comme s'il étoit possible que le Conseil, rési-
dant auprès de la personne du Roi, statuât sur la valeur d'un arpent de
vigne ou de pré situé à l'extrémité du Royaume.   Quel seroit donc le
recours du particulier qui seroit vexé par la cupidité ou l'animosité
d'un Préposé ?   On verroit évidemment que l'injustice qu'on éprouve
ne peut être que le fait du Directeur du vingtieme ; & cependant ce
Directeur répondroit froidement que cela ne le regarde pas ; que les
rôles ont été faits au Bureau général, & que ceux qui se croient trop
imposés, n'ont qu'à faire le voyage de Paris pour se plaindre.

[202] Cet abus, SIRE, n'est pas ancien ; c'est sous le dernier
Ministere qu'il a été introduit : nous croyons qu'il ne subsiste plus sous
le Ministere actuel, & nous espérons qu'on ne le verra plus reparoître

sous votre regne. Cependant il étoit nécessaire de faire sçavoir à VOTRE MAJESTÉ qu'il a existé, & que l'esprit du despotisme & de clandestinité a pu se porter jusqu'à cet excès.

[203] Il nous reste actuellement à expliquer à VOTRE MAJESTÉ, 1°. Comment il est possible que ceux qui ont voulu, dans l'origine, établir en France un impôt réel, aient choisi la forme du dixieme ou du vingtieme, malgré les inconvéniens que nous venons d'exposer ; 2°. Pourquoi on n'a pas changé la nature de cet impôt, quand l'expérience en a fait reconnoître les abus ; 3°. Quel a dû être l'effet de la clause de 1763 pendant qu'elle a eu lieu.

[204] Nous ne devons pas, SIRE, calomnier la mémoire des Ministres qui, en l'année 1710, imaginerent & firent établir le dixieme. On étoit alors dans une situation forcée ; & la régie fut si douce dans ces commencemens, que les inconvéniens ne se firent pas sentir. Le dixieme fut imposé dans un temps où les calamités d'une guerre malheureuse étoient réunies à celle de la famine. Il n'étoit pas question de fixer alors la somme qu'on vouloit lever sur le Peuple : on levoit ce qu'on pouvoit ; & s'il eût été possible de lever des sommes bien plus considérables que ce que produisoit le dixieme, on les auroit employées utilement aux besoins de l'Etat, qui étoient réels & excessifs.

[205] Mais le grand objet qu'on se proposoit pour-lors, étoit de faire payer le dixieme par ceux qui n'étoient pas déja épuisés par la taille, c'est-à-dire par la Noblesse & les privilégiés. Or la plupart avoient affermé leurs biens, & les baux étoient sinceres, parce que jusqu'alors on n'avoit eu aucun intérêt à en faire de simulés. Il ne fut donc fait aucune inquisition des facultés de chaque particulier : on ne monta point de régie dispendieuse ; chacun donna sa déclaration ; l'Intendant en fut Juge, & il pouvoit y suffire, parce que toutes les déclarations appuyées sur des baux n'étoient pas suspectes, & que pour les autres on ne fit aucunes, ou presque aucunes recherches.

[206] Quand la même imposition fut établie en 1733, au commencement d'une guerre offensive, & après vingt ans de paix ; quand, après une interruption de peu d'années, elle fut renouvellée en 1741, au commencement d'une autre guerre, & sur-tout quand le dixieme ou le vingtieme fut continué pendant la paix pour payer les dettes de la guerre, il auroit fallu commencer par fixer la somme que le Roi vouloit percevoir, celle qui étoit nécessaire pour les besoins de l'Etat.

[207] Ce n'est point ce qui fut fait. Les Ministres voulurent tirer

de l'imposition tout le parti possible, & d'autre part les particuliers qui se voyoient imposés d'après leurs baux, employerent aussi toutes les ruses possibles pour se soustraire à l'imposition par des baux simulés, des pots-de-vin, &c. & ce fut alors que le Gouvernement établit une inquisition aussi impracticable qu'odieuse, aussi onéreuse à VOTRE MAJESTÉ pour les frais, que préjudiciable au peuple par les vexations.

[208] C'est alors qu'il auroit fallu reprendre les vrais principes des impôts réels, changer entiérement la nature de l'imposition du vingtieme, & y substituer un autre impôt réel qui n'entraînât ni les frais perpétuels de régie, ni un perpétuel despotisme : mais alors il existoit un autre intérêt que celui de la Finance, celui des Administrateurs.

[209] En effet, après le tableau que nous venons de tracer, il est évident que les Administrateurs ont dans cette partie un pouvoir qu'on ne voit nulle part : car nous pensons, SIRE, que dans les pays même où le peuple est soumis au despotisme le plus décidé, & où la volonté du Ministre peut faire le sort de toute une Province, on n'a pas réservé à ce Ministre le pouvoir de statuer lui-même, de statuer sur le sort de chaque particulier de l'Etat.   C'est cependant ce que nous voyons en France.   Il n'est aucun propriétaire de biens dans le Royaume qui n'ait à solliciter les faveurs de l'Administrateur du vingtieme, ou à craindre les effets de son ressentiment.   Or il n'est pas dans l'humanité que celui qui est revêtu d'un pouvoir si exorbitant s'en demette volontairement ; & si cela arrive quelque jour, il faudra que celui qui fera ce sacrifice, soit doué d'une vertu peu commune.   Voilà, SIRE, pourquoi l'impôt du vingtieme subsiste tel qu'il est ; voilà pourquoi il a toujours été protégé ; voilà pourquoi on a voulu en faire la base de toutes les autres impositions, malgré les abus évidens que l'expérience auroit dû faire connoître.

[210] C'étoit donc la réclamation générale qui devoit obliger à réformer une imposition si vicieuse, & c'est ce qui est arrivé en 1763. Cependant, SIRE, il faut avouer que le cri public ne fut pas encore aussi prompt ni aussi énergique qu'il auroit dû l'être, parce que la politique du despotisme est toujours d'avoir de grands ménagemens pour ceux qui peuvent se faire entendre.   La réclamation fut donc lente, parce que ce n'étoient pas les gens puissans qui avoient le plus à se plaindre de la régie du vingtieme ; & ceci mérite, SIRE, que VOTRE MAJESTÉ y fasse de profondes réflexions.

[211] Ce ne fut donc qu'en 1763 que le Parlement enregistra une prorogation du vingtieme, *à la charge que le prèmier & le second*

vingtiemes, tant qu'ils auront lieu, seront perçus sur les rôles actuels,
dont les quotes ne pourront être augmentées, à peine contre les contre-
venans d'être poursuivis extraordinairement. Nous ne devons point
dissimuler à VOTRE MAJESTÉ que cette fameuse clause de 1763
changeoit entiérement la nature de l'imposition, & la convertissoit en
un cadastre ; & c'est par là qu'elle remédioit à tous les abus, & qu'elle
remplissoit toutes les conditions que nous avons annoncées comme
nécessaires pour l'établissement d'un impôt réel.

1°. La somme imposée sur le peuple par le Roi étoit fixée.

2°. Il n'y avoit plus de despotisme des Préposés à craindre.

3°. Ces Préposés étant devenus inutiles, le Gouvernement devoit
s'épargner tous les frais de régie.

[212] Cette clause ne pouvoit donc être critiquée qu'en disant que
les rôles de 1763 n'étoient pas assez bien faits pour en faire un
cadastre : mais c'étoit avouer que le travail fait depuis bien des années
avec tant de dépenses, avoit été inutile pour l'objet qu'on s'étoit
proposé ; car les Administrateurs n'avoient cessé d'annoncer que par
leurs recherches sur le vingtieme, ils auroient bientôt une évaluation de
tous les biens du Royaume, qui rendroit à l'avenir les répartitions
simples & justes, & préviendroit tous les procès. On auroit donc
conclu que la méthode employée étoit mauvaise, & qu'il falloit recourir
à une autre forme d'imposition.

[213] C'est à quoi les Administrateurs ne vouloient pas consentir.
En conséquence ils se contenterent de murmurer en secret contre la
clause de 1763. Ils prétendoient qu'elle étoit injuste, parce qu'elle
laissoit subsister des impositions injustes ; qu'on ne pourroit plus
décharger ceux qui étoient trop imposés, puisqu'on ne pouvoit pas
augmenter ceux qui ne l'étoient pas assez. Mais tant que l'ancienne
Magistrature a existé, on s'est bien gardé de proposer au feu Roi de
remédier à ces inconvéniens par une loi contraire à la clause, parce
qu'il étoit aisé de prévoir que l'examen de cette loi produiroit une
explication qui pourroit faire découvrir les vices d'une imposition qu'on
vouloit conserver. On prit donc le parti d'attendre des momens
favorables ; & cependant on conserva depuis 1763 jusqu'en 1771, aux
frais du Roi, tous les bureaux & tout les Commis que la clause sembloit
avoir rendus inutiles. On ne fit point non plus le dépôt des rôles,
qui cependant par cette clause devenoit plus nécessaire que jamais ;
car puisque ces rôles devenoient le cadastre de tout le Royaume, il
falloit les rendre publics.

[214] Le moment desiré arriva, ce fut celui de l'anéantissement de la Magistrature.   Un vingtieme fut rendu perpétuel sans la clause de 1763, ni aucune autre clause équivalente ; ce qui a fait revivre tous les abus à-la-fois, & ce qui a donné lieu à la nouvelle inquisition sous laquelle le peuple gémit depuis quatre ans.

[215] Nous nous plaignons, SIRE, premiérement de la perpétuité de l'impôt, secondement de l'abolition de la clause de 1763, & nous supplions VOTRE MAJESTÉ, ou de la rétablir, ou d'y suppléer par une loi qui ait les mêmes effets, qui fixe la somme totale de ce qui sera payé par les peuples, qui dispense VOTRE MAJESTÉ des frais de régie, & qui ne laisse pas le Royaume entier soumis au despotisme des Administrateurs & des Préposés du vingtieme.

[216] Les trois impositions que nous venons d'examiner sont les seuls impôts directs qui se levent dans votre Royaume, & s'il s'en leve d'autres dans quelques Provinces sous différens noms, ce sont des faits dont nous n'avons point de connoissance, & que nous n'avons pas eu occasion de vérifier.   Nous avons aussi indiqué à VOTRE MAJESTÉ les prestations de service corporel, comme la milice & la corvée, & nous n'en dirons pas davantage.   S'il y a des abus, nous ne doutons pas que les Ministres qui président à ces administrations, & en qui le public a la plus grande confiance, ne travaillent à les réformer.

[217] Le logement des gens de guerre est encore une autre espece de service exigé du peuple, & dont la Cour des Aides n'a point de connoissance juridique.   Nous protestons à VOTRE MAJESTÉ que nous sommes bien éloignés de chercher à étendre notre jurisdiction dans ce moment où nous ne devons être occupés que des intérêts des peuples ; mais ce n'est empiéter sur les droits d'aucune puissance que d'avertir VOTRE MAJESTÉ, en qui résident tous les genres de puissance, de ce qui s'est passé à cet égard.   Et dans ce jour, SIRE, où nous présentons à VOTRE MAJESTÉ le tableau des impositions, nous ne pouvons vous laisser ignorer que sous vos yeux & dans votre capitale il se leve une taxe sur beaucoup de maisons, sous le nom de logement de gens de guerre, qui est un véritable impôt réel établi sur vos sujets sans aucune loi, & sans qu'on connoisse les regles d'après lesquelles s'en fait l'assiette.   Nous sçavons que le produit de cette imposition est destiné au logement des troupes, qui est un service militaire ; mais ce n'est pas une raison suffisante pour que l'autorité militaire préside à la répartition.   Quand la taille fut créée sous Charles VII, elle fut destinée à la solde des troupes ; on n'imagina cependant pas de

l'établir sans aucune loi expresse, ni de la faire répartir, juger & lever par les gens de guerre.

[218] Nous ignorons si, sous le même prétexte, on a établi de semblables taxes dans les Provinces, & nous n'avons pas cherché à nous en informer ; nous espérons que ce sera VOTRE MAJESTÉ elle-même qui se fera rendre compte de tout ce qui concerne cette singuliere imposition ; & quant à la ville de Paris, nous la supplions de faire vérifier, 1°. par quelle loi l'impôt qu'on y leve a été établi originaire-ment ; 2°. suivant quelle loi il s'augmente tous les jours ; 3°. par qui & suivant quelle regle se fait la taxe de chaque maison ; 4°. à qui peut s'adresser le propriétaire qui se plaint de sa taxe.   Quand VOTRE MAJESTÉ sera déterminée sur cette objet, nous ne doutons pas qu'elle ne fasse connoître ses intentions par une loi publique ; car le public a droit de demander à connoître les loix auxquelles on veut le soumettre.[1]

. . . .

[219] Nous protestons à VOTRE MAJESTÉ qu'en rapportant des faits particuliers, notre intention n'est point d'armer sa sévérité contre les coupables : mais il faut bien faire connoître quelle a été la con-duite des depositaires du pouvoir arbitraire pendant qu'ils se sont crus affranchis de la censure de la Justice réglée, & nous regardons, SIRE, ce moment où le despotisme, se croyant assuré de l'impunité, s'est montré à découvert, comme un moment précieux à saisir pour démon-trer au Roi ami de la justice, les excès dont nous sommes menacés.

[220] En effet, SIRE, quand nous remontons à la source des abus, & que nous proposons à VOTRE MAJESTÉ des remedes inutiles depuis long-temps, comme celui de faire porter les impositions de tous les genres au département qui se fait dans chaque Province, ou d'ad-mettre à ce même département des représentans du peuple oubliés depuis plusieurs siecles, nous prévoyons bien qu'on dira à VOTRE MAJESTÉ que ce sont des nouveautés que nous voulons introduire dans l'administration.   Il faut donc que VOTRE MAJESTÉ voie clairement que si nous lui proposons ce qu'on appelle des nouveautés, & ce qui cependant n'est que le rétablissement des anciennes regles, c'est parce que le progrès & les véritables innovations que fait tous les jours le despotisme, rendent le rétablissement des vrais principes absolument nécessaire.

[1][*Note de l'Editeur.*]   Il y a encore ici une lacune dans le manuscrit sur lequel on a imprimé : il paroît qu'il étoit question des vexations de plusieurs Ministres & Préposés des finances.

[221] Il ne faut point vous le dissimuler, SIRE, puisque vous voulez faire le bonheur perpétuel de cette Nation qui, dans l'instant de votre avénement, s'est jetée dans vos bras avec une confiance si touchante. Ce n'est point à la réformation des abus particuliers que vous devez borner vos soins, c'est le systême de l'administration qu'il faut attaquer.

[222] On sçait que VOTRE MAJESTÉ aime la justice, on sçait que vos Ministres actuels veulent la faire fleurir ; mais tant que le bien que vous ferez au peuple ne sera fondé que sur votre justice personnelle, ou sur celle de vos Ministres, ce ne sera qu'un bien passager, & la génération future verra le despotisme se venger sur le peuple de la contrainte qu'il aura éprouvée sous votre regne. Il faut donc que le temps de ce regne soit employé à donner au peuple des préservatifs contre le despotisme, & sur-tout contre la clandestinité.

[223] Ce n'est donc point des faits particuliers que nous avons dû nous plaindre, ou au moins nous n'avons dû les employer que comme preuves du système général, & nous devons invoquer cet amour de la justice dont VOTRE MAJESTÉ est pénétrée, pour obtenir des loix qui fassent le bonheur perpétuel de votre Royaume, des loix telles que cette justice qui est dans votre coeur, survive à VOTRE MAJESTÉ elle-même, & se fasse sentir à nos derniers neveux.

[224] Voilà, SIRE, les vues générales qu'ont dû vous présenter d'anciens Magistrats qui, comme les autres citoyens, ont été témoins du malheur du peuple, & qui, ayant consacré leurs vies aux jugemens des procès occasionnés par les impôts, ont vu de plus près quelquesunes des causes de ce malheur. Nous vous présentons ces réflexions avec confiance, parce que nous sçavons que le sentiment qui nous les a dictées les fera agréer de VOTRE MAJESTÉ. Mais nous reconnoissons qu'en agitant un si grand nombre de questions, nous avons pu tomber dans quelques erreurs. Et comment aurions-nous pu les éviter, puisque depuis si long-temps les Administrateurs ne cherchent qu'à se couvrir d'un voile impénétrable, & que le vice .principal de leurs opérations est cette clandestinité, qui ne permet de rien éclaircir & de rien constater ? Mais nous aurions mal rempli notre ministere, si la crainte de nous tromper sur quelques détails nous avoit empêchés de mettre sous vos yeux une masse de vérités utiles & incontestables ; & vous-même, SIRE, nous oserons le dire à VOTRE MAJESTÉ, vous tomberiez dans les pieges que vos tendent les ennemis de votre peuple, si la découverte de ces légeres erreurs vous rendoit suspectes les vérités qu'il étoit si important de vous faire connoître.

[225] Nous n'aurions pas non plus la témérité de croire que d'autres que nous ne puissent pas vous fournir d'autres lumieres, & nous n'imiterons point, SIRE, la présomption coupable de ces Administrateurs qui, depuis plus d'un siecle, ont cherché à écarter du trône tous ceux qui pouvoient éclairer le Roi, comme si la vérité ne devoit parvenir au Souverain que par leur organe. Nous pensons, SIRE, comme toute la Nations sur les Ministres que VOTRE MAJESTÉ a appellés auprès d'Elle ; mais il est encore bien des vérités qui ne vous parviendront ni par les Ministres, ni par les Magistrats.

[226] C'est sur le Peuple entier que pesent les impôts, & leur complication est telle, que chaque Province, chaque Corps, chaque profession est soumise à quelque loi bursale qui lui est particuliere, & a des griefs personnels à exposer à VOTRE MAJESTÉ. Il n'est pas juste qu'un Ministre statue seul & sans contradicteur sur cette multitude d'objets, & il n'est pas possible non plus qu'un Corps de Magistrature soit seul auprès de VOTRE MAJESTÉ l'interprete de cette quantité énorme de différens intérêts.

[227] La preuve la plus réelle que nous puissions donner à VOTRE MAJESTÉ de la sincérité de notre zele, est de lui faire connoître dans quel cas & jusqu'à quel point elle doit être en garde contre les Ministres & les autres Administrateurs, & comment elle peut être garantie de la séduction par d'autres que par les Magistrats, qui depuis long-temps jouissent seuls dans le Royaume du droit de représentation, & sont quelquefois insuffisans pour remplir dans toute son étendue cet important ministere.

[228] La confiance que nous inspire l'administration actuelle, ne doit point nous fermer la bouche. Nous croyons au contraire devoir saisir le moment où VOTRE MAJESTÉ est entourée des hommes les plus instruits & les plus irréprochables, & nous espérons qu'ils se réuniront à nous, & qu'ils desireront autant que nous-mêmes, que VOTRE MAJESTÉ se fasse éclairer sur l'usage du pouvoir qui leur est confié, & dont ils ne veulent point abuser.

[229] Il est certain qu'à beaucoup d'égards, & peut-être sur le plus grand nombre des objets, les Ministres d'un Roi méritent sa confiance plus que personne ; car on peut dire en général que tout ce qui intéresse la gloire de son regne, intéresse aussi celle de leur ministere. Ainsi le Souverain ne peut pas douter que ses Ministres ne prennent le plus sincere intérêt au succès de ses armes, au maintien de son autorité dans l'intérieur de son Royaume, à sa considération chez les Puissances étrangeres.

[230] Mais sur d'autres objets l'intérêt du Ministre n'est pas toujours celui de Roi. Par exemple, quand il est question d'asservir les peuples à tous les suppôts de l'administration, sous prétexte de maintenir l'autorité Royale, ou d'étendre cette administration jusques sur les plus petits objets, il y a une grande différence entre ces deux intérêts : car il n'est pas étonnant qu'un sujet devenu Ministre soit flatté des plus petits détails de la puissance, qu'il ait par-tout des amis à protéger & des ennemis à persécuter, que son orgueil se repaisse de la multiplicité des hommages qu'entraîne la multiplicité des pouvoirs : mais un Roi est trop grand, trop puissant, trop supérieur à ses sujets pour être mu par ces petites passions, & il ne peut voir son autorité intéressée que dans des objets dignes de lui.

[231] Il est un troisieme genre d'affaires dans lequel les Ministres non-seulement n'ont pas le même intérêt que le Roi, mais en ont un absolument contraire. De ce nombre sont toutes celles où il est question d'introduire l'administration clandestine ; car l'intérêt du Roi est toujours d'éclairer la conduite de ses Ministres, & celui des Ministres est quelquefois de n'être pas éclairés.

[232] Il est enfin un grand nombre d'objets sur lesquels l'intérêt du Roi étant contraire à celui des Ministres, le peuple a le même intérêt que le Roi ; mais tous les Grands de l'Etat, tous les gens considérés, tous ceux qui approchent du Roi, ou qui sont à portée de se faire entendre de lui, ont les mêmes intérêts que les Ministres ; & voilà, SIRE, ce qui mérite le plus votre attention, ce qui doit même être l'objet de vos profondes réflexions : car il n'est que trop vrai que cet intérêt des Ministres réuni à celui de tous les gens puissans, l'emporte presque toujours sur celui du Roi réuni à celui du peuple.

[233] C'est ce que nous avons déja fait voir au sujet du vingtieme & de la capitation. Ces deux impositions, où les Ministres & leurs subordonnés se sont réservé le droit de taxer vos sujets ou de modérer leurs taxes arbitrairement & à volonté, donnent lieu à un despotisme odieux à la France, & honteux pour une nation libre ; despotisme contraire aux vrais intérêts de VOTRE MAJESTÉ, même a l'intérêt fiscal, que les despotes sacrifient toujours aux considérations qui leur sont personnelles ; mais despotisme très-utile à tous les gens considérables, parce que ce sont toujours eux qui sont traités favorablement par les Ministres, par les Intendans, par les autres despotes de cette partie.

[234] Tel est aussi l'excès des dépenses. On se propose sans cesse d'y mettre un frein, & tout le monde applaudit dans la spéculation à

5

ces projets de réformation; mais dans l'exécution, tous les Ministres, tous les Ordonnateurs des dépenses s'y refusent, & ils sont appuyés par toutes les puissances de la Cour, & même de la capitale, parce que ce sont toujours des gens puissans qui ont part aux faveurs des Ministres.

[235] Tel est encore l'abus des lettres de cachet accordées sur la demande des particuliers, & que chaque personne puissante dans le Royaume se croit en droit d'obtenir. Et nous-mêmes Magistrats, qui nous regardons comme les représentans du peuple, mais qui sommes aussi du nombre de ces gens considérés qui ont accès chez les Ministres, n'avons-nous pas à nous reprocher de n'avoir jamais réclamé avec assez d'energie contre les abus de ce genre?

[236] Sur tous ces objets, SIRE, il existe nécessairement deux partis dans un Royaume; d'un côté, tous ceux qui approchent du Souverain; de l'autre, tout le reste de la nation. Il faut donc qu'un Roi qui veut être juste, puise ses sentimens dans son propre coeur, & ses lumieres dans celles de la nation entiere.

[237] Mais comment établir une relation entre le Roi & la Nation, qui ne soit pas interceptée par tous ceux dont un Roi est entouré? Nous ne devons point vous le dissimuler, SIRE; le moyen le plus simple, le plus naturel, le plus conforme à la constitution de cette Monarchie, seroit d'entendre la Nation elle-même assemblée, ou au moins de permettre des assemblées de chaque Province : & personne ne doit avoir la lâcheté de vous tenir un autre langage; personne ne doit vous laisser ignorer que le voeu unanime de la Nation est d'obtenir ou des Etats généraux, ou au moins des Etats provinciaux.

[238] Mais nous sçavons aussi que depuis plus d'un siecle la jalousie des Ministres, & peut-être celle des courtisans, s'est toujours opposée à ces assemblées nationales; & si la France est assez heureuse pour que VOTRE MAJESTÉ s'y détermine un jour, nous prévoyons qu'on fera naître encore des difficultés de formes. Ces difficultés seront aisément surmontées quand VOTRE MAJESTÉ le voudra; elles ne sont pas de nature à faire un obstacle réel à ce qui vous est demandé par les voeux ardens de ce peuple que vous aimez. Il est cependant possible qu'elles retardent encore pendant quelques temps le rétablissement de ces Etats tant desirés; & en attendant n'existera-t-il aucune autre voie par laquelle les voeux du peuple puissent parvenir à un Roi qui veut les entendre?

[239] Dans ce moment, SIRE, nous ne vous parlons point une langue qui vous soit étrangere. Toute l'Europe a sçu que le premier sentiment de VOTRE MAJESTÉ, lors de son avénement à la couronne, a

été de faciliter à tous ses sujets les approches de son trône, & qu'elle s'est fait une regle de recevoir tous les mémoires qui lui sont présentés.

Mais la clandestinité de l'administration s'oppose sans cesse à ce desir mutuel que le Roi & la Nation auroient à s'entendre, & rend inutile ce premier sentiment d'un jeune Roi, si précieux pour le peuple qu'il doit gouverner.

[240] Vous recevez, SIRE, les requêtes de tous vos Sujets; mais les grands abus ne peuvent jamais vous être présentés, parce que le tableau des opérations du Gouvernement n'existe nulle part. Il faut donc, pour que VOTRE MAJESTÉ puisse être instruite par les requêtes qu'Elle reçoit, que l'administration ne se tienne plus cachée; il faut que tous les actes d'autorité faits en votre nom soient connus & du public & des particuliers qui ont droit de s'en plaindre; il faut que les motifs soient également publiés, & qu'à chacun de ces actes d'autorité soit annexé le nom de celui de qui il est émané, & qui doit répondre de l'abus qu'il a fait de son pouvoir. Sans cela, les requêtes présentées au Roi n'ont qu'un objet vague, & les abus d'autorité resteront toujours ignorés & impunis.

[241] Vous recevez les requêtes de tous vos Sujets; mais il ne leur est permis de recourir à votre justice que pour leurs affaires personnelles; & cependant les Corps, les Provinces, l'Etat lui-même, restent sans défenseurs. Il faut donc, SIRE, en attendant que VOTRE MAJESTÉ ait rétabli les Etats, qu'il existe au moins des députés de chaque Province, choisis par la Province elle-même, qui remplissent auprès de VOTRE MAJESTÉ & de son Conseil intime, une des fonctions que les Procureurs-généraux remplissent dans les Cours, celle de stipuler les intérêts du public, & sur-tout de la Province qui leur aura donné mission. Cet établissement n'exige point indispensablement celui d'une Assemblée d'Etats dans chaque Province. Nous avons déja observé à VOTRE MAJESTÉ qu'on distinguoit anciennement les pays d'Etats des pays d'Elections. Ces derniers, sans avoir d'Etats, élisoient des représentans, & rien n'empêcheroit de rétablir cet antique usage.[1] En effet, la nécessité évidente a fait appeler auprès du Conseil des députés du commerce de chaque Province : les intérêts du commerce sont-ils donc les seuls que chaque Province ait à stipuler?

---

[1]*Nota.* Il ne faut pas que cet établissement soit dispendieux pour la Province, & il est possible de l'éviter; car il n'est pas absolument nécessaire que ces députés viennent se montrer & solliciter personnellement dans la capitale. Cette fonction pourroit être remplie par les Elus que nous avons proposé de rétablir, & ce seroit par des mémoires

[242] Vous recevez les requêtes de tous vos Sujets ; mais ignorez-vous, SIRE, que le plus grand nombre de vos Sujets, & nommément ceux qui auroient le plus besoin de votre protection, sont absolument hors d'état de l'implorer, parce qu'ils n'ont ni la capacité nécessaire pour faire eux-mêmes un mémoire, ni les facultés nécessaires pour le faire faire par un autre, ni les relations nécessaires pour le faire parvenir à VOTRE MAJESTÉ? Et quelle est la ressource de ceux qui languissent dans les prisons, & qu'on se gardera bien d'en laisser sortir, quand on prévoira que le premier usage qu'ils feront de leur liberté, sera d'implorer votre justice? Il faudroit donc que les représentans de chaque Province fussent spécialement autorisés à se constituer les défenseurs des pauvres, des foibles, des opprimés, sur-tout des captifs, comme en Justice réglée les Procureurs & Avocats-généraux sont les défenseurs-nés des absens, des interdits, des mineurs, de tous ceux, en un mot, qui ne peuvent pas de défendre eux-mêmes.

[243] Vous recevez les requêtes de tous vos Sujets ; mais il est une importante vérité, SIRE, que nous oserons vous dire aujourd'hui, parce qu'il n'est pas possible que l'expérience d'une année ne vous en ait déja convaincu ; c'est que ce recours de tous les particuliers à la seule personne du Roi est absolument illusoire, parce qu'il n'est pas possible que VOTRE MAJESTÉ seule statue en connoissance de cause sur les plaintes & les demandes, souvent indiscretes, de plusieurs millions d'hommes.

[244] Il faut donc que ces requêtes soient renvoyées, & elles le sont dans les différens départemens. Or vous sçavez, SIRE, que c'est renvoyer chaque requête précisément à celui contre qui elle est dirigée ; car on ne recourt à VOTRE MAJESTÉ elle-même que quand on a épuisé toutes les autres voies, & que c'est du Ministre qu'on veut se plaindre. Or nous venons de faire connoître que sur des objets très-

adressés à la Cour qu'ils stipuleroient les intérêts de leurs Provinces. On pourroit aussi avoir à-la-fois deux sortes de représentans qui ne coûteroient rien à la Province, & qui étant ensemble dans une relation continuelle, exerceroient conjointement leur ministere.

Les uns résideroient dans la Province, & en connoîtroient mieux les vrais intérêts que ceux qui résident près la Cour, & ceux-la n'auroient aucune dépense à faire pour tenir mission, puisqu'ils ne se déplaceroient point. Les autres, entraînés par leurs affaires personnelles dans la capitale, se chargeroient gratuitement de suivre les affaires de la Province, & tiendroient à honneur d'en être chargés. Nous croyons que pour que ces représentans soient bien choisis, & que la faveur n'ait aucune part à ce choix, il faut que ces commissions ne soient point utiles.

importans le Ministere entier, & même tous ceux qui approchent de votre personne, ont un intérêt contraire à celui de VOTRE MAJESTÉ & à celui de la Nation.

[245] Puisque ce sont les lumieres de toute la Nation qu'il faudroit communiquer à VOTRE MAJESTÉ, seroit-il possible que ce fût la Nation elle-même qui fît le premier examen de toutes ces requêtes, & que ce fût son suffrage qui indiquât à VOTRE MAJESTÉ celles qui méritent son attention personnelle?

[246] Ici nous devons nous arrêter, SIRE. Nous avons osé avancer que le recours de tous les Sujets à la seule personne du Roi est inutile & illusoire, parce que c'est une vérité évidente dont VOTRE MAJESTÉ elle-même est certainement convaincu ; mais si nous allions jusqu'à proposer d'admettre une réclamation publique contre les abus de l'administration, ne serions-nous pas taxés de témérité? Tous les ennemis de la liberté publique, & sur-tout ceux qui ont le privilege de parler en votre nom, ne diroient-ils pas que ce sont les actions de VOTRE MAJESTÉ elle-même qu'on veut soumettre à la censure publique? Une telle objection est faite pour nous imposer le silence le plus respectueux. Nous vous demandons cependant, SIRE, qu'il nous soit seulement permis de vous rendre compte de ce qui se passe sous nos yeux dans l'administration de la Justice contentieuse.

[247] Celui qui se pourvoit en Cour souveraine a le droit de faire imprimer ses mémoires & de les faire publier ; & quand il est appellant de la Sentence d'un Tribunal inférieur, le mémoire imprimé est nécessairement la critique du Jugement de ce Tribunal. Nous n'ignorons pas non plus que les particuliers qui se pourvoient à VOTRE MAJESTÉ elle-même contre un Arrêt de Cour souveraine par demande en cassation, en révision ou autrement, usent du même droit, & qu'il s'imprime & se publie des mémoires signés d'Avocats au Conseil, où les particuliers critiquent les Arrêts de Cour souveraine par lesquels ils se croient lésés.

[248] Nous sçavons, SIRE, que cette publicité des mémoires n'est pas unanimement approuvée ; on dit qu'il est même des Magistrats qui la regardent comme un abus, & qui soutiennent que les mémoires ne devroient être faits que pour l'instruction des Juges qui doivent prononcer sur chaque procès, mais que le public ne doit pas se constituer le juge des tribunaux.

[249] Pour nous, SIRE, nous avons toujours cru & nous croyons toujours devoir répondre à VOTRE MAJESTÉ & à la Nation, de la

justice que nous rendons aux particuliers ; & s'il est vrai que quelques
Magistrats ne pensent pas de même, nous, qui venons d'avertir VOTRE
MAJESTÉ qu'Elle doit récuser le témoignage des Ministres, quand ils
soutiennent l'administration clandestine, nous devons avouer qu'il faut
aussi récuser celui des Juges, quand ils s'opposent à la publicité des
mémoires.

[250] Au fond, l'ordre commun de la Justice en France est qu'elle
soit rendue publiquement.   C'est à l'Audience publique que se portent
naturellement toutes les causes ; & quand on prend le public à témoin
par des mémoires imprimés, ce n'est qu'augmenter la publicité de
l'Audience.   Si on objectoit que la profusion avec laquelle se publient
les mémoires, est une nouveauté introduite depuis peu d'années, ce reproche d'innovation ne seroit pas une objection suffisante ; car il y a
des nouveautés utiles ; & si l'on avoit rejeté les innovations, nous viv-
rions encore sous l'empire de l'ignorance & de la barbarie.   Mais
d'ailleurs, bien loin que cet usage puisse être regardé comme une innovation dangereuse, nous pensons, SIRE, que c'est le rétablissement de
l'ancien ordre judiciaire de ce Royaume, qu'il tient peut-être à la constitution primitive de la Monarchie ; & cette observation ne sera pas
indigne de votre attention.

[251] Une très-ancienne Monarchie a toujours subi des révolutions
de bien des genres, sur-tout quand elle a été fondée dans des siecles
d'ignorance, & qu'elle a subsisté jusqu'au siecle le plus éclairé.   Si on
considere sous cet aspect l'histoire de cette Nation, on verra que le
progrès des lumieres a mis une différence infinie entre les moeurs & les
lois des différens âges.

[252] Du temps de nos premiers ancêtres, toutes les conventions
des hommes étoient verbales, & il falloit que la foi due aux témoins
suppléât à des actes que personne n'auroit sçu dresser.   On n'avoit
aussi que des loix mal rédigées, & consistant souvent dans une tradi-
tion incertaine, & qui laissoit tout à l'arbitrage du Juge.

[253] Les abus de cette Justice arbitraire étoient énormes.   Ce fut
vraisemblablement l'excès du mal qui fit recourir au remede le plus
simple & le plus efficace, la publicité.   Les Rois rendirent eux-mêmes
la justice à la Nation assemblée dans le champ de Mars, avec un éclat
& une authenticité dont il n'y a pas eu d'exemple dans les temps
modernes ; & à leur exemple, les Grands de l'Etat la rendirent aussi,
chacun dans leur territoire, en presence du Peuple.

[254] Il faut observer que dans ce premier âge l'administration

n'étoit pas encore séparée de la Justice contentieuse ; l'une & l'autre
étoient exercées par le Roi lui-même, aidé des suffrages publics.   Ces
Monarques si redoutés permettoient donc qu'on vînt se plaindre publiquement à eux des fautes de leurs Ministres : ils ne craignoient point
les humbles requêtes de ceux qui venoient implorer leur appui ; mais
ils vouloient se garantir des séductions de ceux qui interposent leur
puissance précaire entre le Roi & le Peuple.

[255] Dans l'âge suivant, on commença à écrire les actes qui
fixent l'état des hommes & leurs obligations, & il se forma aussi un
corps de Jurisprudence écrite, à laquelle il fallut se conformer dans les
jugemens.   Cet âge, qu'on peut nommer celui de l'écriture, eut de
grands avantages sur celui qui avoit précédé, puisqu'alors les droits
des citoyens furent fondés sur des titres constans, & qu'on espéra
de n'être plus jugé par les fantaisies des hommes, mais par la loi elle-
même.

[256] Cependant le nouvel ordre judiciaire eut d'autres inconvéniens
inconnus aux siecles antérieurs.   On eut des loix précises ; mais l'étude
en devint si compliquée, que personne, excepté ceux qui s'y livrerent
entiérement, ne put ni faire la fonction de Juge, ni même avoir connoissance de ses propres affaires.   Il s'éleva dans la Nation un nouvel
ordre de citoyens, qui furent les gens de loi : les uns furent subrogés
aux Grands de l'Etat dans la fonction de rendre la justice, les autres
se chargerent de stipuler les droits des particuliers, & la Nation, dont
la plus grande partie étoit encore livrée à l'ignorance, fut obligée de
leur accorder une confiance aveugle.

[257] Ce fut aussi alors que la Justice cessa d'être aussi publique
que dans les premiers temps.   Elle se rendit cependant encore publiquement dans des Audiences tenues dans l'enceinte de chaque tribunal.   Mais quand les détails d'un procès exigerent un examen de
pieces, les Juges procéderent à cet examen dans des délibérations
secretes, & on perdit l'avantage d'avoir le public pour témoin de la
conduite des Juges.

[258] Nous observons encore que ce fut dans cet âge que l'administration fut séparée de la Justice contentieuse.   Les procès, & sur-tout
les appels s'étant multipliés, & la Jurisprudence étant devenue une
science profonde, il ne fut plus possible que la justice fût rendue par
le Roi ni par les Grands.   Les Rois se reposerent de cette fonction
sur les Magistrats, Jurisconsultes & Gradués, mais ils se réserverent
l'administration ; & comme elle s'exerça par des lettres du Prince, an

lieu de proclamations publiques autrefois usitées, tout se fit dans le secret du cabinet.[1]

[259] Enfin est venu un troisieme âge, que nous nommerons celui de l'impression : c'est celui où l'art de l'Imprimerie a multiplié les avantages que l'écriture avoit procurés aux hommes, & en a fait disparoître les inconvéniens. Les connoissances s'étant étendues par l'impression, les loix écrites sont aujourd'hui connues de tout le monde ; chacun peut entendre ses propres affaires. Les Légistes ont perdu cet empire que leur donnoit l'ignorance des autres hommes. Les Juges eux-mêmes peuvent être jugés par un public instruit ; & cette censure est bien plus sévere & plus équitable quand elle peut être exercée dans une lecture froide & réfléchie, que quand les suffrages sont entraînés dans une assemblée tumultueuse.

[260] L'art de l'Imprimerie a donc donné à l'écriture la même publicité qu'avoit la parole dans le premier âge au milieu des assemblées de la Nation. Mais il a fallu plusieurs siecles pour que la découverte de cet art fît tout son effet sur les hommes. Il a fallu que la Nation entiere ait pris le goût & l'habitude de s'instruire par la lecture, & qu'il se soit formé assez de gens habiles dans l'art d'écrire pour prêter leur ministere à tout le public, & tenir lieu de ceux qui, doués d'une éloquence naturelle, se faisoient entendre de nos peres dans le champ de Mars ou dans les plaids publics.

[261] Ce moment est arrivé ; SIRE, vos Sujets en éprouvent les effets dans la Justice réglée, depuis que l'usage est établi d'instruire & d'intéresser le public par des mémoires imprimés ; & VOTRE MAJESTÉ pourroit faire jouir du même privilege, du même avantage ceux de ses Sujets qui se plaignent de l'administration.

[262] Il semble que le recours à votre Conseil ou à vos Ministres

---

[1] Il n'est pas inutile d'observer que c'est dans le second âge qu'on crut pouvoir se passer des Etats ; car jusqu'alors il falloit absolument que les Rois assemblassent la Nation pour lui faire entendre leurs volontés. Bientôt les Ministres trouverent le moyen de rendre ces assemblées de plus en plus rares, parce qu'il leur convenoit d'écarter de leur gestion des contradicteurs ; ensuite ils trouverent si commode de travailler dans l'obscurité, qu'ils chercherent à épaissir les voiles dont ils s'étoient couverts ; c'est ce qui a donné naissance à cette administration clandestine qui a fait tant de progrès depuis la cessation des Etats généraux jusqu' aux derniers temps : c'est donc dans l'âge de l'écriture qu'a commencé en France la clandestinité de l'administration ; & si c'est dans celui de l'impression qu'elle a fait de grands progrès, c'est que jusqu'à présent le recours contre l'administration par des mémoires publics & imprimés, n'a pas été permis.

contre un Intendant, contre un Commandant de Province, pourroit être aussi public que le recours aux Cours souveraines contre un Tribunal inférieur ; & puisqu'on se pourvoit à la personne même de VOTRE MAJESTÉ par des mémoires imprimés & en présence du public, contre des Arrêts rendus en votre nom dans les Cours supérieures, dans ces Cours si anciennement révérées, dans ces Cours composées d'un grand nombre de Magistrats, dans ces Cours où les Arrêts ne passent qu'à la pluralité des suffrages, & après une longue discussion ; pourquoi ne pourroit-on pas se pourvoir avec la même publicité contre d'autres actes d'autorité qui sont aussi faits en votre nom, mais qui ne sont que l'ouvrage d'un seul homme, qui ont été enfantés dans le secret, & sans aucune discussion préalable?

[263] La difference est, dit-on, qu'on sçait que VOTRE MAJESTÉ ne tient jamais en personne ses Cours de justice, mais qu'on ignore toujours si les actes d'autorité sortis du cabinet, ne sont pas son propre ouvrage : & telle est depuis long-temps la politique des Ministres, que leur personne est toujours à couvert, & que le nom de VOTRE MAJESTÉ, dont il est permis de se revêtir, ou une signature qui ressemble à la vôtre, & sur laquelle le respect ne permet pas d'élever aucun doute, ont mis dans la même classe les actes de votre volonté personnelle, & ceux qui se prodiguent à votre insçu ; en sorte que les citoyens opprimés craignent toujours de s'écarter du respect en se plaignant de l'injustice, & ne sçavent jamais si ce n'est pas manquer à la puissance suprême que de l'invoquer. Voilà donc, SIRE, où l'on en est réduit par la clandestinité des personnes, cette branche du système général que nous avons développée à VOTRE MAJESTÉ.

[264] La France a le bonheur d'avoir un Maître dont le premier désir a été d'être éclairé, & qui a voulu permettre à tous ses Sujets de recourir à sa justice personnelle contre tous les abus d'autorité ; & quand on démontre à VOTRE MAJESTÉ, quand Elle-même a reconnu par son expérience que ce recours est impossible, par le nombre infini de requêtes auxquelles il donne lieu, & que le seul moyen de faire parvenir la voix du peuple jusqu'au Roi, est de permettre à chaque citoyen d'invoquer le témoignage du public, comme dans les Tribunaux où s'exerce la justice réglée, on croit pouvoir opposer à notre zele un obstacle invincible, on croit devoir nous imposer silence en prononçant le nom sacré de VOTRE MAJESTÉ, & on veut que des milliers d'injustices soient impunies à perpétuité, qu'elles soient à l'abri de toutes réclamations, qu'il soit impossible de vous les manifester, par la crainte

imaginaire qu'il n'y ait une occasion où l'on parle avec trop peu de
respect d'un ordre qui se trouvera émané de VOTRE MAJESTÉ elle-
même ; comme si l'on pouvoit douter de l'extrême circonspection
dont useront toujours ceux qui vous adresseront leurs requêtes, & ceux
qui, par état, seront chargés, de les rédiger & de les signer.

[265] Cependant, SIRE, puisqu'on allegue cette crainte, toute
chimérique qu'elle est, puisqu'on veut se prévaloir du respect personnel
dû à VOTRE MAJESTÉ, il ne nous est pas possible d'insister davantage ; mais c'est là le cas où VOTRE MAJESTÉ doit se déterminer
elle-même. Nous vous avons rappellé l'exemple de ces anciens Rois
qui ne croyoient point leur autorité blessée par la liberté donnée à
leurs Sujets de venir implorer leur justice en présence de la Nation assemblée. C'est à vous à juger, SIRE, si ce sera affoiblir votre puissance que d'imiter en cela Charlemagne, ce Monarque si fier, & qui
porta si loin les prérogatives de sa couronne. C'est à son exemple que
vous pouvez encore régner à la tête d'une Nation qui sera toute entiere
votre conseil ; & vous en tirerez bien plus de ressources, parce que
vous vivez dans un siecle bien plus éclairé.

[266] Daignez songer enfin, SIRE, que le jour que vous aurez accordé cette précieuse liberté à vos Sujets, on pourra dire qu'il a été
conclu un traité entre le Roi & la Nation contre les Ministres & les
Magistrats : contre les Ministres, s'il en est jamais d'assez pervers pour
vouloir vous cacher la vérité ; contre les Magistrats, s'il en est jamais
d'assez ambitieux pour prétendre avoir le privilege exclusif de vous la
dire.

Ce sont là, SIRE, les très-humbles & très-respectueuses Remontrances
que présentent à VOTRE MAJESTE

Vos très-humbles, très-obéissans,
très-fideles & très-affectionnés
Serviteurs & Sujets, les Gens
tenans votre Cour des Aides.

A Paris, en la Cour des Aides,
le 6 Mai 1775.

ENGLISH TRANSLATION.

MOST HUMBLE

AND MOST RESPECTFUL

PROTEST

*PRESENTED to the King, our most honored
Sovereign and Lord, by those who hold his
Cour des aides at Paris.*

SIRE :

[1] Your *Cour des aides* has just protested on its own part, and on
the part of the whole Magistracy, against certain articles of the act by
which it has been re-established; but another and more important
duty still remains to be fulfilled.   It is the cause of the people which
we must now plead before the tribunal of Your Majesty.   We must
present a faithful picture to you of the taxes and dues which are levied
in your kingdom, and which constitute the subject-matter of the jurisdiction confided to us; we must make known to Your Majesty at the
beginning of your reign the real condition of the people, whom the
spectacle of a brilliant court can never call to your mind.   Who knows,
indeed, whether the very proofs of joy and affection which Your
Majesty received, at the time of your accession, from all those who
were able to approach your person, may not foster in Your Majesty's
mind a fatal error as to the condition of the rest of the Nation, since
those whom you saw were either a little less miserable than the people
of the provinces or were at least happy in their hopes.   Our Nation,
Sire, has always proved its devotion to its masters by its strenuous
efforts to maintain the splendor of their throne; but Your Majesty
should at least know what these enormous contributions are costing the
unhappy people.

[2] A careful examination of all the taxes would, however, involve
an infinite amount of labor, which Your Majesty cannot yourself undertake.   We will therefore submit special communications on each sub-

(77)

ject, and Your Majesty may hand them over for consideration to those whom you may choose to honor with your confidence. But to-day, Sire, to-day, when it is our precious privilege to speak directly to Your Majesty himself, we shall content ourselves with making plain to you the general and fundamental causes of all the abuses, and with establishing certain facts so simple that Your Majesty may easily be convinced of their truth, and which may sink deeply into your mind. And then, when your intentions are made known and you have given your instructions, it will rest with your Ministers to conform to them in their minute investigation of the various details.

[3] We ought not to allow ourselves to be hampered by any considerations when we have to present matters of such moment to Your Majesty; yet we cannot but regret that we find ourselves obliged to refer to that unhappy period when the absence of Ministers of Justice and the silence of the law left a free field to the avidity of the Financiers[1] and the despotism of the Government Officials. Your Majesty has put a stop to these public misfortunes, and we would that even the memory of them might be completely effaced by that glorious instance of your justice. Had we to complain simply of the persecution suffered by the Magistrates, or even if we had only the disregard of the judicial system during these troublous times to denounce, we should believe that, since everything is redressed, everything should be buried in oblivion. But there is one important fact, Sire, which we cannot, without betraying our trust, avoid bringing to your notice, the fact, namely, that the asserted necessity of strengthening the sovereign authority has served as a pretext for extortions, which have been levied with impunity upon your subjects. A league was formed between the enemies of the Courts and those who cause the people to groan under the weight of arbitrary taxes; the latter lent their influence in annihilating the Magistracy[2] and their services in replacing it, and the reward of their hateful co-operation was the delivering over of the people to their cupidity.

[4] It pains us, Sire, to be obliged in a period of clemency to call your attention to this system of oppression; but laws burdensome for the people were promulgated in a form regarded as legal at the time of

---

[1] The *financiers* were, first and foremost, those capitalists who undertook to collect the indirect taxes for the government under the *Ancien Régime*.

[2] The *Parlements* and the *Cour des aides* had been abolished by Chancellor Maupeou in 1771. See the Introduction.

their enactment, and they still exist to-day, since Your Majesty has made valid all that was done while the administration of justice was suspended. Various important positions are, moreover, still occupied by those who have abused their office; and should new abuses call forth the animadversion of the Courts, it will doubtless be claimed for the offenders that they have sacrificed themselves to maintain the royal authority, and, under pretext of protecting them from the vengeance of their enemies, the attempt will be made to secure their acts from the investigations of justice. It is therefore important, Sire, to rid Your Majesty of a burden of gratitude so prejudicial to the welfare of your people, and to show you that those who have been pretending to labor for the authority of the throne have in reality been successfully endeavoring to usurp for themselves excessive powers over all the Orders of the Realm, which are in no way demanded by the interests of Your Majesty's service.

[5] We would that we might leave it to others, Sire, to acquaint you with these disagreeable truths! Why is it not possible for Your Majesty to abandon those malevolent maxims of government, or rather that political system which was introduced a century ago by the jealousy of the Ministers, and which has reduced all the Orders of the Realm to silence, with the single exception of the Magistracy? Why is it not possible for the Nation itself to expound its own dearest interests? In that case, Sire, with what joy should we intrust to others the task of acquainting you with the excesses committed by the very ministry which would have destroyed us! But since we alone still enjoy the ancient privilege of Frenchmen, the privilege of addressing our Sovereigns and of protesting with impunity against infractions of the law and of national rights, we may not exhibit toward our enemies a generosity which would render us offenders against the entire Nation·

[6] The first matter which we have to lay before Your Majesty is that class of imposts known as the "farmed taxes." We are not imparting anything new to you, Sire, when we assert that these taxes are not so onerous by reason of the actual sums paid by the people into the royal treasury, as on account of the cost of administration and the profits of the Farmers of the revenue, which are assuredly too great, since the Ministers of the previous reign were able to appropriate a part of this profit, not indeed for the benefit of Your Majesty, but in order to bestow it upon their favorites. This fact, which is in everybody's mouth, cannot be unknown to Your Majesty.

[7] You are aware also that aside from the money taken from your subjects the State is deprived, through the farming of the taxes, of the services of a large number of citizens, part of whom are occupied in perpetrating frauds, and the rest in trying to prevent them. And what citizens? Precisely those who might be most useful, either through physical strength and courage, or by reason of their activity and industry : for it is a noteworthy fact that the profession of Clerk,[1] and perhaps even that of smuggler, in spite of its risks, pays better than a soldier's career, and that financial offices procure for those who obtain them more substantial and assured advantages than agriculture, commerce, or manufacture ; and that consequently only such remain in those professions as have not the good fortune, or the talent, to enter a financial career.

[8] Neither can Your Majesty be unaware that in addition to the taxation on individual commodities the production of certain of them is either forbidden or embarrassed throughout the country in the interest of the Farm. Your subjects are, for instance, forbidden to cultivate tobacco, while millions are paid for it each year to foreigners ; salt, too, would prove one of the most precious gifts which nature has bestowed upon France if only the hand of the Financier did not constantly reject what the sea as constantly brings to our shores. Your Majesty cannot be ignorant that there are regions where the manufacture of salt is confined to certain privileged persons, and where, at certain seasons of the year, the agents of the Farm call together the peasants to throw back into the sea the salt which has been deposited on the shore ; that on other coasts salt manufacture, although ostensibly permitted, is nevertheless subject to such restraints that the Farmer can ruin, and ruin effectively, whoever undertakes it against his wishes ; that almost everywhere the exorbitant price of salt deprives the people of the benefits that they might derive from this precious commodity, by using it as seasoning and as a preservative, or for their cattle, or in innumerable useful ways, even for the enrichment of the soil.

[9] Your Majesty knows also that all the other taxes on commodities are prejudicial to production and to commerce ; that France would produce more wine were it not for the excises ; that it would

---

[1] The clerks (*commis*) here referred to were the subordinate officials of the Farm. There were some 30,000 of them. For an admirable account of the system of farming the revenue, see Gomel, *Histoire financière de la Revolution française*, I., 215 *sqq.*

manufacture more merchandise were it not for the interior customs duties. The list of these disadvantages is interminable; we are well aware, Sire, that we cannot give you a complete account of them, because every day we hear of new ones; but this sketch will suffice to show you the injury done to your kingdom by the farming of the taxes, independently of the sums paid by the people for the cost of administration and as profit to the Farmers of the revenue.

[10] It is likewise impossible that Your Majesty should be unaware of the severity of the penal laws against smuggling. You must know that those who commit this offence are sometimes not accustomed to regard it as a crime. There are whole provinces where the children are brought up to it by their parents, have never learned any other trade, and have no other means of support; and when these unfortunates are caught they are condemned to the sort of imprisonment designed for the worst of crimes—sometimes even to death. We doubt not that Your Majesty will be affected by the recital of these cruelties, and will ask how it was possible in the beginning to pro-nounce sentence of death against a citizen for an offence affecting only the revenue.

[11] But there is still another sort of tyranny, of which it is possible that Your Majesty has never heard. Although it does not afford so cruel a spectacle as that of which we have been speaking, it is none the less insupportable to the people, since it affects all the citizens of the lowest class, those who live quietly by labor or trade. It is due to the circumstance that every man belonging to the people is forced to submit daily to the caprices, the insolence, even the insults of the minions of the Tax-farmer. This particular kind of annoyance has never received much attention, because it is only experienced by the obscure and unknown. In fact, if a Clerk shows a want of regard for persons of consideration the heads of the financial administration hasten to disavow their subordinate and to satisfy the complainant; and it is precisely by means of this consideration for the Great that the Farm has been able to subject the defenceless people to an unrestrained and unlimited despotism.[1] Yet this unprotected class is the largest in your realm, and the defenceless certainly have the first claim to the direct protection of Your Majesty.

[12] It devolves upon us, therefore, to explain to Your Majesty the

---

[1] The court is probably guilty of exaggeration here. *Cf.* Gomel, *op.cit.*, I., 325.

real cause of the servitude to which the people are reduced through-out the provinces. That cause, Sire, is to be sought in the nature of the power exercised by the officers of the Farm—a power arbitrary in many respects, which makes it only too easy for them to render themselves formidable.

[13] In the first place, the General Farm[1] has an enormous body of rules and regulations, which have never been collected and codified. It is an occult science which no one except the Financiers themselves has studied, or can study, so that the individual against whom action is brought can neither know the law himself nor consult any one else ; he is obliged to rely on the very same Clerk who is his enemy and perse-cutor. How can a laborer or an artisan help trembling and humbling himself continually before an adversary who has such terrible weapons to turn against him?

[14] In the second place, the laws of the Farm are not only un-known but are sometimes uncertain. There are many doubtful pre-rogatives which the Farmer will exercise according to circumstances. It will readily be surmised that the employees of the Farm make their experiments by preference upon those who have had the misfortune to displease them. It is natural, too, that they are never made except upon those who have not means enough to defend themselves.

[15] Finally, there are other laws which are unfortunately only too definite, but which it is impossible to execute literally, by reason of their extreme severity. The Farmer procures their adoption well knowing that he will not carry them into execution, and he reserves the right to exempt from them when he wishes, but on condition that such exemption, without which the individual subject to the taxes would be ruined, shall be a favor granted arbitrarily either by him or his employees. This is a favorite expedient of the financial adminis-tration which should be fully exposed to Your Majesty. Yes, Sire, the Farmer has been known to say to the citizen : " The Farm must have certain favors to grant and to refuse you ; it is essential that you should be obliged to come and ask for them." This is equivalent to saying,

---

[1] A single great company, " the General Farm," had, since the end of the 17th century, been conceded the privilege of raising the greater part of the indirect taxes, including the salt tax, the excises, the customs duties, &c. For this right the Farm paid the government a lump sum, agreed upon in the contracts, which were renewed at regular intervals. For the somewhat complicated details see Gomel, *op. cit.*, I., 317, *sqq.*

" It is not enough that you bring your money to satisfy our greed—
you must gratify the insolence of our Clerks by your servility." Now,
even if it be true that the greed of the Farmer can be turned to the
advantage of the King, it is certain that the insolence of the army of
Clerks who overrun the provinces cannot profit him in the least.

[16] We have discussed this particular class of abuses, Sire, at
greater length than the others, partly because they are not so well
known, partly because we do not believe it is possible to remedy
them without interfering with the levying of the taxes. We believe,
moreover, Sire, that you have never been made acquainted with the
methods employed by the General Farm in order to win its suits
with individuals.

[17] The first of these methods, Sire—there is no dissembling the
fact—is to have no judge, or what is almost the same thing, to have
no other judge than a tribunal composed of a single man. The *Cours
des aides* and the tribunals dependent upon them have, by their constitution, jurisdiction over all cases connected with the taxes; but the
majority of such cases are removed and referred to a single commissioner of the King's Council, *i. e.*, the Intendant of a province, and,
by appeal, to the Council of Finance, that is to say, to a council which
in reality is held neither in the presence of Your Majesty nor in that of
the head of the Judiciary, where neither Counsellors of State nor
Maitres des Requêtes are present, and which is composed only of the
Controller-General and a single Intendant of Finance, and where,
consequently, the Intendant of Finance is usually the only judge, for
the Controller-General rarely has time to occupy himself with matters
of litigation.

[18] We render full justice, Sire, as does the general public, to
those who hold these offices at present; but the personal virtues of a
mortal man cannot reassure us as to the results of a permanent system.
What we denounce to Your Majesty is the arbitrary system of justice
under which the people have groaned for a century past, and must
continue to groan if protests are made only when the power is in the
hands of those who have the will to abuse it. We must then avail
ourselves of this auspicious moment, when justice has presided over all
Your Majesty's appointments, to convince Your Majesty and Your
Majesty's Ministers of the incontestable principle that the people
cannot be said really to have any judges when only a tribunal consisting
of a single man is granted them. Yet for all those cases which have

been removed from the ordinary course of justice, there is only this tribunal of a single man. In the provinces, the Intendant decides the fate of the citizens, alone in his office, and often in co-operation with the Director of the Farm; similarly, in Paris, where appeals are decided, it is the Intendant of Finance who officiates, and often in co-operation with a Farmer-General. In substantiation of this we believe that we may refer, in good faith, to the very persons upon whom this excessive power has been conferred; we ask them if it is not true that this arbitrary justice is the only sort that your subjects can obtain in all removed cases.

[19] We may add that in such classes of cases as have not yet been removed, and where appeal in the regular course of justice seems still to be permitted, the Farmer-General has found means to render this recourse illusory and make it only an excuse for useless expense on the part of the unfortunate people, by introducing the custom of petitioning the Council of Finance to reverse the decisions of the *Cour des aides*, and in that way bring the matter before that very same tribunal, composed of the Controller-General and the single Intendant of Finance. For, on the one hand, the Farmers maintain that an improper decision should where the King's taxes are involved be regarded by the council as a ground for a petition for removal, and that all the taxes, the collection of which is turned over to them, should enjoy this privilege. On the other hand, the decisions of the Council of Finance relative to petitions for reversal are absolutely in conflict with well-established laws, which are constantly observed in Your Majesty's true Council, for in reversing a decision of a sovereign court the merits of the case are reconsidered without sending the case to another tribunal for a new trial. The consequence is that there is practically no difference between a petition for reversal presented to your Council and an appeal on the merits to a higher court; and the appeal to the Council is only another instance of appeal. Such, then, are the instances of appeal for all cases where the farmed taxes are involved.

[20] The classes of cases which have been removed, such as those involving the registration fees and the *franc-fief*,[1] are taken first before a single person, the Intendant of the province, and subsequently before a single person, the Intendant of Finance, and those classes of cases which have not been removed, such as those relating to the excise dues, are first brought before the *Election*[2] and then before the *Cour*

---

[1] The nature of this due is explained later. See below, ¶ 27. [2] An inferior court.

des aides, but always, eventually, before a single person, the Intendant of Finance.

[21] We know that plausible reasons are assigned for these removals and this delegation of power. Your Majesty will be told that it was desired that both the Farmers and their opponents should be spared the expense and the tedium of the regular judicial procedure, and that the partiality might be avoided which the Financiers assert that they have always experienced on the part of the regular judges. They will even explain to you the reason of this asserted partiality by admiting that the taxes are so onerous and the regulations affecting their administration so contrary to the ordinary judicial procedure that these regulations cannot be satisfactorily observed except by judges who, being initiated into the administration, realize the necessity of having them carried out.

[22] But if the first of these motives were sincere the *Cour des aides* would have been asked to register decrees establishing a shorter and a less expensive procedure—decrees which these Courts would gladly adopt, but which have never been submitted to them for fear of losing the excuse for removal. As to the charge of partiality, if it were true that the sole aim was to grant the Farmer judges who were familiar with the administration, the appeals of the Intendants and the petitions for reversal would be carried to Your Majesty's own Council, which is composed of magistrates who have administered the provinces, and not to the Controller-General and a single Intendant of Finance. It must, therefore, be admitted that the real motive for these removals, the real intention of the government, is to give the Farmer no other judge in his suits than a Minister and those officials who are connected with the administration of the finance—in other words, to make the Farmer himself the judge for himself and for the public at large whenever he may have a preponderating influence in the government offices.

[23] We do not propose, Sire, to enter into these removals in detail, because it would be an endless task to enumerate them, and we are reluctant to dwell upon this subject at great length because, since it affects our jurisdiction, it is a personal matter. It would, moreover, be impossible to produce proofs of the abuses resulting from this system because, as these affairs are not brought before any regular tribunal, it is impossible to prove by any legal document the very abuse that is most loudly attested by public notoriety : but Your Majesty can easily supplement the *Protests* of the Courts by giving ear to the unanimous testimony of the public.

[24] You will learn from that source to what extent the Financiers have abused their arbitrary power in the administration of all the taxes which are farmed under the head of *domaine*,[1] and which are withdrawn from the cognizance of the regular Courts. You will find that all such as come under the head of registration fees and the tax of the *centieme denier*,[2] taxes which are levied upon every contract entered into between citizens, are determined according to the fancy of the Farmer and his agents; that the supposed laws on these matters are so obscure and fragmentary that he who pays can never know what he really owes, that often the agent himself knows no more about it than the taxpayer, and interprets the law more or less rigorously according as he is more or less greedy; and that it is notorious that all these taxes may receive an extension under one Farmer and not under the others, from which it is evident that the Farmer is the sovereign legislator in matters where his own personal interests are concerned. This is an intolerable abuse which would never have arisen if these taxes had been subject to a tribunal of any kind, for where judges are known to exist, fixed and definite laws must be observed.

[25] Your Majesty will be aware that these extensions have of late been carried to an excess hitherto unknown; that the Farmer is no longer satisfied with learning the family secrets recorded in the legal documents which are drawn up from day to day, but pries into the records of the last twenty years on the pretext that the dues have not been exacted with the requisite strictness. A private individual, on the other hand, who is the victim of extortion, may claim redress only within a period of two years.

[26] You will find, Sire, that this sort of annoyance has been carried to such an extent that people are reduced to signing documents privately instead of before a notary; and in those cases where it is indispensable that the document should be drawn up in regular form, those drafting it are often required to distort it by obscure and equivocal clauses, which give rise subsequently to interminable discussions, so that a tax established under the specious pretext of increasing the authenticity of documents and preventing suits at law forces your subjects, on the contrary, to renounce public contracts, and drags them into legal proceedings, which are ruining all our families.

---

[1] These comprised registration fees, the *franc-fief*, &c., as well as the revenue from the royal domain. *Cf.* Necker, *Administration des Finances*, Chap. I.

[2] A tax on sales of real estate.

[27] The right of *franc-fief*—which is also called a domain due—is a due exacted from commoners or non-nobles for the fiefs they hold; it, too, has been included in the arbitrary system of justice. It consists in a year's revenue, which one pays every twentieth year in order to be left in peace for the other nineteen. But when there is a transfer during the twenty years the new possessor is obliged to pay the tax, although the former owner is given no indemnity for the years of exemption which he paid for and has not enjoyed—a usage which may now be sanctioned by some regulation, but which was certainly in the beginning an extortion. Your Majesty will learn besides that eight sous in the livre have been added to a tax that already equaled the whole revenue, that in valuing property no deduction is made for costs, and that there are many other minor abuses. But what will most astonish Your Majesty is to learn that on the pretext of the payment of this tax, the Farmer-General undertakes to decide, through the medium of this arbitrary justice, a most interesting question of state—the question of nobility.

[28] The Intendants have been invested with authority to examine into disputes concerning *franc-fiefs*, registration dues and other similar taxes,—that is, the aim has been to make them judges of the administration of the revenue laws, of the amount to be paid for *franc-fief;* and, at present, if an individual claims that he is not subject to the tax because he is a noble, and the Farmer chooses to contest his nobility, the case must be carried before the same tribunal,[1] so that a noble depends on the will of a single man for the enjoyment of the rank which has been transmitted to him by his ancestors. It is easy to imagine to what lengths abuses of this sort of justice are likely to be carried, and Your Majesty will be still farther convinced by the facts which you may learn from public report.

[29] You will find, for example, that in 1723 the late King called for a confirmation due from all those who had been ennobled during the preceding reign, but that the law did not pronounce the penalty of forfeiture upon those who did not pay the tax; that such forfeiture has since been established by decrees in Council which did not take the form of letters-patent (as though one could be condemned to forfeit his rank by decrees which have not the characteristics of regularly registered laws); and lastly, that these decrees, of which the latest is

---

[1] *I. e.* the Intendant.

dated 1730, have always been considered purely comminatory, and that the Farmers-General themselves have publicly declared that they have never been put into execution. Indeed, their execution seemed impossible, for it would violate every principle of justice to punish the failure to pay a tax by the forfeiture of nobility, an ignominious punishment which is invariably reserved for those who are convicted of capital crimes. Still less possible would it seem to pronounce this penalty upon the children of the person who had failed to pay the tax— to declare forfeit of his nobility a citizen who received it at birth and has lived in conformity with that estate, because his father had neglected, in times gone by, to conform to a special tax law of whose existence he may have been ignorant.

[30] Severities such as these are discountenanced by every one; neither justice nor humanity could ever permit the literal execution of such laws, and the consequence is that that decree in Council of 1730, and many other laws of like character, have remained inoperative. But, Sire, it is in the very nature of arbitrary power that justice and humanity are bereft of their rights when but one man is deaf to their demands. A Farmer appeared who wished to revive the decree of 1730, forgotten since its inception, and a Minister who was willing to abandon to him all the families who had not paid the confirmation tax. Thus a man whose father or grandfather was ennobled as the highest reward for shedding his blood in his country's service, a man who, having passed his life following the example of his fathers, in the expensive profession of arms, has not found himself able to pay the tax, may to-day be deprived of the rights of his nobility because he has fulfilled its duties, and his family may be relegated by the pitiless Financier to the class of commoners, while the Financier himself, ennobled perhaps by the purchase of an office, enjoys the privileges of the highest nobility.

[31] This example will show Your Majesty to what extent a harsh ministry has been able to take advantage of removals too hastily accorded in the past, and you will readily believe that the abuses have not been restricted to the concessions made in earlier times, but that, especially during the absence of the Magistracy, when there was no danger of protest, the public calamities afforded an opportunity to subject new classes of affairs to an arbitrary power.

[32] We may cite as an instance the domiciliary visits made in search of contraband tobacco. The exorbitant price put upon tobacco

has for several years furnished such an incentive to fraud that to prevent it means have been employed which, while they become every
day more outrageous, are nevertheless universally ineffective. The
Farmers-General have obtained such laws as would excite civil war
should they be literally executed. Their Clerks are authorized to search
with the greatest strictness all houses, indiscriminately, without exception, and with no respect for rank, birth or dignities. Similar laws
have been obtained by the Farmers at various times in the past, and
for various objects, but excessive abuse has hitherto been restrained by
established justice, which could rigorously punish the Clerk who abused
the right which the law gave him; to-day that restraint no longer
exists; the last ministry seized the moment of the absence of the
Cour des aides to remove this class of affairs from the regular course
of justice and turn them over to the Commissioners of the Council.

[33] There are many more such removals that might be mentioned,
such as cases having to do with the tax on playing cards, the dues
collected at Poissy,[1] and many others. We wished to give Your
Majesty a few examples only, the rest are reserved for special presentation. When the whole matter has been submitted to Your Majesty
and your Ministers, we trust, Sire, that you will yourself recognize the
necessity of putting a stop to these abuses.

[34] It would seem as if the Farmer-General might have dispensed
with employing so many illegal expedients for avoiding the regular
course of justice, when one considers how many weapons have been
given him with which he can legally triumph over his adversaries in the
face of any system of justice. These methods no longer permit the
judges to attempt to discern where truth and justice lie, for they are
usually obliged to base their decisions upon documents which to the
eye of reason are obviously suspicious.

[35] This will be clear to Your Majesty when we have exposed the
method by which the Farmer discovers and proves cases of smuggling,
for the detection of fraud is the object of most of his suits. We shall
be obliged to weary you, Sire, with tedious details of the continual war
which is waged between two of the most contemptible varieties of
men—smugglers on the one hand, and spies on the other; but since it
is the innocent who suffer, and as the recital may make an impression
upon Your Majesty, we do not feel justified in omitting it.

[1] Upon cattle destined for the Paris markets.

[36] The means of detecting smuggling reduce themselves to two — the reports of Clerks and the information of spies. As to the Clerks' reports, the Farmer-General has the right to exercise, through his Clerks, and with some legal formalities, the most rigorous inspection of the highways, and often of private houses. If in their visits the Clerks believe they have discovered a case of smuggling, they report upon it, and by this report, signed by two Clerks, the facts are considered established and the fraud proved.

[37] If the individual accused in the report claims that the Clerks are slanderers, he cannot legally sustain his assertion except by an *Inscription en faux*. It is necessary to explain to Your Majesty what this means. It is not sufficient for the accused to assert that there are no proofs of facts alleged against him, he must prove the direct contrary; but such proof is by nature often impossible. How is one to prove a negative? How prove to the Clerks the falsity of the facts alleged by them, when the whole affair has taken place inside a house, without other witnesses than the accused and the Clerks themselves?

[38] Moreover, the formalities prescribed for the *Inscription en faux* are extremely complicated, and the omission of a single one deprives the accused of his rightful defense. In order to be permitted to enter the protest it is also necessary to pay a fee, which the majority of the people are not in a condition to pay; one is, besides, given a very short time for making his arrangements, that is to say, for consulting a legal adviser, looking for legal proofs, and borrowing the money necessary for the fee. It must therefore be acknowledged that a man of the people has no possible means of protecting himself against these reports signed by two Clerks.

[39] It is not at all uncommon for one of these Clerks not to be able either to read or write, although he may have been taught to form the characters of his name. The Farmers-General take care to have one in each brigade who can write; it is he who makes out the report, and one of his comrades signs it, and it does not seem necessary to them that he who signs should also be able to read. Your *Cour des aides*, learning of this abuse some time before the dispersion of the Magistracy, issued an administrative decree which forbade Clerks who could not read to sign these reports. The Farmers-General ventured to complain of this as a decree which rendered their administration impossible; and we think, Sire, that during the absence of the *Cour des aides* the decree has been but ill executed.

[40] But there is another abuse which the *Cour des aides* is unable to remedy by its own authority, since it consists of a secret compact between the Farmer and his Clerks, a compact expressly forbidden by law, but of which it is impossible to obtain legal proofs. It is well known that in spite of the legal prohibition the Farmer promises to his Clerks part of the fines to which individuals are condemned through their reports, and this constitutes a part of their wages. So smuggling is considered proved against a citizen by the simple affirmation of two men, who are not only in the pay of his adversary, the Farmer-General, but who expect a remuneration proportionate to the sum which he is condemned to pay.

[41] Such is the judicial method employed in proving smuggling by means of reports. But the Farmer must also have some means of discovering where to look for fraud and how to direct the investigations of his Clerks. It is to this end that it is considered desirable that there should be in every association of merchants, in every house, and in every family, a spy who shall inform the Financier that in such a place and on such an occasion an arrest may be made. The spy does not need to show himself, but the Clerks, warned by him, surprise the person who has been denounced, and either acquire proofs, or manufacture them themselves in their reports. When a warning has been successful a reward is given to the informer, *i. e.*, to the accomplice, the associate, the house-fellow, to the wife who has denounced her husband, to the son who has denounced his father.

[42] Deign, Sire, to reflect a moment upon this picture of the administration of the Farm. Through the confidence placed in these reports a premium is put upon perjury, while by this system of spies domestic treason is rewarded. These are the means by which more than one hundred and fifty millions are every year brought into Your Majesty's treasury.

[43] It is not for us, Sire, to suggest to you other taxes which might replace this immense contribution ; it is not even for us to determine whether the resources of economy might not replace it. It is nevertheless imperative that relief should be afforded to a people burdened by this monstrous system of administration ; and if it is true that economy alone will not suffice to enable Your Majesty to renounce the entire revenue derived from the Farm, at least a certain mitigation of the public misfortunes might be afforded if, by reducing expenses, a certain portion of the revenue could be sacrificed. This is why we

have felt it our duty to show you the terrible spectacle of the most
glorious kingdom in the world groaning under a tyranny which
increases day by day.

[44] It is customary, Sire, to praise and implore Your Majesty's
benevolence at the same moment, but it is your justice that we, the
defenders of the people, would invoke. We know that almost all the
sentiments to which the soul of a king is susceptible, the love of glory
and of pleasure, even friendship, and the desire, so natural to a great
prince, of rendering happy those about him, form perpetual obstacles
to that rigorous justice which he owes to his people, for it is only at
the expense of the people that a king can be victorious over his enemies,
magnificent in his court, and generous toward those who surround him.

[45] France, we might say the whole of Europe, is crushed under
the weight of taxes, and the rivalry of the Powers has led them to vie
with each other in the enormous expenses which have rendered these
taxes necessary; expenses are moreover doubled by a huge national
debt contracted under previous reigns, Your Majesty must therefore
remember that although your ancestors covered themselves with glory,
that glory is being paid for by the present generation; that while they
captivated all hearts by their liberality, and astonished Europe by
their magnificence, that magnificence and that liberality were the
origin of taxes and debts which still exist to-day.

[46] Your Majesty should never forget that the virtuous Louis XII.,
in spite of his passion for war, never believed himself justified in employing means which would have been onerous to his subjects; and in
spite of the generosity which was his characteristic virtue, he had the
courage to expose himself to the reproach of avarice from his courtiers,
because he knew that while a king's economy might be condemned
by a few frivolous or greedy men, his prodigality would make the tears
of a whole nation flow.

[47] That great truth, Sire, is recognized to-day by all the nations
who have learned from the experience of many centuries to require in
their kings only such virtues as make for the general happiness; and
if at your accession all France enthusiastically proclaimed its love for
the race of its masters, stern duty, Sire, obliges us to confess that a part
of those transports were due to the opinion which had been formed of
Your Majesty since your tenderest years, and to the hope that a wise
economy would diminish the public burdens.

[48] But, Sire, while this economy is demanded of you by the voice

of the nation at large, your throne is surrounded by those who believe royal grandeur to consist only in luxury, while the miserable creature whom the heavy taxes deprive of his daily bread is far away, the objects of your benevolence and magnificence are continually before your eyes. It is, therefore, necessary to oppose to them the terrifying but not exaggerated picture of the condition of the people. Oh, that it might be ever present to you, Sire ! Had it been so to your royal predecessors, Your Majesty would to-day be able to follow the dictates of your heart ; and when you learned that the dictates of humanity were violated by the fiscal laws established in your kingdom you would not hesitate to revoke them, and would not be hindered by the necessity of paying the state debt, which is a continual obstacle to the reform of these odious abuses.

[49] For the present, Sire, without venturing to propose to Your Majesty a general reformation of the farmed taxes, special memoirs may be presented to you on various subjects, which may be discussed with your Ministers, for it is impossible that Your Majesty should yourself enter into the details of all the devices that have been invented by the Farmers-General to secure the payment of the taxes, and by the delinquents to elude them. What we do ask at present of Your Majesty personally is to institute an investigation into the manner in which all taxes were extended under the last ministry, and into the removals granted with unprecedented profusion.

[50] You have commanded us, Sire, to accept without examination whatever has received the stamp of law during the period when we were excluded from our functions. A superior power has prevented us from watching over the interests and rights of the people. It becomes necessary, therefore, for Your Majesty to undertake this duty, and in the investigation which you will institute we beseech you to distinguish with the greatest care what is really essential to the collection of the taxes from what has been introduced only through the blind complaisance of the ministry toward the Financiers, in order to gratify their despotism. Your Majesty should eliminate from these new laws, all that goes to establish an arbitrary system of justice. We admit that since there are excessive taxes to be collected it is necessary to have rigorous laws, but these laws can at least be definite ; for no motive, no consideration, no interest, can justify Your Majesty in permitting the fate of the people to depend upon the avidity of a Farmer or the caprice of a government official.

[51] Finally, Sire, although it is not a part of our function to suggest plans to you, and although we must, above all things, avoid sanctioning doubtful systems, there is nevertheless one truth so important, so evident, so calculated to appeal to Your Majesty, that we feel obliged to submit it to you ; that is, that there would be an assured advantage for Your Majesty and an immense gain for the people in simplifying the existing taxes and the laws which provide for their collection.

[52] We have already observed that the regulations established by the Farm form an appallingly voluminous code ; yet there is no one versed either in jurisprudence or in administration who will not testify that only simple laws are good laws. Now, when one considers the taxes the collection of which has given rise to this code, one finds that the dues on the various commodities differ according to the kind of trade concerned, the localities where they are collected, and the rank of the individual taxpayer. Fraud, always active and industrious, profits by this want of uniformity, and makes its way, so to speak, between the sinuosities of the law ; the financial administration is constantly inventing new methods of pursuing it, and the weapons employed against smugglers annoy and embarrass everybody in the enjoyment of their property and the liberty of their persons.

[53] This accounts for the great multiplication of Clerks, who bring their impertinent curiosity to bear upon all the actions of life. In this way the Financiers have acquired the right to inspect merchandise, to enter houses, and to violate family secrets. It is this inequality of the taxes collected in the different provinces which obliged your royal predecessors to divide the kingdom in every direction by customs lines, which it is necessary to guard, like frontiers, with an innumerable army of Clerks.

[54] All this would be remedied, Sire, by simplifying the taxes. Your Majesty's Farmers would save a large part of the expense of administration, and smuggling would become more difficult, for nothing favors it so much as the complication of the taxes and the obscurity of the regulations governing them. The people would enjoy the advantage of being less tormented by the investigations of the employees of the Farm—investigations which are nowhere so annoying as in regions where smuggling is to be expected, notably within the limits of the so-called territories of " the five great Farms," [1] " the *aides*," " the great salt tax," &c.

[1] A portion of central and northern France separated from the rest of the country by a customs line.

[55] We do not claim, Sire, that this simplification would be an easy task. It is, however, evidently possible theoretically, and it would be of the greatest service to the State; but to carry it out, it would be necessary to know in the greatest detail not only the revenue produced by each tax in each district, but the real source of that revenue as well, and to calculate exactly what increase or diminution each of the proposed changes would produce in the amount. It would be necessary to know not only the actual, but the possible product, to consider not only the interests of the Farm, but those of the cultivator, the manufacturer, the merchant, and the consumer, of each commodity. We venture, nevertheless, to assure Your Majesty that this task may be accomplished in spite of its difficulties. There is certainly an enormous amount of material in the registers of the General Farm, in the offices of the Ministers, of the Intendants of Finance, and even of many merchants; it only remains to determine how and by whom it shall be utilized.

[56] Shall the Farmers-General themselves be charged with this task? That has been suggested more than once, Sire. They have been asked to propose plans for reform; but we believe it to be our duty to inform Your Majesty that while the simplification of the taxes would be advantageous to the Farm, the most expert of the Farmers have a personal interest contrary to that of the Farm, because the science which they have been at such pains to acquire would be rendered useless, and it is this profound science, and the complication of the machine which they have to operate, which makes them necessary to the government, and permits them to dictate laws to the Ministers. Can it be doubted, moreover, that the Financiers, if transformed into legislators, would add to the present severity of the taxes whatever might serve to cement the despotism, at once intolerable to the people and useless to Your Majesty, to which they have already subjected the Nation?

[57] Certainly the Farmers-General should be consulted. In spite of the observations which we have made to Your Majesty, there have been those among them who have had sufficient regard for the public welfare to sacrifice to it the interests and prejudices of their position. Nevertheless, in consulting them, it should never be forgotten in what respects their interests are opposed to those of the people and to those of Your Majesty.

[58] You have much to expect, Sire, in this undertaking, from the

zeal and knowledge of the officials at the head of your finances.[1] We even believe that it is important that the work should be done under their direction. But shall they perform the task themselves? Can so great a work be performed by a single man—and a man whose time is, perhaps, already fully occupied by the daily current of affairs in his administration? Doubtless he would employ collaborators; but if the work were put under the control of a single official the same disadvantages which have so often been experienced in the past would inevitably result from being dependent upon one man, and having only a single individual to defend the people against the united efforts of the Financiers. Add to this that his death would some day involve the loss of all the knowledge acquired and of all the work done in that very branch, perhaps, of the subject which it might prove especially necessary to clear up.

[59] It would be well, Sire, if all the details of the administration of the Farms could be known both to Your Majesty, for whom the taxes are levied, and to the people, who pay them. Then, when the people addressed their complaints to you, and asked for relief from their burdens, the remedy might be suggested to you, and Your Majesty would be able to form your own opinion upon it. Since this is impossible in the present state of the laws, it is certainly desirable to endeavor to simplify them. But until this task can be achieved and a new body of laws be given to France, can no restraint be put upon the tyranny of the Farmers, founded as it is upon the general ignorance of the laws and their administration? There is such a remedy, Sire, for you can at once order the Farmers-General to publish exact and circumstantial lists of the taxes to be collected, and a short, clear, and systematic account of such of the regulations to be observed as it is important for the public to know.

[60] They may tell Your Majesty that this work will be long and difficult; nevertheless, no one can honestly refuse to admit that there is no branch of the farmed taxes with which a number of the Farmers or their directors are not especially occupied. Each of them has a complete treatise upon his own division of the taxes, which furnishes him with the data that the General Farm requires from time to time; he has also a set of abridged instructions for the direction of his Clerks, and it is but right that these should be communicated to the public,

[1] The Controller-General is here meant. Turgot was just then at the head of the finances.

since it must always be on the defensive against the attempts of these Clerks. The work is then already done, it needs only to be made public.

[61] But we must warn Your Majesty that the Farmers will not lend themselves readily to this publication, the necessity of which is clearly proved by their very unwillingness. They do not wish the people to acquire a knowledge of the taxes. They desire to keep the country in blind subjugation to the General Farm. They fear that a body of lawyers will arise in each province who, having studied the financial laws, will be able to aid individual citizens in their contests with the Farmer. But it is your duty, Sire, to help your unhappy subjects by increasing their facilities for self-defense. You owe them the support of the laws, and that support becomes only an illusion when the laws are unknown to those who have the right to invoke them.

[62] In thus presenting to you, Sire, a general sketch of the farmed taxes, it has not been our intention to enter in detail into any particular subject. Nevertheless, we must beseech Your Majesty to take into especial consideration the protests addressed to the late King in the month of August, 1770, which up to the present time have received no response.[1]

. . . .
. . . .
. . . .

[1] One might be tempted to look upon the omission here indicated as a device of the printer to stimulate interest by a show of mystery. The court certainly expresses its opinions of the *lettres de cachet* quite clearly in the paragraphs immediately following the gap in the text. It is possible that in the portion of the document which is left out, Malesherbes briefly reviewed the contents of the remarkable protest of August 14th, 1770, to which he here refers, and which, he declares, had been completely ignored by the government. The curious circumstances that called forth this earlier protest against the abuse of the royal orders for imprisonment, helps to explain the attitude of Malesherbes toward the Farmers of the revenue. The Farm, suspecting a merchant, named Monnerat, of smuggling, obtained a *lettre de cachet* from the king's officials, and shut him up in one of the worst of the Parisian prisons. He was first confined in a perfectly dark, subterranean dungeon, with a great chain fastened about his neck. After a month or so he was put into a more tolerable cell, where he was kept for a year and a half. He was then released, and found that he had been imprisoned by mistake, having been unluckily taken for the man for whom the *lettre de cachet* was really intended. The Farmers-General refused to indemnify him in any way for their error, so he brought suit for damages in the *Cour des aides* of Paris, of which Malesherbes was, it will be remembered, First President. The Farmers, however, had sufficient influence to procure the removal (*évocation*) of the case to the Royal Council, and the *Cour des aides* was peremptorily forbidden to pursue the matter farther.

7

[63] Why may we not venture to hope, Sire, that this important investigation may lead you to perform an act of justice which would shed the greatest lustre upón the opening of your reign, namely, to choose men worthy of confidence, and entrust to them the examination of all the orders which to-day detain any citizen in exile or captivity?

[64] Our hopes carry us still farther; for if Your Majesty decides to have this investigation made, we do not doubt that you will improve the opportunity to establish certain principles in this matter where none have been recognized before. One thing at least will become apparent, that orders affecting the personal liberty of citizens should never be granted to private individuals, either for their personal interest or to avenge their private injuries; for in a country where there are laws individuals should have no need of extra-judicial orders; and, moreover, such orders granted to the powerful against the weak, with no chance of redress, constitute the worst form of injustice.

[65] It may perhaps be thought that there are certain exceptional cases in which the public good requires acts of authority that are not clothed with the ordinary formalities of justice. It will be urged that it is sometimes desirable to furnish a substitute for the tardy course of jus-

In the vigorous protest which the tribunal thereupon submitted to the king, it claims that the proceedings which the ministry had so hastily nullified had brought to light " a well devised system of despotism " and a new plan of the financiers to sub- stitute acts of arbitrary authority for the regular legal procedure, not only in cases of smuggling but in any instance where the formalities of the law would embarrass them.

While the tribunal does not deny that the *lettres de cachet* may be legitimate in some cases, especially in order to reach offenders who have taken refuge in some nobleman's residence or other asylum where they are ordinarily exempt from arrest, it maintains that every one who believes himself unjustly imprisoned should be permitted to bring suit for damages against those who obtained the order, for " this is the only protection against the most dangerous form of persecution." The removal of Mon- nerat's case to the Royal Council is, it claims, practically a refusal of justice, " for will an unfortunate victim who has long languished in prison and dungeon, in virtue of an order granted by your Ministers and procured by the Farmers-General, dare to plead in your Council against these same Farmers? "

The worst of it is, moreover, that this abuse has become a recognized principle with the government officials and financiers. " They have established the principle in your Council that to bring suit for damages against those who have committed an injustice in executing an order surreptitiously obtained from Your Majesty, is to set at naught your own royal authority." Now when the Farmers have no other proof for their suspicions than delation, or information which the courts would regard as open to suspicion, they proceed to punish the supposed crime " by means of those orders of Your Majesty which are called *lettres de cachet*." Those who are merely suspected

tice, which might allow criminals to escape ; that police control and the public safety in great cities make it necessary to keep some hold upon suspected persons, and that often public and family interest are at one in requiring the separation from society of an individual who might cause annoyance, and against whom there are no other proofs than those which are controlled by the family itself which is seeking to protect itself from the ignominy of a public trial.

[66] But when all these considerations have been discussed in your presence, and all these abuses have been brought to your attention, you will see, Sire, that these are mere pretexts, which could never have furnished a sufficient justification for permitting the liberty of the citizen to be subjected to arbitrary authority, or that, at least, the right of protesting against wrongs should be secured to the oppressed.

[67] You will perceive that in cases where justice itself demands prompt and secret measures in order that the delays of the law may not permit the flight of the criminal, it is still possible for a Royal Legislator to give greater activity to justice without resorting to illegal methods, and that the necessary celerity would thus be attained with-

of smuggling are in this way cast into horrible prisons or even into dungeons destined for those guilty of the most hideous crimes, as the treatment of Monnerat clearly shows. Should one of these ill-starred victims of the Farm seek justice on the ground that he is no smuggler or that he has been treated with undue harshness, he is prevented from gaining his suit by the removal of his case to the King's Council.

Lettres de cachet are, however, by no means confined to the orders granted to the Farmers. "Consider, Sire," Malesherbes continues, "how enormously the number of these orders has increased, and upon what a variety of grounds and for what strictly personal reasons they are now granted. Formerly they were reserved for affairs of State, and then, indeed, Sire, it was but right that the courts should respect the secrets of your administration. Next they were granted under certain peculiar circumstances—as when the sympathies of the sovereign were aroused by the tears of a family that feared dishonor. To-day they are supposed to be necessary every time a common man has shown himself wanting in the respect due to a person of quality; as if the powerful had not advantages enough already. They are, too, the usual form of punishment for indiscreet remarks, which can never be substantiated except by delation—always an unreliable form of proof, since the delator is, of necessity, subject to suspicion." Further, the orders are granted with great recklessness and are despatched by the clerks in the government offices, and even at the instigation of the subdelegates in the provinces." "The result is, Sire, that no citizen in your realms can be certain that his liberty will not be sacrificed to private vengeance, for no one is so great as to be exempt from the hate of a minister or so insignificant as to be beneath the animosity of a clerk of the Farm."

The text of this *protest* is given by Vignaux's *Mém. sur Malesherbes*, pp. 61–96.

out depriving the person who has been unjustly arrested of redress against his calumniator.

[68] You will perceive that if the public safety demands that some hold shall be kept upon a person who has given just cause for suspicion, the legitimacy of these suspicions should be formally verified, in order that an innocent victim of such precautions may demand and obtain indemnity, or that he may at least know why, and by whom, these violent measures have been taken.

[69] And, finally, you will perceive that in order to shield a family which has itself invoked aid of the government against one of its members who has dishonored it, it is by no means necessary that this kind of justice should be without possible redress. It is, in reality, only the publicity of legal procedure which it is desired to avoid. But without making the affair public, it is possible to record the reason for the royal order in a document signed by the person who issues the order and by those who have obtained it, to preserve this document at least during the whole time of the detention of the prisoner, and to communicate its contents to him.

[70] The prisoner, whatever his crime, should be permitted to present his defense, and even to demand that the reasons for this severe order should be examined afresh by others than those who have issued it, and be reported upon anew to the King, who would naturally choose for this examination men of the most assured and unassailable reputation. But since it is very difficult and often impossible for a prisoner to reach the King himself, it would be necessary, from time to time, that all the royal prisons should be visited and all the existing *lettres de cachet* reviewed by persons unconnected with the administration and of acknowledged integrity.

[71] If it were known that Your Majesty had taken these precautions against being misled, and especially could it be remembered that your reign was inaugurated by a strict investigation of all that the previous administration had been reproached with, we are confident, Sire, that the abuse of these orders issued in your name would become very rare. We can only give you a glimpse of the advantages which would result from such an investigation, but if it is once made you will be able to measure its importance by the gratitude of the Nation. We have indulged in a digression, Sire, which we cannot regret, since it has afforded an opportunity of presenting to you certain observations, which may be of some service, upon the species of abuses which have given

rise to the greatest complaint on the part of one portion of the Nation, and which would be among the easiest to reform.

[72] It is now time to return to the subject of the taxes. The annoyances occasioned by the collection of the farmed taxes have one excuse, viz., the necessity of obtaining for Your Majesty the considerable revenue which these taxes produce. But it does not seem as if there need be the same annoyances in the case of the taxes which are levied directly upon the people. When the amount to be raised is fixed, as it should always be, it should only remain to choose the fairest, simplest, and least wasteful method of apportionment. The administration is therefore inexcusable when in levying these taxes it introduces a despotism as useless it is odious, and augments the tax itself by an expensive system of collection, the cost of which is always borne by the people. But this is just what happens, Sire, in the levying of all the direct taxes, the *taille*, the poll tax and the twentieth; and a part of these annoyances are even felt in connection with the exaction of personal service demanded of the people, as in the case of the militia and the *corvée*.

[73] But the discussion of these abuses brings us to much larger questions. The collection of the taxes upon commodities does not depend upon the form of government, but the apportionment of the direct taxes is intimately connected with the constitution of the monarchy. The faults of this apportionment form part of a general plan of administration which has long existed in your kingdom, and they can only be remedied by a general reformation to which it might please Your Majesty to subject the whole administrative system.

[74] We shall therefore examine the regulations affecting each of the direct taxes in order that Your Majesty may observe the development of this unfortunate system. But we must first consider its origin; we must make plain to Your Majesty its dominating principle and its consequences, and you may perhaps be astonished to see to what extent the pretext of your authority has been directed against that authority itself.

[75] Pardon us, Sire, if we make use of the term *despotism*, hateful as it is; permit us to dispense with vexatious circumlocutions in view of the important facts which we have to lay before you. The despotism against which we protest is that which is exercised without your knowledge, by the emissaries of the administration, persons absolutely unknown to Your Majesty. Not, Sire, that it is our intention to offer

to Your Majesty a useless and perhaps dangerous dissertation upon the limits of your royal authority; on the contrary, it is the right to invoke that authority which we propose to vindicate for every citizen, and by the term *despotism* we mean that sort of administration which tends to deprive your subjects of this right, which is so precious to them, and to shield those from your justice who oppress your people.

[76] The idea of despotism, or of absolute authority, has differed at different times and with different nations. There is, for example, a form of government which is called *oriental despotism*, a government, namely, in which not only the sovereign enjoys absolute and unlimited power, but in which every executor of his orders also exercises unlimited power. The result is, of course, an intolerable tyranny. For there is an infinite difference between the same power wielded by a ruler, whose real interest is that of his people, and by a subject, who, intoxicated by prerogatives to which he was not destined, delights in aggravating the burdens of his equals. This sort of despotism, transmitted from the higher to the lower functionaries, reaches in the end every subject, so that there is not an individual in the whole empire who is safe from it.

[77] The vices of such a government are due both to its constitution and its customs; to its constitution, because the people who are subject to it have neither tribunals, nor codes of law, nor representatives. There are no tribunals, therefore authority is exercised by a single man; there are no fixed and positive laws, therefore he to whom authority is given enacts laws at his own pleasure, which means, in general, according to his caprices; there are no representatives of the people, and therefore the governor of a province may oppress it with impunity against the will and without the knowledge of his sovereign.

[78] The manners and customs of the country favor this impunity, for the peoples who are subjected to this species of despotism are always a prey to ignorance. No one can read, no general intercourse is maintained; the cries of the oppressed cannot be heard outside the borders of the province they inhabit. The innocent victim has not therefore the support of public opinion, which is so powerful a restraint upon the tyranny of subordinate officials.

[79] Such is the unhappy situation of such a people that the most benevolent of sovereigns cannot make the effects of his justice felt except by those who are near his person, and in the few matters of which he can himself take cognizance. The most that he can do for

the rest of his subjects is to choose the higher representatives of his authority as little unwisely as possible, and to urge them to make the best possible choice for the inferior offices. But with all that he can do, the citizens of the lowest class will always be as absolutely subject to the authority of a despot of the lowest grade as the nobles are to the sovereign himself.

[80] It would seem that such a form of government could not exist in nations which have laws, intelligence and habits of refinement; and in civilized countries, even when the ruler possesses absolute power, the condition of the people ought to be very different. However absolute the power, justice may be regularly administered by tribunals governed by fixed laws, and when judges depart from these laws it is possible to appeal to a higher court, and, in the end, to the sovereign authority itself. These appeals are possible because all official acts are duly committed to writing and recorded in public registers, because every citizen may find an enlightened defender, and because the public itself is the censor of the judges. And not only may individuals obtain justice, but societies, communities, cities, and whole provinces as well, but in order to defend their rights they should have assemblies and representatives.

[81] Thus in a civilized country, even though it be ruled by an absolute power, there need be no interest, either public or private, left unguarded, for all the representatives of royal authority should be subjected to three kinds of restraint, that of the law, that of appeal to higher authority, and that of public opinion.

[82] This distinction between the different kinds of absolute power is not a new one. It has often been made by jurists and authors, both modern and ancient, who have written upon the subject of law. It may be derived from a perusal of the history and the descriptions of various countries; but it was necessary to recall it on account of the important truth which we desire to deduce from it. We must make clear to Your Majesty that the government which it is desired to establish in France is the real despotism of uncivilized countries, and that the most highly cultivated nation, in a century of refined customs and manners, is menaced with that form of government in which the sovereign cannot be enlightened, however sincerely he may desire to be.

[83] France, like the rest of Occidental Europe, was governed by feudal law, but each of the European kingdoms has experienced its own particular changes since that form of government was destroyed.

Certain nations have been permitted to discuss their rights with their sovereign, and the prerogatives of both ruler and people have thus been established.   In others absolute sovereign authority asserted itself so speedily that the national rights were disregarded.   This has resulted in at least one advantage for these countries, viz., the absence of any pretext for the destruction of intermediary powers or for the restraint of that liberty, which is the natural right of all men, to deliberate in common upon common interests, and to appeal to the supreme power against the tyranny of subordinate authorities.

[84] In France the nation has always been profoundly conscious of its rights and of its freedom.   Our traditions have been more than once recognized by our Kings, who have even gloried in being the sovereigns of a free people.   Nevertheless the articles of that freedom have never been duly drawn up, and the real power, the power of arms, which under the feudal system was in the hands of the nobles, has been entirely concentrated in the sovereign.

[85] When, therefore, there have been cases of grievous abuse of authority, the representatives of the Nation have not been satisfied with complaining of mal-administration, they have felt obliged to vindicate the national rights.   They have talked not merely of justice, but of liberty; and the consequence of their efforts has been that the Ministers, who were always ready to seize every possible means of shielding their administration from examination, have been artful enough to arouse suspicion in regard both to the governmental bodies which protested and to the protests themselves.   Recourse to the King against his Ministers has been represented as an attack upon his authority.   The grievances of the Estates, the remonstrances of the Magistrates, have been distorted into dangerous measures, against which the government should protect itself.   The most powerful of Kings have been persuaded that they must fear even the tears of a submissive people. Upon this pretext a government has been introduced into France which is more fatal than despotism and is worthy of Oriental barbarism, namely, the clandestine system of administration, which under the eyes of a just ruler and in the midst of an enlightened nation permits injustice to show herself, nay more, to flaunt herself openly.   Entire departments of the administration are founded upon principles of injustice, and no recourse either to public opinion or to a superior authority is possible.

[86] It is this administrative despotism, and especially this system

of secrecy, which we would denounce to Your Majesty, for we have no intention of venturing to discuss the consecrated prerogatives of the throne. It is sufficient for us that Your Majesty has disavowed, in the act which re-established the Magistracy, the tyrannical measures enacted under a ministry which is now dismissed. And we intend to conform to the intentions of Your Majesty in ignoring certain questions which ought never to have been raised.

[87] But it will not be overstepping the bounds of a *due subordination* to lay before you a series of encroachments upon national liberty, the liberty natural to all men, which make it impossible for you to hear the grievances of your subjects or to watch the conduct of your administrative officers.

First, an attempt has been made to do away with the real representatives of the nation.

Secondly, the protests of those representatives whom it has been impossible to do away with have been rendered illusory.

Thirdly, there is an evident desire to make such protests altogether impossible, and to this end the system of secrecy has been introduced. This secrecy is of a double nature; it aims, on the one hand, to shield the operations of the administration from the eyes of the Nation and of Your Majesty himself, and on the other to conceal from the public the identity of the administrative officers. This, Sire, is the outline of the system which we shall now proceed to elucidate.

[88] We state as the first aim of this despotism the attempt to do away with all representatives of the people, and if Your Majesty will but consider the significance of several facts, no one of which is open to doubt, you will be convinced of the truth of this statement.

[89] General assemblies of the Nation have not been convened for a hundred and sixty years, and for a long time before that they were very infrequent, and, we venture to say, almost useless, since what should have rendered their presence especially necessary, namely, the fixing of the taxes, was accomplished without them.

[90] Certain provinces had their own assemblies or Provincial Estates; but some of the provinces have been deprived of this precious privilege, and in those where the Estates still exist, their functions have been restricted within limits which become narrower every day. It is not too much to say that a continual warfare is maintained in our provinces between the representatives of the people and the guardians of arbitrary power, and in this warfare despotism gains fresh victories daily.

[91] The provinces which had no Provincial Estates were called *Pays d'Election*, and certain tribunals once actually existed there called *Elections*, composed of persons elected by the province, who, at least in the matter of the apportionment of the taxes, performed some of the functions of Provincial Estates. These tribunals still exist under the same name, *Elections*, but the name is all that remains of the original institution. Their members are no longer really elected by the province, and, such as they are, they have been almost completely subordinated to the Intendants in the exercise of the functions which remain to them. We shall have occasion to speak later of the *Elections* in considering the *taille*. We shall then inform Your Majesty how they differ from the Provincial Estates; for the present, suffice it to say that the province no longer elects any true representatives.

[92] Each corporation or community still had the right, at least, to administer its own affairs, a right which we will not say formed a part of the original constitution of the realm, for it is more ancient even than that—it is a natural right, a right of all intelligent beings. Nevertheless even this has been taken away from your subjects; and we do not fear to say that the administration has in this matter fallen into excesses which must be called puerile.

[93] Since it has become a political principle with your powerful Ministers, not to permit the National Assemblies to be convoked, things have gone from bad to worse, until the deliberations of the inhabitants of a village have been declared null and void unless authorized by the Intendant. Hence if a community wishes to make an outlay, however insignificant, it must obtain the assent of the Subdelegate of the Intendant, and must follow the plan which he suggests, employ the workmen whom he favors, and pay them in accordance with his dictation. If the community wishes to bring a suit at law, the proceedings must be authorized by the Intendant; the community must first plead its cause before his tribunal before taking it to a court of justice, and if the opinion of the Intendant differs from that of the people, or if their opponent enjoys some influence in the Intendant's office, the community is deprived of the opportunity of defending its rights.

[94] Such, Sire, are the means which have been employed to stifle all municipal feeling in France, to extinguish, if possible, even the sentiment of citizenship. The whole Nation, so to speak, has been declared incapable of managing its own affairs, and has been put under the charge of guardians.

[95] The destruction of protesting bodies was but the first step toward the abolition of the right of protest itself. It has not yet come to an express prohibition of all recourse to the prince, and of all independent action on the part of the provinces; but Your Majesty knows that every petition which deals with the interests of a province or of the Nation as a whole is regarded, when it is signed by a single individual, as a punishable liberty, and if signed by a number of persons, as evidence of a seditious association. It was, however, necessary to make some ostensible reparation to the Nation for ceasing to convoke the Estates, so the Sovereign announced that the Courts of Justice should take the place of these Estates, and that the Magistrates should act as the representatives of the people.

[96] But after having given the Magistrates this new title to console the Nation for the loss of its real representatives, every opportunity was taken to emphasize the fact that the functions of the Judges were limited to their own district and to matters of litigation; hence the right of representation has been restricted within the same limits.

[97] Thus all sorts of abuses may be committed by the administration without ever coming to the knowledge of the King, either through the representatives of the people, since in most of the provinces there are no representatives; or through the Courts of Justice, for they are set aside as incompetent so soon as they venture to speak upon matters of administration; or through individuals, who have been taught by severe examples in the past that it is a crime to invoke the justice of their Sovereign.

[98] In spite of these obstacles the Administrative Officials have always dreaded the voice of the public, a species of protest which can never be wholly silenced; and perhaps they have also been fearful lest a day should come when a King would demand, of his own accord, an account of the secrets of the administration. They were consequently anxious to make such an account impossible, or at least to insure its being rendered by themselves without any chance of contradiction; and it is to this end that they have made such strenuous efforts to introduce a clandestine system of administration.

[99] In order to prove this assertion in all its bearings we should be obliged to enter into the details of all phases of the government, but a few examples will suffice to render its truth apparent. We shall choose our examples from the taxes, which constitute our principal theme, and we shall not hesitate to cite the administrations of those who have

done the most to deserve public approval, for we wish to acquaint Your
Majesty with the intrinsic vices of the system, however much they may
have been neutralized for a time by the personal qualities of the Admin-
istrator himself.

[100] It is acknowledged, for example, throughout Europe that
nothing rendered the previous reign more noteworthy than the construction of roads, which facilitate commerce and double the value of
property in the realm.   The government has believed hitherto that the
corvée was necessary to this great work ; yet the *corvée* is not authorized
by any law of the land.[1]   It would seem that it ought to have been
legally sanctioned, and then it would have been possible to establish
and make public fixed rules for the apportionment of the labor which
is often more burdensome to the people than the *taille* itself.

[101] But this method has not been adopted.   It was urged that there
was reason to fear the sensation which would be excited in the kingdom
should a law be enacted which, by regulating the *corvée*, would seem to
authorize it.   Consequently all the operations have been carried out in
secret, and not even a printed decree of the Council has ever been
issued concerning an exaction from which the people have so long
suffered.   A province learns that the construction of a road has been
decreed only when the work on it has begun and it is too late to oppose it, even if the choice of the route is contrary to the interest of the
province.   If the work is apportioned with injustice, or with too great
harshness, those who have complaints to make have no legal judges
before whom to plead their cause, no fixed rules to oppose to the rigor
of the orders they have received, and no means for legally proving the
injustice which has been done them.

[102] It is said that Your Majesty is desirous of mitigating the
severity of the *corvée*, or substituting for it some other form of taxation.[2]
The Nation awaits these changes with confidence, and already shows its
gratitude ; and we venture to hope that whatever substitute is found

---

[1] The *corvée* was originally the unpaid labor which a lord might exact from his
tenant.   There was no regular royal *corvée* until 1738, when the new interest in highways led the Controller-General to issue a simple instruction to the Intendants author-
izing them to employ forced labor in constructing the roads.

[2] Turgot substituted for the *corvée* a general road tax to be paid by all land owners,
except the clergy.   The preamble to his edict (Feb. 1776) gives an almost sensa-
tional account of existing abuses.   See *Œuvres de Turgot*, edited by Daire, Vol. II,
pp. 287 *sqq.*

for the *corvée* will not be infected with the same secrecy. We never-theless felt constrained to mention the abuses which occur in this branch of the administration, as they are among the most striking examples of the general system.

[103] It is much the same with the tax of the twentieth, except that in this the abuses have a still flimsier pretext. It may be said in regard to the *corvée* that the celerity required in the execution of public works will not permit waiting on the discussion of instances of indi-vidual injustice, but the twentieth has been imposed upon the same land almost without interruption every year for the last forty years. Can it be credited that in all these forty years the rolls of this tax have never been recorded where private individuals might consult them?

[104] This formality has not been omitted through negligence, for the matter was presented to the King by his *Cour des aides* in 1756. The ministry of that period submitted the evidence presented, and the late King consented that such records should be made ; but the Min-isters who followed, after resorting for several years to all sorts of subterfuges which might indirectly obviate the consequences of the King's sacred word, finally succeeded in getting it definitely revoked.

[105] We shall not here recall all the details of a matter that is past for fear of wearying Your Majesty, but, if Your Majesty desires farther information, the facts have not been forgotten and it will be easy to present them to you. We shall content ourselves for the present with observing that the majority of the deceptions practiced by the Collectors of the twentieth are necessarily unknown and unpunished by reason of this secrecy. For example, when a Collector betrays the interests of the royal treasury by favoring some individual, and, in order to conceal his deception from the Ministers, makes up the sum by unjustly aug-menting the quotas of others, the injured parties have no means of proving the injustice without being permitted to inspect the whole list, and this list is kept secret.

[106] Your Majesty will see by this example that this sort of abuse, which is permitted by the secrecy of the rolls, is precisely that which is most opposed to the interests of the King, of the department of finance, of the treasury. It is not therefore in the King's interest that the Administrative Officials have prohibited the publication of the tax-rolls ; it is purely to shield their own conduct from all examination and to. insure impunity to their Collectors.

[107] When all these precautions are found to be insufficient, and

the vexations become so evident that there is no way of palliating them, it usually happens that the culpable persons insure their impunity by means of the second sort of secrecy, which, as we have said, conceals the identity of the Official, and ordinarily makes it impossible to discover who is responsible for any particular abuse of authority.

[108] The administration of your kingdom, Sire, is conducted, in conjunction with Your Majesty, by Ministers, with the aid of their Clerks, and in certain departments by Intendants of Finance, likewise with the aid of Clerks; in the provinces it is managed by the Intendants and their Subdelegates. We shall proceed to consider these different officials, beginning with the lowest order, with those, namely, who approach most nearly to the people.

[109] The Subdelegate of an Intendant is a man without rank and without legal authority, who has no right to sign any orders, hence all those which he executes are signed by the Intendant. It is nevertheless well known in the provinces that the Subdelegate decides upon many details into which the Intendant himself cannot enter. If the Subdelegate abuses his power one can only complain to the Intendant; but how shall people of the lower classes venture to complain when they see that the order is issued in the name of the Intendant himself, and know that this superior magistrate would doubtless consider himself compromised and feel obliged to uphold his own order if it were questioned?

[110] The relation of the Subdelegate to the Intendant, in such cases, is much the same as that of the Intendant to the Minister, and of the Minister to Your Majesty himself.

[111] Whenever it is possible the Intendant avoids making a decision in his own name. In any affair which may compromise him he takes the precaution of securing a decree of the Council, or of obtaining authorization by a letter from the Minister. An individual in one of the provinces, who wishes to protest against the decision of an Intendant and carry his case to the Council or to the Minister, is helpless when he finds himself condemned in advance by a decision of the Minister or a decree of the Council.

[112] As to the Intendants of Finance, whose official position is between the Intendants of the provinces and the Ministers, they are authorities absolutely unknown to those who live at a distance from the capital and the court. It is known in a general way that such officials exist, and that they have real power in the kingdom; but the public

does not understand what classes of affairs they are responsible for, since there are, indeed, no matters directly under their control, and they have no immediate subordinates who are obliged to take orders from them. Their whole administration is carried on in collaboration with the Controller-General, whose signature they obtain for all letters and for those decisions of the Council called *Arrêts de Finance*. The individual who believes himself justified in protesting against such decisions can neither complain to the Intendant of Finance—who signs nothing and may not have had anything to do with the affair, since the Minister is not obliged to follow his opinion and sometimes decides contrary to it—nor to the Controller-General, who might say with reason that he was not responsible for all the documents which he had to sign for the six Intendants of Finance.

[113] Finally, the Minister himself has no status, no direct authority in the State. It is nevertheless in him that all power resides, since it is he who certifies the signature of Your Majesty. He can do all and yet can not be held responsible for anything, since the authoritative name which he is permitted to use closes the lips of whoever might dare to complain.

[114] So, just as the inhabitant of a village dare not defend himself against the petty tyranny of a Subdelegate armed with the authority of an order from the Intendant, we, the inhabitants of the capital, we personally, the Magistrates, whose very office imposes upon us the duty of bringing the truth to the ears of Your Majesty, how often we have seen ourselves accused of audacity for having protested against orders obtained from the King by the artifices of his Ministers!

[115] Let us dare to speak the whole truth to Your Majesty. Orders have been presented to us whose falsity was apparent on their face, and others in which it was evident that the consecrated name had been prostituted to uses unworthy of the King's attention. And when we have exposed the petty vengeances, the petty passions, the petty patronage, for the gratification of which these orders have been obtained, we have been told that to doubt that an order signed by the King was actually given by him was to fail in respect due to royalty. If Your Majesty desires that we should formulate and prove the facts which we allege, you will find that we are in a position to comply with your wishes.

[116] These same Ministers, moreover, have, during the past century, arrogated to themselves jurisdiction in so many affairs of all

descriptions that it is impossible for them to give personal attention to them all. A new sort of intermediary power has consequently established itself between your Ministers and your other subjects, which is neither that of the governors nor of the Intendants of the provinces, but that of Clerks, persons absolutely unknown to the State, who nevertheless speak and write in the name of the Ministers, exercise a power as absolute and as irresistible as theirs, and are even safer from all investigation because they are so much more insignificant.

[117] Thus an individual without patronage, without any relations with the Court, a man, for example, who lives quietly in his own province, may be the recipient of an order of the greatest harshness, without knowing either by whom it was issued, in order to obtain its revocation, nor the reasons for its issue, in order to present his defence. The order is signed by the King, but this obscure individual well knows that the King has never so much as heard his name. The signature of the King is certified by that of a Minister, but he is equally sure that he is unknown to the Ministers. He is in ignorance whether the order has been obtained by the Intendant of his province, or whether one of his enemies has found access to some Clerk at Versailles, of the first, second or third rank, or whether it is one of those blank orders which are sometimes given to the various authorities in the provinces. He knows nothing, and he remains in exile, perhaps even in irons.

[118] We have felt it necessary, Sire, to give Your Majesty some notion of the different kinds of despotism, and especially of the different forms of secrecy in vogue. We may now apply these observations to the three direct taxes, the *taille*, the poll tax and the tax of the twentieth.

[119] The *taille*, the oldest of the direct taxes, is levied upon the unprivileged commoners in those provinces which are called *Pays d'Elections*, that is, in those which have no provincial Estates, and as the *taille* is a personal tax it is paid also by the tenants of ecclesiastics, of nobles, and of members of the privileged classes. Consequently this tax is borne at present by almost all landowners.

[120] The *taille* has been increased by various additions called " supplements," and every year new ones are added. These supplements equal at present, or even surpass, the principal of the *taille*. It is maintained that the principal of the *taille* has not been augmented for a long time; nevertheless the people who pay the tax are constantly complaining of its increase. It is in reality only a question of

words; the principal is not augmented, but the supplements are increased.

[121] We must explain to Your Majesty the manner in which each year the *taille* and its supplements are imposed and assessed. There are four different operations.

1. The warrant [*brevet*] of the *taille* provides for its imposition upon all the *Généralités*. When it is desired to levy a sum supplementary to the *taille* upon the whole Kingdom, or upon a particular *Généralité*, it is by this warrant that it is imposed, and it is also by this warrant that the total sum levied upon the Kingdom is apportioned among the *Généralités*. The warrant of the *taille* is drawn up in the Council.

2. The *commissions* provide for the imposition of the tax upon the *Elections*.[1] Consequently when a sum is to be levied upon a particular *Election* it is imposed by means of the *commissions*, and it is also by the *commissions* that the sum imposed upon each *Généralité* is apportioned among the *Elections*. The *commissions*, like the warrant, are drawn up in Council.

3. The act by which the tax is assessed upon each parish or community is called the *département*. Sums which it is sometimes necessary to raise in a particular parish, are imposed in this way, as, for example, when a house must be built for the priest, or when the community has to pay the costs of litigation or meet other expenses. The assessment among the parishes of the sum imposed upon the *Election* is determined in the same way. The *département* is carried out in the province itself, and at the present time by the Intendant alone, without appeal. The *Elus*[2] and other persons who have a right to be present at the assembly which makes this distribution have no longer a deliberative voice, and the Courts can no longer take cognizance of what goes on there.

4. The roll of the *taille* contains the assessment upon each taxpayer, or, what amounts to the same thing, the apportionment among the taxpayers of the sum imposed upon the whole parish or community. The roll of the *taille* is made by the taxpayers themselves, that is to say, by those who are in turn Assessors and Collectors. Nevertheless the Intendant enjoys the right, in virtue of his position and of his office,

---

[1] The *Election* was the name applied to a subdivison of the *Généralité*, as well as to the inferior court referred to in paragraph 91.

[2] See above, paragraph 91.

of assessing a taxpayer whom he believes to have been favored by the Collectors. He has also a right to send Commissioners into the parish, who call the inhabitants together and have the roll of the *taille* drawn up in their presence, in which case the roll is called *rôle d'office*. The duties of these Commissioners should terminate after informing the taxpayers of the regulations which govern the drawing up of the rolls and obliging them to conform to these regulations. However, in the provinces, the authority of a man sent by the Intendant is so great that these Commissioners draw up the roll as they like ; and this is so clearly recognized that the Intendants often provide their Commissioners with printed instructions indicating the rules according to which they wish the assessment to be made. However, in spite of the assessments made by the Intendant in virtue of his office, and the *rôles d'office* made by the Commissioners, this fourth distribution is not, after all, so completely subject to arbitrary authority as the first three, for individuals whose rights are violated may have recourse to legal proceedings.

[122] We shall now proceed to consider these four operations, first as to the imposing of the tax and then as to its assessment. As regards the imposition of the tax it is obvious that, although the Courts do not cease to maintain that their voluntary registration is necessary for the establishment of taxes, although this maxim is regarded by the Nation as its only safeguard since it has lost its representatives, and although the Kings themselves have conceded the principle in hundreds of instances, new sums are nevertheless imposed every year upon the people without registration and by acts of arbitrary authority such as the warrant of the *taille*, the commissions, and the forms observed in the *département*.

[123] If it is necessary to give Your Majesty some notion of the abuses which may result from this arbitrary method of taxation, there is a recent and notorious incident which we may select as an example. Since 1771 sums have been imposed as supplements to the *taille*, which were deemed necessary both for the indemnification of the Magistrates, whose offices it was desired to suppress, and for the payment of the officers who were destined to form the new tribunal. To-day the old Magistracy is re-established and the new tribunals have been abolished ; nevertheless the tax continues.

[124] It may perhaps be thought by your Council, Sire, that the consequences of the changes made during these four years still entail

outlays too considerable to be met by the ordinary revenues of Your Majesty; and in this respect these recent operations may be compared to a war that has given rise to taxes which are maintained some time after peace has been concluded in order to pay the debts contracted. The pretext will soon disappear; may we hope that the tax will be discontinued? Yes, Sire, we do hope so; we do not even permit ourselves the least doubt; but we must confess that our hope is founded only upon the confidence in your personal justice which is entertained by the whole Nation; for it is a long time since any one in France could harbor the hope of seeing a tax abandoned which might be renewed every year by a secret act of arbitrary authority, such as the warrant for the *taille*. And if Your Majesty would have a report made on all the general and particular taxes which are levied in the kingdom, and which have likewise been established by arbitrary power, Your Majesty would perhaps discover that the greater part of them were originally justified by momentary needs which soon disappeared, and yet the tax continued to be levied.

[125] We shall proceed now, Sire, to consider the four operations, one after the other, from the second point of view, that of their assessment. Let us begin with the warrant of the *taille*, which contains the first apportionment, that among the *Généralités*. We have already said that this is drawn up by the Council of Finance. But Your Majesty knows that, with the exception of the Controller-General and one Intendant of Finance, none of those who are present in this Council can be familiar with the situation of the provinces or with the needs of the State. It is then the Minister alone who determines every year both the amount of the tax and its first apportionment. We are ignorant, Sire, and all France is ignorant, upon what principles this Minister bases his conclusions. We only know that no one has noted any attempt to secure information as to the condition of the provinces previous to the determination of the amount of the tax. The warrant for the *taille* is then, in reality, an act of arbitrary authority, based upon no sufficient previous knowledge, and relating to a matter upon which, above all others, the Orders of the Realm should be consulted.

[126] It is much the same with the *commissions*, which establish the second apportionment, since they are determined in the same Council of Finance, and consequently in accordance with the will merely of the Minister and Intendant of Finance. There is neverthe-

less a difference, since the opinion of the Intendant of each province is asked before the *commissions* are sent out. The fate of each province is, therefore, determined by the report of a single Intendant. Now this Intendant is himself forced to rely upon the opinions of his subordinates, for he cannot familiarize himself with the conditions throughout his *généralité*.

[127] Moreover, it must be noted that the Intendant often has interests opposed to those of his province. Indeed, we cannot but think that the Intendant is commonly a man bent on improving his condition, that he is in constant need of favors at Court, and that he cannot obtain them except through a Minister,—whom one may usually hope to gratify by aiding him to derive the greatest possible results from the taxes. It is also clear that the precarious tenure and uncertain position of these officers oblige them to conciliate all those persons in their province who enjoy credit at Court.

[128] We are nevertheless very far from raising any doubts, Sire, as to the sincerity of the opinions which the Intendants despatch to your Council. We do not doubt that they have the necessary zeal and courage to defend the interests of the province which is confided to their care ; we believe, too, that the strictest justice dictates the account which they give of the relative resources of all the *Elections* in their *généralité*.

[129] It must be urged, however, that the condition of the people should not be represented to you by the Intendants alone, and that it is surprising that neither the corporate bodies nor private individuals in the various provinces are permitted to submit memoirs in the people's interests, before the warrant of the *taille* and the *commissions* are determined.

[130] We observe furthermore to Your Majesty that this warrant of the *taille* and these *commissions* are not only acts of arbitrary authority, but they are also executed in secret, for neither the warrant of the *taille* nor the *commissions* are ever printed or publicly announced ; the *commissions* are simply sent to the *Election*, which must conform to them in making the third apportionment, that of the *département*. The province consequently only learns its fate when this *département* takes place, that is to say, when all is irrevocably determined. It knows nothing of the fate of the other provinces, for nowhere in the kingdom is a general statement to be found.

[131] Thus not only are the provinces judged without a hearing

when the warrant of the *taille* and the *commissions* are fixed, but it is absolutely and physically impossible for them to obtain access to Your Majesty in order to protest against the apportionment. If, in fact, a province is taxed to an excessive amount for imaginary needs, or unreasonable expenditures, it does not hear of it until the moment when the tax is to be raised. If this same province has been unjustly treated in the general apportionment, either through ignorance of the prevailing conditions, or by reason of a predilection of the Minister for other provinces, not only is it excluded from taking any measures against the injustice, but it is not even possible for it to know that such injustice exists.

[132] This secrecy, Sire, is a deliberately conceived system; for we must remind Your Majesty that in the year 1768 the *Cour des aides* decreed that each *Election should send to it each year, during the week succeeding the département, a list containing the total amount of the taxes to be apportioned among the parishes. This statement was to specify the total amount of the taille and its supplements, of the poll tax and of the sums which are added to these impositions at the rate of so many sous in the franc*[1], *and was to give an exact account of the sums assessed each year upon the basis of the tailles.* The *Cour des aides* desired this general account simply in order to present it to the King, and it may be well to add that it had no other possible use for it, for duly registered laws observed for more than a century do not permit the *Cour des aides* to take any official action in regard to what is done in the *département.*

[133] Would you believe, Sire, that the Administration had sufficient influence to have this decree annulled? It is difficult to imagine under what pretext, for they did not go so far, probably, as to say expressly to the late King that they wished to prevent any one from acquainting him with the situation of his people : neither do we believe that they would have dared advance in his presence the barbarous maxim, which has too often been asserted, that the people can easily bear their misfortunes provided the Government is clever enough to conceal them.

[134] Permit us, Sire, one last reflection upon the arbitrary nature of these two apportionments. It is easy to conceive that the Ministers

---

[1] One of the subterfuges of the Ancien Régime consisted in collecting a certain number of sous in addition to each *livre* or franc of the original tax.

who loved despotism should have desired to arrogate to themselves, in the name of the Council of Your Majesty, the right arbitrarily to impose upon the people whatever amounts they saw fit. But it is not easy to understand what interest they could have had in depriving the people of a voice in the apportionment of the burden ; and we do not believe that even those Ministers, despotic as they were, would have established the form of apportionment which exists to-day if the reflections which we have just made to Your Majesty had been presented to them in all their simplicity.

[135] Moreover, since we have undertaken to tell Your Majesty all sorts of truths with no reserve, we must confess that our predecessors were doubtless at fault in not exposing this system of secrecy as they should have done when it was first introduced. Even at that time there were no longer either Estates-General or provincial Estates, nor even representatives of the provinces commissioned by the people to apportion the taxes. This apportionment was made by Judges who had been substituted for the representatives of the Nation, and appeals could be taken from the decisions of these Judges to the *Cours des aides*. It is true that these Magistrates protested against the change, but their efforts ended with demanding the execution of the existing laws, that is, in demanding that the apportionment should be made by them instead of by the Council. Hence these protests appeared at the time to deal merely with a question of jurisdiction, a personal affair of the Courts which was of no interest to the general public.

[136] If these Courts had vindicated for the people the natural right of all men to be heard before being judged, if they had insisted upon the necessity of knowing the condition of the provinces before imposing a tax, if they had, above all, made known to their Sovereigns the difference between despotism and secrecy, it seems to us that the present system would never have been adopted either by the Sovereign or by the chief Ministers, for they had nothing to gain by it. The subordinate Administrative Officials are the only ones who profit by the system, since by means of it they are able to render themselves independent of a higher authority.

[137] We pass now to the third process of apportionment, that made in the *département*, between the parishes or communities of each *Election*. Formerly this apportionment was not arbitrary but was made by the *Elus*, who were actually elected by the province. However, the assembly made up of the *Elus* must not be assimilated to a meeting of

the provincial Estates; the difference between them is, indeed, very
apparent. The provincial Estates grant, or refuse to grant, the *don
gratuit*[1]; they regulate all parts of the administration; they are the
defenders of the rights of the provinces, and these rights are, in general,
those whose maintenance was guaranteed to the province at the time
of its annexation by the Crown. The duties of the *Elus* did not extend to all these matters : they acted as general assessors of the province in apportioning the tax between the parishes and communities,
just as in each parish or community there are assessors who apportion
among the individual tax-payers the sum imposed upon the whole
community.

[138] We must observe, in order to avoid any misunderstanding, that
these former *Elus* also exercised that function which is still retained
by those who now bear the same name, the function, namely, of
Judges in the tribunal of the *Election*. But we shall not consider
them here under this aspect, but as general tax-assessors of the
province.

[139] The fact that this office of general tax-assessor excited the
jealousy of the Administration explains the successive blows which have
been dealt at national liberty in this respect. In the first place, the
real *Elus*, who were actually chosen by the people, were done away
with, and officers appointed by the government, and who procure their
offices by purchase, were substituted for them. In the second place,
the Intendant of the province was introduced into the *département*[2] and
made its presiding officer, and in the end the deliberative functions of
the *Elus* and of all who enjoyed the right of being present in the
département were suppressed. Moreover, the Superior Courts were
forbidden to take cognizance of the proceedings, so that now the apportionment made in the *département* is the work of the Intendant
alone, without recourse or appeal.

[140] Your Majesty will readily observe that the second of the
above changes rendered the first one unnecessary. It is easy to
understand that despotism should have desired to suppress the real

---

[1] *I. e.*, the lump sum paid to the king by the *pays d' état* (that is, the provinces
which retained their estates), in lieu of the taxes which the government collected
in other parts of the realm.

[2] This word *départment*, it will be observed, is sometimes used in the sense of the
act which apportioned the tax among the various parishes of the *Election;* sometimes
it means the assembly which made the apportionments.

Elus as long as they had any real power. But now that the Commissioner of the Council[1] has become the absolute master in the *départe-ment*, and no one else has more than an advisory voice there, no farther reason or pretext remains for refusing to accord to the provinces the right of sending representatives to look after their interests.

[141] Finally, in the third place, a new move was made in 1767, of which we must give an account to Your Majesty. In that year the spirit of secrecy reached such a degree that it seemed desirable that the apportionment made in the *département* should be concealed even from those who had the right to take part in it. With this end in view, the idea was conceived of making two warrants for the *taille*, one of which should be sent to the *département*, while the other was kept secret in order that the Intendant alone might determine its apportionment in his private office. The first warrant dealt only with the principal of the *taille* which, it was argued, never varied, and upon which it was, therefore, useless to consult the province. For the second warrant were reserved all the supplements, all the new assessments, everything which is subject to variation from year to year : in it were noted even the reduction of the supplements of the *taille* granted to those unfortunate individuals whose misfortunes make it impossible for them to pay, reductions which are justifiable, but which nevertheless ought only to be granted to those who can really claim them, since what is deducted from one quota is added to the others. Upon all this, Sire, the Intendant was allowed to decide by himself, without the inconvenient presence of those who took part in the *département*.

[142] The *Cour des aides* addressed to the late King, in the year 1768, certain Protests in which this system of the two warrants was explained. But since for more than a century the *Cour des aides* has not taken legal cognizance of the proceedings in the *département*, it could only enter a protest, and took no farther action. These Protests were probably sent by the late King to the Officers of the Administration, that is to the very persons who were anxious to introduce this new secrecy into the apportionment.

[143] But now that we cherish the hope that Your Majesty is willing to listen to us, we testify that of all the operations undertaken by despotism there is none in which the fatal spirit of secrecy is more

---

[1] An official designation of the Intendant.

manifest than in this system of the two warrants. In a word, since the *Elus* no longer have a deliberative voice, nor indeed any power whatever, in the *département*, we cannot conceive any honest reasons for removing such witnesses.

[144] It only remains, Sire, to speak of the fourth and last apportionment, namely, that which is made among the individual tax-payers by means of the roll of each parish. When the regulations which govern the *taille* were made, despotism had not yet made such progress as we have since seen, and of which we shall speak in connection with the poll tax and the twentieth : no one then supposed that arbitrary authority could decide the fate of each and every individual. That authority had not yet obtained complete control of this fourth apportionment, although it had made several attacks upon it. We have already mentioned two of these encroachments : the one consists in the custom followed by several Intendants of having all, or almost all, of the rolls drawn up in the presence of Commissioners; the other, in the reductions granted upon the simple authority of the Intendant.

[145] As regards the rolls of the Commissioners, the so-called *official rolls*, it is certainly true that the presence of a Commissioner in an assembly of country people is too imposing either to leave the Collectors free to draw up their roll according to their best knowledge and belief, or to permit individuals who believe themselves unjustly treated to defend themselves. This disadvantage was foreseen by the *Cour des aides* when these rolls of the Commissioners were first authorized. It believed that they should only be made at rare intervals, and upon extraordinary occasions, such as, for example, when a new regulation concerning the making of the rolls had been enacted and needed to be explained to the people of the country communities. The Court trusted that it had insured this by forbidding the Commissioners to receive anything from the tax-payers ; it inferred that these commissions would not be frequent when they were not profitable, and that the Intendant would not be led to multiply them by the desire to provide places for his protégés ; nevertheless in several *généralités* everything is done by Commissioners, and certainly they must be well paid. In this way the precautions of the *Cour des aides* have been rendered ineffectual. It does not appear however that the Intendants rely upon the King to meet these expenses ; probably the sum destined for this purpose is levied upon the parishes. This is an extortion prohibited by law, but the Intendant is able to perpetrate it with impunity,

since the amount to be paid by the parishes is determined in the *département* where he is master.

[146] As to the reductions granted to individuals who have suffered losses, we have already observed that they are regarded as favors due to the King's liberality, and they are described as such by the Intendant in the *département*. For if they are not really favors, and if the amount which is deducted from one individual's tax is to be borne by the rest of the inhabitants, those who draw up the tax rolls should be the ones to determine the reductions, otherwise a reduction becomes simply a gratuity which the Intendant grants to a favorite, and for which the people must pay. This was also foreseen by the *Cour des aides*, and it hoped to prevent it by expressly ordering that such reductions and exemptions made by the Intendant should not in any case be re-charged upon other taxpayers; but the Intendants have again evaded this enactment by arranging the matter in the *département*, where they have entire control. As we have already observed, they have taken care to have all such reductions entered in the secret warrant in order to prevent criticism of their conduct.

[147] In reality, any reduction granted to an individual is not a favor but an act of justice, and often, of necessity ; for in a case where fire or storm has made it physically impossible for an individual to pay his tax, it is necessary to make some rebate. These reductions should not, therefore, depend upon the arbitrary authority of the Intendant, and still less should they be provided for in a secret document where all sorts of injustice may be concealed. The *Cour des aides* exposed and explained all these schemes and the resulting abuses in its Protest of 1768 ; nor has justice been done the people, for, as we have already observed, it was referred for examination to the authors of the abuses which it denounced. So the Intendants are still at liberty to grant favors to their protégés at the expense of the people, under the guise of tax reductions.

[148] There are still other violations of justice and infractions of the rules, committed in drawing up the rolls of the *taille*. Perhaps some changes should be made in the existing laws. The majorty of your Admnistrative Officers are said to believe this, and possibly your *Cour des aides* will come to the same conclusion. These changes, how-ever, will necessitate long discussions between Your Majesty and your Ministers ; and we ask Your Majesty if you will not immediately do away at least with the secrecy of the first three apportionments. We

entreat Your Majesty to begin by asking that an account be rendered him of the Protest presented by his *Cour des aides* in 1768. You will find there a discussion of the two warrants of the *taille*, and especially of all that concerns the reductions, and we shall hope that as soon as these explanations are presented to Your Majesty, this whole iniquitous system of secrecy will cease to exist.

[149] But our hopes and our prayers do not end here : we farther beg Your Majesty to reorganize those provincial assemblies called *départements*, by investing them with the power and consequence which they have not enjoyed for a century past. We beg that all the taxes, without exception, which are levied each year in the provinces may be there considered—not only the *taille* and its supplements, but the poll tax, the twentieth, the sums which are levied for the building of presbyteries, and even the militia and the *corvée*. We entreat Your Majesty to ordain that all these taxes shall be publicly announced, and that the apportionments shall be made and the rolls published in time to permit those who believe themselves injured to invoke your justice.

[150] Finally, Sire, it seems to us time to bestow upon your people the right which they formerly enjoyed of choosing representatives to be present in the assembly where the fate of the province is decided. We have already said that the presence of such deputies cannot in any way suggest an analogy between the assembly of the *département* and the provincial Estates ; so that even despotism itself need not take offense. Neither will it in any way prejudice the position of the official *Elus*, who will lose none of the functions which are at present attached to their office.[1] Moreover this measure would not necessitate any change whatever in the provincial assembly called the *département :* it might therefore be adopted at once, without any expense, and without any preparations. We are not proposing to Your Majesty an innovation but a provision of the ancient constitution of the Kingdom, which we only ask you to revive by granting to each province what is everywhere granted to individuals, namely, the right of being heard before being judged.

[151] The former *Elus* were done away with because as assessors of the taxes they exercised some power, and the Ministers of that period wished to destroy all authority which did not emanate from

---

[1] It has not been deemed necessary to translate the note which the Court adds upon this technical matter. See the French version above, p. 44.

themselves ; but now that the Intendant makes the assessment upon his
own authority this pretext no longer exists ; and while the King has not
yet done justice to the Nation in this regard, it is doubtless because
he has never been asked to do so. We have already admitted that
the Magistrates have always failed to insist upon the re-establishment
of institutions which were outside their jurisdiction; and that is the
reason why, when a preponderating voice in the *département* was
given to the Intendants, the Courts did not call attention to the fact
that, since that despotic measure had been enacted, there was no
longer any excuse for refusing to grant to the provinces the right of
choosing their *Elus*.   It may be asked what purpose the mere presence
of such representatives would serve if they possessed no real power,
but is it not well known that the simple presence of a person of consideration constitutes an obstacle to the perpetration of injustice?   The
Administrative Officials of the previous reign certainly recognized this
fact, for by the system of the two warrants they attempted to conceal
their operations even from the knowledge of the official *Elus*, who
certainly would not offer the same opposition that might be expected
from persons chosen by the provinces.

[152] Moreover, real representatives could hardly be refused the
right of recourse to Your Majesty when their protests were not recognized in the *département* where they possessed no authority.   They
would never be able to retard the execution of a measure, but they
might exercise the right which all your subjects should enjoy, and they
might make use of it for the benefit of the province.   We would farther
point out to Your Majesty that even if these representatives chosen by
the provinces should rarely enter protests against the conduct of the
Intendant, and even if those protests which they did make proved
sometimes to be unfounded, it would not follow that their existence
was useless, for the real good they would do would consist in the evil
which their presence would prevent.

[153] We believe, Sire, that should Your Majesty consent to restore
to the provinces their former representatives, and should their presence
give rise to no well-founded complaint against the administration, this
in itself would be one proof of the value of their existence ; and if, in
spite of the infrequency and ineffectualness of their complaints, the
administration should still seek pretexts for freeing itself from this
troublesome criticism, that would simply make the proof more complete.

[154] In presenting to you the annoyances connected with the first

two apportionments, which are determined arbitrarily in your Council, we did not suggest any remedy, for the reason that there is nobody in the provinces at present who has sufficient knowledge of their situation to furnish information in regard to them to the Council. But when there are certain citizens within the limits of each *Election* who attend the assembly of the *département* as official representatives, and when the apportionment of the sum to be levied upon the province is made in their presence, they will be prepared to furnish instructive information ; and we doubt not that Your Majesty will not only permit but will even order them to present such information to the Ministers of Finance and to those who compose the Council. The Intendants will then have opponents, and the people, defenders.

[155] We are confident, moreover, Sire, that the Intendants who govern your provinces at present will not fear to be exposed to such criticism. We believe that both they and the Ministers who at present compose your Council ardently desire to be enlightened and guided in that most important operation, the apportionment of the taxes, which has heretofore been performed only at hap-hazard.

[156] The two other taxes of which we desire to speak to Your Majesty are founded upon different principles from those which govern the *taille*. As we have already observed, the *taille* is the oldest of the direct taxes and was for a long time the only one. It was instituted by Charles VII. for the purpose of providing for the pay of regular troops (which were established at that period in almost all the states of Europe). However, as the Nobility was still subject to feudal military service, it seemed right that they should be exempt from the *taille*.

[157] But during the following centuries military service fell into oblivion, and the Nobility no longer served the State except in the regular paid troops. The privileges of the Nobility came to be less and less respected during this period, because when nobility was attached to certain purchasable offices it fell to the lot of the wealthy. So the financial administration conceived the idea of infringing upon these privileges, though at first only indirectly. The most important of the early encroachments consisted in taxing the commons for the land which they leased from Nobles and other exempted persons. But, finally, Louis XIV., during his later wars, created two taxes to which the Nobility and those otherwise privileged were directly subjected, namely, the poll tax[1] and the tax of the tenth.

[1] The so-called *capitation* was not in reality a poll tax, but a classified income tax.

[158] We shall not dwell long upon the poll tax, for we feel that anything we might say about it would be superfluous. This tax is, in fact, so objectionable, under whatever aspect it is considered, that Your Majesty's Ministers cannot but be convinced of its evils. It was established at that unfortunate period when every expedient was seized upon by the Government without examination. In 1713, when peace was made after an unfortunate war, Louis XIV. did not feel himself in a position to fulfill the promise of suppressing it, which he had made to his people. Since then the fate of this tax has been like that of many others: a vicious tax once registered has been retained, instead of substituting for it a more reasonable one, which would, however, have to be submitted to criticism by a new registration.

[159] Moreover, the arbitrary character of this tax has made it more popular with some Administrative Officials than any of the other impositions. This character is so marked that the surplus from the poll tax, the amount of which is variable and uncertain, is entirely at the disposition of the administration, and they have long reserved this sum for their cherished secret expenditures.

[160] Your Majesty can now understand why the obvious disadvantages of the poll tax have received no attention. Your Majesty may be told that any surplus which the poll tax yields is essential, because it is the only fund which can be used for making improvements in the provinces. If that is the case, Your Majesty should inquire what means were employed for this purpose before the poll tax was established in France.

[161] In fact, Sire, not only is the poll tax fixed by a single man, not only are the rolls secret, but those who are charged with its apportionment, and who have no wish to make it arbitrary, have no regulations to guide them.

[162] Formerly a nobleman from each *généralité* was associated with the Intendant in drawing up the lists. This formality has fallen into desuetude, and there is little cause to regret it, since this nobleman was not chosen by the province, but was appointed by the government, and at the instigation of the Intendant, so that he was simply an idle witness of the latter's operations.

The people of France, from the Princes of the Blood down, were divided into twenty-two classes; those in the first class paid 2000 livres, those in the twenty-second class (soldiers, servants, etc.), only one livre. The tax, however, soon lost all semblance of its original form by reason of exemptions, commutations, etc.

[163] There are, however, certain classes of citizens whose poll tax is not arbitrarily determined.   In the case of those, for example, who are subject to the *taille*, the poll tax has become an adjunct of the *taille*.   Corporations of artisans in certain large cities are, moreover, permitted to apportion the tax among themselves and thus remedy its arbitrary character.   But what law or regulation determines the entire sum to be imposed upon each body of artisans?   We know of no such law, and it is more than probable that the matter rests entirely with the Administrative Officials.

[164] There is also another class of Your Majesty's subjects whose poll tax is a fixed amount, namely, those who pay by having a part of their salaries withheld.   But although this may not be arbitrary it is unjust, since the poll tax is not a tax upon real property affecting only the property of the taxpayer, but a personal tax which should be proportionate to all his resources.   There is often a great variation in the fortunes of those who hold similar offices, nevertheless they must all pay the same poll tax.

[165] For all those who pay the poll tax neither through the retention of part of their salaries, nor by contribution as members of an association or guild, nor as an adjunct to the *taille*, the tax is entirely arbitrary, a shameful subjection of all citizens to the Officials of the Administration.   Should we attempt to expose to Your Majesty all the resulting abuses, we fear that we should be suspected of exaggeration.   For instance, would Your Majesty credit it if we asserted that the Intendants had been known to boast of threatening the inhabitants of their *généralités* with doubling the amount of the poll tax if they did not consent to arrangements which these Officials doubtless believed to be for the good of the province, but which nevertheless they had no right to force upon the citizens?

[166] It is impossible, Sire, to demonstrate the truth of such facts, since one of the chief vices of the tax is its secrecy.   There is, however, one abuse which is committed every year, and which is of so serious a nature that we feel obliged to inform Your Majesty of it; and although we are not in a position to prove it, it would be easy for Your Majesty to do so.

[167] Will you not deign, Sire, to ascertain whether it is true that in many towns a poll tax is levied upon the officers of justice which is greater than they can be compelled to pay, which consequently forces them to ask favors of the Intendant and so puts them completely in

his power? And who are the victims of this tyranny? The Judges who determine the fate of their fellow-citizens, whose liberty and independence it is therefore most necessary to preserve. You see, Sire, what are the results of arbitrary and secret taxes, and to what length a tyrant will go who is sure of being neither watched nor criticised. As a matter of fact, if the Intendants, without being deprived of any of their power, were simply obliged to publish the rolls of the poll tax, it would be impossible that every Judge should be taxed each year to an exorbitant amount, which is always reduced, except when the Judge has displeased the Intendant.

[168] We shall say no more upon the subject of the poll tax. We deem it necessary, however, to assert our right of jurisdiction. The poll tax is one of the regular taxes, and should therefore be subject to the jurisdiction of your *Cour des aides*, which cannot do otherwise than claim its rights under all circumstances; for it ought never voluntarily renounce any part of the jurisdiction which has been given it for the good of the people and the maintenance of justice.

[169] We would most urgently request Your Majesty to abolish the poll tax altogether, or at least completely to revise it, for it is an inexhaustible source of injustice. We do the Municipal Magistrates of Paris and the Intendants of the provinces the justice to believe that they ardently desire to be relieved from this fantastic assessment, which is as abhorrent to those Magistrates who love order, as it is dear to those who desire to take advantage of the existing system.

[170] We must now take up the question of the tax of the twentieth, which is at present the subject of the most vigorous protests on the part of the people, for it had always been regarded as an extraordinary measure, to be reserved for times of special need, until the absence of the Magistracy offered the opportunity of making it a permanent tax. We should be open to the just reproach of the whole Nation, Sire, if we did not do all in our power to induce Your Majesty to fix a term to its existence. Even if it be true that it was necessary to continue this tax after peace was concluded, in order to pay the war debts, the people need not at least be deprived of all hopes of its removal. Why afflict the Nation with the prospect of its perpetuity?

[171] This tax has been renewed, almost without interruption, for forty years; and Your Majesty knows how little resistance has been made to each of the renewals, which have simply offered an opportunity for bringing the miserable condition of his people to the atten-

tion of the King; and surely they, who suffer so much, should not be deprived of that consolation. But we are confident, Sire, that under your rule the protests made on the part of the people will bring something more than their own consolation.

[172] We beseech Your Majesty to recall what we have but just said in regard to the poll tax. If the duration of that tax had been determined after the war of 1701, and if it had only been continued by successive renewals, there might have come a favorable moment when the Courts could have exposed its abuses; and in any case the Administration would not have ventured into such excesses, had they known that at each renewal their conduct would be subject to criticism.

[173] This is exactly what happened, Sire, in the case of the twentieth before it was made permanent. In 1763 this tax, already burdensome enough in itself, had become more so by reason of the inquisitorial methods employed in levying it, and when the time came to renew it, the *Parlement* of Paris attempted to put an end to these methods by a provision which prohibited augmenting the rates of 1763. This action was imitated by all the other Courts and was not disapproved by the King. But this amendment, which was designed to remedy the abuse, was displeasing to those who desired to perpetuate it, and consequently, when the tax was renewed during our absence, the amendment was not included either in the text of the law or in the records of those who had taken our places.

[174] The people soon felt the cruel effects of the re-establishment of the tax without the amendment of 1763. Your subjects found their taxes raised almost immediately without any reason being given for the sudden increase, and new investigations, of unexampled severity, were instituted throughout the kingdom, as if the Administrators wished to avenge themselves for the constraint under which they had suffered from 1763 to 1771. If we may venture to say so, Sire, it seemed as if they wished to make plain to the people all that they had lost in losing their former Magistrates.

[175] Matters have now reached a point where the perpetuity of the tax is perhaps less burdensome to the people than the despotism which it involves. We hope, Sire, that Your Majesty will deign to occupy yourself with this matter, for we believe there is none more worthy of your attention. The real nature of these taxes must be considered, and we shall endeavor, therefore, to elucidate the fundamental principles of this department of the administration.

9

[176] If we merely asked your Majesty to fix the duration of the tax of the twentieth, we should only need to invoke your love for your people; but in order to demonstrate the necessity of re-establishing the amendment of 1763, or of substituting for it some equivalent provision, it is necessary to give Your Maesty a clear and simple idea of this tax, which has existed in France since the commencement of this century, first under the name of the tenth, and later under that of the twentieth, the *sou pour livre* of the tenth, etc.; and to render this account intelligible we must return to first principles and determine the true nature of real taxes.

[177] A real tax is one which is levied upon the property of a subject and not upon his person: accordingly each possession, each bit of real estate, is taxed in proportion to the income it produces. When it is necessary to establish such a tax, it would seem that one should begin by determining the total sum which the King desires to obtain from his people, and then seek the form of apportionment and collection which would be most economical for the King, and which would expose the people as little as possible to arbitrary power and to the annoyances which inevitably result from it.

[178] That was not, however, the method pursued in levying the tenth and the twentieths. Every individual was required to pay into the Royal treasury a certain part of his income, and for the execution of this law a system of administration has been developed, particularly in recent years, which has the double disadvantage of subjecting the King to large expenses and the people to arbitrary power. In regard to this method, we would observe to Your Majesty, in the first place, that a real tax of which the total sum is not fixed is an injustice to the Nation; and in the second place, that this species of tax is vicious in itself because it necessarily involves both expense and arbitrariness.

[179] We venture to observe to Your Majesty that such a tax is an injustice to the Nation, because it violates the great principle that a ruler should never exact from his subjects either more or less than the necessities of the State demand. If a tax such as the tenth or the twentieth produces less than is required by the State it is necessary to seek other resources, and there are certainly those to be found which are less burdensome to the people than a direct tax. If, on the contrary, the tenth or the twentieth produces more than is necessary you can hardly doubt, Sire, that this surplus is employed in expenses for which it would have been unjust to levy a new tax.

[180] As we have said, this kind of tax is necessarily both expensive and arbitrary. To render this more comprehensible we must acquaint Your Majesty with the various forms of apportionment employed in the different provinces for raising those taxes of which the total amount is fixed. We shall examine as briefly as possible their respective advantages and disadvantages, and it will be easy to demonstrate that the apportionment of the twentieth combines all the disadvantages. It occasions more expense, more tyranny, and more injustice of every kind, than any other form of apportionment, and the amendment of 1763 was a necessary remedy for abuses which had become unbearable.

[181] There are some localities where, when the amount of the tax has been determined, the inhabitants are permitted to apportion it among themselves. There are others where a cadastre is made, that is, a fixed valuation of all the property of the tax-payers, in accordance with which the amount of the tax is apportioned each year by a simple arithmetical operation, with no personal interference from anybody. There are reasons for and against both of these systems of assessment.

[182] It may be said in favor of the annual apportionment by the tax-payers themselves that it does not involve any expense and does not subject the people to any tyranny on the part of the subordinate officials sent by the government. It may be urged, too, that the tax-payers themselves are the only ones who can make a just apportionment; for there is no farmer who does not know perfectly well the value of his neighbor's land, and it is impossible that a stranger should ever acquire so exact a knowledge. It is maintained also that all cadastres are unfair, that they are admitted to be so in the provinces where they exist, and that this injustice arises either from the fact that the cadastre was originally made by those who were incapable of doing it well because they were strangers to the parish, or from the fact that since the cadastre was drawn up there have been unexpected variations in the value of property, which may, and often do, arise, from a thousand different causes.

[183] The partisans of the cadastre maintain that in the provinces where it exists the apportionment is neither expensive nor arbitrary. They admit that the cadastre is drawn up in the first instance at enormous expense and by the despotic authority of the Commissioners of the cadastre, who are permitted to determine the fate of each individual; but this unhappy period once passed, they maintain that the tranquility of the people is forever assured. In fact, in those districts

where the cadastre prevails, not only is there no expense and no arbitrariness, but there are no law-suits, while the annual apportionment by the tax-payers is an inexhaustible source of envy, dispute and division.

[184] To the objection that the tax-payers have greater reciprocal knowledge of their possessions than a strange Commissioner can have, it may be answered that they have also personal interests and passions which prevent fair dealing. It is claimed that all this is avoided by having the cadastre drawn up by a Commissioner who, being a stranger to the parish, can have no other interest than justice, and that if he lacks local information he can acquire it by listening to the contradictory statements of the tax-payers, whose common interest gainsays individual statements.

[185] It is claimed also in favor of the cadastre as against the annual assessment by the citizens, that the tax-payer's knowledge of his neighbor's possessions can only be of use to the inhabitants of a single community; but the taxes must be apportioned also among the communities of each province and among all the provinces of the kingdom, and it is asserted that these apportionments can only be made justly by means of a cadastre and by government Commissioners.

[186] It may be well to observe to Your Majesty that this last objection to the system of assessment by the citizens themselves can only hold good so long as the communities and provinces have no representatives, for if they had representatives there would be nothing to prevent all the communities from assembling through their deputies and apportioning among themselves the sum levied on the province, just as the inhabitants of a community apportion among themselves the sum levied upon the community. Could not the advantages of both systems be combined by having the cadastre made by the tax-payers themselves instead of by Commissioners? After it was once made there would be no farther expenses, no arbitrariness, no law-suits; and since it would have been made by those who are personally acquainted with the value of the property taxed, and whose common interest consists in treating every individual with justice, there is reason to believe that such an apportionment would be more just than any other.

[187] This kind of cadastre would have the farther advantage that when variations in the value of property occurred which rendered its revision necessary, the community would itself see this necessity and might proceed to make the revision without waiting for it to be ordered by the government.

[188] Finally, in drawing up the cadastre by this method, all the expenses, which are now so great as often to prevent the employment of this form of apportionment, would be saved. The cost incident to the successive sojourns of the Commissioners in all the villages would no longer exist, and we believe that the expense of surveying might also be avoided. We can understand that a survey is necessary for a strange Commissioner who, knowing nothing of the relative value of land, could otherwise only inform himself in general as to which tracts were good, bad, or indifferent, and levy the tax upon each piece according to the acres which it contains and which he supposes to be good, bad, or indifferent in quality : but the country people themselves, who have a direct knowledge of the value of each piece of land, would be spared this labor and could make their cadastre without a preliminary survey.

[189] We may say even more : the cadastre would make itself, without any order from the government, provided the tax to be apportioned among the citizens were a real tax, a tax levied upon each parcel of land, each tract being definitely designated. As a matter of fact, when the tax-roll had once been carefully made in a parish, it would contain a valuation of all the real estate. It would be acknowledged that the roll of that year had been well made, since the inhabitants of a community constitute a public, and a public never refuses to recognize plain facts. This tax-roll, once recognized as a good one, would become the cadastre.

[190] Although the *taille* is apportioned each year in certain districts by the citizens themselves, the rolls have never produced a cadastre, because the *taille* is not a real tax. It is not levied upon each piece of property, but upon all the resources which the individual possesses, the amount of which changes from year to year. The considerations of trade and industry, as well as of personal privileges, also enter into the assessment. So that a commoner who is subject to the *taille* may be taxed one year for a piece of property which the next year may be in the possession of a person exempt from the *taille*, and thus the rolls of one year are of no use in succeeding years.

[191] This is about all there is to be said of the two methods of apportioning a tax of which the amount is fixed in advance. Opinions differ in regard to them, and we do not wish to espouse any one, but simply to present to Your Majesty certain indisputable truths bearing upon the subject. Now it is an indisputable truth that a tax like the

tenth or the twentieth, which does not consist of a fixed sum to be apportioned but in which a certain part of his income is exacted from each individual, involves by its very nature more inconvenience, more expense and more injustice than either of the methods of apportionment which we have described. We propose to demonstrate this to Your Majesty and subsequently to show how, in France, a needless secrecy has been added to the inherent vices of the tax.

[192] We have observed that apportionment by the citizens themselves is not accompanied·by expense or arbitrariness, but does involve a continual resort to legal processes : and that in the system of the cadastre there is no expense, no arbitrariness, and no law-suits, when the cadastre is once completed, but that the making of it involves large expenditures and is presided over by arbitrary authority, unless it is made by the tax-payers themselves.

[193] In the case of the twentieth, an accurate collection of it involves each year all the expense which would be involved in making a cadastre ; the people are continually subjected to the same arbitrary power to which the making of the cadastre subjects them for a limited period ; and finally, there are continual law-suits, just as in the regions where the apportionment is made each year by the tax-payers without producing a fixed valuation.

[194] All these annoyances connected with the twentieth are due to a common cause, namely, that in the present method of levying this tax there is an interminable dispute between the King and every individual in his kingdom in regard to the value of each piece of land.

[195] In order, therefore, that the tax shall be satisfactorily collected the King must keep a man in every village to look after his interests. The whole of France must be covered with an army of Clerks ; and although the number of these Clerks is not at present so very great, it is only because the tax has never yet been collected with the strictness with which it might be, and certainly will be, collected some day unless Your Majesty provides a remedy by revising the law. It is certain that this rigor and the expenditures that it involves have been constantly on the increase ever since the tax was instituted, except during the period when the amendment of 1763 was in force. And its arbitrary character is as perpetual as its costliness, for it is impossible that the power of the government agents should be other than arbitrary. It is said that the Intendant is their judge, but is it possible that the Intendant should be qualified to decide as many suits as there are

parcels of land in his *généralité?* How can he inform himself upon all these cases? He is absolutely obliged to depend upon the subordinate officials, and they become, therefore, the real judges of the people.

[196] Can it be doubted, Sire, that the government rewards each of these under officials whenever he succeeds in increasing the product of the twentieth in his locality? Who, in fact, would be willing to expose himself gratuitously, and without such encouragement, to the hatred of an entire district? It is then certainly true not only that arbitrary authority presides over the collection of the tax, but that the person in whom this authority is vested has an interest in oppressing the people. Nevertheless it would appear that the inducements to oppression are not yet sufficient always to secure the interests of the government, for there are always some among the tax-payers who are able to offer the officials still more powerful inducements to treat them with leniency. Condescend, Sire, to consider, in this connection, the double vice of arbitrary taxes : the weak are oppressed on the pretext of the King's interests, while the powerful and the intriguing are favored against the King's interests.

[197] Finally, we assert that the twentieth cannot fail to be, like the *taille*, an inexhaustible source of litigation. This must continue to be true until the suit of the King against all the tax-payers of his Kingdom is decided, once for all, by making a cadastre from the rolls of the twentieth. But we fear, Sire, that it will never be terminated in this way, or at least only very gradually and very imperfectly, for the following reason, which Your Majesty must certainly find plausible.

[198] It is admitted that only the inhabitants of a district can have a reciprocal knowledge of the value of their property and that the cadastre can be well made only by them, or at least with their assistance. In accordance with this, we have suggested that the best method of obtaining a cadastre is to delegate the task to the community. On the other hand, we have observed that if a Commissioner from the outside be charged with the work, he may receive much assistance from the people themselves, since it is for the general interest that the operation should be performed as justly and accurately as possible, and since the declaration of any individual may often be contradicted by the voice of the community at large. But an agent concerned with the twentieth has no means of obtaining reliable information, because no one has any interest in enlightening him ; on the

contrary, it is for the general interest to deceive him, since he is the
common enemy of the whole country.

[199] As we have said, the vice of secrecy has been added unneces-
sarily to the disadvantages springing from the nature of the tenth and
the twentieth, and moreover both the kinds of secrecy which we defined
above are present, namely, that of the transactions and that which
conceals the persons involved.

[200] As to the secrecy of the transactions, we have already shown
Your Majesty that the ministry has made every effort in its power to
prevent the rolls of the twentieth from being put on record, which is
equivalent to admitting that they desired perfect freedom either to
grant favors or to commit malversations.

[201] As to the secrecy of the persons concerned, Your Majesty must
be informed of the change which was introduced during the last ministry.
Formerly a person who believed himself unfairly treated addressed
himself to the Intendant of the province. It was perfectly understood
that the Intendant would refer the matter to the subordinate official
concerned, but at least the Intendant, the official and the tax-payer all
lived in the same province where the property in question was situated.
There was, therefore, an opportunity for a thorough discussion, and it
was possible to verify the facts alleged by both parties. Under the last
ministry it would seem that the Ministers themselves became jealous
of the authority of the provincial Intendants. There came a time
when those who complained to the Intendant were told that now they
must address themselves directly to the King's Council—as if it were
possible for the Council, sitting near the person of the King, to decide
upon the value of an acre of vineland or meadow situated at the
extremity of the realm ! What redress remained under such a system
to an individual who had been made the victim of the cupidity or dis-
like of a government agent? It might be clear that the injustice from
which he suffered was due to the director of the twentieth : nevertheless that officer might reply indifferently that he was not responsible,
that the tax-rolls were made out in the central office, and that those
who believed themselves too heavily taxed had only to make the
journey to Paris in order to present their grievances.

[202] This is not an abuse of long standing, Sire. It was only
introduced under the last ministry ; we believe it no longer exists
under the present one, and we trust that it will not reappear during
your reign. Still Your Majesty should know that it has existed, in order

to realize the excesses to which the spirit of despotism and secrecy may lead.

[203] It now remains for us to explain to Your Majesty, first, how it happened in the beginning that those who desired to establish a real tax in France chose the form of the tenth and the twentieth, in spite of the disadvantages of which we have been treating : second, why the nature of the tax was not changed when experience had demonstrated the abuses of which it was susceptible : and third, what was the effect of the amendment of 1763 while it was in force.

[204] We do not wish to slander the memory of the Ministers who conceived and established the tenth in the year 1710. The country was in a critical situation at the time, and the administration of the tax was so mild in the beginning that its disadvantages were not felt. It was a period in which the calamities of an unfortunate war were added to that of famine. There was no question of fixing a certain sum to be levied upon the people, but only of obtaining from them whatever they were able to give ; if it had been possible to levy a much larger sum than the tenth produced, it could have been utilized for the necessities of the government, which were real and urgent.

[205] But at first the principal object of the originators of the tax was that it should be borne by those whose resources were not already exhausted by the *taille*, viz., by the Nobility and the privileged classes. The land of the majority of these was let, and the leases represented its real value, because, up to that time, there was no motive for concealing it. No investigation was made, therefore, into the resources of each individual, and there was no necessity for a costly administration. Each person made his declaration, and the Intendant acted as judge ; this he was able to do because there was no doubt as to the honesty of those declarations which were based upon leases, and as for others, they were accepted with almost no examination.

[206] When the same tax was imposed in 1733, at the commencement of a war of aggression and after twenty years of peace ; when, a few years later (in 1741), it was again renewed at the commencement of another war ; and particularly when the tenth or the twentieth was continued during times of peace in order to pay war debts, the sum which the King desired to obtain and which was demanded by the necessities of the government should have been fixed in advance.

[207] But this was not done. The Ministers wished to make the tax yield as large a sum as possible and, on the other hand, tax-payers,

finding that their quotas were based upon their leases, seized all possible means of eluding the tax, such as false leases, bribery, etc. And it was at this period that the government established those inquisitorial methods which are equally odious and impracticable, and as burdensome to Your Majesty on account of their cost, as they are prejudicial to the people by reason of the annoyances which accompany them.

[208] This would have been the time to return to the true principle of real taxes, to change the character of the twentieth altogether, and substitute for it another real tax which should not involve perpetual expenses of administration and perpetual despotism. But unfortunately there were other interests concerned than those of the treasury, namely, those of the Administrative Officials.

[209] It is in fact evident from the sketch we have just given that the Administrative Officials in this department of the government have greater power than in any other. We believe, Sire, that even in the countries where the people are subjected to the most absolute despotism, and where the will of a minister may make or mar the destiny of a whole province—even in these countries, we believe that a minister would not be permitted to decide, and decide by himself, the fate of every individual in the State. Nevertheless this is what we see to-day in France. There is not a landed proprietor in the kingdom who is not obliged either to solicit favors from the agent of the twentieth, or to fear the consequences of his spite. Now it is not in human nature that a person who is invested with such excessive power should lay it down voluntarily; should that ever happen, the person who makes this sacrifice must needs be endowed with extraordinary virtues. These then are the reasons, Sire, why the tax of the twentieth exists in its present form, why it has always been carefully guarded, and why, in spite of the obvious abuses which experience has demonstrated, an effort has been made to make it the basis of all the other taxes.

[210] It would seem, therefore, that only a general protest could serve to bring about the reform of so objectionable a tax; and in 1763 there was such a protest. It must, however, be admitted, Sire, that the voice of the public did not make itself heard so promptly and vigorously as it should have done, for it is a part of the policy of despotism especially to favor those who might secure a public hearing. The protest was tardy because the people of influnce were those who had the least to complain of from the administration of the twentieth; and this fact, Sire, merits Your Majesty's careful attention.

[211] Finally, in 1763, the *Parlement* registered an extension of the twentieth on condition *that as long as the first and second twentieths existed they should be collected in accordance with the existing rolls, the assessments in which were not to be augumented; the violation of this ordinance to be punishable by special penalties.* We ought not to conceal from Your Majesty that this famous clause of 1763 completely changed the nature of the assessment of the tax and converted it into a cadastre. By this means all the abuses were done away with, and the conditions which we have mentioned as necessary to the establishment of a real tax were obtained. First, the sum levied by the King upon the people was fixed; secondly, the despotism of the officials was no longer to be feared; thirdly, those officials being no longer necessary, the government might save all the expenses of administration.

[212] This amendment was not, therefore, open to criticism, except by asserting that the tax-rolls of 1763 had not been made with sufficient accuracy to justify converting them into a cadastre. But this would have been to admit that the work performed at such expense for so many years had not attained its object, for the Administrative Officers had constantly maintained that their investigations in connection with the twentieth would presently result in a valuation of all the land in the kingdom, which would render future assessments at once simple and just, and would prevent all disputes. If this result had not been attained, the inference was that the method employed had been bad and that some new form of apportionment must be devised.

[213] To this, however, the Administration would not consent, and consequently they had to content themselves with secretly complaining against the amendment of 1763. They asserted that it was unjust because it permitted the continuance of unfair assessments, and that, since it forbade increasing the assessment in cases where it had been too low, it made it impossible to diminish it where it had been too high. But as long as the former Magistracy existed, they did not venture to propose to the late King to remedy this disadvantage by a law contrary to the amendment, because it was easy to foresee that the registration of such a law would bring about a discussion which would expose the vices of the system of apportionment which they wished to retain. They waited, therefore, for an auspicious moment, and in the meantime, viz., from 1763 to 1771, all the offices and all the Clerks which the amendment had seemingly rendered unnecessary were maintained at the King's expense. Furthermore, the tax-rolls were still left

unrecorded, although this amendment rendered a record of them more necessary than ever; for when these rolls became the cadastre of the kingdom, they should have been made public.

[214] The longed-for moment arrived when the Magistracy was dissolved. The twentieth was made a perpetual tax, without the amendment of 1763 or any equivalent clause : this occasioned the revival of all the abuses at once, and furnished an excuse for the institution of those inquisitorial methods from which the people have suffered for the last four years.

[215] We protest first, Sire, against the perpetuity of the tax, and secondly, against the abolition of the amendment of 1763; and we entreat Your Majesty either to re-establish it or to substitute for it some other measure which would produce the same effects, that is, which would fix the total sum to be levied, spare Your Majesty a costly administration, and not leave the whole kingdom in subjection to the despotism of the Administration and the agents of the twentieth.

[216] The three taxes with which we have been dealing are the only direct taxes which are levied in your Kingdom as a whole, and if similar ones are levied in certain provinces, under different names, we do not take legal cognizance of them, nor have we had any reason for investigating them. We have also mentioned to Your Majesty the exactions of personal service, such as the militia and the *corvée*, and we shall not discuss them further. We do not doubt that if there are abuses connected with them, the Ministers who preside over this portion of the administration, and in whom the public have the greatest confidence, will do all in their power to reform them.

[217] The lodging of troops is another kind of service demanded of the people, of which the *Cour des aides* does not take legal cognizance. We protest to Your Majesty that we are far from seeking to extend our jurisdiction at this juncture, when we should be occupied only with the interests of the people; but it will not infringe upon the rights of any authority if we inform Your Majesty, in whom resides every species of authority, of what goes on in this connection. In presenting this account of the taxes to you, Sire, we can not leave you in ignorance that in your capital and under your very eyes an assessment is levied upon many houses, nominally for the lodging of troops, which is in reality a real tax imposed upon your subjects without being established by law and without any knowledge on the part of the public of the regulations which govern its assessment. We know that the product of this

tax is destined to pay for the lodging of the troops, which is a military service, but that is not a sufficient reason for permitting the military authority to control its apportionment. When the *taille* was established under Charles VII., it was destined for the payment of troops, but nevertheless there was no thought of establishing it without any express law, nor of having it apportioned, judged, and levied by the troops themselves.

[218] We do not know, and we have made no effort to inform ourselves, whether similar taxes have been established upon similar pretexts in the provinces; we trust that Your Majesty will yourself investigate all that concerns this peculiar exaction. As to the city of Paris, we entreat you to investigate, first, by what law the tax which is there levied was originally established? secondly, what law governs its constant increase? thirdly, by whom and according to what rule the tax is levied upon each house? fourthly, to whom may a house-holder address complaints in regard to the tax? When Your Majesty has satisfied yourself upon these points, we do not doubt that you will make known your intentions by means of a public law; for the public has a right to demand a knowledge of the laws to which it is to be subjected.[1]

. . . .
. . . .

[219] We assure Your Majesty that it is not our desire in citing these particular facts to arm your severity against the culprits, but it is well that you should know how those in whom arbitrary power is vested have conducted themselves during the period when they believed themselves free from the censure of established justice. We cannot but regard the moment, Sire, when despotism, believing itself assured of impunity, shows itself openly, as an auspicious one for pointing out to the King, the friend of justice, the excesses with which we are menaced.

[220] We foresee, Sire, that we shall be accused of wishing to introduce innovations into the administration when, in reality, we are only turning back to the source of the abuses, and proposing to Your Majesty remedies which have long fallen into disuse, such as having the taxes of all kinds considered in the *département* which is held in each province, or of admitting to this *département* the former representatives

---

[1] [Note by the original editor.] Here again there is a gap in the manuscript; the passage omitted seems to have dealt with the vexations caused by several Ministers and Supervisors of the Finances.

of the people, who have been ignored for several centuries. Your Majesty should therefore clearly understand that if we propose what are called innovations, but which are really only the re-establishment of former regulations, it is because the progress of despotism and the real innovations which it is constantly introducing render a return to sound principles absolutely necessary.

[221] We dare not deceive you, Sire, for we know that it is your desire permanently to establish the happiness of the Nation, which at the moment of your accession demonstrated its devotion to you with so touching a confidence. Your efforts must not be restricted to the reformation of individual abuses; you must attack the whole system of administration.

[222] We know that Your Majesty loves justice, we know that your present Ministers desire to promote it. But so long as the welfare o your people is founded only upon your personal justice, or that of your Ministers, it will prove but a fleeting blessing, and the coming generation will behold despotism avenging itself upon the people for the constraint which it has suffered during your reign. The period of this reign should therefore be utilized to establish barriers for the people against despotism, and especially against secrecy of administration.

[223] We have not deemed it our duty therefore to protest against particular abuses; or rather we have only used them as illustrations of the general system. But we would invoke that love of justice which peculiarly characterizes Your Majesty, in order to obtain laws which will establish the permanent welfare of your kingdom; such laws as will enable that justice which fills your heart to survive Your Majesty and to make itself felt by our most distant posterity.

[224] These then, Sire, are the general views of some of your former Magistrates who, like other citizens, have been witnesses of the people's misfortunes, and who, having devoted their lives to the trial of law-suits arising from the taxes, have had peculiar opportunities for observing some of the causes of these misfortunes. We present these reflections with confidence, for we know that the sentiments which dictated them will recommend them to Your Majesty. We realize, however, that in dealing with so many questions we may have fallen into some errors. How, indeed, could we have avoided that, since the Administrative Officials have so long been endeavoring to envelope themselves in an impenetrable veil, and since the chief vice of their operations is the secrecy which makes it impossible to investigate or prove anything?

We should have but ill fulfilled our duty if we had permitted the fear of being mistaken in some details to prevent us from laying before you a mass of important and incontestable facts; and you, Sire—if we may venture to say so—will fall into the trap set for you by the enemies of your people, if the discovery of these slight mistakes makes you suspicious of the truths which it is so important for you to know.

[225] We are not, moreover, so rash as to suppose that others than ourselves cannot further enlighten you.   We shall not imitate, Sire, the guilty presumption of those Administrative agents who for more than a century have sought to keep at a distance from the throne all those who might be able to enlighten the King, as if the truth were never to reach the Ruler except through them.   We esteem, Sire, as the whole Nation esteems, the Ministers with whom Your Majesty has surrounded yourself, but nevertheless there are many facts which you will never learn either from the Ministers or from the Magistrates.

[226] It is the people at large who bear the burden of the taxes, which are so complicated that each province, each association, each profession, is subjected to some particular revenue law, and has its own grievances to put before Your Majesty.   It is not right that a single Minister should decide, without restraint, upon such a multitude of cases, and it is equally impossible that any one body of Magistrates should alone interpret to Your Majesty this enormous number of conflicting interests.

[227] The strongest proof of the sincerity of our zeal which we can give is to inform you in what cases and to what degree you must be on your guard against the Ministers and other Administrators, and how you can shield yourself from deception, by listening to the representations of others than the Magistrates, who have so long been the only persons in the kingdom who exercised the right of protest, and who are sometimes incapable of fulfilling that important function in all its bearings.

[228] The confidence which we feel in the present administration shall not close our mouths.   On the contrary, we believe that we should take advantage of this moment when Your Majesty is surrounded by the most learned and the most irreproachable of men, and we hope that they will unite with us, and that they will desire as ardently as ourselves that Your Majesty should be enlightened as to their exercise of the power which has been confided to them, and which they can have no wish to abuse.

[229] In many respects certainly, and perhaps in most, the Ministers of the King deserve his confidence more than any one else, for it may be said, in general, that every thing which affects the glory of his reign affects also that of his Ministers. The Sovereign cannot doubt that they take the sincerest interest in the success of his arms, the maintenance of his authority at home, and his dignity and consideration among foreign powers.

[230] But there are other matters in which the interests of the Ministers do not coincide with those of the King : they differ widely, for example, when the people are subjected to slavery by the tools of the Administration upon the pretext of maintaining the royal authority, or when the Administration is extended until it includes the most insignificant matters. It is not surprising when one of your subjects becomes a Minister that he should be flattered by the pettiest attribute of authority, that he should everywhere have friends to favor and enemies to persecute, and that his pride should feed upon the variety of attention and homage which accompanies a multiplicity of powers. But a King is too great, too powerful, too far above his subjects, to be moved by these petty passions, and he cannot feel his authority affected except by important considerations.

[231] There is a third class of affairs in which the interests of the Ministers not only differ from that of the King, but are absolutely opposed to it. To this class belong all questions relating to the introducing of secrecy into the Administration, for the interest of the King is always served by throwing as much light as possible upon the conduct of his Ministers, while such light is by no means always welcome to the Ministers themselves.

[232] There is, finally, a large class of questions in which the interest of the King, although opposed to that of the Ministers, coincides with that of the people, while all persons of rank and consideration in the State, all who are privileged to approach the King or to gain his attention, are on the side of the Ministers. And what most deserves your attention in this connection, Sire, what is worthy, indeed, of being the subject of your most profound attention, is the fact that the nterests of the Ministers united to those of all people of influence, almost invariably outweigh that of the King and the people.

[233] We have already called attention to this consideration in connection with the twentieth and the poll tax. These two taxes, in the administration of which the Ministers and their subordinates have

reserved the right to tax your subjects, or arbitrarily to modify their taxes at will, have given rise to a despotism in France which is at once odious and shameful to a free nation. This despotism is contrary to the real interests of Your Majesty, and even to the fiscal interests, which the despots are always ready to sacrifice to personal considerations; but it is most serviceable to persons of position and consideration, for they are always treated with favor by the Ministers, the Intendants, and the other despots in this department of the government.

[234] The excessive expenditures furnish another example. Propositions are constantly being made for restricting them, and everybody applauds these proposals in theory; but when it comes to putting them into execution all the Ministers and those controlling the expenditures refuse to carry them out, and they are supported in this refusal by all the influences of the Court and even of the capital; for it is always the people of influence who benefit by the favors of the Ministers.

[235] Still another example is the abuse of *lettres de cachet* granted to individuals. Every person of any authority in the kingdom considers it his right to ask for them. And we Magistrates, who regard ourselves as the representatives of the people, but who still belong to that favored class who have access to the Ministers, must we not reproach ourselves with never having protested energetically enough against this abuse?

[236] In regard to all these questions, Sire, there are necessarily two parties in the kingdom; all those, on the one hand, who are privileged to approach their Sovereign, and on the other, the rest of the Nation. Consequently a King who loves justice must seek his motives in his own heart, and enlightenment in the hearts of the Nation.

[237] But how can any communication be established between the King and the Nation which shall not be intercepted by those who surround the King? Once more, Sire, we must not disguise the truth. The simplest and most natural means, and at the same time the most conformable to the constitution of this Monarchy, would be to listen to the voice of the Nation itself assembled, or at least to permit assemblies in each province. To tell you otherwise were cowardly; you must not be left in ignorance that the unanimous wish of the Nation is to obtain either the Estates-General or, at least, the provincial Estates.

[238] But we well know that for more than a century the jealousy òf the Ministers, and perhaps of the courtiers as well, has constantly opposed these national assemblies, and if France is ever so happy as to

10

have Your Majesty pronounce in favor of such assemblies, we foresee that formal difficulties will still be raised. Such difficulties can easily be surmounted if Your Majesty desires it; they cannot constitute a real obstacle to the realization of the ardent desires of the people you love. It is, however, possible that they may postpone for a period the re-establishment of the longed-for Estates; in the meantime, is there no other avenue by which the petitions of the people may reach the King who is waiting to hear them?

[239] We do not speak now in a language strange to you, Sire. At the time of your accession, all Europe knew that the first wish of Your Majesty was to facilitate the approach of all your subjects to your throne, and that you made it a rule to receive all the petitions which were presented to you. But the secrecy in the Administration constantly opposes the mutual desire of the Monarch and the Nation to come to an understanding, and has neutralized that first wish of a young King, which was so important to the people whom he was to govern.

[240] You receive petitions, Sire, from all your subjects; but the crying abuses can never be laid before you because there is no record in existence of the transactions of the government. In order, then, that Your Majesty should be enlightened by the petitions which you receive, it is necessary that the operations of the Administration should no longer be secret, and that all acts of authority issued in your name should be made known both to the public at large and to the individuals who are chiefly affected. It is necessary also that the motives of these acts should be made public, and that each act should bear the name of the person from whom it emanates, who should be held responsible for the use which he makes of his authority. Otherwise the petitions presented to the King will serve but little purpose, and abuses of authority will remain unknown and unpunished.

[241] You receive petitions from all your subjects; but they are only permitted to invoke your justice in their personal affairs, and consequently associations, provinces, and even the State itself are without defenders. Therefore, until Your Majesty shall have re-established the Estates, there should at least be deputies from each province, chosen by the province itself, who would perform for Your Majesty and your inner Council one of the functions which the *Procureurs-généraux* fulfill in the Courts—that of defending the interests of the public, and particularly of the province they represent. This institution would not necessarily involve an assembly of Estates in each province. As we

have already observed, a distinction was formerly made between the *pays d'Etats* and the *pays d'Elections*, for in spite of the fact that the latter elected representatives, they had no Estates; and there is nothing to prevent the re-establishment of this old usage.[1] The Council has been forced by obvious necessity to summon commercial deputies from each province. Are the interests of commerce the only ones in which the province should be represented?

[242] You receive petitions from all your subjects; but you cannot be unaware, Sire, that the majority of your subjects, and particularly those who most need your protection, are absolutely incapable of invoking it, for they have not the necessary intelligence for drawing up a memoir, nor the necessary means for getting it drawn up by others, nor the necessary facilities for getting it into the hands of Your Majesty. And what resource have those who languish in prison, and who are not likely to be permitted to escape, when it is foreseen that the first use that they will make of their liberty will be to implore your justice? The representatives of each province should therefore be especially authorized to constitute themselves the defenders of the poor, the weak, and the oppressed, and, above all, of prisoners, just as, in the established system of justice, the *Procureurs* and *Avocats-généraux* are the natural defenders of the absent and the incapacitated, of minors, and, in a word, of all those who cannot defend themselves.

[243] You receive petitions from all your subjects; but there is one important fact which we venture to bring to your attention because it is hardly possible that the experience of one year should already have demonstrated it, and that is, that this right of the individual to appear before the King in person is, in reality, utterly illusory; for it is impossible that Your Majesty should decide justly and with a knowledge of the facts upon all the complaints and demands—often unwarranted enough —of several millions of persons.

[244] Consequently these petitions must be, and are, referred to the different departments of the administration; which means, Sire, that each petition is referred to precisely that person against whom it is directed. For no one appeals to Your Majesty until he has exhausted all the other resources, and is obliged to complain against the Minister himself. But we have made plain that there are very

---

[1] The Court develops certain details of its plan in a note, which may be found in the French original, p. 67 *sq.* above.

important cases in which the whole Ministry, and even all those who surround the person of Your Majesty, have interests directly contrary to those of Your Majesty and of the Nation.

[245] Since it is essential that Your Majesty should avail yourself of the knowledge and experience of the Nation at large, would it not be possible for the Nation itself to examine, in the first instance, all these petitions and then to indicate by vote which ones deserve Your Majesty's personal attention?

[246] Here we must pause, Sire. We have dared to assert that the recourse of all your subjects to the King in person is ineffectual and illusory, because it is an obvious fact, of which Your Majesty must yourself certainly be convinced. But if we should go so far as to propose allowing public protests against the abuses of the administration, we should be accused of audacity. All the enemies of public liberty, and especially all those who are privileged to speak in your name, would assert that we wished to submit the acts of Your Majesty himself to public criticism. Such an objection is calculated to impose the most respectful silence upon us. Nevertheless we ask your permission, Sire, to give you an account of what goes on before our eyes in the administration of contentious justice.

[247] A party who appears in a Sovereign Court has the right to print and publish a memoir of his case, and if he is appealing from the decision of an inferior tribunal, the printed memoir is necessarily a criticism of that tribunal. We are aware also that individuals who appeal to Your Majesty himself against a decision of a Sovereign Court by a petition for reversal, revision, or otherwise, enjoy the same right, and that memoirs signed by an *Avocat au Conseil* or by private individuals are printed and published, which contain criticisms of the decisions of the Sovereign Court by which they believe themselves wronged.

[248] We know, Sire, that the publication of these memoirs does not enjoy unanimous approval. It is even said that there are some among the Magistrates who consider it an abuse, and who maintain that memoirs should only be used for the instruction of the judges who have to decide the case, and that the public should not be made the judge of the Courts.

[249] As for ourselves, Sire, we always have believed, and always shall believe, that we are responsible to Your Majesty and to the Nation for the justice we mete out to individuals; and if there are some Magistrates who think otherwise, we, who have warned Your Majesty

to challenge the testimony of the Ministers when they defend the secrecy of administration,—we must admit that you must also challenge that of the Judges who oppose the publication of memoirs.

[250] It is, in fact, a fundamental principle of the judicial system in France that its operations should be public. All suits should naturally be argued before the audience of the general public, and to take the public to witness by means of public memoirs is simply to increase this audience. It may be objected that the profusion of these printed memoirs is a novelty of recent origin; but the charge of innovation does not constitute a sufficient objection, since there are desirable novelties, and if we had rejected all innovations we should still be living under the empire of ignorance and barbarism. However, we believe, Sire, that this institution, far from being a dangerous innovation, is only the re-establishment of the old judicial procedure in this Kingdom, and that it may perhaps be derived from the original constitution of the Monarchy. This observation, Sire, is not unworthy of your attention.

[251] A long-established Monarchy, particularly one which was founded in centuries of ignorance, and which has maintained its existence until a period of unexampled enlightenment, must have experienced revolutions of many kinds. In considering the history of this Nation under this aspect, it will be seen that the progress of enlightenment has given rise to an immense difference between the customs and the laws of different periods.

[252] In the times of our earliest ancestors, all contracts and agreements between men were verbal, and faith in the testimony of witnesses took the place of documents, which no one would have known how to draw up. The laws themselves were but ill-formulated and often consisted in vague traditions which left everything to the interpretation of the judge.

[253] This arbitrary justice was subject to the most heinous abuses, and it was doubtless their enormity which led to the adoption of the simplest and most efficacious remedy, namely, publicity. The Kings themselves administered justice to the Nation, in the Assembly of the *Champ de Mars*, with a dignity and authority unknown to modern times, and the great Nobles followed the King's example and rendered justice in the presence of the people, each in his own territory.

[254] It must be remembered that in this first period the administration was not yet divorced from contentious justice; both were exercised by the King himself with the aid of public opinion. The

redoubtable rulers of that period permitted public complaint to be made to them of the conduct of their Ministers. They did not fear the humble petitions of those who came to implore their aid, and they endeavored to secure themselves against the deceptions of those who attempted to interpose their doubtful authority between the King and the people.

[255] In the following period it became customary to write down the enactments which determined the condition and the obligations of men, and a code of written law came into existence, to which all decisions had to conform. This period, which may be called that of Writing, had great advantages over the preceding one, since the rights of citizens now rested upon a permanent foundation, and they might hope to be judged henceforth by the law itself instead of by the caprices of their fellowmen.

[256] The new judicial system nevertheless involved difficulties unknown to previous centuries. There was now a body of definite laws, but the study of them had become so complicated that no one who did not devote himself entirely to it could perform the functions of a judge, or even administer understandingly his own affairs. A new order of citizens arose in the State, namely the lawyers, some of whom took the place of the Nobles in their function of judges, while others undertook to secure the rights of private individuals and of the Nation, the greater part of which was still in a condition of profound ignorance and so was forced to repose a blind confidence in them.

[257] The administration of justice also became less public than in the earlier period. Each tribunal still held its public sessions, but whenever the details of a case required the examination of documents, the judges made such examination in secret deliberations, so that their conduct was no longer wholly open to public criticism.

[258] We must observe, moreover, that it was during this period that administration was separated from contentious justice. Lawsuits, and particularly appeals, had multiplied to such an extent, and jurisprudence had become so profound a science, that it was no longer possible for the King and the Nobles to administer justice in person. The Kings therefore confided this function to the Magistrates, lawyers, and graduates, while they reserved to themselves the administration, and as it was exercised by means of royal letters instead of the public proclamations of earlier times, everything was done in the secrecy of the King's cabinet.[1]

---

[1] It may be worth while to observe that it was in this second period that the Gov-

[259] Finally there came a third period, which we shall call the Age of Printing, in which the printing-press has multiplied the benefits of writing and obviated its inconveniences. Learning has been diffused by printing; the written laws are to-day known to every one, and every one may apply them to his own affairs. The legal profession has lost that superiority which general ignorance once gave to it. The Judges may themselves be judged by an intelligent public, and such criticism is far more severe and far more just when it is made quietly and deliberately by reading the printed page, than when opinion is at the mercy of a tumultuous assembly.

[260] The art of printing has then given to writing the same publicity which in earlier times invested the spoken word in the presence of the assembled Nation. But it has required several centuries for the discovery of that art to produce its full effect. It has taken a long time for the whole Nation to acquire the taste and the habit of informing itself by reading, and for the education of persons skillful in the art of expressing themselves, who can lend their services to the public and take the place of those who, endowed with natural eloquence, were able to gain the ears of our fathers in the *Champ de Mars*, or in the early Courts.

[261] But that moment has arrived, Sire. Your subjects already enjoy its benefits in the regular system of justice, where the custom of interesting and instructing the public by printed memoirs has been established; and Your Majesty may ordain that those of your subjects who have complaints to make against the administration may enjoy the same privilege and the same advantage.

[262] It would seem that recourse to your Ministers against an Intendant or a provincial *Commandant* might be as public as the appeal to a superior from an inferior court. And since a citizen is

ernment first found it possible to do without the Estates. Up to that time the Kings had been absolutely obliged to assemble the people to make known their commands. The Ministers straightway found means of making these assemblies more and more infrequent, since they desired to remove, as far as possible, all critics of their administration, and they soon found it so convenient to labor in seclusion that they sought to thicken the veil in which they had enveloped themselves. It was therefore the age of Writing which gave birth to that secrecy of administration in France which has made such progress from the period of the suppression of the Estates-General up to the present time; and if its growth has been fostered during the age of Printing, it is because the recourse to printed complaints against the administration has so far been forbidden.

permitted to appeal publicly to Your Majesty by means of printed
memoirs, against the decisions rendered in your name by the Superior
Courts,—tribunals long held in veneration, and composed of a large
number of Magistrates, whose decisions are only reached after long
discussion and by a plurality of votes—why may not that citizen protest with the same publicity against other acts of authority also done
in your name, but which are the work of a single man, and which are
conceived in secret and with no preliminary discussion?

[263] The difference, it is said, is that every one knows that Your
Majesty never holds your courts of justice in person, whereas one can
never know whether the acts of authorty which emanate from your
cabinet are your own work or not. The Ministers long ago adopted a
policy which is calculated always to shield their persons; the name of
Your Majesty, with which they clothe their acts, and a signature which
resembles yours and which may not be questioned without failing in the
respect due to Your Majesty, have sufficed to put into one and the
same class the acts which represent Your Majesty's personal desires
and those of which you know nothing. The consequence is that your
oppressed subjects always fear that they may seem wanting in respect
when they complain of injustice, and are never sure that in invoking
the supreme power they may not be offending against it. These are
the results, Sire, of keeping secret the responsible official,—one of the
evils of the general system which we have described to Your Majesty.

[264] France enjoys the happiness of having a ruler whose first
wish is for enlightenment, and who desires to enable all his subjects to
invoke his personal justice against all abuses of authority. But when
Your Majesty has been convinced by the representations of others, and
by your own experience, that this recourse is impossible on account of
the almost infinite number of petitions to which it gives rise, and that
the only means of providing that the voice of the people shall pene-
trate to the King is to permit every citizen to call on the public as a
witness (as he may already do in the tribunals of established justice),—
even then, our opponents believe that they can still confront our zeal
with an insuperable obstacle and impose silence upon us by pronouncing
the revered name of Your Majesty. They would leave a thousand
cases of injustice forever unpunished and shielded from all protest, so
that it would be impossible ever to expose them to you, all for the
sake of the imaginary fear that an occasion might sometime arise in
which an order which emanated from Your Majesty himself should be

treated with too little respect: as if there could be any doubt of the extreme circumspection which will always be exercised by those who address petitions to you, as well as by those who, in virtue of their position, are commissioned to draw up and sign these petitions.

[265] However, Sire, since this fear, chimerical as it is, has been given expression, since our opponents take advantage of the personal respect due to Your Majesty, it is impossible for us to insist farther; we must leave this matter in the hands of Your Majesty. We have reminded you of the example of those early Kings who did not feel their authority endangered by the liberty of their subjects to implore their aid in the presence of the assembled Nation. It is for you to judge, Sire, whether your power will be weakened by imitating Charles the Great, that proud Ruler, who laid such great stress upon the prerogatives of the crown. If you will follow his example, you may still reign over a nation which shall be in its entirety your Council, and you will find its resources far greater than he did, because you live in a far more enlightened century.

[266] Deign to reflect, Sire, that on the day when you accord to your subjects this precious liberty, it may be truly said that an alliance has been concluded between the King and the Nation against the Ministers and the Magistrates; against the Ministers, if ever there are any so perverse as to desire to conceal the truth from you, against the Magistrates, if ever there are any so ambitious as to claim the exclusive privilege of telling you the truth.

These, Sire, are the very humble and very respectful protests presented to Your Majesty by

> Your most humble, most obedient,
> most faithful and most loving
> Servants and Subjects who hold
> your *Cour des aides*.

In the Cour des aides,
Paris, May 6, 1775.

ERRATUM.

The quotations from the *Mémoires Secrets* given in the Introduction (pp. vi.–vii.) should not be attributed to Bachaumont, but to Mairobert, who continued the publication of the "memoires" after the death (in 1771) of their originator.